D1231375

ENGLISH EDITION
World Apostolate of Fatima, USA

A PATHWAY UNDER THE GAZE OF MARY

ENGLISH TRANSLATION
James A. Colson

EDITED BY
Barbara Ernster

CARMEL OF COIMBRA

A PATHWAY UNDER
THE GAZE OF MARY

Biography of
Sister Maria Lucia of Jesus and the Immaculate Heart O.C.D.

Foreword by David Carollo

World Apostolate of Fatima, USA

Nihil Obstat
Rev. Msgr. Luciano Guerra

Imprimatur
Coimbra, August 23, 2013
✠ Virgilio Antunes
Bishop of Coimbra

We affirm the imprimatur for the 2013 Portuguese edition of this book by the Bishop of Coimbra. The nihil obstat and imprimatur for this English edition are pending.

Reverend John G. Hillier, Ph.D.
Censor librorum
Diocese of Metuchen

Author
Carmel of Saint Teresa – Coimbra, Portugal

English Editors
Barbara Ernster
Mary Kay Fier, proofreader
Edward Goryl, proofreader

Photographs
Archives of the Carmelo of Coimbra and the Shrine of Fatima

Design
Meghan Jones

Cover Design
Megan Pritchard

English Edition Publisher
World Apostolate of Fatima, USA
P.O. Box 150
Washington, NJ 07882-0150
www.bluearmy.com

Printed in the United States of America
Harmony Press Inc. Easton, PA 18042
© 2015 World Apostolate of Fatima. All rights and International rights reserved.

Second Edition
June 2015

ISBN Number
978-0-578-15863-1

CONTENTS

CHAPTER IV
AFTER THE APPARITIONS

CHAPTER V
I'M HERE FOR THE SEVENTH TIME

CHAPTER VI
STUDENT

CHAPTER VII
BEGINNING OF RELIGIOUS LIFE

CHAPTER XVIII
ENCOUNTERS WITH THE BISHOP DRESSED IN WHITE

CHAPTER XIX
ONLY SOME MORE TIME

FOREWARD

We are pleased to bring the English edition of A Pathway Under the Gaze of Mary to you. The story of Fatima has been told many times and the accounts of Sister Lucia have been written so that we have come to understand the requests of the Lady come from heaven.

Our Lady told young Lucia that Francisco and Jacinta would go to heaven soon, but that she would have to stay on earth awhile longer. She lived eighty-eight more years, most of that time in the Carmelite convent at Coimbra. This book gives a better understanding of what her daily life was like, from the apparitions to her journey to Carmel, and ultimately to her joyful and holy death. Sister Lucia shows us through her simple life how to live the requests of Our Lady, teaching us the essential part: "The sacrifice of each one requires the fulfillment of their own duty and observance of My Law" (Letter of April 20, 1942 to Bishop José Correia da Silva.).

There is always controversy that follows Marian apparitions, and Fatima has had its share. Sister Lucia grew tired of trying to correct false statements and rumors, pleading instead to just do what Our Lady asked. Our hope is that this book brings you to a stronger understanding of the message of Fatima, and inspires you to "make of everything you can a sacrifice and offer it to God as an act of reparation for the sins by which He is offended ..." so that we can bring down peace upon our nations and change the world.

God bless you,

David Carollo
Executive Director
World Apostolate of Fatima, USA

PREFACE

Sister Lucia was a prominent figure of the Portuguese Catholic world of the 20th Century. As the Shepherdess of Fatima who, together with Francisco and Jacinta saw Our Lady in 1917, she is regarded as a child blessed and chosen to spread the message of peace and salvation of God throughout the world. As a Carmelite nun, she was known as a privileged person dedicated to God and in service to His Church, one in whom people placed enormous confidence based on her role as Our Lady's confidant.

In addition to Portugal, Sister Lucia is also an essential figure in the world, particularly in Europe. Since the apparitions with their references to the conversion of Russia, the spread of the errors of atheism, and the political changes that have occurred in the Old Continent, she is seen as someone involved in this prophetic mystery that pervades our contemporary history. From a personal point of view, many men and women from numerous countries on five continents still maintain a great admiration for Sister Lucia and pray to her to ask her intercession before God for the spiritual graces they need.

The contemporary history of the Church would hardly be complete without the inclusion of Sister Lucia's role. The references to the Holy Father and to his sufferings since the apparitions, as well as the revelation of the third part of the Secret of Fatima and the dramatic events experienced by the Church in the late second and early third millennium do not allow us to ignore Sister Lucia.

Reading the *Memoirs of Sister Lucia* allows us to enter into the heart of the Message of Fatima and to understand the human and spiritual personalities of the three shepherd children through the eyes of Lucia. Although she focuses on Francisco and Jacinta, we discern the greatness of her soul as an apostle among people, her determination to seek the truth, and her fidelity to God and to His holy Mother. Her book, *Calls from the Message of Fatima,* reveals a way of living and commitment that marked her convictions and actions throughout her entire long life.

Now her biography, *A Pathway Under the Gaze of Mary,* gives us a broader perspective of Sister Lucia's personality. Written by the Sisters of Carmel of Coimbra, it reflects their personal knowledge of her daily life and writings, and provides testimonies that mirror the depth of her soul.

This book will help readers appreciate the distinctive qualities essential to the life of Sister Lucia: love of God, devotion to Our Lady, unconditional fidelity to the Church and commitment to the salvation of lost humanity. After all, the Message of Fatima according to her interpretation, her existence, and her testimony renews the invitation to conversion and the proclamation of the Good News of salvation in Jesus Christ, and impels each and every one of us as Christians to fulfill our pathway under the gaze of Mary.

Coimbra, February 13, 2013
✠Most Reverend Virgilio Antunes
Bishop of Coimbra

INTRODUCTION

-I am here for the seventh time.
Go; follow the path the Bishop wants you to take.
This is the will of God.
-Yes, I will do what I promised.[1]

"He left his land, and family, and his father's house and went to the land that he was shown."[2] And the shepherdess, her eyes fixed upon God Who spoke to her, obediently took upon her fragile shoulders the responsibility to make known to the world devotion to the Immaculate Heart of Mary. We accompany this simple soul on her long journey where obstacles were not lacking. Like the crystal clear water from a spring flowing towards the sea, she surged ahead, strengthened by the love that accompanied her along her passage through the world that was for her *the only path to God.*[3]

It was a life of love with Mary. When her path became overwhelming from answering the numerous questions of many people, she would courteously reply, *"It is all because of Our Lady!"* And Our Lady would say to all who listen, *"Everything is for the sake of Jesus!"* Yes, because everything is directed to Him in our lives. And when Mary came to earth to bring a message, it was for the glory of God and the salvation of His children, to point us in the Way, the Truth, and the Life, and to remind us that something is not right. From a very young age, Sister Lucia's life had the seal of Mary. This love from early childhood marked all of her steps during her long vocation. It was always to Jesus through Mary.

---

1 Seventh apparition of Our Lady at the Cova da Iria, June 15, 1921.
2 Genesis 12:1.
3 Archives-Carmel of Coimbra, *My Pathway*, 1, p.208.

◀ Lucia in the center with her mother at her side; in back row, her brother, three sisters and a niece. Photo taken in 1919 after her father's death.

▲ Maria Rosa, mother of Lucia, with her daughters Teresa, Carolina and little Lucia.

▲ Maria Rosa, mother of Lucia.
▼ Family house of Lucia.

CHAPTER I
THE CHILDHOOD OF LUCIA

1 | Birth and Baptism

Near the end July 1906 after an intense day of work in the fields and chores in the house, the lady Maria Rosa, a mother of five children (one died prematurely at birth) had news to give to her husband.

-Antonio, we're going to have another child!

With his gentle and kind heart, Mr. Antonio dos Santos replied to her:

-Don't be troubled! It is one more blessing from God. Therefore, there will be no lack of bread in the drawer or oil in the pot.[4]

For them, receiving news of another child was like a surprise gift from God, given when and where He desired. And so they filled the house with the joyful laughter of innocent children who were loved and always happy, even with the many problems placed upon them. There was never an expectation of *gifts*, but the heart of the mother was a center of love, equally given and unique for each one of them. Whenever Sister Lucia referred to her parents, she did so with great veneration, extolling their qualities that she always admired. They were the best and most wise parents in the world! Even when recounting the time of the apparitions of Our Lady, Lucia never complained about her mother, who could be quite severe as she tried to discern the truth, but always apologized with great integrity.

While waiting for the child to be born, Maria Rosa prepared a new outfit, not needing many since the outfits of her other babies were saved and scented with aromatic herbs, preserving them from moths and keeping them always pleasant.

The day of March 28, 1907, was Holy Thursday. In the morning Maria Rosa attended Mass and received Communion, intending to return in the afternoon for a visit and adoration of the Blessed Sacrament. She could not return, however, because the *"shepherdess"* was born. The fact that her mother had received Communion that morning was a great pleasure for Sister Lucia who liked to say she made her first Communion before birth.

Antonio did not want to wait too long to have his child baptized, but knew the parish priest would refuse to administer baptism on Holy Saturday to a child who was less than eight days old, and it was a very busy day. He also did not want his girl to spend Easter without being baptized, and wanted to avoid having two feasts on the same day – Easter and Baptism. Thus, he solved the problem with a *"white lie"*— he registered the girl as being born on March 22 so the pastor could not refuse. This is why Sister Lucia always celebrated her birthday on March 22

---

4 Memoirs of Sister Lucia, Volume II, 5th Memoir, No. 2, p. 21 (4th edition). (From now on, we will cite the book "Memoirs of Sister Lucia" with the abbreviation MSL, followed by other indications.)

and only learned of her true birthday later in life when she heard her mother's explanation to a family friend, Fr. Formigão. In the last years of her life Lucia celebrated her birthday on two days – the 22nd for the outside world, and the 28th for the Community of Carmel because the 22nd was always too busy with correspondence and visitors, and the Community could hardly be with her.

Because time was pressing, Antonio and Maria Rosa began to think of a name for their girl and their choice of godparents. They asked Mr. Anastasius Vieira, an uncle, to be the godfather. He agreed, and therefore his wife Aunt Teresa was asked to be the godmother, to which she also agreed. It was customary at that time for a baby being baptized to be given the name of a godparent or a close family member. Antonio insisted, however, that the baby would be called Lucia. Everyone thought this was strange because no one in the family had this name. The reaction was similar to when Zechariah insisted on the name John for his son, St. John the Baptist. She was to be called Lucia, which means *Light* – a little light that would shine the light of God throughout the world.

She was baptized on Holy Saturday, March 30, 1907, by the parish priest, Fr. Manuel Marquest Ferreira, during the ringing of the bells announcing the Resurrection of Christ (at that time Holy Saturday was called Alleluia Saturday, and had the lively presence of a paschal feast). Those who heard the bells knew they were the bells of Easter, but in this joyful announcement there was another announcement the world did not yet know. Lucia appeared in the light of the day like a flower that blooms in the spring, a child who after a few years would receive the mission of conveying to humanity a message of salvation. It was no accident that her baptism into the Church was on Holy Saturday, a day especially dedicated in a liturgical memorial to the Mother of God. The Blessed Virgin surely was present on this special Saturday to take under her protection this little creature who would soon be her confidant and messenger.

The feast of Baptism was a popular family event, well-attended, a lot of work, and one of the reasons Lucia's father wanted to avoid a second feast at home. Certainly the oven was lit in the old house so that a good lamb could be roasted, as it was during the time when the new spring lambs were about three months old. After the Baptism, the dos Santos house would be open to everyone for a celebration meal. The family was modest, but very generous and hospitable, a trait passed on to Lucia.

2 | Getting Started

Now there was a new girl in the house who was the center of everyone's attention. Lucia's older sister, Maria of the Angels, was 16 years old and Carolina was the youngest at age five. Carolina was in a good position to be queen of the house, but found Lucia to be very special and wanted to comfort her little sister. Since they did not have dolls, the older sisters could be playful and motherly with Lucia.

Maria Rosa taught her children with a tender, but firm heart. Because she loved her children very much, she did not allow them their tantrums, but taught them to control this inner tendency so common in early childhood so that it would not become rooted in adulthood. Little Lucia, like any child, had her tantrums and was no exception to the rule. She was a very lively and clever child, but could also be a rascal, knowing very well how to circumvent the situation when she saw that one of her pranks could result in harm.

Since the dawn of her life, Lucia learned to share. A neighbor's mother could not breastfeed her baby so Maria Rosa nursed both. When Lucia took her milk, she must have felt the intimate presence of the "brother" who shared her meals. She always recalled this fact that her mother shared with her with great emotion. She learned generosity, a characteristic of her mother, who tried to teach her children not only by word but especially by example.

When a poor person knocked at their door for alms, it was from the hand of the smallest child the alms were to be received. It was sweeter for the poor and less humiliating, and the child learned to give, doing so with great joy. It was the parent's rule never to dismiss a poor person without giving him something, and it was the oldest who was at home who should decide what was to be given.

One day Lucia and her brother were alone. A poor person knocked at the door, and being the younger, Lucia called her brother who rushed to meet the beggar. Lucia explained this account of the day:

I realized there was a poor beggar woman knocking on the door. I called my brother to come and give her alms. He came, went into the kitchen and opened the drawer in the kitchen table where my mother had left a pork bone with quite a bit of meat on it, intending when she returned to use it for the family meal. My brother took the meat. He then lifted down a whole loaf from the tray that hung from the ceiling where my mother used to put the bread to cool when she took it out of the oven and went to give the lot to the woman. As he gave it to her, he realized it would not fit in the bags she was carrying. She began to lift up her apron, but my brother told her to wait. He went back into the house and into the weaving room where he grabbed a bag that was hanging on the beams of the loom in which the balls of thread to fill the shuttles were kept. He tipped them all into a basket, put the meat bone and the bread into the bag and gave the lot to the woman. The woman was astonished and said:

-Are you giving me all of this, or do you want me to bring the bag back the next time I come?

My brother said:

-Take all of it and pray for me.[5]

The poor woman went away praying the Our Father and singing from within. Lucia who participated in the whole incident was happy.

Shortly after, her mother and sisters returned, ready for their sewing and work on the loom while the meal was prepared. As soon as Maria of the Angels sat at the loom she noticed the balls of thread in the basket and the missing bag. She asked Lucia what she had done with it. This time Lucia was innocent and told her what happened. Her sister was grieved because she needed the bag. But their mother did not reproach Manuel for giving alms, and to avoid upsetting him said: *-Do not worry, we can make another bag. We have many pieces left over from the dressmaking...Lucia will make one.*[6] Their mother chose odds and ends from the leftovers of Teresa's sewing and had Lucia align them. Although her little hands were clumsy trying to pick up the needle, Lucia worked with all her heart. Soon Maria had a new bag for the balls of thread and Lucia felt very proud of the work that she had done. Maria Rosa always said: *-Whatever we gave to the poor people was never needed!*[7]

3 | Some Mischief

Lucia began early in life to take an interest in work, becoming industrious and careful as she observed in the rest of her family. It was the blossoming of what would be in her entire life.

One day at a very young age she noticed some hens that always showed up at the time when her mother gave them corn, but then disappeared. Full of zeal, though frowning, she said to her mother:

-Those hens are eating the corn and then go away and don't lay their eggs here![8]

Her mother was unconcerned, but Lucia followed the hens to see where they were going. As they climbed through the middle of a thorn bush and went behind a beehive, Lucia chased them with a stick and was attacked by bees. Hearing her screams, her mother helped her escape the angry bees and told her it would have been better if she had been obedient and left the hens in peace. But

---

5 MSL II, 6th M, No. 17, pp. 93-94.

6 *Ibid.*

7 MSL II, 5th M, No.2, p. 16.

8 MSL II, 6th M, No. 20, p. 100.

the young one was not satisfied and continued to complain about *the hens eating the corn and not laying eggs!* She had an inner sense of justice and would only give in if something was the truth, and she thought this was true about the hens.

After some time she was surprised that one of those vagrant hens returned, surrounded by a large brood of chicks! What a joy! The little chicks struggled to follow their mother up a few steps but could not climb them. Lucia was very happy to guide them, but the mother hen did not understand her friendly gesture and attacked her. Soon she shouted to her mother again: -*Oh mother, help! That hen wants to bite me!*[9] Her mother attended to the incident, teaching her what she should have done.

One day while going through the kitchen, there was no one around and Lucia felt a temptation. The shelf on the wall contained a barrel of honey. Because it was too high up for her small size, she looked around and found a solution. Grabbing a tall bench, she stood on top of it to reach the barrel, which was very full and a little too heavy for her strength. But her desire for it was stronger! With both hands she took hold of the barrel, uncovered it, and began to tilt it so that the honey would flow into her mouth. Once her appetite was satisfied, she would put it back and go on her way. But it was a disaster! The barrel weighed too much and the honey not only went to her mouth, it flowed down on her and to her feet! Without savoring the taste of the honey that cost her so much to achieve, she lifted the barrel as best she could and started screaming for her mother, who did not need an explanation. Maria Rosa gave her a bath, clean clothes and washed her soiled clothes while telling her one should not eat in secret or with greediness. Lucia, wanting to explain, said: -*Oh mother, but it was the barrel that fell!* [10]

Once during recreation—a time in the Carmel especially dedicated to visiting between the sisters—Lucia described with immense grace an incident that occurred with the pedals of the loom. Now that was an irresistible temptation! Her mother and sisters told her that she was not to swing around the poles of the loom, as this was prohibited. One day she was by herself and could not resist the temptation to swing again. But this time the rope broke and one of the pedals fell. What a disaster! She was terrified, thinking of the consequences that would soon befall her—a scolding and a spanking.

Before her mother and sisters returned, Lucia thought hard how to suppress her guilty conscience, knowing she would get what she well deserved. Quietly she hid under the table, her back flat against the wall so they could not find her. When her sister returned and began to loom, she found the pedal that had fallen and

9 *Ibid.*
10 Oral Narration of Sister Lucia.

soon guessed who had been there. But she could not find the little one. Finally she found Lucia, who saw the vine and knew a beating was coming, so she began screaming, banging her hands and feet on the floor, which was frustrating to all. In all her sadness, she did not see that each one of them had left her and returned to their work.

When the commotion passed, she quietly curled up in her mother's lap and asked for clemency: -*Mother, you're not going to hit me, are you?*

Her mother gently reprimanded her for her disobedience and asked her to be better in the future. Little Lucia very seriously replied: -*But the rope broke!*

Even when her mother told her husband what had happened, the little one stubbornly replied again: -*It was the rope that broke!* [11]

After the day's work, the family gathered at the table and relived these delightful episodes, which while funny, were used to educate. Her father supported the lessons her mother had given during the day and so Lucia grew up admiring their wisdom. While her mother and sister cleaned the kitchen, her father would go out onto the patio with her and continue to teach. He taught her to call the sun the lamp of the Lord, and the moon the lamp of Our Lady, and the stars the lamps of the Angels. Then he danced with his girl who liked to dance and spin like a top. Afterward, she would sit on his lap and he would answer her questions. He told her she came from Heaven in a wicker basket carrying flowers so that when she dressed like an angel, she could throw the flowers in a procession of the Blessed Sacrament. His little girl was very happy!

One day another disaster happened. Lucia loved to play with the little rabbits. Her mother told her not to take them out of the rabbit burrow because they could escape. But the temptation was so great! While there alone, she opened the burrow and pulled out a rabbit. Very pleased, she was calming the animal who did not desire to be handled. The rabbit broke free and ran like a thoroughbred while she stood idle and breathless—she knew she could not catch that rabbit!

Very remorseful, she went looking for her mother to confess what she had done. The truth had to be told. With her head bowed down, she received her scolding, promising not to do it again. As she got up she thought to herself: *My mother said I am bad; my father said I came from Heaven in a wicker basket with flowers.* Then she asked her mother:

-*So, then in Heaven are there bad things?*

My mother replied:

-*Well yes, there were angels in Heaven who were demons, and because they did*

---

11 Cf. MSL II, 6th M, No. 17, p. 96.

evil God put them out, and now they go about tempting everyone. As for you, He sent you here below to see if you'll be good, so as to be able to return there.

    And I replied:

    -But I do not remember!

    -Of course not, responded my mother, because you were asleep and you are very forgetful.[12]

Later while playing some games she thought about her mother's response, and in the evening when they were all at the table she told her father of her doubts, which delighted all.

    -Oh father, mother told me I must do good to go to Heaven!

Her father, with his peaceful and benevolent smile, replied:

    -This is for when you are older; as for now, you are very small. Therefore, you still have a lot of time to become good.[13]

Recalling these enchanting scenes in later years, she said God was waiting for her to do well so He could bring her to Heaven, but concluded: *He is the one Who has to make me good, so I may be there with Him.*

4 | A Childhood Marked by Family Charity

In her memoirs, Lucia wrote about her parents with the clarity of a crystal fountain and described her comfortable family environment as it was before the apparitions of Our Lady. They were simple people, dedicated to the work by which they lived. They gave their children a solid Christian education without being scholarly, and although the children did not attend school, they were rich in their values. They learned to respect others and to treat poor people with dignity. From early on their mother taught them to think of others. Lucia gave some details of this education:

    I asked my mother to let me make a blue woolen shawl with red stripes to wear at Christmas when I went to kiss the Child Jesus. My mother said I could, but I would have to make two, one for myself and one for one of the little poor girls who went around begging and had none.

    I did not think there would be time, but I got hold of the wool and sitting down on the ground I started to crochet busily.

    When my father returned home that evening I said to him:

    -Don't come asking me to dance, papa, because I can't go.

    -You can't? What has happened then? he asked.

---

12   MSL II, 5th M, No. 2, p. 27.

13   *Ibid.*

Family house of Lucia.

Interior of Lucia's house.

Family loom.

Maria of the Angels, sister of Lucia, working at the loom.

Sisters of Lucia.

Maria of the Angels, older
sister of Lucia, spinning.

Gloria, sister of Lucia.

Manuel, brother of Lucia.

Teresa, sister of Lucia.

Lucia and her mother.

◀ Maria Rosa, mother of Lucia
and Olympia, mother of
Francisco and Jacinta.

▼ Bedroom of Lucia and her
sister Carolina.

I told him I had asked mother to let me make a blue shawl with red stripes to wear for the first time when I went to kiss the Child Jesus at Christmas and that mother said I could, but I had to make two, one for myself, and the other to give to one of the poor children who went around begging and had none of their own. I added that I did not think there would be time to make them both.

My father responded:

-You'll have time all right, I'll help you.

-But you don't know how to crochet!

-That's true, he replied, but I can wind the wool for you.

He drew up a chair close to me and then went to the drawer of the machine to get an empty cotton spool. He took a skein of wool out of the bag, threaded it into the wool winder and sat down beside me to wind it.

My mother, who was busy in the kitchen, realized what was happening and came in smiling and hugged my father from behind saying:

-What a good man you are! But look, you don't wind wool in the same way as cotton; you wind wool on your fingers so as to make a fluffy ball so that the wool does not lose its softness.

She taught my father how to wind the wool on the fingers of his left hand. My father looked at my mother smiling and said:

-Now I have learned to do one more thing, to wind the wool on my fingers.

And to the squeaking sound of the wool winder, the thump of the combs in the loom where my sister Maria was weaving, and the noise of the sewing machine wheel which my sister Teresa was turning slowly, he began to sing:

The name of Mary,
How good it is.
Save my soul
That it is yours.

For it is yours,
It has to be.
Save my soul
When I come to die.

When I come to die,
When my days are over,
Take my soul
To a good place.

To a good place,
To Paradise.
Save my soul
On the day of Judgment.

While sitting on the floor at my father's feet busy with my crochet needle, I gradually heard the voices of my mother who was busy in the kitchen and my sisters who were working at the loom and the sewing machine. Thinking of the phrase 'take me to paradise' I stopped and asked:

-Papa, is the paradise to which Our Lady is going to take us the one where Adam ate the apple?

-No, he replied, the place Our Lady is going to take us is Heaven.

-Oh, well, that's all right then, I said, because I don't want to go to where Adam ate the apple. There are snakes wrapped around the trunks of the trees there, and so you can't eat those apples. But those snakes were able to talk, and the ones you see when you go up on the heath don't.

-No they don't, my father said. The fact is that they lied when they deceived Eve so that she would disobey God and eat the apple. So God punished them. They were struck dumb and forced to slide along the earth.

In the meantime, my mother came to call us to supper as everything was ready. Patting me on my shoulder, she said:

-So you see, little one, you must not tell lies otherwise God will punish you as He punished the snakes and you will be struck dumb like them and made to crawl along the ground and eat dust.

-Oh, but I don't tell lies.

And we went to have our supper. [14]

Thus, both playfully and seriously, little Lucia received an education and a love for the truth. In a simple manner it was engraved in her mind. In another episode, Lucia asked her mother to let her make a red jumper. Her mother said 'yes' and she got to work hard on the jumper she wanted to debut on All Saints Day (known as Little Cake Day). When it was finished, it so happened that a poor girl about Lucia's age was very badly dressed. Her mother seeing this sympathized with her and gave Lucia's new jumper to her. Lucia complained to her mother:

-So you gave her the jumper I made and now I have nothing new to wear on All Saints Day! [15]

Her mother did not miss the opportunity to give her a lesson on true

---

14 MSL II, 6th M, No. 15, pp. 86-87.
15 MSL II, 6th M, No. 15, p. 84.

charity, helping her to think first of others and then teaching her to make another even more beautiful jumper. How happy Lucia was on All Saints Day in her new jumper and seeing the poor girl at her side with the other. She learned how much joy you receive when you give to others. She grew up in this happy environment, playing games and learning the responsibilities of family life, until the day that the "Lady more brilliant than the sun" came into her life.

5 | First Communion

As Marie Rosa was the area catechist, children would gather at her home for catechesis lessons. From an early age, Lucia would sit on her mother's lap and participate in the lessons, and soon would know the whole doctrine on the tip of her tongue. With her wit and good memory, she had no difficulty memorizing doctrines and when she did not understand, she would ask for clarification. If she did not understand a response from her mother, at meal time she would ask her father who would give her further explanation.

The time had come for the parish priest to examine the children and decide which ones were prepared for First Communion. Lucia was only six years old and the parish priest did not allow children under seven to make First Communion. She explained:

The eve of the great day arrived, and His Reverence sent word that all the children were to go to the church in the morning so he could make the final decision as to which ones were to receive their First Communion. To my displeasure His Reverence called me to his side and gently told me that I had to wait until I was seven years old! I began to cry at once, and just as I would have done with my own mother, I laid my head on his lap and sobbed. It happened that another priest who had been called in to help with the confessions entered the church. Seeing me in this position he asked the reason for my tears, and being informed, he took me into the sacristy and examined me on the catechism and the mystery of the Eucharist; then took me by the hand and led me to the parish priest and said:

-Father Pena, you can let this child go to Communion. She understands what she's doing better than many of the others.

-But she's only six years old, objected the good priest.

-Never mind! I'll take the responsibility if the good pastor wants, he replied.

-All right then, the good priest said to me, go and tell your mother that you are making your First Communion tomorrow.

I could never express the joy I felt. Off I went, clapping my hands with delight and running all the way home to give the good news to my mother. She at once set about preparing me for the Confession I was to make that afternoon. My mother took me to the church and when we arrived, I told her I wanted to confess to the other priest. We went to the sacristy where he was sitting on a chair hearing confessions. My mother knelt down in front of the high altar near the sacristy door together with the other mothers who were waiting for their children to confess in turn. Right there before the Blessed Sacrament, my mother gave me her last instructions.

When my turn came I went and knelt at the feet of our dear Lord, represented there in the person of His minister, imploring forgiveness for my sins. When I had finished, I noticed everyone was laughing. My mother called me and said:

-My child, don't you know confession is a secret matter and it is made in a low voice? Everyone heard you! There was only one thing nobody heard and that is what you said at the end.

On the way home, my mother tried several times to discover what she called the secret of my confession. But the only answer she obtained from me was complete silence. Now, however, I am going to reveal the secret of my first confession. After listening to me, the good priest said these few words:

-My child, your soul is the temple of the Holy Spirit. Keep it always pure so He will be able to carry on His divine action within it.

On hearing these words I felt myself filled with respect for my interior, and asked the kind confessor what I ought to do.

-Kneel down there before Our Lady and ask her with great confidence to take care of your heart, to prepare it to receive her beloved Son worthily tomorrow, and to keep it for Him alone.

In the Church there was more than one statue of Our Lady. But, as my sisters took care of the altar of Our Lady of the Rosary, I usually went there to pray. That is why I went there on this occasion also, to ask her with all the ardor of my soul to keep my poor heart for God alone.

As I repeated this humble prayer over and over again, with my eyes fixed on the statue, it seemed to me she smiled, and with a loving look and kindly gesture, assured me that she would. My heart was overflowing with joy I could scarcely utter a single word.[16]

Pierced with this glance that was marked in the depths of her soul, Lucia returned home in the hand of her mother, keeping this secret in her heart that made her so happy! When they arrived home, her mother asked Teresa, an apprentice of sewing, to make a dress of white fabric for Lucia's First Communion. It was a lot to ask, but she did not refuse her mother. With the help of Maria of the Angels they went to work. They worked well into the night by the light of a candle. They too

---

16 MSL I, 2nd M, Ch.1, No. 3, pp. 69-71 (18th edition).

were happy for Lucia. As for her, she was so happy she could not sleep. She gave all of her heart to God and she did not think of anything else until dawn, which was the Feast of the Sacred Heart of Jesus, May 30, 1913, when she was to receive Jesus for the first time. Several times in the night she visited her sisters, who worked fervently to make the dress for the *bride of Jesus*. It was a night of vigil, a vigil of love initiated by the smile of Mary that was her first consecration, made with an innocent heart and complete surrender to the Mother. And whoever surrenders to Mary belongs to her Son, because it is the pathway that leads to Jesus.

Finally it was dawn of the big day, but the clock seemed to never ring nine o'clock! Having to wait for the Beloved always intensifies the desire to possess Him more. Before leaving the house, in the company of five people and dressed in white with a wreath, the eldest took Lucia to the kitchen where she was to ask pardon of her parents and ask for their blessing. Her mother blessed her and suggested what she should ask Jesus when she received Him in her heart:

-*Above all ask Our Lord to make you a saint.*[17]

With a devotion befitting a daughter that was nourished from the qualities of her mother, she memorized these words so that when she received Communion, she would say them first to Jesus. And she took this into account.

And so adorned in the immaculate white dress, a symbol of the purity of her soul, her brother Manuel took her to the church.

They arrived very early, but Lucia, being preoccupied, ran to the altar of Our Lady of the Rosary to peer again on the motherly charm that had captivated her with a lovely smile the day before. Soon the hour sounded for the solemn Mass to begin presided by the parish priest Reverend Father Pena, and assisted by two other priests, one of whom was the Rev. Padre Cruz, S.J.

There were four rows of children from the rail to the back of the church. Since Lucia was the smallest, she was placed with the *Angels*—girls dressed like angels who held a towel for the children to take communion on their knees. Lucia tells about this unforgettable encounter:

As the Mass began with singing and the great moment drew near, my heart beat faster and faster in expectation of the visit of the great God, Who was about to descend from Heaven to unite Himself to my poor soul. The parish priest came down and passed among the rows of children, distributing the Bread of Angels. I had the good fortune to be the first one to receive. As the priest was coming down the altar steps, I felt as though my heart would leap from my breast. But he had no sooner placed the Divine Host on my tongue than I felt an unalterable serenity and peace. I felt myself bathed in

17 MSL I, 2nd M, Ch. 1, No. 5, p. 72.

such a supernatural atmosphere that the presence of our dear Lord became as clearly perceptible to me as if I had seen and heard Him with my bodily senses. I then addressed my prayer to Him:

-Oh Lord, make me a saint. Keep my heart always pure for You alone.

Then it seemed that in the depths of my heart, our dear Lord distinctly spoke these words to me:

-The grace granted to you this day will remain living in your soul, producing fruits of eternal life.

I felt as though being transformed in God. [18]

In an intimate note written on January 13, 1944, Sister Lucia mentions that these words, *at the bottom of my soul*, made sense at the time she made her consecration to Our Lady, on the eve of her First Communion. She wrote:

I saw the Mother smile! I heard her 'Yes!' And I heard the sound of her voice:

-My daughter, the grace that is given to you today will remain forever alive in your heart, producing fruits of eternal life.

It was not an apparition, but a presence. These words were etched so indelibly in my soul; they are still the bind of my union with God. [19]

With her little hands folded on her chest and recalling that nothing could disturb her, she sang more from the heart than the voice. The lyrics of the song that the choir performed while Communion was distributed were:

O Angels, sing with me!

O Angels, praise without end!

Give graces, I cannot!

O Angels, give them to me! [20]

Throughout her life whenever she heard this song, Sister Lucia relived the sensation and memory of her First Communion.

It was almost one o'clock before the ceremonies were over. Since the children were also renewing their Baptismal promises, the ceremony was very long. The celebration had started later than anticipated because the priests who were assisting arrived a little late. And the children were fasting! Lucia explains:

My mother came looking for me, quite distressed, thinking I might faint from weakness. I was feeling so satisfied with the Bread of Angels that I found it impossible to take any food whatsoever. After this I lost the taste and attraction for the things of the world and only felt at home in some solitary place where, all alone, I could recall the

---

18 MSL I, 2nd M, Ch. 1, No. 6, p. 73.

19 *My Pathway,* 1, p. 1.

20 *Sing To The Lord,* editorial L.I.A.M., 6th edition, 1972.

delights of my First Communion.[21]

Someone once said, *"A First Communion well done marks the whole life."* Lucia was marked, and more than that, it was imprinted on her inside. She did not talk about her frequency at Communion, although it was not unusual at that time to take Communion every day. It is assumed she had the Bread every Sunday because none of the family missed Mass. Because of her desire to receive Holy Communion and the fervor with which she made her First Communion surely she would have wanted the Bread of Angels frequently. After this day her visits to the Blessed Sacrament when she passed by the parish church were more time consuming and customary. She was already very intimate with Jesus Who was there! He was her Jesus. Maria Rosa advised her children to always enter the church when they passed by, and Lucia was obedient. Even at her age she was able to think of some reason that would make it necessary to visit her Friend.

Later when she was a religious of Saint Dorothy in Spain, Sister Lucia knew that there were people who wanted to buy her First Communion dress, a business she did not like at all. She wrote to her mother asking that it be sent to her promptly. As soon as the dress was in her possession, she took it apart and made several bonnets for sleeping. She kept one for herself and offered the others to some nuns, including her Mother Provincial, who really appreciated it.

The white dress Lucia wore on this unique day was a simple and inexpensive imitation cotton fabric. But the fact that it was white was more valuable than the quality of the fabric because it symbolized the whiteness of lilies, her favorite flower, and her pure soul because of God. She was the "lily of the mountain" which is reflected in the *lily of the valley,* [22] and became the property of the Spouse of Virgins! Each time she received her Hidden Jesus, in thanksgiving she sang in her innocent heart: *I am my Beloved's and my Beloved is mine!* [23]

---

21 MSL I, 2nd M, Ch. 1, No. 6, p. 73.

22 Sg 2:1.

23 Sg 6:3.

◀ Parish Church of Fatima where Lucia was baptized and made her First Communion.

▶ Baptismal font in the Church of Fatima where Lucia was baptized.

◀ Fr. Manuel Marques Ferreira, parish priest of Fatima at the time of the apparitions (1914-1919).

▶ Fr. Cruz

Statue of Francisco, Jacinta and Lucia praying during the apparition of the Angel.

CHAPTER II

THE APPARITIONS OF THE ANGEL
1915 – 1916

1 | Early Life of the Shepherdess

Lucia was now seven years old and her mother began to think about giving her some responsibilities. Besides the cheerful playing with other children and especially with her cousins, Francisco and Jacinta, her mother wanted her to be like her other sisters and get used to being occupied and having chores. Her mother insisted on this and Lucia began to take the sheep out to graze. It was healthy work that lent itself much to child's play, which added a sense of responsibility.

She knew she was going to guard the sheep with all the other shepherds in her company but when the day came, she was met in the hills with a crowd of shepherds and herds. Confused, she asked three companions who agreed to go to the opposite side where it was more peaceful. The following day there were four shepherds with their sheep at the Cabeço. After a morning of games, singing and running, jumping rope and throwing stones, they sat down to eat a snack each had brought, and Lucia invited her companions to pray the Rosary, a request her mother made when she left the house. Devotedly they began to pray and suddenly on the trees they saw a figure made of snow that was almost transparent by the rays of the sun. The three frightened companions asked:

-*What is that?*

Lucia responded:

-*I don't know!* [24]

They continued to pray the Rosary always looking at the mysterious figure that faded as they finished. Afterwards they continued to play until it was time to go home. Lucia did not speak of this to anyone. From a very early age she proved to be reserved, able to keep a secret, and withstand strong emotions undisturbed. A few days later when she arrived home, her mother asked Lucia what she had seen because her companions had told their families and they talked about it. She was surprised that any importance was given to the event and not being able to explain what she saw, simply said:

-*It looked like a person wrapped up in a sheet… you could not see any eyes or hands.*

Her mother, with a gesture of disgust, concluded: -*Childish nonsense!* [25]

The apparition was repeated twice more in the company of the same girls, who returned home to tell their parents. Lucia's mother again heard about it from the outside and called her daughter who had said nothing and ordered her very seriously to tell her all that they had seen. The little one, a bit intimidated, replied:

---

24 MSL I, 2nd M, Ch. II, No. 1, p. 76.
25 *Ibid.*

-I don't know, mother. I don't know what it is! [26]

Her mother was silent, but questions remained in her heart.

After her First Communion, Lucia liked to retire from time to time to think about her Jesus. Once her sisters began to tease her playfully and asked her if she saw someone wrapped in a sheet. She was humiliated but kept silent. These were the first thorns in her path, and were particularly painful because she was accustomed to the affection of the whole family; she was the little girl of the house. But here the sky began to darken her life with clouds and she felt the first thorns of the Way of the Cross.

Her companions playing in the house were her cousins Francisco and Jacinta, but they were not allowed to accompany her when she became a shepherdess. Their mother Olympia felt that they were still too young to go with the sheep, so they resigned themselves to wait all day for their cousin Lucia. Although they were tempted to disobey, what their father or mother said was sacred. Expecting at the end of the day to get together again, all three went to look at the lamp of Our Lady, the moon, and those of the Angels, the stars, as Lucia's father taught them. The sun was the lamp of Our Lord Who alone illuminated the day, but they liked more to see the lamps at night because they were gentler to look at.

These moments were short and the cousins persisted in asking their mother for permission to go with Lucia to watch over the sheep. After much insistence from the little ones, their parents talked among themselves and finally allowed them to accompany Lucia. What a joy for all three; Lucia never again wanted any other company. Always together they led the sheep only to the lands of the two families, and thus no longer mingled with other shepherds. It was God's hand leading the paths of these three children to be responsible for delivering the Message brought by Mary to the world.

2 | First Apparition of the Angel of Peace

In the spring of 1916 while walking to keep the herd in a property called Old Chousa, a drizzling rain began to fall. They climbed the hill to find shelter in the crevices of a rock. The rain soon passed and the sun returned and they remained there. At noon they ate their lunch after praying an abbreviated version of the Rosary so they could play. They were always told to pray the Rosary and they had to obey, but they liked playing very much, so they solved the problem: the three sat down and Francisco, being the leader, counted the beads saying *Our Father,*

---

26 MSL I, 2ⁿᵈ M, Ch. II, No. 2, p. 77.

Hail Mary, Hail Mary... and at the end of the decade very slowly, Glory be... Thus ended the rosary and the games began. But on this day their lives would change. Lucia tells it this way:

We had enjoyed playing for a few moments only when a strong wind began to shake the trees. We looked up, startled to see what was happening, for the day was unusually calm. We saw coming toward us above the olive trees the figure I have already spoken about. Jacinta and Francisco had never seen it before, nor had I ever mentioned it to them. As it drew closer, we were able to distinguish its features. It was a young man, about 14 or 15 years old, whiter than snow, transparent as crystal when the sun shines through it, and of great beauty. On reaching us, he said:

-Do not be afraid! I am the Angel of Peace. Pray with me.
Kneeling on the ground he bowed down until his forehead touched the ground and made us repeat these words three times:

-My God, I believe, I adore, I hope and I love You. I ask pardon of You for those who do not believe, do not adore, do not hope and do not love You.

Then, rising, he said:

-Pray thus. The Hearts of Jesus and Mary are attentive to the voice of your supplications. [27]

Leaving them absorbed in a supernatural atmosphere, the Angel disappeared; they remained there for a long time and repeated the prayer that was engraved supernaturally in their hearts. They had no desire to talk to each other, penetrated by the strong feeling of God's presence that did not fade for several days. It was not necessary to express themselves to each other. None of them felt the desire to speak to anyone of what had happened. Francisco did not hear the voice of the Angel. While the two girls repeated the prayer the Angel said, he, like an echo, repeated what he heard from them.

3 | Second Apparition of the Angel of Portugal

After a few months, on a summer day the three shepherd children gathered the sheep during the hottest hours. They spent the hour of their siesta time at the Angel's well, which they called Arneiro, in the backyard of Lucia's home. While they were playing at the well, the Angel appeared to them again and with a gentle reproach asked them:

-What are you doing? Pray, pray very much. The most holy Hearts of Jesus and Mary have designs of mercy on you. Offer prayers and sacrifices to the Most High.

---

27 MSL I, 2ⁿᵈ M, Ch. II, No. 2, p. 78.

-*How are we to make sacrifices?* Lucia asked.

-*Make of everything you can a sacrifice, and offer it to God as an act of reparation for the sins by which He is offended, and in supplication for the conversion of sinners. You will thus draw down peace upon your country. I am its Guardian Angel, the Angel of Portugal. Above all, accept and bear with submission the suffering which the Lord will send you.*[28]

A few moments after the Angel disappeared Francisco asked his cousin what he had said. She was surprised that he had not heard. As in the first apparition he heard no dialogue, but Francisco didn't reveal this. Lucia, feeling unable to speak, asked him not to ask her anything that day, promising to tell him everything the next day. Francisco did not persist, and he confessed to her the next day that he did not sleep as he was thinking about what the Angel might have said. Together, Lucia and Jacinta told him what they heard. He wanted explanations about the meaning of the words, but again Lucia asked to leave the question for one more day. Since they still had not recovered their physical strength, Jacinta went on to tell her brother a little about it.

From this second apparition, the three shepherds found new ways on many occasions to make sacrifices of everything that gave them pleasure and offer them up for peace and for the cross they would soon receive. There was among them a natural cooperation, and they eagerly embraced a sacrifice as something sweet, but always with the utmost discretion so no one realized anything.

Under solitude in the midst of the trees or inside the cave that had become a hermitage for them, the three seers spent a lot of time praying the prayer the Angel taught them, prostrate and without fear of being seen. They remained that way until they were too tired to go on, especially in the first few weeks. Little by little they returned to their innocent playing.

4 | Third Apparition of the Angel of Portugal

In autumn, the three shepherds decided to pray in the cave and for this reason had to make a long and difficult journey with the sheep. For them it was already a sacred place. They prostrated themselves and began to pray the prayer they learned in the first apparition. Suddenly they felt enveloped by an intense light and rising saw the Angel holding in his hand a chalice with a Host suspended above it, from which a few drops of blood fell. The Angel did not say anything, but leaving the chalice with the Host suspended in the air, the Angel knelt down

---

28 *Ibid.*

Well at the house of the parents of Lucia, site of the
second apparition of the Angel.

▲ The path traveled by the shepherds with their flock.

◀ Site of the first apparition of the Angel to Lucia, Francisco and Jacinta.

◀ Statue of Francisco, Jacinta and Lucia praying during the apparition of the Angel.

beside them with his face to the ground. The shepherds followed his gesture and this time prayed a prayer much longer than the first:

-*Most Holy Trinity, Father, Son and Holy Spirit, I adore You profoundly, I offer You the most precious Body, Blood, Soul and Divinity of Jesus Christ present in all the tabernacles of the world, in reparation for the outrages, sacrileges and indifference with which He Himself is offended. And, through the infinite merits of His most Sacred Heart and the Immaculate Heart of Mary, I beg of You the conversion of poor sinners.*[29]

Praying very slowly they repeated it. As in other times, Francisco repeated the prayer after hearing his sister and cousin. Then rising, the Angel took the Chalice and the Host in his hands. He gave the Host to Lucia and the Chalice to her cousins to drink, as he said:

-*Take and drink the Body and Blood of Jesus Christ, horribly outraged by ungrateful men. Make reparation for their crimes and console your God.*[30]

He fell prostrate again, repeating the prayer three times, then disappeared. The shepherds did not notice the Angel had left; they had Jesus in their hearts. The two cousins had received their First Communion on this day. Totally absorbed by this experience so sublime, they were not aware of the time that passed, nor were they occupied by the sheep. But God took care of the sheep and did not allow them to escape or damage the nearby properties.

So taken were they by the supernatural presence, they lost all track of time. Francisco, who could hardly walk, alerted his companions of the coming of the night. Like the Apostles on Mount Tabor, they would say in their hearts: *It is good that we are here!*[31] They returned home in silence, and without the notice of family members, lived a few more days in this other world. Lucia referred to this impressionable time with great emphasis. She was to be more intensely designated, given a very special mission that she would take on her own shoulders. She used to say her cousins were chosen to be witnesses. Once they had given their testimony, Mary came to bring them to Heaven as she promised in the first apparition, while Lucia would remain here to go through a long and difficult path.

5 | Effects of the Apparitions of the Angel

After the visits and guidance from the Angel, the shepherds began to look eagerly and more perseveringly for ways to offer sacrifice for the conversion of sinners and to console Jesus. From this common experience, the three could not

---

29 MSL I, 2nd M, Ch. II, No. 2, p. 79.
30 *Ibid.*
31 Mt 17: 4.

be separated. Lucia had a magnetism that drew her cousins to her. For them it was always preferable that just the three of them could be together to talk about the secret they carried within themselves and to help find ways to console their God as the Angel requested in the last apparition. Lucia, still so young, was already a catechist and counselor of her two cousins as well as other children who liked to listen to her. It was an innate gift that remained all her life—she taught what she knew and was happy to be heard.

Under the solitude of the foliage where they were shepherding the flock, or at home in a place protected from outside glances, the three gave themselves to prayer, repeating with their hearts on fire the prayers they learned during the visits with the celestial Catechist.

During the winter, not being able to go out with the flock, they gathered together for games, but always reserved time to console Jesus, especially since the taste for children's play was taken from them.

Now older, Lucia was initiated into handling needles. She learned quickly to use them with skill and perfection. Lucia was already a master of the craft and with immense pleasure taught Jacinta to crochet. She demanded perfection in the work and it was well done without the need for a compliment.

6 | The First Farewell

Lucia was nine years old when her older sister Maria dos Anjos was married on August 23, 1916, to Antonio dos Santos Valinho. For a nine-year-old at that time these family events were not very memorable. On the day of the wedding, as she told, before leaving for the church, there was a ceremony in the house of the bride where all the guests gathered to follow in procession on horseback.

When the bride was ready she appeared in a new dress and a kerchief and scarf adorned with pieces of gold. Surrounded by her entire family who were in the main room, the groom stood in the doorway and asked her parents:

-*Will Mr. Antonio and Mrs. Maria Rosa give permission for Maria of the Angels to accompany me to the church to get married?*

Amid great commotion, the father asked his daughter if she wanted to go, and she, weeping, replied yes. Then she tearfully hugged everyone as they told her:

-*God be with you and make you very happy in your new home.*

Lucia, seeing them all crying and especially her sister, ran to the groom and pushed him out and said:

-*Go away, because she does not want to go. Do you not see how she cries!*

Her mother smiled in spite of her tears and they all left for the church and the feast followed in good harmony. This separation troubled Lucia and she did not understand why her sister would now live in a house with Antonio.

-Oh, mother, why is it that Maria now will not come to our house? [32]

Her mother explained to Lucia that with this wedding, it was the beginning of leaving her parents' side. Six months later, on February 14, 1917, Lucia's sister Teresa also married, and she moved further away so that they would only see her on Sundays.

---

32 Oral narration of Sister Lucia.

Valinhos, site of the third apparition of the Angel.

Image of Our Lady of Fatima.

Lucia with cousins Francisco and Jacinta in 1917.

CHAPTER III
THE APPARITIONS OF OUR LADY
1917

1 | Dark Night Under the Bright Sun

The visits of the Angel did not change the children's demeanor in the eyes of the family. No one realized anything, but everything changed when on May 13, 1917, the Lady appeared to them and asked:

-Are you willing to offer yourselves to God to bear all the sufferings He wills to send you, as an act of reparation for the sins by which He is offended, and in supplication for the conversion of sinners?

-Yes, we are willing.

-Then you are going to have much to suffer, but the grace of God will be your comfort. [33]

The life of Lucia and her cousins, as well as their families, were inflicted with much suffering from then on. Lucia's family especially suffered greatly and her mother felt much pressure because she did not believe in the apparitions as so many other people did. Compelled by her tender heart, she began punishing her child who until recently was surrounded with pampering. Only God knows the pain by which she was doing it. For righteousness and truth she could not bear that her daughter had become a liar, bringing so many people to pray in front of a tree!

Mr. Marto, Jacinta and Francisco's father, believed them from the start. Their mother doubted at first, but then soon she also believed the claims of the children. For Lucia, her mother was not so gentle. Her father, not wanting to get involved in the subject, never challenged or affirmed it, but her mother could not agree to such a thing.

This disagreement was providential because if the two families had accepted everything the children said then perhaps it would have led to the belief that this was a story arranged and taught to the children, which happened nonetheless. Lucia, being the oldest and considered the head of the three, suffered the most because of this disbelief. Together the children suffered the humiliation of being treated poorly by many people who went to the Cova da Iria and did not believe. They came often seeking Lucia, but dared not seek her cousins because their parents did not allow it. Lucia, being at home, did not feel well. It was a great affliction that fell upon her. The people ruined the area by the Cova and the surrounding property belonging to her parents. This was a great loss to the economy of the house. Her mother and sisters told her when she wanted to eat that she should ask the Lady for food or she could have what grows in the Cova da

---

Iria. It became distressing to her to eat any morsel of bread! Only with her cousins could she feel relief and they, being smaller, sought to comfort her by reminding her of the words of Our Lady: *Therefore, you will have much to suffer.* They suffered with her, offering their affliction, and almost envied her fate because they wanted to be like her and have many sacrifices to offer for the conversion of sinners and to console Our Lord. It was extraordinary at this age to be so eager for sacrifices. The Lady had communicated to them a fire of charity that made them able to suffer severe hunger, not thinking about themselves but for the salvation of those who were at risk of being lost forever.

Lucia tells in detail these visits of our heavenly Mother.

2 | Apparition of Our Lady on May 13th

It was Sunday, and after they had gone to Mass in the church of Fatima with their families, the three shepherds were free to take the sheep to graze. They chose their desired site, which was not difficult at this time of year because it was the height of spring and the grass was abundant everywhere. Still very young, they understood Psalm 23: *The Lord is my Shepherd, I shall not want. He leads me to lie down in green pastures, He leads me beside the still waters and comforts my soul.*[34]

This day Lucia chose the property of her parents, the Cova da Iria. They went slowly, leaving the sheep to graze along the way. After arriving there, while the sheep quietly grazed, the three began to build a wall around a thicket, the site where the Basilica dedicated to Our Lady of the Rosary would later be built. Lucia describes:

We suddenly saw what seemed to be a flash of lightning.

-We'd better go home, I said to my cousins, that's lightning; we may have a thunderstorm.

-Yes, indeed.

We began to go down the slope, hurrying the sheep along toward the road. We were more or less half-way down the slope, when near a large oak tree we saw another flash of lightning, and some steps later we saw on a holm oak a lady dressed all in white, brighter than the sun and radiating a light more clear and intense than a crystal glass filled with sparkling water when the rays of the burning sun shine through it. We stopped, astounded before the apparition. We were so close that we were in the light which surrounded her, or rather, which radiated from her, maybe five feet away, more or less.

---

34 Ps 23:1-3.

Then Our Lady spoke to us:

-Do not be afraid. I will do you no harm.

-Where are you from? I asked her.

-I am from Heaven.

-What do you want of me?

-I have come to ask you to come here for six months in succession on the 13th day at this same hour. Later on I will tell you who I am and what I want. Afterwards I will return here yet a seventh time.

-Shall I go to Heaven?

-Yes, you will.

-And Jacinta?

-Also.

-And Francisco?

-Also, but he must say many Rosaries.

Then I remembered to ask about two girls who had died recently. They were friends of mine and used to come to my home to learn weaving with my oldest sister.

-Is Maria da Neves in Heaven?

-Yes, she is.

It seems to me that she was about 16 years old.

-And Amelia?

-She will be in purgatory until the end of the world.

It seems to me that she was between 18 and 20 years of age.

-Are you willing to offer yourselves to God and bear all the sufferings He wills to send you, as an act of reparation for the sins by which He is offended and in supplication for the conversion of sinners?

-Yes, we are willing.

-Then you are going to have much to suffer, but the grace of God will be your comfort.

As she pronounced these last words Our Lady opened her hands communicating to us a light so intense that its rays penetrated our hearts and innermost soul, making us see ourselves in God, Who was that light, more clearly than we see ourselves in the best of mirrors. Then on an interior impulse that was also communicated, we fell on our knees, repeating in our hearts:

-Oh most Holy Trinity, I adore You, my God, my God, I love You in the most Blessed Sacrament. After a few moments, Our Lady added:

-Pray the Rosary every day to obtain peace for the world and the end of the war.

Then she began to rise serenely, going up toward the east until she disappeared in the immensity of space.

The light that surrounded her seemed to open up a path before her in the thickness of the stars; we sometimes said we saw Heaven opening.[35]

On May 13, 1917, enveloped in light and peace, gentle as the rain on the green grass, the Blessed Virgin appeared in Fatima as a helpful Mother for the good of her children whom she saw in danger. She revealed that she came from Heaven and then delivered to three innocent children a message of salvation for the world: The movement of atheistic materialism will come from the source of communism. Heaven deigned upon the world a blaze of light illuminating the dense night that threatened to envelop humanity completely. When the world closed its eyes to the supernatural and turned its back on God, the Mother of God came to warn humanity of impending danger and showed the way to avoid it, asking for prayer and conversion.

It was thus silently that everything began.

From that day this unknown place began to attract the eyes of all social classes to Jesus, Who was *a sign of contradiction.*[36] And today all roads lead to Fatima.

At the same time on that day May 13, 1917, a bishop was consecrated in Rome; Eugenio Pacelli would become Pope Pius XII in 1939. This pope had several decisive roles in Fatima throughout his legacy, always showing great appreciation for the message brought by the Mother of God.

2-1 Radiant like the Sun

When the vision disappeared the shepherds were absorbed in the aftermath of the surprise visit, but not in the way the visit of the Angel had left them. After the two girls informed Francisco of what Our Lady had said because he could not hear her, they spent the afternoon in a thoughtful mode. When Lucia told him Our Lady would take him to Heaven but he had to say many Rosaries, he exclaimed:

-*Oh, my dear Lady! I'll say as many rosaries as you want.* [37]

Lucia, anticipating what would happen when she told him, said:

-*I can just see you still going to tell someone.*

-*No, I won't, he answered, don't worry.*

But then he exclaimed:

---

35 MSL I, 4th M, Ch. II, No. 3, pp. 174-176.
36 Lk 2:34.
37 MSL I, 4th M, Ch. I, No. 4, p. 143.

-Oh, what a beautiful Lady! [38]

At dusk they gathered the herd and returned to their homes. In Lucia's house everything went normally. They noticed nothing on her face or in her behavior. She already had a great capacity to withstand such strong emotions. They dined and rested. The long days of May meant the nights were shorter for resting after a day's work. At the home of Lucia's aunt and uncle, it was not the same. When the children arrived, the parents still had not come from the market. Jacinta, driven by an inner force, waited for her parents and when she caught sight of them, she ran into the arms of her mother and though breathless told her:

-Oh mother, today we saw a beautiful Lady in the Cova da Iria! [39] Her mother returned her hug and received the news with some irony, almost not paying any attention. At night when they were all at the table, Jacinta was asked what they had seen. She jumped up and with joy in her eyes repeated the exclamation while she danced all around:

-We saw a beautiful Lady in the Cova da Iria! Her hands were so (she imitated the position of the hands of Our Lady)*and she had a Rosary that was so beautiful!* [40]

Once the words came out of her mouth, she was no longer able to hide what had happened. Francisco remained silent and downcast. He knew of the promise he made to his cousin so many times in the afternoon, and to see that his sister had not been able to keep the secret worried him. At one point he also was interrogated and could not lie. He confirmed what she saw without saying anything further. Mr. Marto soon declared his belief in the apparition and ended the conversation in peace. They prayed their evening prayers and then rested.

In the home of Lucia nothing of the like transpired. Certainly she was concentrating on the day though nothing drew attention to the fact she was withdrawn. She was at peace with the secret in her heart.

Thus, it was no surprise to her when on the following day Francisco warned her that Jacinta had told. Being very sorry, she said tearfully that she had a strong impulse in her heart and could not conceal so great a joy. Lucia had anticipated what might happen and told her cousin not to cry and not to say anything more of what the Lady said to them.

-But I've already told them, Jacinta replied.

-What did you say? Lucia asked firmly.

-I said that the Lady promised to take us to Heaven!

And immediately she said:

---

38 Cf. MSL I, 1ˢᵗ M, Ch. I, No. 7. p. 45.
39 Fernando Leite, S.J., *Jacinta*, 1951.
40 *Ibid.*

-Forgive me, I won't tell anybody anything ever again! [41]

Lucia knew now that life was not going to be easy. She had already experienced what happened when her friends told about the vision of the mysterious figure in the early days of grazing. Now it was going to be more serious. But the inner joy and the certainty that the Lady gave them of taking them to Heaven gave her strength to be afraid of nothing.

As soon as news reached Maria Rosa, she was startled and even more so by the silence of her daughter. Why was it that she had to find out everything from the outside and not a word from her? But after requesting that she not invent these stories, she gave them no importance, saying they were things that children do. However, when so many people came to her house to ask questions she began to get worried and tried to dissuade them from making such tiring trips, and said to them:

-Don't take any notice of it. It is all children's talk. What I don't know is how it came into their heads to say such a thing! It's incredible that people actually believe them! How can it be? God help me. I could have done without all this! [42]

The people continued to come to the house, however, and each time in greater numbers, always annoying Maria Rosa with the same questions. Some were well-intentioned and with devotion, but others made fun and asked tricky questions blaming Lucia's poor mother. Her father, not yet annoyed with these questioners, looked for ways to avoid the house and only returned when he knew that no one would be there. All of this was merciless suffering for her mother, and when Lucia came home from grazing the sheep being already exhausted, she scolded her and sometimes gave her a few slaps or the broom handle, blaming her for all this suffering.

-You have to tell these people you lied so they don't all go around wasting their time on fairy tales and making me waste my time, as I can't get anything done! [43]

The little one did not respond. Full of bitterness, she would look into the bottomless well to free her pain, recalling the words she had heard from the Angel and what Our Lady had told her:

-Then, you are going to have much to suffer, but the grace of God will be your comfort. [44]

This was carved into her heart, but the night was very dark and she felt alone when she was at home. Seeing that her cousins were believed, she felt even

---

41 Cf. MSL I, 1ˢᵗ M, Ch. 1, No. 7, p. 45.
42 MSL II, 6ᵗʰ M, No. 33, p. 128.
43 *Ibid.*
44 MSL I, 2nd M, Ch. II, No. 4, p. 83.

greater pain. It seemed to her that her parents no longer liked her. This feeling in her 10-year-old heart was very hard, especially since she had been queen of the house. Suddenly she was treated like a criminal and blamed for all the suffering that happened in her family. She ached for her mother's suffering, a mother whom she idolized as the best mother in the world. If only she could suffer alone without others being drawn into this path. Like Calvary, it was necessary to drink the cup that was presented. She had to see her mother suffer at her side just as Jesus suffered alongside His Mother at the cross.

In her book *Memoirs of Sister Lucia, Volume II,* she recounted how great was her suffering, describing the Calvary of the entire family, especially her mother. Throughout her life, Sister Lucia always praised her mother and never referred to her with any bitter memories. If her mother caused her suffering, it was always in the sincere search for righteousness and truth.

Little Lucia said 'yes' to God, a 'yes' so honest from her innocent heart that God took possession of her entirely. From that day on she became the property of God. Despite her nature and human weakness, she wanted to proclaim her feelings and was able to say before Him, *I will do God's will just as His Son in His mortal life.* It was true. Her 'yes' on May 13, 1917, was a solemn consecration of her entire being and all her life to God through Mary. Each time she was visited by suffering she brought herself to that blessed place at that hour on that day and renewed her unconditional surrender. This 'yes' marked her life forever.

June 13th drew nearer and the shepherds continued to take their sheep to graze. The first apparition had totally changed them, and now they prayed the full Hail Marys and discussed how they would make sacrifices. Before they would allow themselves a choice of games, but now it was a choice of sacrifices: to give up their lunch to the sheep, and later to the poor people, spending days without food from morning to evening. Instead they chose to eat acorns for their midday meal because they were bitter. They also passed the days scorched by thirst, making frequent novenas, and even going a whole month without drinking much water. [45]

3 | Apparition of Our Lady on June 13th

June 13th was a test for Lucia. As one fond of festivities, her family watched what she would do on this feast day of Saint Anthony. Having no other entertainment, the children in the village looked forward to the feast days and

---

45 Fernando Leite, S.J., *Jacinta.*

would not miss them. Lucia's mother and sisters said to her:

-*We've yet to see if you'll leave the festa just to go to the Cova da Iria and talk to that Lady!* [46]

On the 13th everyone kept quiet. Traditionally this day was free from shepherding the flocks. Lucia came out very early with the flock, intending to gather them in time to go to Mass at 10 a.m. Just before eight o'clock her brother called her. Some people had arrived and wanted to talk to her though she was with the herd. The group of people had come from an area about 25 miles from Fatima, and they wanted to accompany her to the Cova da Iria. As it was still very early, he invited them to go to Mass first and then to the Cova. When they returned from Mass, the people waited for her in the shade of the trees. Lucia felt angry and as silence from the family prevailed around her, at 11 o'clock she went to meet her cousins. Accompanied by the people they made their way to the site of the apparitions. They prayed the Rosary while they waited for the arrival of the Lady. The apparition was announced by lightning. When the Lady appeared Lucia asked the same question as in May:

-*What do you want of me?*

-*I wish you to come here on the 13th of next month, to pray the Rosary every day, and to learn to read. Later, I will tell you what I want.*

I asked for the cure of a sick person.

-*If he is converted he will be cured during the year.*

-*I would like to ask you to take us to Heaven.*

-*Yes, I will take Jacinta and Francisco soon. You are to stay here for some time longer. Jesus wants to use you to make me known and loved. He wants to establish in the world devotion to my Immaculate Heart. To those who accept this, I promise them the salvation of their souls and they will be loved by God like flowers placed by me to adorn His throne.*

-*Am I to stay here alone?* I asked sadly.

-*No, my daughter. Are you suffering a great deal? Don't lose heart. I will never forsake you. My Immaculate Heart will be your refuge and the way that will lead you to God.*

At the moment when she spoke these last words, she opened her hands and for the second time she communicated to us the rays of that same immense light. We saw ourselves in this light, as it were, immersed in God. Jacinta and Francisco seemed to be in that part of the light which rose towards Heaven and I in that which was poured out on the earth. In front of the palm of Our Lady's right hand was a heart encircled by thorns

46 MSL I, 2nd M, Ch. II, No. 4, p. 83.

which pierced it. We understood that this was the Immaculate Heart of Mary, outraged by the sins of humanity and seeking reparation. [47]

The shepherds were so moved that they felt more protected not revealing all that the Lady had said to them, but this was to be the cause of new suffering. Lucia began to experience an inward darkness and great loneliness. She suffered so much knowing that her cousins were going to Heaven soon and she would be alone in the mission entrusted to her. It was comforting when Lucia recalled the Lady's promise, that her Immaculate Heart would be her refuge, but still very painful. How impressive to see a 10-year-old child carrying so much responsibility and suffering! Then the voice of temptation came, because the devil does not let God's work be done without tempting those whom He calls. It is a time of trial, a difficult time, but if it is put to good use it will allow faith to take root and strengthen the foundations of life.

After the June apparition, seeing that instead of everything waning, the events continued and took on even greater proportions, Lucia's mother was very worried about the alleged lies of her daughter, nephew and niece. She was relieved when the parish priest sent word to her to bring Lucia to the parochial residence for questioning. It was the first step of the Church.

Thinking the parish priest was going to resolve the problem in her home, Maria Rosa very seriously conversed with Lucia, and with some satisfaction in her voice said:

-*Tomorrow we're going to Mass the first thing in the morning. Then you are going to the Reverend Father's house. Just let him compel you to tell the truth, no matter how he does it; let him punish you; let him do whatever he likes with you, just so long as he forces you to admit that you have lied. Then I'll be satisfied.*[48]

That evening Lucia spoke with her cousins and confessed the apprehension she felt in the face of her mother's threats. They informed her that the parish priest also sent for them, but they were not afraid. They encouraged each other, concluding:

-*Patience! If they strike us, we suffer for the love of Our Lord and for sinners.* [49]

They always thought about the good of others, desiring to save souls.

The next day to her surprise, Lucia, who was anticipating a threatening man of iron, was questioned with much gentleness and kindness, although the interrogation was meticulous and boring. The pastor, however, was not convinced and left her in a sea of suffering by telling her *it could very well be a deception of the*

---

47 MSL I, 4th M, Ch. II, No. 4, p.177.
48 MSL I, 2nd M, Ch. II, No. 5, p. 85.
49 *Ibid.*

devil. [50]

This was a sharp arrow that pierced the depths of her conscience. Hence came sleepless nights and terrible nightmares. She experienced discouragement, stopped the practice of sacrifice, was willing to abandon everything and say it was all a lie. She began to formulate a firm resolution not to return to the heavenly apparition in thirteen days. When she informed her cousins about her resolution, Jacinta said to her with a strong conviction:

-No, it's not the devil! They say the devil is very ugly and he's down under the ground in hell, and the Lady is so beautiful! We saw her going up to Heaven! [51]

They talked her out of saying she didn't see anything because then she would be lying. Francisco and Jacinta helped their cousin with great prayer and sacrifices. They were a wonderful light to her. Knowing her sufferings, the two shepherds consoled and advised her as best they could, more in silence than with words. In these moments silence was more effective. Suffering greatly, Lucia prayed and offered sacrifices. By confessing her temptations the battle was half-won because God opens the door to His help and places it beside the one that is suffering. Lucia had beside her those two angels who were enlightened by the Holy Spirit to advise her as if they were great teachers, and she received the help with humility.

It was a month of unprecedented suffering for her and there seemed to be no end to it. Her two cousins watched, distressed at seeing the thirteenth of July getting closer and Lucia still affirmed she would not go with them to speak to the Lady. Tormented by nightly nightmares in which she saw herself in the claws of the devil being dragged into hell, she looked for every opportunity to escape. Even in the company of her sincere friends, she would not listen to reason.

On the 12th she was still determined not to go. In the afternoon she informed Jacinta and Francisco of her resolution. They answered her:

-We're going, the Lady told us to go there.

Jacinta volunteered to speak to the Lady, but she was so upset over my not going that she started to cry.

I asked her why she was crying.

-Because you don't want to go.

-No, I'm not going. Listen! If the Lady asks for me, tell her I'm not going, because I'm afraid it may be the devil. [52]

Lucia hid behind a thorn bush to avoid having to answer the many people who had already begun to arrive. Her two cousins were desolate, but they did not

---

50 *Ibid.*
51 MSL I, 2nd M, Ch. II, No. 6, p. 86.
52 *Ibid.*

lessen their intercession for her nor their confidence in Our Lady. In the evening when she returned home, her mother scolded her for spending all day playing— another thorn suffered in silence without any apology. If her mother could only see inside her little one's heart.

4 | Apparition of Our Lady on July 13th

On the morning of July 13 after a troubling night of insomnia, Lucia did not mention the heavenly appointment to her family, which caused some surprise but no one questioned her. As the hours progressed, however, something big was stirring inside her. The enormous responsibility weighed heavily on Lucia and, unconsciously like Jesus in Gethsemane, she tried to ward off the Cup. The Blessed Virgin watched over her little confidant and did not let her succumb. Lucia related:

Suddenly I felt compelled to go by a strange force, which I could not resist. I went on the path to my uncle's house to see if Jacinta was still there. I found her in the bedroom with Francisco kneeling at the foot of the bed, crying.

-Aren't you going then? I asked them.

-Not without you! We don't dare. Do come!

-Yes, I'm going, I replied. Their faces were full of joy, and they set out with me. [53]

The hand of Mary chased away the terrible temptation that overwhelmed her entire being and imbued her with much strength. She was back on the path ready to go forward:

It was as if a huge burden was lifted directly from my heart. It was a new day that dawned. Upon arriving at the site, we began to pray the Rosary with the people that were present until we saw the reflection of the customary light and Our Lady was on the holm oak.

-What do you want of me? I asked.

-I wish you to come here on the 13th of next month, to pray the Rosary every day in honor of Our Lady of the Rosary in order for you to obtain peace for the world and an end of the war, because only she can help you.

-I would like to ask you to tell us who you are and to work a miracle so that everybody will believe that you appear to us.

-Continue to come here every month. In October I will tell you who I am and what I want and I will perform a miracle for all to see and believe.

Here I made some requests but I cannot recall now just what they were. What I

---

53 *Ibid.*

▶ Jacinta and Lucia in Reixida
   September, 1917.

▼ Lucia, Jacinta and Francisco
   in Aljustrel, 1917.

do remember is that Our Lady said it was necessary for such people to pray the Rosary in order to obtain these graces during the year. And she continued:

-Sacrifice yourselves for sinners and say many times, especially whenever you make some sacrifice: O Jesus, it is for love of You, for the conversion of sinners, and in reparation for the sins committed against the Immaculate Heart of Mary. [54]

5 | The Secret

5-1 *The Vision of Hell (Part 1)*

In saying these last words, she opened her hands, as in the past two months. The light seemed to penetrate the earth and we saw, as it were, a sea of fire. Plunged in this fire were demons and souls in human form, like transparent burning embers, all blackened or burnished bronze, floating about in the conflagration, now raised into the air by the flames that issued from within themselves together with great clouds of smoke, now falling back on every side like sparks in huge fires, without weight or equilibrium, amid shrieks and groans of pain and despair, which horrified us and made us tremble with fear. (It must have been this sight which caused me to cry out, as people say they heard me.) The demons could be distinguished by their terrifying and repellent likeness to frightful and unknown animals, black and transparent like burning coals. Terrified and as if to plead for succor, we looked up at Our Lady, who said to us so kindly and so sadly:

-You have seen hell where the souls of poor sinners go. To save them, God wishes to establish in the world devotion to my Immaculate Heart. If what I say to you is done, many souls will be saved and there will be peace. The war is going to end; but if people do not cease offending God, a worse one will break out during the pontificate of Pius XI. When you see a night illumined by an unknown light, know that this is the great sign given you by God that He is about to punish the world for its crimes by means of war, famine, and persecutions of the Church and of the Holy Father.[55]

5-2 *Devotion to the Immaculate Heart of Mary (Part 2)*

-To prevent this, I shall come to ask for the consecration of Russia to my Immaculate Heart and the Communion of Reparation on the First Saturdays. If my requests are heeded, Russia will be converted and there will be peace; if not, she will spread her errors throughout the world, causing wars and persecutions of the Church.

---

54 MSL I, 4ᵗʰ M, Ch. II, No. 4, p. 178.
55 *Ibid.*

The good will be martyred, the Holy Father will have much to suffer, various nations will be annihilated.

In the end my Immaculate Heart will triumph. The Holy Father will consecrate Russia to me, and she will be converted, and a period of peace will be granted to the world. In Portugal, the dogma of the Faith will always be preserved, etc. [56]

5-3 Call to Penance (Part 3)

Many years later on January 3, 1944, obeying an order from the Bishop of Leiria, Sister Lucia wrote the last part of the Secret, which remained guarded in her heart:

At the left of Our Lady and a little above, we saw an Angel with a flaming sword in his left hand; flashing, it gave out flames that looked as though they would set the world on fire; but they died out in contact with the splendor that Our Lady radiated toward him from her right hand. Pointing to the earth with his right hand, the Angel cried out in a loud voice: 'Penance, Penance, Penance!' We saw in an immense light that is God something similar to how people appear in a mirror when they pass in front of it, a bishop dressed in white (we had the impression that it was the Holy Father), and other bishops, priests, and men and women religious going up a steep mountain, at the top of which there was a big cross of rough-hewn trunks as of a cork tree with the bark. Before reaching there the Holy Father passed through a big city half in ruins, and half trembling with a halting step, afflicted with pain and sorrow, he prayed for the souls of the corpses he met on his way. Having reached the top of the mountain, on his knees at the foot of the big cross he was killed by a group of soldiers who fired bullets and arrows at him, and in the same way there died one after another the other bishops, priests, men and women religious, and various lay people of different ranks and positions. Beneath the two arms of the cross there were two Angels each with a crystal aspersorium in their hand, in which they gathered up the blood of the martyrs and with it sprinkled the souls that were making their way to God. [57] *'Do not tell this to anyone. Francisco, yes, you may tell him.'* [58]

Then Our Lady requested:

-*When you pray the Rosary, say after each mystery: O my Jesus, forgive us, save us from the fire of hell. Lead all souls to Heaven, especially those who are most in need.*

---

56 MSL I, 4th M, Ch. II, No. 5, p. 179.
    Author's note: with this etc., the narrative was suspended in the third part of the secret, which remained a secret until it was revealed on May 13, 2000.
57 *The Message of Fatima (the Secret)*, Congregation for the Doctrine of the Faith, or MSL I, Appendix III, Part III of 'The Secret' p. 215.
58 *Ibid.*

After this, there was a moment of silence, and then I asked:

-Is there anything more that you want of me?

-No, I do not want anything more of you today.

And as before Our Lady began to ascend toward the east, until she finally disappeared in the immense distance of the firmament. [59]

The Lady asked them to keep secret what they had seen in this apparition, but since June the shepherds were compelled by an inner strength to guard the secrets as Lucia stated: *Our Lady did not tell us at this time to guard the secret, but we felt that we were moved by God.* [60]

6 | The Heart of the Message in the Hearts of the Children

After this apparition, Lucia regained peace and strength to embrace all suffering. How could such young children bear the full weight of this vision and guard its content so faithfully? The vision of hell impressed them so much to the point that, as Lucia explained, they almost died of fright. It drove them to embrace a generous charity for sinners, doing everything they could to prevent more souls from being tormented in hell, and to make reparation to the Immaculate Heart of Mary, which was revealed to them surrounded by thorns. The three of them spoke among themselves about the deep impression it left on their hearts and helped each other to think of ways to save sinners from hell. Jacinta from time to time was petrified by the thought of an eternity of torment. Once after contemplating this for a long time, with an immense sadness in her voice she asked her cousin:

-But listen! Doesn't hell end after many, many years, then?

Lucia, a little more educated and in the same sad tone, responded:

-No! Hell never ends! [61]

The three were immersed in pain to see so many souls lost forever. They prayed, made sacrifices and cried with an intense love, especially for those who do not love. Sometimes questions remained in their hearts: *"How can anyone not love God, if He is so good?"* And they prayed the prayers taught by the Angel, prayers of adoration, supplication and reparation: *"My God, I believe... Holy Trinity... "* They prayed prostrate until they were exhausted. They would intercede for long hours before God for those not willing or those who had no desire to do so. In this apparition, it was the third time that the Lady opened her hands and this time she lowered them. According Sister Lucia's interpretation, this position of Our Lady's

---

59 MSL I, 4th M, Ch. II, No. 5, p. 179.

60 MSL I, 4th M, Ch. II, No. 4, p. 177.

61 MSL I, 1st M, Ch. I, No. 8, p. 46.

hands signified the gesture of a caring mother who raises her little child who has fallen. The left hand gathers the child from the floor and the right hand supports and caresses the child. Our Lady is always lovingly attentive to her children who have fallen into the marshes of pain and sin. She offers everyone her protection and wants to help them stand up and walk on the right path, which is the only way to happiness.

7 | A Deep Love for the Bishop Dressed in White

After this vision the Holy Father was in the hearts and prayers of the three shepherds. They did not know who he was or his name, but that man in white staggering under the weight of suffering came into their hearts forever. He was a central figure in the third part of the Secret, a suffering person who was targeted. He was the Pope but not any particular Pope. Lucia told of a particular vision of the Pope that Jacinta alone saw:

One day our siesta was spent down by my parents' well. Jacinta sat on the stone slabs on top of the well. Francisco and I climbed up a steep slope in search of wild honey among the brambles in a nearby thicket. After a little while, Jacinta called out to me:

-Didn't you see the Holy Father?

-No.

-I don't know how it was, but I saw the Holy Father in a very big house kneeling by a table with his head buried in his hands, and he was weeping. Outside the house there were many people and some of them were throwing stones; others were cursing him and using bad language. Poor Holy Father! We must pray very much for him.

At another time we went to the cave called Lapa do Cabeço. As soon as we got there we prostrated on the ground, saying the prayers the Angel had taught us. After some time Jacinta stood up and called to me:

-Can't you see all those highways and roads and fields full of people who are crying with hunger and have nothing to eat? And the Holy Father in a church praying before the Immaculate Heart of Mary? And so many people praying with him?

Some days later, she asked me:

-Can I say that I saw the Holy Father and all those people?

-No. Don't you see that that's part of the secret? If you do, they'll find out right away.

-All right! Then I'll say nothing at all. [62]

Even with these visions, the little seers were not sure who the Pope was. Only later

---

when two priests visited them and advised them to pray for the Holy Father did they realize who he was.[63]

8 | A Promise about Portugal

In Portugal the dogma of the Faith will always be preserved. This promise of the Lady does not mean that the Portuguese are protected in advance against evil or that they can do whatever they want and will always be safe. Although Sister Lucia was a person of few words when she commented about the Message of Fatima and especially avoided making personal interpretations, some time ago she let this affirmation slip out as she was meditating: *-If Portugal does not approve abortion then it is safe, but if approved it will have much to suffer. For the sin of the person, that person is responsible and pays for it, but for the sin of the nation all the people pay for it because rulers who enact unjust laws do so on behalf of the people who elected them.*[64]

Today Portugal is under the weight of three social sins that require reparation and conversion: divorce, abortion, and the civil marriage between persons of the same sex. It is the great moral crisis that explains all other crises. A body sick with gangrene does better with treatments, but while the disease improves, treatment does not eradicate the source of evil, and death will be the end. So it is in the social fabric. While immorality rages as a deadly plague, all the people groan and have much to suffer. But the promise will be fulfilled, because there will always be a *remnant poor and humble*[65] *that will be like yeast in the dough.*[66] Victory over evil is always and only from God and He does not triumph by power, but always through the small and poor.[67] Snow lilies will sprout in the middle of the swamp.

9 | Prepared to Fight

The three seers, like the martyrs of Christianity, helped and encouraged each other in their prayers and sacrifices during the times when they were alone with the sheep. Nobody knew about their sacrifices. One cannot imagine the fasts they imposed on themselves, the burning thirst which devoured them, and the floggings they made with nettles, etc., all to help save those who stood in the pit of sin. This intense, fervent prayer stemmed from their hearts, which burned with the flaming fire of love for God and neighbor. Whatever would come, this flame of

---

63 MSL I, 1st M, Ch. I, No. II, p. 50.
64 Oral Narration.
65 Is 10:18-22.
66 Lk 13:10-21.
67 Jgs 6:15-16.

love clothed them in a strength that did not succumb to the cries of nature.

Meanwhile Maria Rosa, seeing the increasing influx of people to their home and unable to believe in the cause that brought them, experienced a great deal of concern and anguish. Her house, already full of people, was intruded upon by strangers coming through the door uninvited. Even when they couldn't speak with the seer they would not leave. Lucia and her cousins hid themselves from the people who, with good or bad intentions, waited for them to appear. The family also could not prepare meals. It was a life of disorder. After a few days, Lucia's mother told her to go again to talk with the parish priest and confess the lie. She was the cause of everything and it had to end! Lucia quickly went to her uncle's house and told Jacinta what she was going to do. Francisco was also informed and the two remained to pray confidently for the help of Our Lady. On the path outside, Lucia's mother was advising her to tell the truth and say the visions were a lie. Upset and on the verge of tears, Lucia said:

-*But mother, how can I say that I did not see when I did see?* [68]

Her mother swallowed and said nothing, but thought 'that's my girl…' They walked the short distance in silence and went up the stairs to the parish house. Her mother turned to her daughter and said:

-*Just you listen to me! What I want is that you should tell the truth. If you saw, say so! But if you didn't see, admit that you lied.* [69]

Without saying anything more they went in. The parish priest received them and spoke to the little one with kindness and affection. He tried to trick her to see if she would contradict herself or be inconsistent in her statements. Shrugging his shoulders, he said to her mother:

-*I don't know what to make of all this!* [70]

Her mother returned home heartbroken that the pastor could not solve the problem. The coming and going of people did not stop and Maria Rosa had to always go searching for Lucia to come home and contend with them, because they would not budge without seeing her. Daughter and mother both suffered, and the pain which became so much greater and the silence so much heavier was kept in these two hearts that loved each other so much.

After the apparitions began, Lucia was blamed for many areas of their land being destroyed because of the influx of people to and from the Cova da Iria. The family livelihood was affected. Her other two sisters, Gloria and Carolina, served faithfully in homes to earn a living. Her father would not meet with all the

68 MSL I, 2nd M, Ch. II, No. 7, p. 89.
69 *Ibid.*
70 *Ibid.*

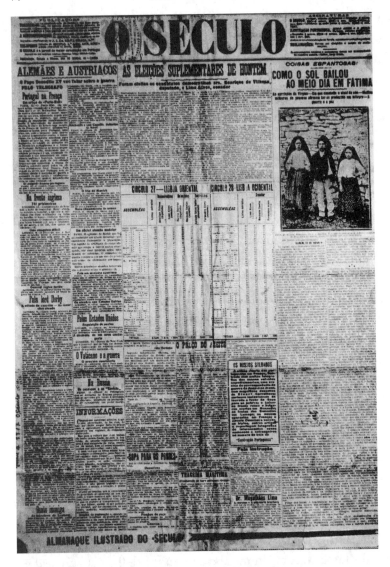

Journal "O Século" that disclosed the events of Fatima.

◀ Francisco, Jacinta and Lucia together at the Church of Fatima.

▶ Lucia, 10 years old.

people intruding into their home asking endless questions that he did not feel comfortable answering. Upon returning from work, he visited with his friends in the tavern and only returned home when there was no one there. Lucia's mother absorbed all this bitterness without the consolation of being able to admit that her youngest daughter was telling the truth!

Of her, Our Lady also asked a lot of sacrifice, although she did not tell her in words. Next to those that God chooses for a special mission, He always places "unnamed saints" that will help them accomplish what He asks, because the work is always the work of many. The shepherdess did not walk alone, though she often felt the weight of loneliness. Beside her there was a great tier of helpers raised up by God, so that together they could fulfill the Message brought from Heaven. And the work continues today because Fatima is *a small fountain that became a river, a light that became the sun.*[71]

10 | Facing the "Judges"

On August 10th, the shepherds' parents received an order from the authorities to appear before the Administration of Vila Nova de Ourem with the little ones the next day. Mr. Marto agreed to go but would not take his children because they were too small for the walk and too young to go to a court. Lucia's father did not agree, stating:

-*Mine will go; let her answer. I understand nothing of these things. And if it is intentional, it is good that she is punished.* [72]

Lucia was mounted on a donkey, tired from so much sacrifice and many sleepless nights. With the melancholy sound of a dull conversation between her father and uncle and rocked by the rhythmic steps of the donkey, she was overcome by sleep and three times slipped off the donkey and landed on the ground. The ground was not far from the small donkey and the shepherdess suffered nothing more than to be startled. Years later during recreation when referring to this episode, she recounted it with her fine sense of humor and never with bitter memories. Meanwhile, her two cousins were weeping and praying for her, thinking that she would be killed. Lucia suffered from the feeling that her parents did not love her, because unlike her aunt and uncle, they would indulge the authorities' wishes. A child this age has much fear of things related to police, judges, and such. All the way there in the silence of her heart, the little one offered to God and Our Lady this sacrifice and repeated the act of offering that Our

---

71 Esther 10:4.
72 MSL I, 2nd M, Ch. II, No. 8, p. 89.

Lady had taught her: *O Jesus, it is for love of You, for the conversion of sinners, and in reparation for the sins committed against the Immaculate Heart of Mary.* [73]

At the administration office she was questioned by the administrator, Mr. Arturo dos Oliveira Santos, in the presence of her father and uncle and other unknown persons. He used all ways to get her to reveal the Secret that the Lady had given her. His promises did not entice her nor did his threats frighten her. He tried to intimidate her into promising not to return to the Cova da Iria, but Lucia would not make that promise. The child perhaps insulted him with the innocence of her crystal clear gaze, a gaze that reflected a soul completely immersed in God, and one that told the administrator she would return to the Cova da Iria.

The administrator assured her that he would find out even if it was necessary to take her life, and after giving a stern reprimand to Mr. Marto for not bringing his children, he sent them away. Mr. Marto cared nothing about his reprimand. It went in one ear and out the other. He did not have a way to bring children so small on such a long trip. They returned by the same route, after having eaten something from the provisions they brought with them. Upon their arrival home, Lucia jumped to the ground and made a quick visit to her friends and confidants who were at the well crying and praying for her. She embraced them and told them that they did not kill her and that she managed to guard the Secret. When they saw her they hugged her, crying with joy after having believed one of Lucia's sisters who told them that she had been killed.

11 | August 13th - In Prison

On the morning of the thirteenth day there was a large turnout of people at the house of the shepherds, who were bombarded by numerous questions and pulled at from all sides. Each person wanted their sole attention. At one point Lucia's father who was with her at the Marto house was warned that they were expecting the administrator. Although Antonio dos Santos did not want to get involved in the events, this time he had to be with them. Maria Rosa encouraged him saying:

-*Who knows, maybe this time, with Francisco and Jacinta as well, they will succeed in getting the children to say that they lied and bring this whole affair to an end. Go on, go there and see!*[74] Her father took her by the hand and walked with her.

Another unsuccessful attempt was made to compel the children to tell about the Secret and to promise not to go to the Cova da Iria. They were young

---

73 MSL I, 4th M, Ch. II, No. 5, p. 178.
74 MSL II, 6th M, No. 40, p. 138.

and uneducated, but firm as a rock. The administrator, however, would not be duped by those mountain children! Then he told the children's parents to take them to the parish priest to be interrogated in his presence. While there, Lucia told the administrator:

-I do not lie and say only what I saw and heard from the Lady. If people go to the Cova da Ira, it's because they want to; I did not call anybody there.

-Is it true that the Lady told you a secret?

-Yes, sir. But I did not say if you want, I'll go down to the Lady and ask her if I can tell about the secret, and then tell you.[75]

As the answers were always the same, the administrator made a very perceptive statement:

-These are supernatural things! Let's go![76]

All the while he had told the shepherds not to return to the site of the apparitions, but now wanted to take them himself to the site in his car. The children were suspicious and didn't want to accept his offer but he insisted and helped them into his car. Then he mischievously drove along at full speed, taking a different route to the Cova da Iria. Lucia realized it and told him it was not the right way. Thinking he had made a simple mistake, she told him she would go first to talk to the parish priest of Vila Nova de Ourem and return in time for the hour of the apparition. But the truth of their situation was soon understood. The shepherds found themselves taken to Ourem, a location Lucia already knew.

The parish priest of Fatima was now in great trouble and tried to appease the tempers of the crowd who judged him as an accomplice in the kidnapping of the children. Before the rumor could spread (that he was aware of the plot to abduct the children) he published his own defense in the "Messenger of Leiria" [77] and two other newspapers.

Lucia's mother was not at all distressed when Olympia, crying, gave her the news. She said:

-So! They're not going to lie! Don't be afraid, godmother, they will not submit to them! [78] She was hopeful that it was over. However, at the Cova da Iria, fifteen to eighteen thousand people prayed and lamented the absence of the seers who were not at the site. At the regular time of the apparition they were graced by manifestations of the presence of the Lady, who, not finding her confidants there, desired that the crowd at least leave comforted.

---

75 Conego C. Barthas, *FATIMA*, chp. 6, p. 92 - 93.

76 Fernando Leite, S.J., *Jacinta*.

77 *Ibid.*

78 Antonio Maria Martins, S. J., *Documents of Fatima*.

When the shepherds reached Ourem, they found themselves in the same situation as other prisoners and were delivered into the hands of strangers. After many attempts, the administrator shouted furiously:

-*They will be imprisoned until they give up the Secret. And if they take too long, they will be boiled in oil.*[79]

The children were locked in a room and given something to eat and a place on the floor to sleep while the administrator's wife kept watch. They were tired and with clear consciences fell asleep. Sleep, however, did not eliminate the reality of their situation: being locked up and away from their families. In the morning that reality was painfully felt.

August 14th was an intense day. The three children were intensely tested between interrogations and death threats, offers of rich gifts, and the experience of real prison in the company of a group of men who at first were not very friendly. But nothing persuaded them from their loyalty to the promise made to the Lady that came from Heaven. The prisoners must have found it very strange that three small children were placed in a cell with them. Perhaps some of them already knew of the events at Fatima, or had heard the threats uttered by the guards when they locked them up and recognized the shepherds. With good intentions they advised the children to tell the Secret so they could be freed. But the shepherds would not give in.

Lucia, still so young herself, put her own sorrows and pain aside to console her cousins, especially Jacinta who was so small and frightened, crying for her mother. To gain strength they started praying a Rosary before a medal that Jacinta had, which they hung on the wall. Gradually all the prisoners joined them with respect and devotion. After the Rosary, Jacinta began to cry because no one from her family came to visit her. Lucia, suppressing the river of tears that threatened to drown her innocent heart, reminded Jacinta of sinners, and again the three of them offered up this painful moment. Like a torch burning in a dark night, Lucia was like a mother to her younger cousins, forgetting herself while comforting and strengthening them, always asking the Lady to lift their spirits. Seeing Jacinta so sad, one of the prisoners tried to distract them and began to play his harmonica for everyone to dance and help pass the time. As Jacinta was very little, one of them took her in his arms to dance. The innocent child accepted the offer, but her tears continued to flow from her sweet eyes. She confessed that most of her pain was because she would never see her mother again, convinced that death awaited them. But Francisco comforted her with the assurance that they would soon see

---

79 Conego C. Bathas, *FATIMA*, chp. 6, p. 94.

Our Lord and Our Lady. Like the early days of Christianity when the martyrs encouraged each other in their common struggle, the three children were also encouraged by their common plight, even to death if that was necessary.

After some time, the prison door opened abruptly and a guard appeared. In a dry, irate tone he ordered them to follow him to the administration. The three shepherds followed him promptly, their hearts oppressed by the uncertainty of what was to follow. Anyone in similar circumstances would be afraid, but one thing was certain: come what may, they would not tell the Secret. He gave orders to prepare a boiler of oil for them and withdrew from his office leaving them alone. This moment seemed like an eternity and they did not speak, but rather prayed in their hearts. A few minutes later the door opened again. Jacinta was the first to have to choose between telling the Secret or be boiled in oil. She did not hesitate and without force volunteered for martyrdom. The same thing happened with Francisco. Lucia was alone with the anguish of what was happening to her cousins and what was in store for her, but without hesitating a moment responded negatively to the guard's order to reveal the Secret. She followed him to the torture that she generously accepted in her heart. Oh, astonishment! Instead of a boiler where she thought she would find her cousins already dead, she found them in another room, and they hugged each other warmly. The guard told them not to rejoice too much because if they did not tell the Secret all three would go to the boiler. But they did not hesitate in their purpose of fidelity.

Again that night they were put in the care of the administrator's wife, served a good meal and given mattresses on which to lie down. The next morning after more attempts, the fury of the administrator was like towering waves on the sea but he was not able to break the wills of the children who were as firm as a rock. He returned them to their families without achieving his objectives. He brought them to the church at Fatima in his car, precisely at the hour the faithful were leaving the church. It was August 15th, the Solemnity of the Assumption of Our Lady into Heaven.

Since everyone knew about the case, the people drew near to Mr. Marto and asked him if he knew about the children. He replied with a sad shrug that he knew nothing of them. Then someone shouted and pointed to the balcony of the parish house: -*Oh, Ti Marto, look, they come with the administrator. They are on the porch of the parish priest.*[80] When all the people coming out of Mass saw them they wanted to climb the stairs, but the administrator made a gesture with his hand to stop them. However, the shepherds' fathers would not be contained and went up

---

80 Fernando Leite, S. J., *Jacinta.*

the stairs while the mothers waited in the churchyard. After hugging their fathers, the children rushed to their mothers. Mr. Marto stayed and was arguing with the administrator. Sister Lucia said he gave the administrator a verbal thrashing. The people were also outraged by what the administrator had done. Although Mr. Marto had serious reasons to ask for justice, he was a man of peace and knew how to curb his indignation, but not without giving him a piece of his mind. So that everything would end peacefully, he invited the administrator to have a drink in the tavern next door. Administrator Santos, realizing his tactic, accepted the invitation. The two of them went with the driver which led people to say: -Look. Ti Marto was not silent and now he is going to jail![81] However, tempers calmed and all went to their homes. The administrator was personally reluctant to return.

Everyone wondered if the children were treated badly. Lucia, being the oldest, said no; for her, there was no mistreatment or beatings. They arrived home and had lunch. During the meal everyone questioned her about what had happened at the Administration and then drew their own conclusions. Lucia did not realize during this first hour home that there had been no reprimands. Her mother was somewhat relieved during these days of 'vacation' because no one was coming to the house for the shepherds. But as soon as the news spread that they were home, the procession started again. Her mother decided that Lucia would take the sheep to graze, a fact that very much grieved the little shepherdess who felt coldness in her mother, different from her aunt Olympia who on this day did not let her children go. Lucia obeyed without resisting her mother. She generously received these small thorns that were being pressed into her heart, and offered them up in silence to soften the pain of thorns that surrounded the Immaculate Heart of Mary, for the conversion of sinners, and for the Holy Father. By this point she no longer indulged in play when she was alone, but her spirit grew, fueled by the suffering that she was served in abundance.

12 | Apparition of Our Lady on August 19th

On Sunday, August 19th, after spending many hours in the company of Francisco and his brother John, Lucia took the sheep to graze in Valinhos, closer to home. As John was not one of the three visited by Our Lady, Lucia and Francisco did not share the same intimacy with him as they did with Jacinta. She was very sad not to go with them, but her mother thought she was still too exhausted from the emotional days in jail. At one point, Lucia noticed something supernatural

81 *Ibid.*

happening and recognized that it was Our Lady approaching. She told Francisco. He immediately thought of Jacinta who would feel bad if she was not present. Lucia asked John to go get her but he had no desire to help her. She promised to give him all of her money, two pennies, if he would go. He accepted the deal and ran as fast as he could for Jacinta. When he arrived home he told his mother:

-*Lucia asked that Jacinta come quickly because Our Lady is coming, because they saw signs in the sky.*[82]

His mother told him to get Jacinta at her godmother's house and return home with her. When John gave his sister the message, she did not hear the order to return home and ran as if she had wings toward Valinhos, followed by John. Upon her arrival the Lady appeared on the holm oak, preceded by the customary lightning, and the dialog began:

-*What do you want of me?*

-*I want you to continue going to the Cova da Iria on the 13th and to continue praying the Rosary every day. In the last month, I will perform a miracle so that all may believe.*

-*What do you want done with the money that the people leave in the Cova da Iria?*

-*Have two litters made. One is to be carried by you and Jacinta and two other girls dressed in white; the other one is to be carried by Francisco and three other boys. The money from the litters is for the feast of Our Lady of the Rosary, and what is left over will help toward the construction of a chapel that is to be built here.*

-*I would like to ask you to cure some sick persons.*

-*Yes, I will cure some of them during the year.* Then, looking very sad, Our Lady said:

-*Pray, pray very much, and make sacrifices for sinners; for many souls go to hell, because there are none to sacrifice themselves and to pray for them.*

And, as usual, she began to rise toward the east. [83]

They cut off the branches of the holm oak in which she had placed her feet. Jacinta wanted to remain there until the end of the day, but not having her mother's permission, Francisco decided they must go and gently escorted her home. The little one had in her hand the branches of the holm oak and passing by Maria Rosa's house cried out to her with overflowing joy:

-*Oh Aunt, we saw Our Lady again in Valinhos!* Her aunt, half distressed, responded:

-*You are always seeing Our Lady. But you are one great liar.*

---

82 Fernando Leite, S. J., *Jacinta*.
83 MSL I, 4th M, Ch. II, No. 6, p. 180.

And the little one full of enthusiasm said:

-*But this is what we saw. She had one foot here and one here* – and showed her the branches that she took. Her aunt wanted to see and was surprised with the wonderful scent the branches exuded. She did not know what to say.[84]

Since August 13, even in the absence of the shepherds, people who were at the Cova da Iria reported seeing some signs of Our Lady and Maria Rosa had become a little less skeptical. She stated:

-*There were other people who saw, who believed; but now so many people say that they have seen and I just do not believe!* [85]

It always seemed to her that something this big could not happen in her family. Faced with this news Maria Rosa concluded:

-*If this Lady comes now, appearing here in Valinhos it is still good, because maybe these people will come here and stop going to the Cova da Iria. Here in Valinhos, they do not cause much damage, because it is not cultivated land.* [86]

But when she heard that the Lady told the shepherds to continue going to the Cova da Iria, she said:

-*Oh, my God, we're still in it! Not even the government officials are able to end this.*[87]

That afternoon the branches disappeared and no one knew what became of them. Shortly before the Beatification of the Shepherds, the Rev. Father Luis Kondor handed to Sister Lucia a few cases with relics of the seers and explained where the small particles of the holm oak came from: on August 19, 1917, Ti Marto hid the branch Jacinta had placed under his mattress and kept it always with him until he delivered it to the Vice Postulator of the Cause of the Shepherds. Knowing this, Sister Lucia sighed and said:

-*Well, that was very competent of Ti Marto!*

13 | Lucia's Mother Struggles with Doubts

Lucia told of an episode that happened at that time when a visitor with a charming simplicity came and was conversing with her mother:

Among other people, a little man arrived at our house who came from Casais to ask what had happened during the days that the administrator had the shepherds imprisoned: what was it they wanted, were they mistreated, etc.

84 Fernando Leite, S. J., *Jacinta*.
85 MSL I, 2nd M, Ch. II, No. 12, p. 94.
86 MSL II, 6th M, No. 43, p. 146.
87 *Ibid.*

My mother replied: -They say they were not mistreated. What I hoped was they had been forced to admit that they lied, and thus reasoning with all these people would end. But, complications! Things are the same as always.

The little man replied: -But look there, oh Maria Rosa, why do you want the government officials to make the little shepherds confess, saying they lied if they do not confess? They do not want anything to do with the priests or with friars, or with nuns— they already put them all outside Portugal; they closed the churches and they do not let the bells ring or have processions; they steal everything that is of the Church. Look, even in our small church which had a few olive trees that gave the oil for the lamp of the Blessed Sacrament, they've stolen everything. They say it is theirs and voila! Now we have to make the oil to light the Blessed Sacrament! But this is still not the worst: the worst thing is they've meddled in wars, leading our children to go there to die, pierced by bullets in front of the guns. Maria Rosa, who knows if Our Lady will come here to save us!

Her mother responded: -Our Lady? We wish that it was Our Lady! But what! Here in my house I never have peace or quiet. So many people come knocking on the door and don't let me do anything. And time makes me lose touch. And then with the girl, they want to see her and she's out there with the sheep, and I don't have anyone to send for her and stay there guarding the sheep in her place! I am tormented and do not know where to turn. God help me! [88]

When someone asked if she was grieved to learn that her daughter was imprisoned, Maria Rosa replied with her characteristic candor:

-No, I thought if it's true that they saw Our Lady, she will preserve them; but if they lied, it is good to oblige them to say that they lied. To them, the three children, so young, can do great evil, and the government officials who want nothing to do with God or with Holy Mary might be able to force them to say they lied and end this once and for all. Ai! God forbid! [89]

14 | New Sacrifices

During the apparition in August, the Lady made a request of them. It was a painful secret that gripped the shepherds internally. Now they were making many sacrifices, with a more intense thirst for saving sinners. They shared with each other how they increased their sacrifices and eagerly welcomed these new opportunities.

In her memoirs, Lucia always presented her cousins as mentors because

---

88 *Ibid.*
89 *Ibid.*

many times they would propose to her a new sacrifice. Thus, for example, she remembered the rope around her waist was divided into three pieces. She wrote:

-Some days later, as we were walking along the road with our sheep, I found a piece of rope that had fallen off a cart. I picked it up and just for fun I tied it round my arm. Before long I noticed that the rope was hurting me.

Then she said to her cousins:

-Look, this hurts! We could tie it around our waists and offer this sacrifice to God. [90]

When they agreed to the idea, the three divided it by placing it across a stone and striking it with the sharp edge of another. They made three pieces, in which they tied some knots to increase the sacrifice, and each one placed it tight around their waist. They did not remove it until the apparition of September 13, when the Lady maternally advised them not to sleep with it. They managed to use the rope without anyone finding out. Later Sister Lucia confessed to feeling very sorry for having burned the ropes her cousins gave her, Francisco's just before his death and Jacinta's before she went to the hospital. She kept the ropes until she left Fatima to go to Asilo de Vilar. She always kept hers, however, and continued to use it as much as she could, but only after authorization from her confessor or spiritual director. Today it is a precious relic.

After her death the rope was found with some other instruments of penance that she used. It is a rope of sisal, which commonly was used to hold the animals, measuring 1m 16cm long and 1cm thick with five knots. To keep it from fraying Sister Lucia stitched the rope at both ends. Currently this rope is on exhibition among other objects of hers in the museum located next to the Carmel of Coimbra, "Memorial of Sister Lucia."

An important detail to note is that since the beginning of the apparitions of Our Lady, Lucia's life changed immensely. Both in the family and in her meetings with people of her homeland and from afar, she was the one who was held responsible for the alleged lies of the three. She confided to her cousins that it seemed as if the devil was in her house, and stated: *-Since I saw these things, I haven't had any more joy and well-being in our house.*[91] She suffered a great deal because of this and *had to eat the bread of tears and drink abundant weeping.*[92]

Like any child she liked to play, not sacrifice herself. Although she along with Jacinta and Francisco renounced the joy and innocence of play to take on a pastoral life, they did not cease having the desire to do so. Thus the discovery

---

90 MSL I, 2nd M, Ch. II, No. 12, p. 93.

91 MSL I, 2nd M, Ch. I, No. 6, p. 86.

92 Ps 80:5-6.

of sacrifice with the rope was a beautiful enhancement. Her heart continued to be that of a child, free and prone to spontaneous joy because she was at peace. There was one constant in the lives of the three children, and that was one heart and one soul—they had seen and understood the sorrow that God and Our Lady had for the sins of the world, and for the people who did very little to console them. The shepherds wanted to help convert sinners to avoid the horrors of hell that the Lady had shown them. Forgetting themselves they thought only of their love for sinners. They continued to give their lunches away to the sheep and to the poor people they met on their way, and spent many days without water under the scorching sun.

They were very young and knew nothing about the world. Lucia had a great maternal love for world peace that grew in her heart and accompanied her all her life. Ever since the Lady had shown them hell and the Secret, she knew that sin was the cause of all the evil in the world and the Holy Father's suffering. Never discouraged, she carried her heavy cross faithfully, always with a motherly love for the salvation of humanity. Right up to the end of her life when she would hear of new outbreaks of war, she would sigh:

-*Men do not know how to live in peace!* With each new cross, she repeated with all her heart: *O Jesus, it is for love of You, for the conversion of sinners, and in reparation for the sins committed against the Immaculate Heart of Mary.* [93]

Oh, the sorrow of God! The hearts of the shepherds were painfully carved with the sadness that they saw and felt in God. God is sad not for Himself but for humanity, for *"God is infinite Joy,"* a beautiful definition by the young Carmelite, St. Teresa of Jesus of the Andes. [94]

God is sad. When a mother sees her child run the serious risk of going astray and does not heed her loving advice, the mother is saddened and her only consolation is to see the child return to self-restraint. God is so, and infinitely more! The shepherds understood so deeply the reason for this sadness and that nothing was impossible. They were able to give joy to God by helping their brethren who went astray return to the Heart of the Father. They were a loving restoration for the Heart of God, living with intensity St. Paul's assertion: *Complete in my flesh what is lacking in the afflictions of Christ on behalf of His Body which is the Church.* [95]

---

93 MSL I, 4th M, Ch. II, No. 5, p. 178.
94 1900-1920.
95 Col 1:24.

15 | Apparition of Our Lady on September 13th

Around noon the shepherds came out of their homes and headed towards the Cova da Iria. They did so with great difficulty because of the huge influx of people who pressed everywhere wanting to see them up close, touching and talking to them. Lucia said it was a little like what Jesus went through as He walked through Galilee and Judea. She wrote that some gentlemen helped pave a path through the crowd for them:

We finally arrived in the Cova da Iria near the holm oak and began praying the Rosary with the people. Shortly afterwards we saw the flash of light and then Our Lady on the holm oak.

-Continue to pray the Rosary in order to obtain the end of the war. In October Our Lord will come, as well as Our Lady of Sorrows and Our Lady of Mount Carmel. St. Joseph will appear with the Child Jesus to bless the world. God is pleased with your sacrifices. He does not want you to sleep with the rope on, but only to wear it during the daytime.

-I was told to ask you many things, the cure of some sick people, of a deaf-mute.

-Yes, I will cure some, but not others. In October I will perform a miracle so that all may believe. Then Our Lady began to rise as usual and disappeared.[96]

A tender Mother, Our Lady is concerned with her children who have no one to lead them to do penance. Her words were a balm in the midst of all the suffering that would come to them: *-God is pleased with your sacrifices.*[97] But God would not let any more time pass before sending someone to help them see His will and lead them in the right way. He usually wants His chosen ones to go through human mediation, so they walk safely in the light of obedience according to His will.

On September 13 the Rev. Manuel Nunes Formigão arrived in Fatima. Fr. Formigão came to investigate the shepherds and events at Fatima. He was present at the time of the apparition but saw nothing unusual except a slight decrease in sunlight, which could mean little or nothing. That day he did not speak to the seers or anyone there. On the September 27 he was back in Aljustrel and proceeded with the first interrogation. Lucia was able to breathe easier with the visit of this holy priest who questioned her and her cousins and gave them practical advice for life:

He interrogated me seriously and thoroughly. I liked him very much, for he spoke to me a great deal about the practice of virtue, and taught me various ways of exercising myself in it. He showed me a holy picture of St. Agnes. He told me about her martyrdom

---

96 MSL I, 4th M, Ch. II, No. 7, p. 182.
97 *Ibid.*

and encouraged me to imitate her. His Reverence continued to come every month for an interrogation, and always gave me some good advice, which was of help to me spiritually. One day he said to me:

-My child, you must love Our Lord very much in return for so many favors and graces that He is granting you. These words made such an impression on my soul that, from then on, I acquired the habit of constantly saying to Our Lord:

-My God, I love You, in thanksgiving for the graces which You have granted me.[98]

Then she shared this ejaculation with her cousins who recited it frequently. What belonged to one belonged to all—a passion among early Christians who had everything in common, material and spiritual goods, and who walked with each other.

The storm in Lucia's home intensified after September 13. She had hoped her mother was becoming more convinced of the apparitions during the month of August, but Maria Rose became discouraged and her suffering took on new proportions. In addition to her painful doubts about the apparitions and Lucia's truthfulness, the irretrievable loss of crops from their land due to the crowds, and the constant harassment from people coming to their home to see and talk to the little one caused great emptiness in her that was felt in her family.

It was hard for mother and daughter. Lucia suffered silently her personal cross and saw her mother whom she idolized filled with so much pain and without any relief. In the midst of this dark night, Lucia looked up to Heaven and trusted in the Lord from Whom she knew aid would come [99]and repeated in her wounded heart: *O Jesus, it is for love of You, for the conversion of sinners, and in reparation for the sins committed against the Immaculate Heart of Mary.* [100]

How this child grew spiritually inside of just 10 years!

16 | Apparition on October 13th and the Miracle of the Sun

The 13th of October was approaching, the day of the last apparition and the promised miracle. The media spread the news throughout the country without intending to draw people to the site, at a time when communications were very slow. The newspaper men who were arriving from far and wide were the means that Heaven used to gather a greater number of people. There came the simply curious, believers and unbelievers. Rumors spread that the authorities would place a bomb on the site of the apparitions and kill everyone. That did not stop people

---

98 MSL I, 2nd M, Ch. II, No 10, p. 91.
99 Ps 120:1-2.
100 MSL I, 4th M, Ch. II, No. 5, p. 178.

◄ The seers together at the
   arch with pilgrims.

▼▶ Miracle of the Sun on
   October 13, 1917.

from being there, much less the three seers who gave nothing to the thought they might die that day. Hearing this, Lucia's parents wanted to accompany her for the first time.

I recall what my mother said to my father on October 13ᵗʰ:

-If our daughter is going to die there, we want to be there to die with her. [101]

Under a heavy sky and persistent rain, the roads in Fatima since the evening before were like human rivers flowing into the Cova da Iria, which like a motherly shelter was welcoming everyone. Wet to the bone, but unconcerned about any health problems that this could cause, each one just wanted to be closer to the little holm oak, which had increasingly become more difficult to achieve. At each apparition the 'sea' of people extended further out, but every face was turned toward the lower part of the mountain and all eyes looked toward the sky waiting to see something of the invisible. Still early, Lucia left home *in torrential rain and harsh wind, facing danger.* [102]

She was in the hands of her parents and it was her father who escorted her to the foot of the holm oak. Despite many threats to the seers nothing happened, but Lucia's parents were frightened that if there was no miracle they would be lost among so many people who would feel duped. Someone annoyed with the rain and biting cold shook Lucia, called her a liar, and asked her why she continued to deceive all the people. She very calmly told him the truth saying she had not asked anyone to come there, and she was on land belonging to her family. It was they who had come onto someone else's property.

Lucia described the last apparition:

Having arrived at the Cova da Iria, near the holm oak, I was moved by an interior impulse. I asked the people to shut their umbrellas and say the Rosary. A little later, we saw the flash of light and Our Lady appeared on the holm oak.

-What do you want of me?

-I want to tell you that a chapel is to be built here in my honor. I am the Lady of the Rosary. Continue always to pray the Rosary every day. The war is going to end, and the soldiers will soon return to their homes.

-I have many things to ask you: the cure of some sick persons, the conversion of sinners.

-Some yes, but not others. They must amend their lives and ask forgiveness for their sins. And looking very sad, Our Lady said:

-Do not offend the Lord our God anymore, because He is already so much offended. Then, opening her hands, she made them reflect on the sun, and as she

101   MSL II, 6ᵗʰ M, No. 76, p. 192.
102   *Ibid.*

ascended, the reflection of her own light continued to be projected on the sun itself. This is when I cried out, 'look at the sun.'

My aim was not to call the people's attention there, because I was not even aware of their presence. I was moved to do so under the guidance of an interior impulse.

17 | The Promised Miracle

After Our Lady disappeared into the immense expanse of the firmament, we saw beside the sun St. Joseph with the Child Jesus and Our Lady robed in white with a blue mantle. St. Joseph and the Child Jesus appeared to bless the world, for they traced the Sign of the Cross with their hands. A little later this apparition faded. I saw our Lord and Our Lady; it seemed to me it was Our Lady of Sorrows. Our Lord appeared to bless the world in the same manner as St. Joseph had done. This apparition also vanished, and I saw Our Lady once more, this time resembling Our Lady of Carmel.[103]

While the children gazed at these latter visions, the miracle of the sun occurred, the promised sign to confirm the truthfulness of the apparitions. The shepherds did not see the miracle. It was not intended for them, but for the crowd, so that all might believe.

Suddenly the rain stopped, the clouds parted like a curtain pulled back to let the rays of the sun through, which dried up all the mud and the soaked clothes of the crowd. This was sufficient to show a presence of the Blessed Virgin, but the miracle would be bigger and inexplicable. Three times the sun with its rays whirled on itself darting about with shades of yellow, blue, green, purple, and this phenomenon was observed from afar. The people took on the colors of the sun. At one point, the whole crowd started screaming, terrified, confessing aloud their sins, making acts of faith and asking for forgiveness. It seemed that the sun was loosed from the firmament and was coming toward the earth to burn all the people.

After the miracle, all the people wanted see and talk to the children. Lucia claimed not to know how she spent the rest of the afternoon. Questions and requests poured in from everywhere; each of the shepherds was taken by the mob and like waves dragged about without being protected. Lucia hung onto the neck of Dr. Carlos Mendes, who was tall and managed to keep her safe for some time, holding her above the grip of people. But he could not see the bumps on the path and at one point fell, leaving the shepherdess floating on the waves of the crowd.

Lucia responded to numerous questions, finally getting home at night

---

103 MSL I, 4th M, Ch. II, No. 5, p. 178.

exhausted. Even there, she had to talk to those waiting for her, among whom was Rev. Formigão, who made his interrogation. Seeing the fatigue of her child, Lucia's mother asked him to be careful and protect her because of the danger to her health. Maria Rosa fumed:

- *This is a real mess. Everyone wants us to refuse others, but to them say yes! What am I going to do? How do I get these people who come here to be resigned and go away without seeing and speaking to the little one? They put up with me here at home, but they do not leave without seeing her! This is easy to say, but it is very difficult to achieve! God help me, I do not know if He will give my life back!*[104]

Lucia, who had not eaten since morning, was exhausted from hunger, fatigue, and the weight of the emotions that filled her heart. She dropped unceremoniously to the floor and fell asleep. It appeared that all those who still remained waiting to question her were leaving. Finally, the family could eat a light meal and rest.

When Maria Rosa opened the door at dawn the next day, she gasped to see there were people already waiting. Those who had come from afar did not want to leave without speaking to the little seers. They stayed there, waiting for their turn. It was an endless line at both houses. It recalls what the Gospel said about Jesus: *They had not time to eat.*[105]

Lucia explained some contradictions found in interviews after the last apparition as due to the repetition of questions and the fatigue that subdued the three shepherds. So many people pulled at them and asked questions that they ended up saying yes to everything. It was very hard! It was a great cross, especially for Lucia, who was considered the main spokesperson for the three because it was she who spoke with Our Lady. It was also a great cross for her mother. All through October they thought and hoped the line of people would diminish and they could again live their lives in peace and the family could return to cultivate the Cova da Iria and shepherd the flock. They had been a year without their income which was necessary for their livelihood. Antonio and his wife expected things would return to normal again. But no! Our Lady had taken possession of that land forever. The Cova da Iria already belonged to the people of God. This was a new flock that began to come here to find subsistence, and the *Immaculate Mother of God of the new life* [106] was going to be there always to help with their needs.

The miracle had happened. The ones who saw Our Lady with the right intention believed. There were always those who did not want to believe, who

---

104 MSL II, 6th M, No. 51, p. 157.

105 Mk 3:20.

106 Hymn of the Fiftieth Anniversary of the Apparitions.

even if the world fell at their feet or if they surrendered internally to the evidence, would not give in. As Sister Lucia said, *'It was not the case.'* The Lady of the holm oak had promised to say who she was and what she wanted. She said she was the Lady of the Rosary, a name familiar to everyone in Fatima, because it was a known invocation. She asked that a chapel be built there and that everyone pray the Rosary every day, a request she made in each apparition. With great sadness on her face, she said: *-Do not offend the Lord Our God anymore, because He is already so much offended.*[107] This is the reason for the Lady's visits and for all her requests. A caring Mother came to warn against the danger of letting oneself be chained by sin, and gave the remedy for this supreme evil because *what good is it for one to gain the whole world but lose his soul.*[108]

18 | A Qualm

Increasingly more and more priests were arriving to question the shepherds, some with orders from their superiors. It was the duty of the Church to take the apparitions seriously, but for the children it was very humiliating. In her memoirs, Sister Lucia confesses that some people used her in little ways to gain her trust and then left her to suffer. They drove into her spirit the sharp and painful thorn of uncertainty because they doubted her truthfulness when she did not reveal any details. When her cousins were unable to help her discern she took refuge in a fervent prayer to Heaven for help:

-Oh my God and my dearest Mother in Heaven, you know that I do not want to offend you by telling lies; but you are well aware that it would not be right to tell them all that you told me! [109]

And Heaven responded. The Vicar of Olival, Father Faustino José Jacinto Ferreira, came to interrogate her. Little Lucia felt relaxed and confident with him. God sent him to give her peace. After answering his questions, Lucia asked for advice about her indecisions and he helped her. She wrote: *One day, however, I sought the advice of a holy priest regarding my reserve in such matter, because I did not know how to answer when asked if the most Blessed Virgin had told anything else as well. This priest, who was then Vicar of Olival said to us: You do well, my little ones, to keep the secret of your souls between God and yourselves. When they put that question to you, just answer: Yes, she did say more, but it's a secret. If they question you further on this subject, think of the secret the Lady made known to you, and say: Our Lady*

107 MSL I, 2nd M, Ch. II, No. 16, p. 97.
108 Mk 8:36.
109 MSL I, 2nd M, Ch. II, No. 17, p. 100.

told us not to say anything to anybody; for this reason, we are saying nothing. In this way, you can keep your secret under the shelter of Our Lady.[110] *How well I understood the explanation and guidance of this venerable old priest! From then on, he never lost sight of my soul. Now and then, he called in to see me, or kept in touch with me through a pious widow called Lady Emilia. She was very devout, and often went to pray at the Cova da Iria. After that, she used to come to our house and ask to let me go and spend a few days with her, and then she took me to the house of the Vicar. His Reverence was kind enough to let me stay two or three days in his house as company for one of his sisters. Then he had the patience to spend long hours alone with me, teaching me the practice of virtue and guiding me with his wise advice.*

Even though at that time I did not understand anything about spiritual direction, I can truly say that he was my first spiritual director. I cherish, therefore, these grateful and holy memories of this saintly priest. [111]

---

110   MSL I, 1st M, Preface, No. 2, p. 35.
111   MSL I, 2nd M, Ch. II, No. 17, p. 101.

Stained glass window commemorating the miracle of the sun.

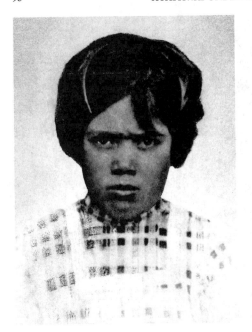

Lucia, 1918.

Pilgrims on the way to the Cova da Iria.

First outdoor Mass celebrated at the Chapel of the Apparitions, October 13, 1918.

CHAPTER IV
AFTER THE APPARITIONS

1 | Influx of More People

As time passed, the influx of people wanting to talk to the shepherds intensified, which was certainly the greatest penance for them. In order to avoid always having to waste time going to find them on the paths and call them home, Francisco and Jacinta's parents decided that John would start watching the flock and the two seers would stay at home. It was a hard decision for the three shepherds because they wouldn't have this time alone to help each other pursue faithful correspondence to Heaven's requests and speak freely what was in their souls.

If the pasture was close to home, her two cousins went with her, but otherwise Lucia went alone with her sheep and only at night would they see each other. It was one more sacrifice that they offered for the conversion of sinners. Lucia's mother said:

-*When the three are alone, they talk a blue streak. Yet, however hard you listened, you could never catch a single word from them, and as soon as someone comes, they lower their heads and never say a word! I can't understand this mystery.*[112]

With this new situation everyone suffered and Lucia became more isolated. She suffered in the absence of her confidants. She could now only vent her heart to the Heart of the Mother of Heaven who promised never to leave her, and she abandoned herself to this love that she trusted.

She continued for some time with the flock, but was constantly sought. Her sister, who did not have any work, took her place. 'It' did not end after the apparitions! On the contrary, the crowd grew larger. After determining that they could manage the house without the yield of the sheep, Lucia's parents decided to sell the herd and send her to school. After all, it was a request of Our Lady that she learn to read. A teacher would help them solve the problem.

All three of them started to go to school in 1918. Jacinta and Francisco accompanied Lucia for a short time until they fell ill at the end of October. Sometimes Lucia noticed that Francisco walked very slowly and asked him the reason. He replied that his head ached and when walking he had more pain. She advised her cousin not to come. He said he wanted to go but not to school, rather, he would stay in the church with the Hidden Jesus. School was no longer of any use to him anyway because of his health. Jacinta also only attended for a short time. In the meantime, Lucia went to school and when she returned home she began to learn sewing and weaver's work. She recalls not being able to do much work

---

112 MSL I, 1st M, Ch. III, No. 4, p. 62.

because she had to meet those who sought her and often accompanied them to pray the Rosary at the Cova da Iria. On her return from school, she almost always visited her sick cousins, who asked her to tell the Hidden Jesus that they missed Him. When she returned to their house she brought them the sweetness of these visits. At times she was not always able to be alone with God. While Jacinta was still attending school, she did not understand how the people knew that during recess they were in Church and she was astonished that soon there would be many people there asking them questions and making requests.

2 | Her Mother's Sickness

Full of worries and sufferings, Maria Rosa who never fully admitted to the veracity of the apparitions, fell ill with such severity that the whole family thought this was the end of her life, because the doctor said that nothing could be done. She received the Sacrament of the Anointing of the Sick and dismissed the whole family. Lucia was the last to receive a goodbye hug and blessing. But her mother could not let it end without saying:

-*My poor little girl! What will become of you without your mother? I am dying with you stuck in my heart.*[113]

As I was still hugging her and sobbing bitterly, my oldest sister pulled me forcibly away from her, and took me out to the kitchen, and forbid me to go back into my mother's room, saying:

-*Our mother is dying of sorrow because of you and all the trouble you have caused. I knelt down and put my head on the bench and with a deep sadness the likes of which I had never felt in my life before, I offered my sacrifice to God, and begged that my mother would recover. Shortly afterwards, my two sisters Maria and Teresa came up to me and said:*

-*Lucia, if you really did see Our Lady, go right now to the Cova da Iria and ask her to heal our mother. Make her whatever promise you like; we will fulfill it. And then we will believe.*[114]

Without hesitating, Lucia ran to the Cova da Iria, praying the Rosary and weeping bitterly. It was so painful to know her mother was about to leave her and to hear that she was responsible. So as not to been seen, she took some shortcuts that she knew. Then at the place of the apparitions, kneeling and praying, she cried and begged Our Lady to cure her mother. And she made a generous promise:

-*I would go there for nine consecutive days, together with my sisters, pray the*

113 MSL II, 6ᵗʰ M, No. 48, p. 152.
114 *Ibid.*

Rosary and go on our knees from the roadway to the holm oak tree; and on the ninth day we would take nine poor children with us, and afterwards give them a meal.[115]

After praying and unburdening her heart to the Heart of the Heavenly Mother, Lucia stood up and confidently returned home. St. John said in his first letter that *when we make a request believing that God will grant it to us, we will have the grace granted.*[116] Thus Lucia believed and was answered, because when she reached the house, she had the joy of finding her mother better. Her sister Gloria informed her.

My father, who was in the room keeping my mother company, came to me, took my hand, and said:

-Come hug your mother who is already better.

My mother was sitting up in bed taking a small bowl of soup. My father held the bowl so my mother could hug me:

-Where did you go, my daughter? Were you asking Our Lady to heal me? asked my mother.

-Yes, I answered.

-I already feel better, thank God.[117]

Then her father asked her what promise she had made and Lucia explained. Her father nodded saying that as soon as her mother recovered her strength, they would all go to fulfill the promise that she had made. And all of them dined in a good mood with her godmother Teresa and her husband, who had already prepared to help the family in their mourning. After a few days, the family kept Lucia's promise and made the path on their knees, and this was the start of a gesture that has been repeated by thousands of people, asking or thanking Heaven for help in moments of great pain and distress.

3 | The Epidemic of Pneumonia

1918. There emerged like an uncontrollable fire an epidemic of pneumonia that decimated entire families. War never comes alone; it always brings companions like hunger and plague. After death is sown on the battlefields, plague is the dark blanket of war extended over the earth, silently spreading to entire populations, sowing death in every household.

Once again charity filled the heart of Maria Rosa. Without worrying about the danger of infection, she went from house to house with her daughter Gloria,

---

115 *Ibid.*
116 1 Jn 5:15.
117 MSL II, 6th M, No. 49, pp. 153-154.

tending the sick and taking the children of parents who were sick to her own home. Not long after, Ti Marto warned Antonio about the danger that they faced. He had prohibited his own wife from continuing to help sick families. Maria Rosa heard all her husband had to say, then replied:

-You have a good point. It's just as you say. But look here, how can we leave those people to die without anyone there to give them a glass of water? It would be better if you came with me to see how these people really are, then we can decide what has to be done. [118]

Antonio followed her, helping to bring the broth Lucia had made at home to distribute to their patients. Shortly afterwards he returned with a baby, giving him to Lucia and Gloria, and a little later returned with two more children. Ti Marto saw the needs of those families and from that day on became the first to go help them without fear of infection.

During this period, Lucia was the delight of the children. She cared for and played with them in a tender and motherly way, making them feel better in the absence of their parents. Her responsibilities did not diminish the procession of people, now under the violent storm of the epidemic, who flocked to the sacred place of the apparitions to implore the Mother of Heaven for her protection for their families. The little seer started to draw the attention of some visitors who feared for her health. One day, Dr. Carlos Mendes from Torres Novas came to ask Maria Rosa if she would allow him to take Lucia to his house so that he could educate her and give her a place to study. Her mother agreed to this, subject to her father's approval. Even though it would be very painful for her to be separated from her daughter, Maria Rosa wanted to see if interest in the apparitions might end, and advised her husband that it would be good to let her go. He agreed, but did not give in very easily.

Lucia spent some time with this family where, surrounded by love, she could relax without the stress of the pilgrims. Some close family friends asked if she could come to their house as well, which was also more relaxing than in Aljustrel. One day Dr. Mendes and his wife took her for a walk around the village and she saw a train for the first time. She was amazed by all the people at the windows waving goodbye as the train was moving. When she arrived home, she hurried to describe this novelty to the children that gathered around her, who listened intently, their mouths open with admiration:

-I saw many small houses, trotting along one behind the other, without either horses or donkeys to pull them, and with lots of people inside looking out the windows,

---

118 MSL II, 5th M, No. 2, p. 19.

with a great chimney in the front belching out smoke and it seemed a whole lot of horns sounding at once. [119]

Upon hearing the story, my mother who also had never seen a train was outraged and reprimanded me harshly saying:

-What's that you are saying? All we needed was for you to invent yet another story. Where did you see houses on wheels? What are you thinking of? Don't let me hear you saying such things again. [120]

Lucia obeyed and stopped telling the story, which her listeners regretted because she had a special gift for storytelling, helping people see and understand with their imaginations. Later, while in Lisbon with her mother she finally had the opportunity to show her a train. She was so proud to show her the "houses" that passed by so rapidly:

When we were at the station waiting for the train, I made my way to the front to look down the track and see as it approached. As soon as I spotted the train coming, I pulled my mother by the arm, saying:

-Come here and look. Look! Can't you see the chimney whistling and belching out smoke, and the little houses trotting along one behind the other and all the people inside?

Her mother replied:

-You're right. I have never seen such a thing. What you said was true. [121]

4 | Orphaned by Her Father

The state of health was getting worse for the two young shepherds whom the Lady at the Cova da Iria had promised to take to Heaven soon. On April 4, 1919, the first Friday of the month, Our Lady took Francisco, the Consoler of Jesus, to Heaven. It was the first ache that struck Lucia's heart, an earthly bond that had been broken. Soon another even stronger bond would break that no one expected—her father.

On July 30, 1919, Antonio dos Santos felt sick. They called the doctor who diagnosed him as having double pneumonia and prescribed the required medication available at that time. Because the disease was already very advanced or because the medication was not adequate her father continued to get worse. The next morning he felt his departure from life was imminent. He asked the family to call the priest to hear his confession and administer the Anointing of the

---

119 MSL II, 6th M, No. 53, p. 158.
120 *Ibid.*
121 *Ibid.*

Sick. Lucia's mother warned him that she very likely would only be able to find the parish priest, to whom for some time he did not like to confess. He was already glimpsing the light of eternity where all our human aversions are overcome, and said:

-Don't worry about that! It doesn't matter. [122]

Maria Rosa sent for the pastor, who, thinking the patient's condition was not so urgent, lingered awhile and came too late. Antonio dos Santos died in the arms of his faithful wife and his sister Olympia, repeating the ejaculations that the two prayed between painful sobs:

-Jesus, Mary, Joseph save my soul which belongs to You! Lord Jesus, have mercy on me by the merits of Your Life, Passion and Death on the Cross! Father, into Your hands I commend my spirit! [123]

After less than 24 hours of becoming ill he took leave of his earthly abode. Thank God he was prepared, as the Lord Jesus advises in the Gospel, because no one knows the day or the hour.[124] A few days earlier, he had gone to Our Lady of Ortiga where he confessed and received Communion at the Mass of the Feast, which is celebrated on the second Sunday of July and extended for three days. Twelve-year-old Lucia accompanied her parents to the feast and then they went to dinner at her sister Teresa's home close by. Later this memory was a solace for Lucia who was at peace knowing that her father, who was not able to confess at the time of his death, had done so a few days before. He was prepared, as her memoirs state:

I feel entirely at peace with respect to the eternal salvation of my father, certain that the Lord received his beautiful soul into the arms of His infinite Mercy and presented him into the full possession of the immense Being of God, our Father. [125]

Later in Carmel, upon learning of a film about Fatima in which her father was presented as an addicted, drunken person, Sister Lucia thought it was her duty to defend his memory. She made the following disclosure to Bishop Ernesto Sena de Oliveira of Coimbra:

My father is in Heaven through the mercy of God and it pains me, not just for me, but especially for my sisters, to hear something which is not true, and it seems to me a duty of charity and justice to respond. My father died recently, victimized by double pneumonia in the short time of 24 hours. His death left me in great distress because of having died without confessing though he had requested the confessor, who

---

122 MSL II, 5th M, No. 2, p. 36.
123 *Ibid.*
124 Cf. Mt 25:13.
125 MSL II, 5th M, No. 2, p. 36.

not supposing it was such a serious case, delayed coming and thus did not arrive in time. Thanks to the immense goodness of the beloved Mother of Heaven, I later learned that he had been saved, due to his desire to confess and the act of contrition my mother suggested before he died. His soul was in purgatory expiating his faults, which the media sought to release about him. On a day in which I had knowledge of a gift that had been sent to me, I asked my Superior the favor of employing Masses for his eternal rest. This authorization was denied. I offered then to Our Lord my vow of poverty; I deprived everything of myself for His love instead of the Masses I wanted to provide for his eternal rest. Again by my dear Mother in Heaven, I knew God had accepted his soul and he was already in Heaven. How great is the goodness of God! [126]

Lucia's loneliness was greater with each death. The loss of her father with whom she had such an affinity wounded her heart and undermined her health. Whenever she could, she went to the cemetery and sat on the graves of her father and Francisco, praying, crying and confiding the pain in her heart to those whose remains rested there. Then she took refuge in the Loca Cabeço praying the prayer taught by the Angel. No one suspected she was here and she was not sought. She no longer had her confidant—Jacinta—who had gone to the hospital in Ourem. Before she went to the hospital, Lucia told her:

-*It won't be long now till you go to Heaven. But what about me?*

At that Jacinta replied:

-*You poor thing! Don't cry! I'll pray lots and lots for you when I'm there. As for you, that's the way Our Lady wants it. If she wanted that for me I'd gladly stay and suffer more for sinners!* [127]

One would be hard-pressed to find two children at this age with such a sincere and profound friendship. The Lord asked for more and Lucia faithfully repeated in her torn heart: *It is for love of You, my God in reparation for sins committed against the Immaculate Heart of Mary, for the conversion of sinners and for the Holy Father.* [128]

At age 12 she already had a huge burden of responsibility upon her shoulders. Perhaps some began to notice her pale color and declining strength and became worried. Some ladies from the O'Neill family who lived in Lisbon and spent seasons in Valado asked Maria Rosa if she and Lucia could spend a few days of rest in their home in Lisbon. She accepted the offer because she too felt burdened by the family's suffering and the continuous stream of visitors. Lucia and Maria Rosa were well-received in their home. They rested comfortably and

126 Cf. MSL II, 5th M, Appendix, p. 37-40.

127 MSL I, 1st M, Ch. III, No. 2, p. 60.

128 MSL I, 2nd M, Ch. III, No. 16, p. 98.

returned to Aljustrel renewed with energy.

5 | In Lisbon

Father Manuel Nunes Formigão was sincerely interested in the case of Fatima and the shepherds. After Jacinta's death on February 20, 1920, in the D. Estefania Hospital in Lisbon, he became worried about Lucia's future. He was well-known in Fatima, and during his visits was invited to stay in the homes of some friends. He began to take the necessary steps in regard to Lucia and spoke with a lady friend in Lisbon, who offered to receive the shepherdess and keep her protected from the public.

Having a place for her to go, he spoke with Maria Rosa. Previously he had made the same request, but her husband would not consent. Now that he had died, she alone could make the decision. Lucia's mother was hesitant to let her go, wanting to respect the will of her husband. Fr. Formigão reassured her by inviting her to also go to Lisbon to consult with a good doctor for her ailments and at the same time see where her daughter would stay before making a decision. At the beginning of July, mother and daughter went to the home of Miss Maria da Assunção Avelar e Silva. This woman received them with much affection and arranged for Maria Rosa to be attended by good doctors and to be chauffeured to the city for her appointments. After her medical consultations and seeing that Lucia was in good hands, she returned to Aljustrel without her.

Maria da Assunção was a single woman from a noble family. To avoid the difficulties in those early years of the Republic, she withdrew to her house where she had a chapel of the Blessed Sacrament and a chaplain who celebrated Mass every day.

The mistress wanted a good education for her guest and searched for a tutor for Lucia. She placed her under the supervision of a "Miss," as Sister Lucia called her, who taught her reading and writing. The mistress taught her the refinements of social etiquette and grooming to which Lucia was not accustomed. Lucia, who up to now had lived a comfortable and modest lifestyle with the simple clothes of the mountain life, had difficulty seeing herself in more stylish fashions. During Lucia's stay, the mistress did not know that she was the 'Shepherdess of Fatima,' only that it was necessary to accustom her to urban society. She was 13 years old, already a young woman, not very tall but well-formed. The mistress took great pride in taking care of her. She tended to her sunburned skin from the Serra de Aire and had someone cut her braids and arrange her hair, which had grown down to her shoulders. On one of her visits, the mistress wanted to give her another

▲ General view of the site of the apparitions.

◄ Pilgrims in the Cova da Iria.

▲ Thousands of pilgrims in the
Cova da Iria.

■ Chapel built at the apparition site of
Valinhos.

◄ Bishop José Alves Correia da Silva,
Bishop of Leiria - Fatima.

refinement—a corset. After rigorously arranging it on her, she went down with her to the dining room.

The poor mountain girl who was transformed into a city girl fell silent and distressed because she could hardly breathe. Sitting at the table she felt even more distressed because she couldn't eat! Quietly, she slipped out of the chair and left unnoticed by the visitors who were conversing about things that she didn't know much about. 'Miss,' who sat beside her, did not give much importance to her leaving.

Once out of the room, Lucia ran hastily up the stairs to her room where she quickly took off the adornments that were suffocating her and put on the clothes that she had brought from Fatima. Wearing the velvet hat adorned with colorful feathers, she came down smiling and in a good mood. When she entered the room, everyone burst out laughing from the depths of their souls. Only 'Miss' was not amused, and being quite upset, asked her:

-*Young lady, what are you doing?*

Lucia very naturally replied:

-*Ma'am I just could not eat! As tight as it was, I only saw my mother cinch a burro this tight!!!* [129]

There was general laughter among the guests. The mistress could not have tried more, but it was not for Lucia. Her body was accustomed to penance for the love of God, not penance for the sake of vanity, and therefore rejected it.

Fr. Formigão began to make contacts to place the young seer in a place safe from the curious who were beginning to discover her whereabouts in the capital. Some of her relatives who lived in Lisbon had come to invite her to their homes. Lucia, in her simplicity, sometimes answered the phone, a novelty at that time, and presented herself truthfully saying:

-*You are speaking to Lucia… Yes, ma'am, to Lucia of Fatima.*[130]

Thus, the secret of her identity was becoming known.

Fr. Formigão spoke to Mother Superior Lindim, a Dorothean Sister, and they agreed to a solution: Lucia would be an intern at the Casa do Largo de Santa Marinha in Lisbon, a shelter for the protection of girls opened by Miss Emilia Brandão Palha who was president. Arrangements were made by Mother Superior and Maria da Assunção and a trousseau was prepared. However, Miss Emilia Brandão thought it would be imprudent to receive Lucia, and this plan was canceled. It appears Lucia had no knowledge of these steps, because in her memoirs she presents a different reason for not returning to her father's house:

---

129 *Sister Lucia, A Memory that We Have of Her*, p. 8.
130 Joaquim Maria Alonso, *Fr. Formigao, Man of God and an Apostle of Fatima*.

-*My stay in Lisbon was beginning to become known until one day Lady Assunção Avelar was warned that the civil authorities were trying to discover my whereabouts.* [131]

In Fatima her mother was quite tormented by the people who continued to come, seeking to talk to Lucia. According to Sister Lucia, her mother was called to the Administration to tell them where her daughter was, to which she responded with her natural straightforwardness:

-*My daughter Lucia is where she wants to be and where I also want her to be. I will not say where she is because I do not want people to go to her to interrogate her and hinder her studying, as they were doing here in Fatima. Where she is, she is to be educated and study. By her leaving Fatima, I also want to see that this ends and I can still one day live in peace in my house, which I cannot with so many people continuously knocking at my door.*[132]

The authorities heard her and smiled, knowing that Maria Rosa had no interest in the visits that she received.

Lucia spent a few days in Santarem, accompanied by Fr. Formigão and his sister Miss Maria Antonia Formigão. She was given the chance stay to a little longer to study in the College of Madre Luisa Andaluz, but Lucia returned to Fatima on August 12, 1920, to appease the people there who tormented her mother, wanting to know her whereabouts. Later she would return to Santarem to the college of Madre Andaluz.

There were many people of goodwill who wanted to help Lucia, but Our Lady would soon show the path God wanted her to follow. God was arranging the right people to guide her according to His will. Fr. Formigão gave his opinion to the Bishop of Leiria, but their opinions differed. However, the Bishop of Asilo de Vilar in Porto, who was the director of interning, prevailed. He knew the Dorothean Sisters very well because they were responsible for the boarding school. They did not know the family names of the religious who stayed there. The following year, in June 1921, Lucia entered the school.

6 | The Shepherdess Finds the Shepherd

Bishop José Alves Correia da Silva was the first consecrated bishop assigned to the Diocese of Leiria after it had been restored. Although he was totally indifferent to the case of Fatima, it was within his jurisdiction and he was obliged to handle it and study it. It was an added responsibility to many others in his diocese. Knowing that the only seer still alive was in Fatima, he asked a

---

131 MSL II, 6th M, No. 66, p. 176.
132 *Ibid.*

woman friend, Miss Gilda, to bring her to the Episcopal Palace. Miss Gilda had no difficulty obtaining permission from Maria Rosa, who would not oppose an order from the bishop.

It was very amusing how Lucia first communicated with her bishop. When Lucia arrived at Miss Gilda's house where she stayed for the evening meal, she was asked if she wanted to accompany her to Mass on the following day and if she wanted to confess before communion. Responding yes, the woman asked if she would like to confess to the Bishop. Lucia said no, she would be too embarrassed, to which the lady smiled. The next morning the two sat near the confessional with the priest. They waited for their turn; the lady was first and then Lucia. The confessor and penitent could not see each other, but Miss Gilda told him who was coming after her. The shepherdess made her confession with her characteristic simplicity and to her astonishment when she returned to her place, she saw that the one who left the confessional was none other than the Bishop! With her eyes popping out of their sockets, she turned to the lady and said:

-*So he was the Bishop!*[133]

After Mass they conversed with His Excellency and then followed him to his home. Thus began a deep friendship. Father C. Barthas, author of the book *Fatima*, said that this first contact with the shepherdess left the Bishop a bit cold. However, in his sequel to this book, Father Barthas related that Sister Lucia said Bishop José was a teacher, guide, and father for her.

After questioning her about the apparitions, the Bishop asked her if she wanted to leave Fatima and study in Porto. She informed him that it was already agreed that she would go to Lisbon. Then the Bishop explained to her that Porto would be better, presenting all the conditions in which she would live in this "college," which she noted:

I would not speak about the apparitions in Fatima to anyone, or about my parents and family, except to give their names, without saying where they lived. No one would visit me except the women to whose care he intended to entrust me. These women were also very good and would not leave me lacking anything. I should not write to anyone except my mother, who was to send my letters to the Vicar of Olival, and through His Reverence, hers would be sent to me. I would not return to Fatima for a holiday or for anything else without his permission. [134]

On the inside Lucia was very happy. This new prospect made her smile. She was pleased that she could live in a home without constant exposure to the curious and the interrogations, both of which made her very tired. She would

133 MSL II, 6th M, No. 68, p.179.
134 MSL II, 6th M, No. 69, p. 180.

not commit herself, however, without the permission of her mother. The Bishop discussed it with her mother and everything was set; it became a secret shared between the two. Lucia could not say anything to anyone about this conversation. For her there were many secrets!

She arrived in Fatima, thinking about the conditions under which she would go to Porto, and began to feel mortal anguish. She weighed each of the conditions that the Bishop presented to her and pondered them in her heart. Her feelings ranged from denial to acceptance of this huge sacrifice, and she suffered silently, not discussing it with her mother. During her hours alone, or at night when she could not sleep, she would think about the future and an immense sadness entered her heart, as Jesus in Gethsemane:

I remembered Lady Assunção, whom I liked very much and thought of as my friend, my sisters whom I could not continue to contact or write; my uncles and other family members; my father's house where I had spent a childhood being innocent and happy: Cova de Iria, Cabeço, Valinhos, and the well where I had enjoyed the delights of Heaven! And leaving everything so, once and for all to go to Porto. I don't know exactly where it is, and I do not know anyone there.

And she continued:

These thoughts and reflections were causing me such great sorrow that the idea of going to Porto seemed to me like being buried alive in a grave and being alone. I said -No, I will not go. I prefer to go to Lisbon or Santarem. Being there I can, from time to time, go to Fatima, see my family, and keep in touch with them. Going to Porto, nothing! No, for this reason I do not want to go! I said 'yes' to the Bishop, but now I say that I regret it and do not want to go there.[135]

When Lucia was in the arms of her mother, she was willing to vent all the bitterness that she felt, but always remained faithful to the secret. She lived with this torture for several months, praying, offering her sacrifice, and asking for help to be able to say yes to what was asked of her despite her lack of strength to do so. She received no consolation and it seemed that Heaven abandoned her to herself, alone in the middle of a dark and cold night. It was all for Our Lady!

At the end of May the parish priest of Fatima told Maria Rosa that the Vicar of Olival wanted to talk to her and Lucia at his residence. This trip would be difficult made on foot because it would be too painful for their horse. It was Maria Rosa's intention not to go, but after meditating, she resigned herself to the sacrifice to avoid any grief. The two of them walked the distance, offering it as a sacrifice, and rested at times by the roadside while praying the Rosary. They

---

135 MSL II, 6th M, No. 69, p. 181.

divided the walk into two parts, staying overnight at the house of a friend who lived in Soutaria.

The Vicar wanted to convey to Maria Rosa the Bishop's desire to take Lucia to Porto and to tell her of the conditions for which he sought her approval. Her mother, who already compromised by letting her go to Lisbon, was bewildered and wanted to know the reason for this change. The Vicar reassured her, saying that Fr. Formigão would negotiate and inform the Lady Assunção. Maria Rosa, whose heart was bleeding, consented to the Bishop who would be responsible for Lucia, but she reserved the right to pick up her daughter if she knew Lucia was not well. Her mother hoped again that *it would all end*. When the Vicar asked Lucia if she wanted to go to Porto, she replied with her characteristic sincerity:

-I would have preferred to go to Lisbon, but in order to do what Your Excellency, the Bishop asks, and subject to the conditions outlined by my mother, then I will go to Porto. [136]

Very happy with the response, the Vicar asked the two of them to maintain secrecy and then invited them for lunch, after which they returned to spend the night at the home of Lady Emilia in Soutaria. On the return to Fatima, in a moment of rest, her mother asked Lucia if she would really be glad to go to Porto. Lucia assured her:

-I would have been happier to go to Lisbon, but as they say the Bishop represents God, I will do his will and go to Porto. If I am not happy there, my mother will come for me.

And with this idea we cheered each other up. [137]

When they were alone at home, noting the look of sadness on Lucia's face and thinking about their next separation, her mother asked her:

-Are you sad? Do you not want to go to Porto? See there, we did not put it into writing. If you do not want to go, don't go!

The shepherdess responded:

-I would rather go to Lisbon or Santarem, but as the Bishop wants me to go to Porto, I'll offer the sacrifice to Our Lord and I'll go to Porto. [138]

And each one concealed her pain, so as to not make the other suffer.

---

136   MSL II, 6th M, No. 70, p. 184.

137   MSL II, 6th M, No. 71, p. 185.

138   *Ibid.*

Pilgrims in the Cova da Iria.

First chapel built on the site of the apparitions in 1918.

Our Lady of the Rosary.

Lucia, 13 years old.

CHAPTER V
I'M HERE FOR THE SEVENTH TIME

1 | Farewell to Fatima

Lucia's departure day from Fatima was June 13, 1921. Many pilgrims were in Fatima on this day to sing and pray to the heavenly Mother, and among them was an unknown lady who, having been sent by the Bishop, arrived at the home of Maria Rosa to take Lucia to Porto. The timing was good so as not to arouse suspicion. The lady was Filomena Miranda, born in Santo Tirso. She conveyed the two orders of the Bishop: that they would take Lucia to Leiria on this day where they would stay until the 16th, and then Lucia would go with her alone to Porto. Lucia listened in silence and felt a chill in her soul seeing the hour she feared had arrived, but she did not respond. Her mother, however, did not agree. Three days in Leiria for what? She wanted to keep her daughter in her company for these three days and then she would accompany her to Leiria. Lucia warned her mother that this sacrifice would not be good for her poor health, but her mother would not budge. And the Lady Filomena returned to Leiria without Lucia.

The three days were long and short at the same time: long, because each lived with the anticipation of the impending pain of parting; short, because of the swift ending of intimacy of mother and daughter. Their hearts were bleeding! Each one desired to strengthen the other with an embrace but wanted to spare the pain this gesture would bring forth, so they swallowed the tears that flooded their souls.

The 15th came, the last day! Early in the morning, Lucia went to Mass at the Fatima church and received the Bread of Heaven to gain strength for the journey which lay before her but was unknown by others. She prayed with unusual intensity, feeling so lost! After the thanksgiving she looked beseechingly at the statue of Our Lady of the Rosary that had smiled on the eve of her First Communion, and left the church holding her hands tightly to her chest as if to hold back the force of that communion, knowing she was receiving there for the last time in her life. Upon her soul everything was dark and there arose a terrible storm of doubts. She was running out of time and felt no strength to move forward. She described this time of pain, turning to Our Lady:

It was June 15, 1921, when I felt myself struggle with the indecision and the regret of the 'yes' that I had given earlier, with the uncertainty of what I would find in my determination to go back; the knowledge that I had left and the yearning that stayed in my heart!

Goodbye to all this in the bloom of youth to the home of my dear Lady Assunção Avelar and others who treated me with maternal affection, but also equally the sorrow of leaving Aljustral and my paternal house. Concern about the uncertainty of what

I would find was oppressing my heart and making me envision what I did not want to think about! No. I will tell my mother I do not want to go and we'll not arrive tomorrow in Leiria and everything would be settled. Then I would go back to Lisbon or Santarem to the home of my dear Lady Adelaide or to Leiria to stay with the women in the Patricio family (these women became friends of the families of the seers during the time of the apparitions), *or any of the sites which would be better for me so I can study and obtain a good future.*

Where the Bishop wants to send me, I do not know how it will be and it is with the condition of not returning home; then I would never see my family anymore or the Cova da Iria, Loca do Cabeço, Valinhos, the well, and the church where my Hidden Jesus is and where I have received many graces! The smile at my First Communion! Vila Nova de Ourem where Jacinta was, and the cemetery where the mortal remains of my beloved father and Francisco are! Never to return to tread on this blessed land, but to go only God knows where! Without even being able to write directly to my Mother! Impossible! I will not! [139]

It was in the afternoon of this day with this multitude of thoughts trampling each other, that I went through all the places connected with the apparitions and with a special connection to my heart. When I arrived at the Cova da Iria I knelt down next to the grid which protected the site where Our Lady appeared on the holm oak, and I let the tears run down from my eyes, while I was asking Our Lady's forgiveness for not being able to offer her at this time this sacrifice that seemed beyond my strength. I remembered that most beautiful day May 13, 1917, when I gave my 'yes,' promising to accept all the sacrifices that God wanted to send me. This memory was like a light in the bottom of my soul, a scruple that did not give me peace, and made me pour out a torrent of tears! [140]

It was a struggle between nature and grace, for *the spirit is willing, but the flesh is weak.*[141] At this time Lucia had no one to turn to for advice and came to seek Heaven's aid. The Virgin Mother who had promised never to abandon her in her time of anguish came to bring peace to her soul, thus fulfilling the promise made on May 13, 1917, to return here a seventh time. Lucia continued to pray:

So helpful, once again you have come down to Earth; and then I felt your helping hand and maternal touch on my shoulder. I looked up and I saw you, it was you, Blessed Mother, holding my hand and showing me the path, and your lips unveiled the sweet timbre of your voice and light and peace was restored to my soul. 'Here I am for the seventh time. Go, follow the path which the Bishop wants you to take, this is the will of

---

139 *My Pathway*, I, p. 10.
140 *Ibid.*
141 Mt 26:41.

God.' I repeated then my 'yes,' now much more conscious than on that day of May 13, 1917.[142]

2 | Leave and Follow Me - First Time

An enormous weight was lifted from her. Lucia was at peace and strengthened to move forward, now certain of the will of God. Though it was difficult, it only mattered where He wanted her to walk. Now quiet, appreciating the time alone after watching the Virgin return to Heaven, she replayed the wonderful experiences she had in this place four years earlier. Her heart rose to the first sign of a religious vocation:

I remembered Our Lady of Mount Carmel, and in that moment I felt the grace of a vocation to religious life and the attractiveness of the Cloister of Carmel. I took as my protection my dear Therese of the Child Jesus.[143]

Days later, on the advice of the Bishop, I took the standard rule of obedience and the motto of the words of Our Lady narrated in the Gospel, "Do whatever He tells you."[144]

Stronger, relieved of the temptation that had oppressed her, she continued her pilgrimage to all the holy places, some of which at that time were only known by her, such as the place of the Angel's apparitions. In her uncle's house she spent a few moments in the rooms of her cousins, Francisco and Jacinta. She didn't catch the attention of anyone, because every once in a while she would make this visit. Returning home in the evening, she contemplated one last time the lamps of Our Lady and of the Angels from her childhood in the company of her father and cousins:

This longing was pinching like a dagger being driven into my heart, but I promised that I would be faithful! I renewed my 'yes' and I asked the help of my Guardian Angel and the Angel of Portugal, precursor of the Virgin Mother.[145]

Then Lucia and Maria Rosa sat at the table, which at one time was so populated, and for the last time shared a light meal in silence. They went to bed early because soon they would have to get up and go out into the night. Her mother was not aware of Lucia's interior struggle. Although Our Lady had pacified her, giving her the certainty of doing God's will, nature did not cease to suffer. The waves of temptation returned, making their way into her 'small boat' where Jesus

---

142 My Pathway, I, p. 6.
143 Saint Therese of the Child Jesus, a Carmelite in Lisieux, France (1873-1897).
144 My Pathway, I, p. 12.
145 Ibid, p. 13.

slept. [146]

Lucia described her farewell from the home where she was born and raised:

At 2 a.m. on June 16, 1921, when the whole village was asleep, I got up in the company of my dear mother, who was far from suspecting the fight that was raging in my heart. Like Abraham, who climbed the mountain to offer his son Isaac to God, and in the company of this poor laborer who was taking us to Leiria, we went by the way of the Cova. He took us there so I could pray my last farewell Rosary.

When this ended, He put us back on track. I was lagging behind and turned to say my last goodbye, and in that place where now stands the Basilica I saw a figure of light. I had the impression that it was my dear Mother in Heaven who came to inspire me and give me courage with her maternal blessing, but I do not know. Perhaps it was just a reflection left in my mind of what happened the day before, or it may have been the glare of the moon among the trees. [147]

Once in Leiria, her mother bought Lucia a handbag in which to carry little items. She did not take clothes, just some underwear, books and notebooks. Her mother did not want her to leave empty-handed, but did not know what she would need. Lucia was given to the lady whom the Bishop sent, and she would provide everything that Lucia needed. After this arrangement was made, they went to her uncle's house where they had lunch and then were visited by Carolina, who was nearby taking care of a sick child. With great joy Lucia visited with her mother and sister, none of them realizing when they might meet again. Lucia continues:

By 2 o'clock in the afternoon we were in the Leiria station and I gave my mother a farewell embrace. She was immersed in tears, and as always, tortured by doubt, but bid me goodbye saying:

-Well, my daughter, if it is true that you saw Our Lady, she will protect you, but if you lied, then you will be miserable.

And fulfilling the prophecy of my dear mother, Our Lady has protected me, saved me, helped and defended me leading my footsteps. [148]

Lucia got on the train and at the window waved goodbye to her beloved mother with her handkerchief, letting the tears run, which flowed together in the same river that came from the eyes of her mother.

---

146 Cf. Mt 8:24.
147 *My Pathway,* p. 14.
148 *Ibid.*

Pilgrims continue to come to the Cova da Iria.

Lucia, age 13.

CHAPTER VI
STUDENT

1 | The Institute of Arcediago Van Zeller In Vilar

Lucia made the trip to Porto in the company of Miss Filomena Miranda, whom she did not yet know. Arriving late in the evening, they could not go to Asilo de Vilar, the Institute of Arcediago Van Zeller where the Sisters of St. Dorothy were to receive her, so they looked for a hotel, but they were all full. Lucia stated:

-As in Bethlehem, the Holy Family had no place.[149]

Miss Filomena decided to knock on the door of a family friend who lived in Rua da Boavista. The lady of the house was Rosalina Menezes Faria.

The maids told them that the owners were not there, but not long after the couple arrived and arranged for the two to stay the night. Miss Filomena could not reveal the identity of the mountain girl who accompanied her, so gave the excuse that she was slightly indisposed from the trip. Therefore, the owners proposed that they have a small dinner served by their maids and then retire to their rooms. But Miss Filomena insisted they would just eat a snack and then the two would sleep in the same room; she would sleep in a recliner so the girl could rest. The homeowners respected their guest's desires and sent them an extra bed, placing it on the floor of their room. After a cup of tea, Lucia retired to the bed on the floor and soon fell into a deep sleep. She was going into the unknown, missing everyone she loved, especially her mother. Despite her forlorn heart she slept serenely, as if everything was normal. Lucia had an incredible ability to control her emotions and handle things so maturely at the age of 14.

The day dawned: June 17, 1921. The two guests rose at 5:30 a.m. and left without breakfast in order to arrive at the Institute in time for Holy Mass and Communion. Overwhelmed by the uncertainty of her future, Lucia received the Eucharist on this day with a renewed fervor, entrusting herself to the only one who would accompany her and make her path clear. Mary would be her strength. Lucia sought refuge in her heart with faithful confidence, but felt unceasingly the pains of the cross.

After thanksgiving, the two were accompanied by Madre Maria das Dores Magalhães, Mother Superior of the Institute. They went into the sacristy where they were received by the chaplain and confessor, Msgr. Manuel Pereira Lopes. These people were the only ones who knew the secret of her identity. No one else would know who she was. After greeting her, the chaplain asked her some questions, which she answered with her natural shyness, then repeated to him the recommendations of the Bishop of Leiria. He then said:

---

149 *My Pathway*, I, p. 14

-The girl will now change her name. Therefore she will be called Maria das Dores (Mary of Sorrows). If you are asked where you are from, only say that you are close to Lisbon and nothing more. Do not speak of Fatima or your family, nothing.[150]

With her heart in a knot Lucia nodded affirmatively. This was another unfamiliar place for her and she noticed that the silence she expected was missing. But her gaze was fixed inwardly on her Mother who promised to lead her forever and she repeated with all her soul the prayer taught to her in the Cova da Iria, *-O my God, it is for love of You.*

After this brief encounter with the chaplain, who would be her confessor while in the Institute of Arcediago, she took leave of Miss Filomena and was taken to the schoolmistress who gave her the boarding school uniform, a scratchy pinafore of black and white squares that made her equal to everyone else. Then she was led to the craft room and everyone was excused from silence so they could welcome the new classmate. Naturally, the questions began. Lucia says of this first meeting:

No one there suspected who I was, not the teachers or students and, of course, soon they began to rain questions:

-What is your name?

-Mary of Sorrows.

-And your nickname?

-None.

-Where are you from?

-Near Lisbon.

-But, there are many places near Lisbon! Is it Cascais?

Naturally, I remained silent.

-So you do not know the name where you are from? Is it Sintra?

-No.

-Is it Santarem?

-No.

-Is it Parede? Etc...

-And your parents' names?

I kept silent, and naturally, I was taken for a fool.

-What a mystery! They were commenting, a little 14-year-old who does not know where she is from, does not know her parents' name, and does not have a nickname. I felt that, you know, oh dear Mother and our Good Lord knew how I felt! But recalling my 'yes,' I repeated it softly day by day, next to Your altar at the foot of the tabernacle.[151]

---

150 *Ibid,* p.17.
151 *Ibid,* p.18.

This first encounter, highlighted by the candid smiles of the other girls who were already accustomed to the boarding school, eventually made Lucia depressed with dark clouds. The shepherdess in her silence experienced bitter tears in her heart, but reasserted her unconditional 'yes,' despite the temptation to give up.

And I remembered the promise of May 13, 1917:

-Then you are going to have much to suffer, but the grace of God will be your comfort. [152]

Like a mountain climber who perseveres with eyes fixed on the goal to be achieved, Lucia embraced all the sacrifices, keeping her eyes on Mary and Jesus, Who gave her everything. Whenever possible she took refuge in the chapel, the place of her petition and where she felt peace. There she vented her heart and received the courage to pursue her path with love and grace, not focusing on her sufferings. She confessed:

I always tried to hide my suffering, my disappointments and internal struggles, especially so my mother would not suffer because of me or think to come after me. I wanted to offer to God my holocaust and all that was possible with joy, and this was the happiness to which I referred in my letters. Immolate myself for love, for souls, in fulfillment of my 'yes.' [153]

On June 21, Maria das Dores wrote her first letter to her mother, and perhaps the first letter of her life. It had several errors, but was full of affection for all:

My dear Mother,

Firstly I cherish your health and of our whole family, I am fine thanks be to God.

My dear mother I can finally tell you that my trip was very good thanks be to God.

Now, I appreciate knowing that your trip went well and you found our entire family well.

Fortunately I am very happy and content. My dear mother, I ask you to please tell me if the boys already made amends and how it is and was. I would ask you to please give my regards to our whole family and give many kisses to my sisters Maria and Teresa. Give our bountiful praise to the boy and tell my godmother that I miss her very much.

And for you a longing embrace from your daughter who wishes you well.

Maria das Dores of Jesus

My beloved mother when you want to write, write to the Rev. Bishop of Leiria

---

152 MSL I, 2nd M, Ch. II, No. 4, p. 83.

153 *My Pathway*, I, p. 19.

and he will send me your letter. [154]

2 | Adapting to a New Life

One day during Confession, Msgr. Pereira Lopes asked me if I was happy. It had been suggested to conceal all that I was suffering, but since I was asked by him in the place of God, I thought I should tell the whole truth and sincerely express the suffering that invaded my soul. But I received no consolation. The confessor with a little sweetness in his voice told me that Jesus had suffered more. Therefore, I shouldn't complain. I was Maria das Dores and I should not refuse.

But there was someone who understood her and treated her with paternal tenderness and affection—Bishop da Silva, the bishop of Leiria, who visited her regularly. The shepherdess was at ease with him and trusted him openly with her heart. His Excellency was demanding and firm with her when he administered spiritual direction, but was truly a father, teacher, and guide.

In a common dormitory with very little room, I could not be at ease to say the prayers taught by the Angel in the position that we learned how to pray. But love is inventive and I did not give up in the face of the difficulties.

With the permission of the confessor, I continued to use the rope as a belt. It was very difficult to pray the prayers of the Angel with my arms crossed or lying prostrate, without being noticed. I did not have a private room. I slept in a common dormitory without curtains and when I was Sacristan, I could do a little in the tiny hallway behind the main altar. Sometimes I would ask for permission to leave the recreation of the night to go make a visit to the Blessed Sacrament. It would happen that I would be alone, but it was rare because some of my companions would ask for permission to accompany me. I was also responsible for the recreation of children in the playground and in this case I could not leave. I was limited to pray on my knees when time allowed. [155]

Ah! I miss the nostalgia of the fields of Fatima ... I long for the Loca do Cabeço, a silent witness of so many wonders and so much love!

Attracted by the compassion that radiated from their new companion, the students forgot the mocking attitude of that first encounter and began to enjoy her. Lucia was always a good person to be around, but by this time she stopped being playful and mischievous like everyone else. A week after she arrived it was the feast of St. John. Lucia was dazzled by the fireworks show. She marveled at them! She had already seen the unique beauty of the Mother of God and was also excited by this beauty created by human art. The following year, she remembered

---

154 Sanctuary of Fatima, Critical Documentation of Fatima [DCF], Volume III, 3 (1920 - 1922), Doc. 623, p. 141.
155 *My Pathway*, I, p. 26.

this beauty and that this innocent pleasure could be offered as a sacrifice for an unrepentant person about to enter into eternity. She chose not to see the fireworks and convinced her companions to do the same. All of them offered this sacrifice for a soul to open itself to the grace of God.

The next year was a different picture. The schoolmistress ordered that everyone should go to sleep; no one could see the fireworks. What a pity! They were so close but they could not see them. But the young people had no difficulty coming up with a solution. There is always one in the group that sheds a light for the others.

The bedroom had two doors leading to the balcony from which you could see the fireworks very well. Since the schoolmistress did not sleep in the dormitory they would use one door to go to the balcony and have one student remain to watch if she was coming. If she came, they would be warned and everyone would silently sneak back to the bedroom through the other door and get into their beds pretending to sleep.

The schoolmistress, knowing that with young people you can always expect some mischief, came upon some of the girls on the balcony but did not catch any of them behaving badly and the girls returned to their rooms. Once in their rooms they stifled their laughter underneath the sheets, and waited for her to retire so they could return to savor the beauty of that night of St. John in Porto. Maria das Dores shared this adventure joyfully and with the freedom of God's children. Having a delicate conscience, but without being scrupulous, she did not have guilt about it. Within her coexisted a great cross and infectious joy that came from God, and those who approached her felt it.

Regarding this initial phase of her life, they say that *"one who runs for pleasure does not tire."* Lucia complied generously and without reservation with the bishop's proposal, but the impact of having to renounce her home and family and go to Lisbon and the home of a stranger was not lost on her. It is natural to feel uncomfortable and suffer in a strange place, and the cross is always different than what we think it will be in our eagerness to embrace it. Because it is a cross it has to really hurt. The great 16th century Spanish Mystic St. John of the Cross once wrote to a spiritual daughter: *Where there is no love, put love, and you will find love.*[156] Lucia did not know his writings, but already knew how to apply them in her life. She described this time:

My first impressions were disappointing; everything seemed so sad and uncomfortable! The way students were treated, the house, the yard, compared with my

---

156 St. John of the Cross, letter 22-159.

Serra de Aire...where I came to be immersed in Holy God! It seemed to me a grave in life. There in that place, she just smiled at me in that beautiful chapel where my good Jesus is hidden and you, O Mother, how many times have you offered Him my sacrifice, my resignation, my devotion repeated every day, renewed with this Love that I was only able and silently to place in your blessed hands. [157]

Thus did Maria das Dores live, suffering in silence while adapting to a new life with rules to which she was not accustomed. The shepherdess—a pupil with no last name, no family, and unknown to all—offered all these thorns with love.

Her internal suffering was also accompanied by poor nutrition. It was postwar and food was scarce. Lucia was used to eating simple but wholesome and plentiful food. When Miss Filomena visited her a month later, she was very worried. She talked to Bishop da Silva, who was also concerned and soon visited and met with his contact and protector, Maria da Conceição Maldonadeo Bento Pereira. She arranged for Lucia to spend a few holidays in her home or in the Quinta da Fonte Pedrinha in Braga, to regain her strength. It was during these times that Maria das Dores became acquainted with Miss Maria Eugenia Pestana, a girl almost her age, and this sincere friendship lasted a lifetime.

In order to help strengthen her, the lady Maria da Conceição brought her an abundant supply of fruit and other food that she could save and eat when needed. But the shepherdess did not only think of herself. Shortly before lunch time, whenever she could do it without being noticed, she would go to the places in the cafeteria where the poor would hide, and bring them some fruit or a slice of cheese. She was pleasantly surprised when she was received with a grateful smile. No one spoke, but they wondered who their benefactor was.

Maria das Dores knew how to attract and entertain the other students with such beautiful stories of Our Lady and of the Angels, and was herself enraptured before the image of Our Lady. This drew the attention of the students to go to the chapel where she would be. Through their deep profound meditation, they noticed something very special inside this girl of the mountain and would question her. With an innate sense of righteousness Maria das Dores would sometimes unfairly judge them and answer with a sharp tongue, but she softened her character, taking advantage of this as a new form of sacrifice. She became an enjoyable companion for all of them during recreation and devotion, and the students began to follow her as their role model.

She began to arouse the attention of more astute companions who began "spying" on her to discover who she was. One of the students remembered having

---

157 *My Pathway,* I, p. 18.

seen her face, and one day found a newspaper behind a drawer that told about the Fatima apparitions. There was a picture of the three shepherds. She had no doubt; it was she! She and the other students shared their thoughts, ideas, and questions about the spirit of Lucia, and her real identity started to make sense. They had even thought that she was deaf when she didn't respond to her name, Maria das Dores, to which she was not accustomed. They remembered, too, when she marked her clothes with an "L," which caught the attention of the schoolmistress who did not know the "secret." Lucia told her it was clothing that had been given to her by the lady who took her to the orphanage.

The one who found out the identity of the little shepherdess did not lose a moment in conveying her discovery to Lucia, which left her in a sea of tears and grief. She turned to the chaplain and confessor of the orphanage, thinking that she was guilty of having revealed the secret that had been imposed on her when she entered. He consoled her as best as he could, telling her that she should have been notified by the Superior of the house, that her exit from Porto with the schoolmistress was arranged and concealed, and that during the internship absolute silence was imposed on the subject of Fatima. But the secret circulated by word of mouth and soon resulted in a certain respect between Lucia and her companions.

3 | Hard-working Student

Lucia attended classes, having been placed in the intermediate category until entering the Novitiate. Besides their academic preparation, the students were given exams in high school, where they learned cooking, sewing, embroidery, painting, drawing and music. They were prepared to become good housewives. Lucia specialized in embroidery, particularly embroidery with gold and silver. The work required much attention to detail. She also learned the technique of binding.

She did beautiful work, and she was very happy to share her knowledge. She could say in all truth: *I learned with loyalty; and communicated without envy.* [158] However, another sacrifice awaited her. She offered it with love, but the pain from it left a deep wound. She prepared with determination for the 4th year examination, the highest level at the Institute of Arcediago. According to her protector's wish, she was also prepared for the entrance examination for college, which she would attend after her 4th year, to continue her studies. Lucia really liked this and wanted to study, and always had very good grades.

---

158 Wis 7:13.

However, the Bishop of Leiria wanted to keep her anonymous and it was not possible for her to take an official examination without presenting an identity card, thus exposing her. The examination of the 4th year was very important at that time and was done in the high school. Instead she was examined individually by Dr. Regos, who went to the institute to give the final details to the students who were taking the exam. There was one more rejection and it was big! She had received several offers from colleges, which was a cherished dream of hers for a long time, but she had to turn them all down. Now she saw herself with clipped wings. Gracefully she embraced this new sacrifice, but she felt its thorn all her life, especially when later she needed to write by obedience her memoirs, or correspond with highly educated people. Addressing these issues of great responsibility and feeling uneducated and insufficiently prepared to do so, she later confessed:

On earth I have not found anyone who could understand the words of Our Lady "learn to read" or those who wanted the honor of giving me fulfillment in instructing me, so that the work that took place in me is all of the Holy Spirit. To Him is due all honor and glory. [159]

Most sacrifices after they are borne stop hurting, but this was always present in her and repeatedly accepted. Sometime near the end of her life, while reflecting again on this bitter memory, she concluded that this waiver that had been asked of her was for the glory of God. It was one more seal of authentication of the Message of Fatima. It had flourished despite her being its principal transmitter. She said:

-If I had studied and knew how to write correctly, it would seem that when writing my Memoirs as a literary work, it would not be in the genuine purity of simplicity. It was only I who knew how to say what I saw and heard, without the careful art of a language. God does everything well and leads our steps always in the best way. Blessed be God forever! [160]

When she was informed that she would not take the exam like the other girls, a huge storm arose in her mind. She recalled several offers made to her years ago and her willingness to give up everything and take the reins of her life into her own hands. She longed to study, not to make herself notable, but to better convey the message that Heaven had delivered. Without an education, how could she do it and be heard credibly? As to her departure from Fatima, Heaven calmed this storm. She was on her way to the chapel to tell her Confidant in the Tabernacle the suffering that troubled her soul. He anticipated her arrival and told her these words:

159 Letter to Bishop Ernesto Sena de Oliveira, October 1, 1955.
160 Oral Narration of Sister Lucia.

-Do not be sad. You will not study, but I will give you my Wisdom. The Message is in the care of my Hierarchy. [161]

She guarded these words that gave her such peace in her heart and continued forward with her eyes on God.

4 | Path with Thorns and Flowers

When her protector, Maria da Conceição, learned Lucia could not study, she became worried and offered her a portion of her property to secure a future without material concern. Lucia thanked her and talked to Bishop da Silva at the first opportunity. His Excellency listened in silence, and with fatherly concern for the good of his pupil, explained that it would not be prudent to accept this generous offer. There would be occasional murmurings, which could and should be avoided by surrendering this as well. Lucia was in the glow of her adolescence, a fruitful period of sweet dreams, and she felt very deeply that this sacrifice was asked of her for the sake of the Message she was responsible for conveying to the world. How lovely to see her so human: graced by heavenly favors, yet blindly and humbly walking her path; suggesting her own ideas as was her nature, yet accepting the guidance of human mediations. Later, she would be grateful to God for having given her a guide so prudent and concluded it was very good to have been so. Lucia, or rather Maria das Dores, no longer indulged the demand for sacrifices, but was moved by the fervor of her heart, the desire to save souls and console the Hearts of Jesus and Mary. The fidelity to obedience was growing in her and she began to understand that *obedience is better than sacrifice.*[162] She submitted to her confessor, sacrificing her own desires and obediently offering up the true sacrifice—the sacrifice of the will.

On June 8, 1923, the Feast of the Sacred Heart of Jesus, she was chosen by her companions to be the caretaker of the Sacred Heart of Jesus. Later, on August 26, without going through the normal process, she was admitted as a member of the Daughters of Mary. With her confessor's permission, she was inspired to fervently devote herself in a special way to Our Lady, devoting herself entirely to God by the perpetual vow of chastity. [163] She was now 16 years old.

On this day she was guided by the hands of Mary, the Lady of her life, who was present with her shepherdess in a very sensitive way. The Mother was beside her daughter at such an important moment! During the consecration, members

---

161 Oral Narration of Sister Lucia.

162 I Sam 15: 22.

163 *My Pathway,* I, p. 25 - 26.

receive a medal of Our Lady to wear over their chest. Sister Lucia kept this her whole life, and in her grave it rests on her heart. She walked her path of thorns and flowers always with great love and a surrendered disposition. Intimate joys were a balm for her soul to smooth the way, fresh water in the desert that was sometimes very hot, intoxicating wine that strengthened her in her search for God's will and loyal fulfillment of her mission. Saint Teresa of Avila says that God sometimes intoxicates souls so that they will not be frightened of the great sacrifices that arise on the horizon.[164]

Later in her life it was enchanting to see and hear Sister Lucia relive that distant time when she was among her cheerful companions and could be playful and joyful like them. She was lively as ever and never refrained from any proposed activities.

One day she participated in a prank: the girls were not allowed to eat the fruit in the backyard. But temptation didn't just happen in the Garden of Eden—a student passing near a park saw a pear that seemed to say: *Come to me!* The young girl looked at the tempting fruit and not needing to be encouraged by any snake reached out and ate the pear. Others saw this act and turned in the poor transgressor who was called to account and punished.

The punishment was exemplary, to serve as a lesson for all. However, the others were supportive of their companion who had taken the forbidden fruit because of hunger and being of an age when the appetite is not lacking. Together they considered the grapes that were also inviting. During recess they sought out the Sister who accompanied them and asked her to sit next to a column at the back door where they formed a circle around her while joyfully singing and dancing. Without the Sister's notice, Lucia left to eat some grapes and carry some in her apron pocket. She returned to the circle with another girl who did the same. When recess ended, the Sister did not notice that the grapes had been harvested. Lucia and her companions took all the grapes to eat during their study time.

Then the other side of the coin came: the weight of the conscience. Lucia was already a member of the Daughters of Mary. She drew attention to what they had done, which was not pleasing to God, and advised them all to confess. At the first opportunity for confession, there was a collection of sinners waiting. Lucia went first. She confessed her sin with much contrition. To her surprise her confessor asked if the grapes that she ate were evil; she said *no!* Then the priest said, *do not worry.*[165] He knew their stomachs were not very well-nourished, so this did not qualify as a sin. This lightened her soul, but the adventure was not

---

164 Cf. St. Teresa of Avila, *The Way of Perfection*, ch. 18, p. 129.
165 Oral Narration of Sister Lucia.

repeated. [166]

Sister Lucia had fond memories of this distant time as a pupil in the Vilar Institute. Those four years were very vivid in her life. Living anonymously, not being able to take exams like the other students, and distinguished by an "I don't know" response to questions made her stand out among her companions. She was respected and loved even by the schoolmistress. When necessary, they gave her responsibility over the younger girls, which she had already experienced in her childhood. She enjoyed their company, even though at times it was inconvenient, especially when she wanted to leave the playground to pay a visit to the Blessed Sacrament. When alone she would lie prostrate, praying the prayers taught by the Angel. Sometimes friends would ask to join her, so she could not pray as such. She accepted their company with a lovely smile and prayed in silence, her heart prostrated before the Lord of her life.

One winter season almost all the girls became seriously ill with flu and it seemed that it would take many of their young lives. Given the severity of the girls' state, the Mother Superior came to the ward one day and spoke to them with maternal concern, saying that their condition was very serious and that medicine was having no effect on the illness. Given that they were doing everything they could, she advised that they go to confession and receive the sacrament of Anointing of the Sick. The Sacrament would help them better withstand the illness and heal if that was God's will, or better prepare them for Heaven. They all listened in silence and agreed to her proposal. One of the girls began to cry and protested that she did not want to die. The Mother Superior approached the girl's bed and with great gentleness tried to console her by talking about Heaven. She asked her:

-*So, Miquelina, you do not want to go to Heaven?*

The subdued girl responded with great strength, perhaps incited by the high temperature:

-*Yes, Madam, I want to go to Heaven, but I want to live!*[167]

They all confessed and received Communion as Viaticum and the Holy Anointing. Their conditions improved and they came out unscathed from the disease. Only Miquelina worsened and went to Heaven, having received the Sacraments as proposed.

---

166 *Ibid.*
167 *Ibid.*

5 | Fatima Without the Shepherds

Since the two younger seers had died[168] Lucia was the principal figure in the Fatima movement. If everything was invented, as her mother thought, then the movement would fade away. Gamaliel once said of Christianity to the Sanhedrin: *If this is the work of men, ultimately it will fail, but if it comes from God, you will not succeed in destroying it.*[169] And so it happened with Fatima.

The shepherds were God's only instruments used to convey the message of salvation to the world through the maternal Heart of Mary. Despite government prohibitions against visiting the Cova, people continued to come to Fatima, seeking Our Lady's intercession and protection. They came from all corners of the country and later the world, and from all walks of life—all roads led to Fatima. Troubled souls felt the warmth of the Mother's shelter. They could not explain it, but there they felt right. Some people went to Fatima to ask for favors, others went in thanksgiving for favors received; some went for love of Mary, to console her Heart, and to rest in this shelter that was available. They experienced the deep peace that only God can give, and returned with renewed hearts and the strength to embrace their daily crosses, which were sometimes quite heavy.

Lucia was asked to draw the world's attention to the Heart of the Mother, but had to sacrifice the joy of savoring *this fountain that was pouring forth in gushes and that was transformed into a torrential river.*[170] She was even told to be absolutely silent on the subject. If someone next to her was talking about Fatima, she ignored the conversation, but within her ran hot tears that she drank with pleasure. Only with the Bishop of Leiria, during his visits to her or on holidays in Braga, could she open her heart and ask him news of her native home.

On July 8, 1924, Lucia was again subjected to questioning, this time as part of a canonical procedure. In 1922 the Bishop of Leiria had opened the Canonical Process, an official church investigation into the events of Fatima. The same bishop appointed a commission composed of the Reverend Fathers João Quaresma, vicar general; Faustino Jacinto Ferreira, prior of Olival and archpriest of the Council of Ourem; Manuel Marques dos Santos, seminary professor; Joaquim das Neves Ferreira Gonçalves, pastor of Santa Catarina de Serra; and Agostinho Marques Ferreira, parish priest of Fatima. Because Lucia resided in Porto, the Bishop of Leiria recused himself and the Bishop of Porto proceeded with the official interrogation of the shepherdess in his jurisdiction. Permission

---

168 Francisco died on April 4, 1919, and Jacinta on February 20, 1920.
169 Cf. Acts 5:38-39.
170 Cf. Esther 10:6.

was granted and Lucia was questioned by Reverends Manuel Nunes Formigão Junior, Manuel Marques dos Santos and Manuel Pereira Lopes from the Diocese of Porto and confessor of the respondent. [171] She was 17 years old.

As she did all her life, she recalled from her memory and in her heart all she heard and saw at Fatima and responded simply and sincerely to the questions that had already been posed so many times, maintaining the Secret and events pertaining to the apparitions of the Angel, which so far were not known. She wrote about this event:

I knew nothing about such formalities at the time, and I did not call any more attention to this interview than any other of the many I was accustomed to. I tried to respond with truth and clarity to what I was asked, being very careful not to move forward or reveal that which I still kept in silence. But I think I had no obligation to say so, and do not know, but I have the impression that it is more joyful when you retain things that are only between the soul and God. At least to me it has happened.[172]

It pained her to have to talk about such intimate things that she wished to keep to herself. It is a common repugnance to all who receive favors of this kind. They never like to reveal information and if they do, it is only by obedience.

In June of 1929, Bishop José Alves Correia visited his spiritual daughter who was then a religious sister in Tuy. In their private conversations, he clarified some doubts that he still had at the conclusion of the study, which he would crown with solemn approval the following year. During this visit, His Excellency spoke broadly of the expansion of the devotion to Our Lady of Fatima not only in Portugal, but throughout the world. Lucia listened and gave thanks in her heart. The message continued to expand, even in her absence, even with her silence. Her life given for love was a stream of fresh water benefitting souls; it was a hidden fire, which warmed so many hearts frozen by sin.

6 | Vacation in Braga

Going back to the time during the period of the Institute of Arcediago in Vilar, Lucia enjoyed a healthy and restorative vacation with Maria da Conceição Maldonado Bento Pereira, who became her protector and who was authorized to take her periodically to the Quinta de Fonte Pedrinha. This was the farmhouse offered to Maria das Dores that she rejected to avoid scandal. Despite this, the shepherdess was well supported by the Bishop who asked his good friend Maria Isabel Vasconcelos to take care of her in his absence. This promise was fulfilled

---

171 DCF, Vol. II, Doc. 7, p. 123-135; Doc. 8, p. 137-146.
172 *My Pathway*, I, p. 37.

▲ Blessing the foundation stone of the Basilica.

▶ Basilica of Our Lady of Fatima.

▲ Blessing the foundation stone of the Basilica.

▶ Chapel of Apparitions.

◄ Maria Isabel Vasconcelos and family.

▲ Maria da Conceição Maldonado Bento Pereira.

▼ Lucia, 16 years old.

with heart and soul.

Once a year Lucia was allowed to leave the Institute and receive a visit from her dear mother. The two hearts were strengthened in their love for each other. Her summer vacation was spent at the Quinta da Formigueria, which belonged to the Bishop of Leiria, accompanied by Miss Filomena Miranda. When His Excellency ended his holiday, the shepherdess would spend the remaining time in the Quinta da Fonte Pedrinha with her protector.

During this holiday time, Lucia felt very comfortable with the Bishop who observed her faithfulness in obedience. She described this time of distinction with her Bishop:

During the day the Bishop did not want me to walk with my head uncovered in the sun, and he sent Miss Filomena to me with a large straw hat. At first, as I wasn't used to it, I forgot to put it on and I came out of the house without it. The Bishop realized this and beating his palms on the window, called me and wondered where the hat was. Then I had to climb the stairs and kneel before the Bishop and ask for forgiveness. His Excellency told me, you still did not learn to obey, my daughter! I fetched my hat and returned to reading a book or magazine. Not to forget it again, I hung the hat on a wire of the trellis at the bottom of the stone staircase, since I would pass by it and see it. The Bishop laughed and told me that someday when I was putting the hat on, I would find a nest of birds inside it. But that never happened.

At night when the servants had already completed their work, all of us assembled in the chapel to pray the Rosary. The Bishop opened the tabernacle and Miss Filomena sang with me the Salutaris and Tantum Ergo and at the end a hymn to Our Lady. The Bishop intoned the Rosary, held Benediction with the Blessed Sacrament, then allowed us to kiss his sacred ring and we went to rest.

Sometimes he sent me songs to sing that he knew from college, The Athenaeum, from his childhood, or the Sierra. Those that Miss Filomena knew she sang with me and those that she did not know, I had to sing alone. At first I was bashful and it was hard for me, but when I got used to it I did not have any difficulty. There were verses that I modified from his letters and the Bishop loved to send them to me and we sang them often. One was as follows:

In Heaven there is a small window
Portugal is seen by her
When God feels sad
He will sit next to her.

I said:

> *Fatima is seen by her* [173]

At the table, sitting next to the Bishop, she thought it was more important for her to serve, and she did so with pleasure. If sometimes Lucia showed resistance, the Bishop would say to her:

-Here now, my daughter, mortification and fasting is obedience.[174] He was forming her in obedience but with gentleness and Lucia devoted herself to this obedience without embarrassment.

7 | Meeting with Her Mother and Invitation to Religious Life

In the summer of 1925 during a holiday period, Maria Rosa and Lucia enjoyed a longer time together. Neither of them dreamed that it was the last time they would enjoy such intimacy in the Formigueira home; soon Lucia would enter into the religious life. She was 18 years old and already felt strongly the call of God. She said in her memoirs:

> *I took advantage of the opportunity to ask my mother's permission to become a Religious.*
>
> *She responded: -Look, daughter, I know nothing about such a life. I will ask the Bishop.*
>
> And she went downstairs to look for the Bishop, who was reading on a bench opposite the balcony under the shade of the trellised vines. As soon as His Excellency saw my mother, he called her over to him and made her sit down on the bench beside him. I was watching from the balcony. I did not hear what they were saying, but when my mother came back after a *long conversation with the Bishop, she was very pleased to be able to say 'yes' to my request, on condition that I agreed to let her know if I was not happy, so that she could come and take me.*[175]

Mother and daughter spent many pleasant moments conversing and singing the songs of the Serra de Aire. They walked together in the Quinta, remembering past times and Lucia's life as a child. Lucia wrote:

> *One afternoon, my mother and I went for a walk in the Quinta in order to take advantage of the freshness of the afternoon air. We came to a quarry situated a little lower down, and made our way to the bottom of it, where we sat down on a stone. My mother asked did I still remember some of the old songs we used to sing in Fatima. I said I did. Believing that no one could either see or hear us, the two of us began to sing:*

---

173 *My Pathway,* I, p. 32.

174 *Ibid,* p. 28.

175 MSL II, 6th M, No. 74, p. 190.

I love God in Heaven
And I love Him on earth.
I love the fields, the flowers,
I love the sheep on the hillside.

I am a poor shepherdess,
I always pray to Mary.
In the midst of my flock
I am the midday sun.

I love God...

With my little lambs
I learned to jump.
I am the joy of the hillside
I am the lily of the valley.

I love God...

When we came to the end, we heard someone laughing. We looked up and there was the Bishop at the top looking down at us and laughing. We got up in order to go back up and greet His Excellency, but he made a sign to us to stay where we were and he himself came down. When he reached us, he sat down on a stone next to us and told us to go on singing as he enjoyed listening to us. So then we sang some verses in honor of Our Lady:
Chorus

It's true, it's true (repeat)
Heaven is my home!

Heaven is my home,
I long to be there
And it will be mine, never fear (repeat)
Close to the Mother of God, the beloved.

Heaven is my home,
Home of eternal bliss.
There I shall always be happy,

Close to the Mother of God, the beloved.

It's true, it's true…

Afterwards, we returned to the house because it was nearly time for supper, which we all shared in a happy frame of mind. [176]

8 | Confirmation

Maria Rosa attended the intimate ceremony of Lucia's Confirmation, as she had not yet received this sacrament. The Bishop had taken holidays to help her through the rigorous preparation.

On August 24, 1925, my godmother Miss Filomena Miranda joined me on this occasion as I received the name of Lucia of Mary. I was always called Maria Lucia of Jesus Rosa dos Santos, and this was changed to Maria das Dores to conceal my usual name.

I really enjoyed receiving this Sacrament because I substantially felt the presence of the Divine Holy Spirit. In the three days preceding this, the Bishop very carefully prepared me to receive the gifts and fruits of the Holy Spirit and he explained the meaning of the Sacrament of grace working in my soul, etc.

In the evening, in the conservatory, he had me sit next to him on a big couch of straw in the presence of Miss Filomena Miranda and my mother, and gave me a thorough examination on the catechism. Thanks be to God, I responded to everything. At the end Miss Filomena said:

-If Your Excellency examined me in this way, I would not be able to answer even half of your examination.

-By saying this, the bishop answered, I will put the catechism in hand for you to study.

In the afternoon of that day, I received the Sacrament of Confession in a confessional by the door of the Chapel, and the next day after the Holy Mass and Holy Communion, he administered to me the Holy Chrism. [177]

During this holiday time, it was a pleasure to share many walks with Carlinhos, the farm steward's son and a seminarian. He delighted in telling her about Fatima, the shepherds and pilgrimages, and concluded:

-The oldest one is still alive, but no one knows her, and added, I would like to see and talk to her, but I don't know her![178]

Lucia laughed inside, and at night when Carlinhos was no longer there, the

---

176 MSL II, 6th M, No. 75, pp. 190-191.

177 *My Pathway*, I, p. 33.

178 *Ibid.*

Bishop heard about these conversations and laughed as well. When Lucia received her Confirmation, Carlinhos' mother was there and found out who Maria das Dores was. Carlinhos said to Lucia:

-But I tell you the things of Fatima and you are her![179]

The parents were sorry to have not known this before, because the Bishop was also confirming their youngest daughter. He offered to confirm their daughter the next day and have Maria das Dores be the sponsor of Mary of Jesus. Only he did not make the examination so strict.

---

179 *Ibid.*

Asilo de Vilar in 1921.

The original interior of the Chapel in Pontevedra.

House of Dorothean Sisters in Pontevedra.

CHAPTER VII
BEGINNING OF RELIGIOUS LIFE

1 | The Religious Vocation

Lucia had the consent of her mother to give her life to the Lord. But where? How?

On June 15, 1921, in her farewell to the sacred place of the apparitions, Lucia had contemplated the seventh time with the *Lady more brilliant than the sun.* She retraced in her memory the events that happened there four years ago and while thinking of the vision of Our Lady of Mount Carmel on October 13, 1917, during the miracle of the sun, she felt for the first time the desire to consecrate herself to God in Carmel. Also coming to her mind was the image of St. Therese of the Child Jesus, who was beatified on April 29, 1923. She, too, was born with the desire to be a Carmelite.

She guarded this ember in the depths of her heart. However, she confessed, this tiny flame bore the winds of the world in her adolescent years, still wanting to cling to earthly assurances. Because of this, the inheritance promised by her protector was tempting. She confided:

I confess that this decision of the Bishop was a great sacrifice for me. Silently I retired to my room to cry. The tiny flame which God had lit in my soul for the religious vocation certainly grew, but so slowly that sometimes it seemed to die out, and then what would become of me? They told me that for Carmel I did not have the health, but the other order did not attract me. Also, I liked the beautiful house and the Quinta da Fonte Pedrinha on the slopes of the Mount of Good Jesus! But I meditated on the beautiful words of Our Lord in the Gospel: The birds of the sky do not sow or reap, and yet the Heavenly Father takes care of them. The lilies of the valley would not spin or weave and in truth neither Solomon clothed them with so much magnificence! I made one more act of abandonment to Divine Providence, and transporting this flower to the feet of the Blessed Mother, I renewed my 'yes' asking her to take me to the throne of our God. [180]

The innocent shepherdess was granted special favors from Heaven, but not for her personal benefit. She was chosen to convey a message to the world from Heaven and was asked to live this message of salvation, to which she sought to be faithful throughout her life. Until the end of her days on earth she suffered and fought for this message and for the truth. But her own path was not a simple one; she did not receive a special light from above to see. Like anyone else, she had to figure out in faith and with much prayer what God's will was for her. Our Lady never told her what path to follow, though she sometimes confirmed for her that

180 *My Pathway,* I, p. 35.

she was on the right path. Often she walked in darkness.

Because of the political situation at the time, the Republic expelled many religious orders from Portugal and Lucia was not able to choose her vocation path. The Sisters of the Institute of St. Dorothy could continue in the school of Vilar, but without calling themselves sisters. They were *"ladies"* who took care of the education of the female students. As for the contemplative orders, they were swiftly and completely swept from Portuguese soil. In particular, the sisters of the Convent of St. Teresa of Coimbra were expelled on October 10, 1910, five days after the introduction of the new regime.

Lucia did not lose her courage. Before Our Lord she contemplated her life and her dream which began to take a more concrete form. In early 1925, Miss Filomena Miranda invited Lucia to accompany her on a trip to Rome to attend the Canonization of Saint Therese on May 17. Lucia confessed her enthusiasm to participate in this solemn celebration and immediately made a plan:

If the Bishop grants me permission, I would like to pass through Lisieux to ask for my admission in Carmel. [181]

She spoke to the Bishop and permission was granted. But after a conversation with the Mother Superior of the Institute of Vilar, while pondering prudent measures with regard to her state of anonymity, the Bishop withdrew the authorization. She had to have a passport to leave the country and then her identity and whereabouts would be known, and for now they did not want to compromise her safety.

The Mother Superior, learning of Lucia's desire to go to Carmel, prudently pointed out to her that her health was weak and she was prone to anemia. She invited her to join the Institute of Saint Dorothy to see if she felt comfortable there. Lucia consented without asking for admission.

She talked about her vocation with the Bishop, who told her: *though it seemed that I did not have the health for Carmel, he was leaving the decision completely free to what I wanted.* [182]

She spoke to the ladies who were her protectors and friends, and knowing of her desire to enter the Carmel of Lisieux, they counseled her to wait longer. She asked the Bishop if she could stay home with these ladies, where she could study the French language with a particular professor. She decided to follow this idea and returned peacefully to the Institute of Vilar.

---

181 *Ibid*, p. 38.
182 *Ibid*, p. 39.

2 | Postulant

On October 22, 1925, the Mother Superior of the Institute informed Lucia that she wanted her to talk to the Mother Provincial.

I was led to her office and there I met with the Rev. Mother Monfalim. After greeting me, she asked if I wanted to accompany her to Tuy, because she had heard that I wanted to become a nun, and she was certain that in her Institute I would find it good. I apologized, saying that I had not prepared clothing or documentation to cross the border. The Bishop also was not informed. Her Reverence replied that it did not matter, even if it took two days, there still was not enough time to tell the Bishop and to buy anything that was necessary, and we could do it in the Novitiate. Documents for crossing the border were also not available but going with Her Reverence, who was well known by the police, allowed us to pass without difficulty. [183]

Lucia confessed her intention to study French in order to fulfill her desire to enter the Carmel of Lisieux. Mother Monfalim, already very much moved by Lucia's experience and prudence, although she did not tell this to her, chose Lucia from among all her daughters to confide in her soul, and told her: -*The idea of Carmel was an illusion; I had not the health for an Order so austere, etc. I could study French in the novitiate which had sisters who spoke it very well and could give me lessons. After this, if I thought it was the will of God, I could relocate to a Carmel in Spain where there were many. If I wanted, I could even enter Vilar as a postulant for only 6 months and then be able to wear the Holy Habit.* [184]

Lucia gave her 'yes,' which was sealed with an emotional embrace by Mother Monfalim, who received her as a postulant and promised not to reveal her identity.

Time was pressing. It was necessary to find a small trousseau for her departure within two days and say goodbye to persons with whom she had formed deep bonds of friendship. She did so by making a visit to her friends' house during the short time she had left. The Bishop of Leiria, having been advised of Lucia's departure for Spain, made a surprise visit to the Institute on the morning of the 24th:

It was reported how I decided at the last minute to become a postulant under the conditions which they advised me and that I must always tell His Excellency what I might need. [185]

In the future his visits would be more rare because of the greater distance

---

183 *Ibid*, p. 40.
184 *Ibid.*
185 *Ibid*, p. 41.

and because she would be out of the country. His paternal solicitude, however, remained with her forever.

As she was already a postulant, she was invited to the midday meal with the community, but she chose to eat for the last time with her companions, to say goodbye and offer them a medal of Our Lady of Grace. After she removed the medal from the gold chain, she replaced it with the image of Our Lady in the Chapel of the Daughters of Mary.

Sometime earlier, Lucia had given away her earrings in an act of compassion. When a classmate named Alda died, she went to her burial at the cemetery. When she returned, Alda's mother was weeping in the entrance hall. Lucia tried to console her. The poor mother confessed that her tears were not only for the pain of losing her daughter, but because she had no money to return home to Lisbon. Lucia had no money, but her heart was filled with charity and she took out the gold earrings and gave them to the poor lady telling her, -*Go sell them at the jewelry store and you will have enough to pay for the trip.*[186]

The poor mother was eternally grateful to that unknown girl and expressed that she had such a good heart. For the shepherdess it was a fragrance in her soul, *because there is always a little perfume on the hands that offer roses and know how to be generous.*[187]

3 | Leave and Follow Me - Second Time

Lucia set her feet on the path without great emotion or sentiment. She knew that one who gives oneself up to God is not forgotten by Him. With her eyes fixed on Christ and Mary, in whose heart was safe refuge, she went to the unknown foreign land. Suffering homesickness as any postulant, she noted: *No one is surprised to see a postulant crying, the longing is so natural.*[188]

On October 25, 1925, she left for the S. Bento station, accompanied by her Mother Provincial, Mother Monfalim of the Institute, and Mother Costa. The train was leaving at two o'clock in the afternoon, and they were waiting to say goodbye to their friends and benefactors, Maria da Conceição and Maria Isabel Vasconcelos, who wanted to travel with Lucia to the exit at Braga. Fr. Barros, a Jesuit, also accompanied them and together they went by taxi to Tuy, where they arrived at night. The taxi left the three travelers at the bottom of a staircase, Lucia

---

186 Oral Narration of Sister Lucia.

187 Author's note: in the book ' Sister Lucia, The Memory that We Have of Her, ' due to lack of information, it was written that this poor woman was the mother of Miquelina.

188 *My Pathway, I,* p. 41.

relayed:

We climbed the stone steps to enter the lobby, and a group of sisters immediately came forward, whom I saw for the first time with a habit. With expressions of joy, they welcomed the Rev. Mother Provincial and helped to take the suitcases from the car and brought them into the house.

Meanwhile I said goodbye to the Rev. Barros who gave me a blessing and I entered the house, following the procession that went ahead of me. I came across an open door that led to a Chapel. I entered and knelt in the front pew where I was left alone for a long time before the tabernacle and a beautiful image of Our Lady of Lourdes. Then I heard the sound of festive voices passing. [189]

Having been in the chapel for some time Lucia felt she may have been forgotten and began to shed many tears. Oh, the longing—her friends and benefactors in Porto, her classmates, the internship, her mother who was now further away and would also suffer because the distance would hinder more visits. Everything came at once bearing down on her sensitive heart which now felt exiled. At each step in her path, the Lord called for greater solitude in her heart so that it would be entirely His. She listened again to the depths of her soul, to the promise of the Lady in the Cova da Iria: -*Don't lose heart. I will never forsake you. My Immaculate Heart will be your refuge and the way that will lead you to God.*[190]

She knew that she was protected and would not be forsaken. This heart so young was weighed down with a great responsibility as the Shepherdess, and now would begin a new path as a nun. It was not going to be easy to combine these two things, and all these thoughts came flooding in, disrupting what should have been a time of great spiritual joy. On May 13, 1917, Lucia and her cousins had agreed to offer their lives to God and to embrace all the sufferings that He wanted to send them. After their consent, the Lady announced they would have much to suffer, but the grace of God would be their comfort. This cross appeared with open arms at every turn of her life.

In the meantime, what had happened to the sisters and the Mother Provincial? Because Lucia's decision had been made so quickly, no one knew anything about her coming. For her admission to be authorized there had to be at least an introduction to the Council. Her Mother Superior spoke with the Council and Lucia was admitted. In a normal situation this would have been done in advance without the postulant being there, but in this circumstance Mother was obliged and in a hurry for the authorization. While Mother was taking care of this, Lucia was left in the chapel next to the Tabernacle, alone with Jesus Whom

---

189 *Ibid*, p. 43.
190 MSL I, 2nd M, No. 4, p. 83.

she loved. In His presence she would not feel immersed in a night of desolation.

Finally a sister helpmate touched her gently on the shoulder and asked her to follow her to the cafeteria where she was served supper. Lucia was so overwhelmed that this first meal taken in the convent was etched in her memory—she was served rice with cod, coffee with milk, and bread.

After the meal, which was eaten in silence, she was presented to the Mother Superiors who were waiting in the recreation room. She suffered a great disappointment—which she later understood but which grieved her at this moment—upon realizing they already knew who she was when the Mother Provincial had promised to keep her secret. She said:

Then they took me to the recreation room where I was with the Rev. Mother Provincial and some other Mother Superiors who embraced me and welcomed me. They did not notice my disappointment in looks, gestures and words, and almost everyone knew I was a postulant. While hugging me one said:

-From where was this said to me, that the Mother of my Lord should come to me! [191]

Another, pointing to the small image that was on the bureau:

-What do you want of me? [192]

They proceeded as if nothing was known, but in my heart I wondered to myself how it was. Mother Provincial assured me that no one knew who I was, and I noticed that almost everyone knew it! Today, I understand that Mother Provincial could not fulfill this promise, because she could not tell this to me without telling our advisers, such as the Mother Teacher, etc. [193]

Later, in Carmel, Lucia wrote a note protesting against what was said in the book, *Fatima: Altar of the World*, about the purpose of this period:

I read in the work 'Fatima: Altar of the World'[194]*page 136, Section 18, that no one in the house knew who I was, and that the Mother Superior of the Novitiate house had imposed the obligation not to talk about me or the apparitions or things about Fatima or Our Lady. This is not true. It was I who asked Mother Provincial not to say who I was to the Community or to outsiders, which Her Reverence promised me but failed, perhaps forced by her duty, I do not know; what is certain is that on the same day that I arrived in Tuy, I already noticed that several Mother Superiors knew it.* [195]

The next day she received a new bitter surprise that tempted her to go back. After Mass when she was waiting to officially enter the Novitiate, which was on

---

191 Cf. Lk 1:43.
192 MSL I, 4ᵗʰM, No. 3 p. 173.
193 *My Pathway,* I, p. 44.
194 Cf. Fatima: Altar of the World, Vol. II, 1954, p. 136.
195 *My Pathway,* I, p. 357.

the top floor of the building, the Provincial Mother called her into her office and told her that in a few months she would go to Pontevedra, but would return in time to wear the Holy Habit in May. Lucia gulped. Very quickly it went through her mind that she made a wrong decision, which her natural disposition dictated to her:

I felt more comfortable returning to Porto rather than going to Pontevedra, but I thought that it was a sacrifice I was denying to Our Lady, and therefore I tilted my forehead in silence and I renewed my 'yes' of May 13, 1917. [196]

Always the bells of Fatima resounded in her heart! Before they rang from the top of the Basilica, they sounded an alarm in the heart of the shepherdess. And she, feeling the cry of nature to deny that it hurt, imposed silence and with heroic strength thought as Eva Lavallière (French actress and Catholic convert): "Burst, if you want, but obey!"

4 | Pontevedra

Lucia went to Pontevedra the following day, on October 26, 1925. She did not understand this decision—did Our Lady want to reveal herself therein, or did she reveal herself there because Lucia was there? Maybe both, because God leads us and also follows us and transforms into grace and goodness everything in our life that can be wrong because *we know that in everything, God works for the good of those who love Him.*[197] She related her arrival at this new destination:

Accompanied by Mother Pino on the train, we reached Pontevedra at night. The Rev. Mother Superior Magellan, the one who received me in Vilar, welcomed me with a great demonstration of esteem, and joined me in the chapel praying among other things the Act of Consecration to Our Lady (Oh My Lady). Next she led me to the dining room where I had supper and then we went to the recreation room where the community gave me a hug and welcome. Her Reverence asked me to sit next to her and gave me news of the Vilar in Porto, etc.[198]

The second night passed in this foreign land, in this house where she would only be known by the Mother Superior. To all the others, she appeared ambitious for the religious life in the Congregation of St. Dorothy, founded by St. Paula Frassinetti. The next morning she was surprised to be placed among the Sister Helpers. Her Superior who was ordered to fulfill it confessed that she also was surprised by this decision. Lucia knew that the by-laws prohibited the Sister

---

196 *Ibid,* p. 45.
197 Rom 8:28.
198 *My Pathway,* I, p. 45.

Helpmates[199] from learning to read, yet she had been promised that she could study the French language.

Once again I kept silent and cordially renewed my 'yes.' [200]

Lucia's identity was always hidden behind the name of Maria das Dores so she could better live the religious life. She found the order of Sisters to be humble and silent, which preserved her simplicity—a jewel that was entrusted to them. She thought of the promises made by Mother Monfalim, but Mother could not decide on this placement of Lucia alone, and did not want to entice Lucia with her promise, or to seek to do what she promised and then proceed otherwise. Maybe Mother's heart bled in altering her plan, but the decision of her Council must have weighed more.

In certain matters the Superior may not go against a decision of the Council, and this would be such a case. If the new postulant had no school exams, and was not made to take them, and she was not illiterate, she was placed among the group who were admitted to Helpers. They could not fall in the category of schoolmistress, who intended to pursue teaching in the schools of the Congregation. There could have been an exception, but this was not always possible. The shepherdess accepted to walk this path that was proposed to her, trusting in God's hand that guided and impelled her from within. Yes, because people are merely instruments in the hand of God. It is always His hand that shapes us and leads us where He wills.

The first work that was asked of Maria das Dores was to garden. Perhaps they thought that this kind of work was familiar to her, being the daughter of farmers, but she had never done this before. Before she could learn the skill of handling a hoe, Our Lady inspired an offering for a different kind of work. She was assigned to help clean the house, in the kitchen and the cafeteria. However, the environment of the house did not satisfy her desire for recollection.

The atmosphere of the house was like a home. The internal students were for primary and secondary schools, and normally almost every hour, came and went in groups to the school. They were studying and talking loudly throughout the house, singing etc. There were two boarding schools with their playgrounds for the rich and poor girls. There was such a movement of families who came to bring them and pick them up, and finally, with all the coming and going, it looked more like a public square than a convent. I had hoped for the gathering of a cloister for a more quiet life consecrating

---

199 Author's Note: Sisters Helpmates were Religious who did not have preparation to devote themselves to teaching, but lived their vocation assuming the performance of domestic work.

200 *My Pathway,* I, p. 46.

myself to the Lord... [201]

Another direction for her life was churning around in her mind—the Carmel—but thinking they would believe her conceited and that it would *undermine in its principle the glory of God and Our Lady, I offered God my sacrifice for Him and for the poor of the Institute.* [202]

She continued her generous surrender without showing on the outside what she suffered within. She offered to God her interior martyrdom, renewing the offering that Our Lady taught her: -*O Jesus, it is for love of You...* [203] *I morally suffered a true martyrdom, but I tried to portray whenever He was not visible externally, especially in my letters, that I was happy, and my only happiness was to suffer for the love of Our Lord, for my dear Mother in Heaven, for the conversion of sinners, the Holy Church, the Holy Father and (for) Priests.* [204]

Lucia opened her heart to the Lord in intimate prayer, entrusting faithfully her pain, with the certainty of being understood:

-*But, O, my Beloved, that You give me the desire of a more collected life, more alone with You? Will it only be to ask me for this sacrifice, this renunciation? I had to go through this like You in the agony of Gethsemane. As You also said: Father, if it be possible, let this cup pass from Me, but not My will, but Your will!*

O Jesus, it is for love of You, for the conversion of sinners and in reparation for sins committed against the Immaculate Heart of Mary! Yes, because since I saw You, I never stopped looking for the light of Your face, like in an immense mirror the streams of humanity pass in front of You. Nothing escapes You in this uncreated Light that penetrates and absorbs everything in You, where everything reflects like shadows passing, focused on the Eternal Infinite Being. I love You my Jesus. Hail Mary! Being happy, I consider souls receiving the Lord's illustrious thanks, which go through life guarding them in silence in the secret of their heart! But each soul will follow the path that God has mapped out: You did not choose Me, but I chose you. And St. Paul tells us: a few chosen for Apostles, the others for Prophets, Doctors, etc., each one has to follow the path that God gives him. [205]

---

201 *Ibid*, p. 47.
202 *Ibid*, p. 48.
203 MSL I, 2nd M, Ch. II, No. 6, p. 87.
204 *My Pathway*, I, p. 48.
205 *Ibid*, p. 49.

House of the Dorothean Sisters in Pontevedra.

Lucia's bedroom in Pontevedra, where on
December 10, 1925, Our Lady appeared.

Present appearance of the room transformed
into a chapel.

▲▶ Courtyard of the House in Pontevedra, where
the Child Jesus appeared.

CHAPTER VIII
THE GREAT PROMISE

1 | You at Least...

Misericórdias Domini in aeternum cantabo! (I will sing the mercies of the Lord forever!)

During a very troubling time, the Mother of God deigned to come again to meet her poor daughter to whom she had promised her special protection.

It was December 10, 1925. I was in my room, when suddenly the room lit up and it was the light of my dear Mother in Heaven who came with the Child Jesus on a luminous cloud. Our Lady, as if wanting to instill courage, rested her hand on my shoulder, and as she did so, showed me her Immaculate Heart encircled by thorns, which she was holding in her other hand. The Child Jesus said:

-Have compassion on the Heart of your most holy Mother, covered with thorns, with which ungrateful men pierce it at every moment, and there is no one to make an act of reparation to remove them.

Then Our Lady said:

-Look, my daughter, at my Heart surrounded with thorns with which ungrateful men pierce me every moment by their blasphemies and ingratitude. You at least try to console me and say that I promise to assist at the hour of death, with all the graces necessary for salvation, all those who on the first Saturday of five consecutive months, shall confess, receive Holy Communion, pray the Rosary, and keep me company for fifteen minutes while meditating on the mysteries of the Rosary, with the intention of making reparation to me.

After this grace, how could I take myself away from the least sacrifice that God asks of me to console the Heart of my beloved Mother in Heaven, happy that Mary depletes the bitter drops of the Chalice. [206]

The grievance of the Heart of the Mother made known to her confidant was not only intended *for* her, but *through* her as a maternal request to every person who would listen and live it. Our Lady presented another rung on the ladder of salvation to her children increasingly oppressed by sin, to help them live in the grace of God. It was a new invitation to conversion by a Mother who, grieved and concerned about the dangers and fears that her children face, patiently guides them along a more secure path.

For love of Mary, one is asked for five consecutive months to receive the sacrament of Confession, receive Holy Communion, pray the Rosary, and keep Our Lady company for fifteen minutes while meditating on one or more mysteries of the Rosary. By spending time with Mary in meditation, inspired by her love,

---

206 *Ibid*, p. 51.

one's heart will slowly grow in the desire to live every day in the spirit of the First Saturday, i.e. in self-denial and avoiding sin. Those who practice this devotion will inevitably desire more and more to be like Mary, imitating Jesus and pleasing to the Father. Then one's focus on the benefit of the Promise changes to an inward focus on living life as an act of reparation to the Heart of the Mother because it pleases God.

That is the reason Mary visits her children: to point them to the way of happiness and freedom. A person is so much more happy and free when living a virtuous life absent of sin. *It is the freedom in your being and your life, freedom of virginity, the freedom of the Spirit of Christ.* [207]

In the heart of every human being is the innate desire to be happy. Who does not feel it? But what a lot of mistakes are made in the search for happiness! Happiness is confused with pleasure and love with fleeting passion. How much more the heart chases after foolish fantasies that leave it empty and hungry. For this reason the gentle voice of Mary comes to point us toward the true source of happiness so desired. Everyone who discovers this can exclaim with Saint Augustine: *"Thou hast made us for You, Lord, and our heart is restless until it rests in You."* [208]

2 | Apparitions of the Child Jesus

Lucia relayed a second apparition of the Child Jesus from February 15, 1926, to her confessor and to her Mother Superior. The Superior said that little could be done and advised her to write to Msgr. Manuel Pereira Lopes who had been her confessor at the Institute of Vilar. The humble postulant obeyed, although she preferred to address this subject with the Bishop of Leiria. Her letter received no immediate response. Knowing that Maria das Dores could not make herself understood well in Spanish, and so that she would understand her confessor, her Superior advised her to go to a Portuguese Jesuit priest who was at that time in Pontevedra. This priest was Fr. Francisco Rodrigues and he was a great help to her.

Msgr. Lopes eventually did respond to her letter, which described the apparition of February 15 as follows:

Most Reverend: With all due respect I would like to thank Your Reverence for the lovely little letter of charity that you wrote to me...The next day when I received Jesus in the Eucharist, I read the letter to Him and said:

-O my Jesus! I, with Your Grace, with prayer, mortification and confidence will

---

207 Luis Kondor, SVD, *Do You Want to Offer Yourselves to God?*, p. 228.
208 St. Augustine, *Confessions of St. Augustine*, Book I, Chp. I, p. 27.

do all in obedience that You allow me and You inspire me. The rest I will leave to You.

On the 15th, I was very busy at my work and was not thinking of [the devotion] at all. I went to throw out a pan full of rubbish in the yard, where, some months earlier, I had met a child, whom I had asked if he knew the Hail Mary. He answered that he did. I asked him to say it so I could hear him. But, as he made no attempt to say it by himself, I said it with him three times over, at the end of which I asked him to say it alone. But as he remained silent and was unable to say the Hail Mary alone, I asked him if he knew where the Church of Santa Maria was. He told me that he did. I told him to go there every day and to say this [prayer]: O my heavenly Mother, give me your Child Jesus! I taught him this, and then left him....

Going there as usual, I found a child who seemed to me to be the same one whom I had previously met, so I asked him:

-Did you ask our heavenly Mother for the Child Jesus?

The child turned to me and said:

-And have you spread throughout the world what the heavenly Mother asked you to do?

With that, he was transformed into a resplendent Child. Realizing then, that it was Jesus, I said:

-My Jesus, you know very well what my confessor said to me in the letter that I read to You. He said it was necessary for this vision to be repeated, for further happenings so it is believed, and that the Mother Superior alone could do nothing to spread this devotion.

-It is true that the Mother Superior on her own can do nothing, but with my grace, she can do everything. It is enough that your confessor gives you permission and that your Superior speaks of it, for it to be believed, even without people knowing to whom it has been revealed.

-But my confessor said in the letter that this devotion was not lacking in the world, because there are many souls who receive You on the First Saturdays in honor of Our Lady and of the 15 Mysteries of the Rosary.

-It is true, my daughter, that many souls begin them, but few finish them, and those who do finish them, do so to receive the graces that are promised. It would please me more if they did five decades with fervor and with the intention of making reparation to the Heart of their heavenly Mother, than if they did fifteen decades in a tepid and indifferent manner. [209]

The seer asked for clarification, that if some people cannot go to confession on Saturday, would He permit that a confession within eight days be valid? *Jesus*

---

[209] Antonio Maria Martins, S. J., *New Documents of Fatima*, No. 32, p. 116.

replied:

-*Yes, and it can be longer provided that when they receive Me on the First Saturday they are in the state of grace and have the intention of making reparation to the Immaculate Heart of Mary.*

I asked again: -My Jesus, what about those who forget to make this intention?

Jesus replied: -They can do so at their next confession, taking advantage of the first opportunity to go to confession.[210]

Lucia felt a mixture of indescribable happiness and stinging pain. Seeing God so offended she wanted... *to suffer all the torments to repair the Immaculate Heart of Mary, my dear Mother, and one by one take from her all the thorns that lacerate it. I understood that these thorns are the symbol of the numerous sins that go against the Son, crossing the heart of His Mother. Yes because of them, many children are lost forever.* [211]

Later Msgr. Lopes confided that he did not want to continue with these responsibilities and advised Maria das Dores to treat the things of her soul with the Bishop of Leiria, and therefore, there were no more letters from the seer to this priest.

Humbly she gave an account of this apparition to her Mother Superior. She was quite worried and told Lucia that to embark on this extraordinary path, she certainly could not continue at the Institute. The postulant was not distressed. It seemed to her that if this was an impediment, it would be God's way to lead her to a cloister.

Speaking with her confessor, she was advised not to talk anymore about these things to her Mother Superior but to write down everything. She promised to consider the life of contemplative devotion (prayer and penance), and by doing this would comply with Heaven's request. Lucia felt that she understood everything Jesus asked of her, which gave her great peace. Her confessor was a secure support for Lucia, helping the postulant in her first steps into the religious life, while carrying the burden of responsibility to deliver the Message that Heaven had asked her. Feeling thankful and with increased fidelity to that obedience, she continued with her daily work in spite of the inner struggle and difficulties that obstructed her desires. She longed for the cloistered life.

She did everything with love and for love, even appearing cheerful so that her tribulation was not visible on the outside. Sometimes when Lucia was serving the girls in the cafeteria they would speak in a language different than her Portuguese, causing her to make some humorous mistakes. Once they asked her for some *salsa*

210 *My Pathway*, I, p. 52.
211 *Ibid*, p. 53.

and Maria das Dores brought them a bunch of parsley, which generated much laughter by all. Another time they asked her to bring a convoy, meaning a cruet. Lucia thought they wanted to see the train, so she diligently watched the tracks until she saw one coming and went to tell them. Even she laughed with pleasure, presenting a light mood without revealing what she carried inside, and never projecting her dark nights. Lucia learned to live within herself, able to say like Saint Paul: *I know how to live in abundance and suffering if necessary!* [212]

---

212 Phil 4:12.

The appearance of the primitive courtyard of the house of the
Dorothean Sisters where the Child Jesus appeared to Lucia.

The novitiate group of the Dorothean Sisters. Lucia is
the fourth from the left on the top row.

Our Lady of Fatima.

Interior of the Chapel in Tuy.

CHAPTER IX

THE WAYS OF GOD GUIDED BY MARY

1 | Back in Tuy

In the absence of a sister who was ill, Maria das Dores was put in charge of accompanying the girls back and forth to school and home among other errands. On several occasions when she was going for water at the public fountain, she was approached by a boy who had intentions of dating. This was perfectly normal and was a great mortification for her. Her interior struggles were growing as the young postulant searched for answers to her life. One day, while going on an errand, she passed the Convent of the Poor Clares. She entered the chapel for a visit to the Blessed Sacrament and asked to speak to the Abbess who received her in the locutory. Lucia wrote:

I told her that I was Portuguese and was a postulant at the College of Dorothean Sisters, but preferred to be in a cloister, and I asked if it was possible to be admitted there. The Rev. Mother said yes, but would rather she request the information from my Rev. Mother Superior and my confessor. I replied that my confessor was Father Francisco Rodrigues, a Jesuit, who could address her whenever she wanted and her Reverence agreed. My Mother Superior did not know I had gone there because I had done so, taking advantage of the opportunity when I was sent out with a message. I told her Reverence that I would return later or I would write. I gladly said goodbye, thinking that soon I would be admitted in that Monastery. On my way back I stopped at the residence of the Jesuits to speak to Rev. Rodrigues, who answered me:

-It is okay, but if your aspiration is Carmel, it will be better to deal with Carmel and send you there. [213]

When Lucia arrived home, she told Mother Superior what had happened. Mother was a bit disturbed by the news but did not say anything to her postulant. She must have called the Mother Provincial in Tuy to prevent what was happening. Then on July 18, 1926, Mother Superior called a woman associate to take Lucia on the first train in the morning to Tuy. Lucia was not surprised when she saw the associate arrive in Pontevedra at 10 p.m. They quietly departed at dawn. Lucia would have spoken to her confessor, who understood so well, but there was no time. Sheltered in the heart of her Mother, she knew that she would always be well and at peace. She was anchored in that heart, which no one could take away no matter what happened. It was her cell of intimacy with God. She blindly trusted in God Who would lead her in His way, and although she could not clearly see the path, He was present in her heart.

They reached Tuy at 9 a.m. and went to Mass in the Church of St. Francis.

---

213 *My Pathway*, I, p. 57.

Then they went to a house which at that time was still a temporary convent on the street of Ordonez where they were received by Mother Provincial:

The Reverend Mother Provincial received me very well, and spoke at length with me about various things, mostly about my desire to go to a cloister. She told me that it seemed to her a temptation and she was certain that in the novitiate I would feel comfortable, and I should avoid future inconveniences that I feared. She promised I would be in the novitiate house forever, since it was always necessary to have some professed members.

Then she directed me to the Reverend Mother Teacher, who led me to the novitiate and introduced me to the novices who hugged me, giving me a warm welcome. The schoolmistress assigned me to the job of the black linen closet, where I worked in the company of Sister Joan.

In the environment of the novitiate, being sheltered and having silence, I felt good, but the doubt of the future always remained with me. The promise of the Reverend Mother Provincial was that I would be there forever. Would it be like my time in Vilar, without any accomplishment? Who would fulfill my work? Would it not be reckless living in uncertainty like this?

Our confessor was Rev. Aparicio da Silva, Superior of the Jesuit residence. I talked to him about everything. His Reverence was of the opinion that, given the promise that the Reverend Mother Provincial made to me, to stay forever in the novitiate house, and that I must profess there, that if God did not want me there He would have not have led my steps there, etc. As to what the Reverend Rodrigues had told me, to write and to burn everything. So I did it and was well pleased, because I had no place to store things properly, and I was afraid that someone would see them.

On Thursdays and Fridays there were holy hours until midnight, and the Blessed Sacrament was exposed all night on the First Fridays, filling my soul with happiness because I was then in the presence of my Lord! There were so many graces granted to me that I could not even think of refusing Him the least sacrifice. It was necessary to give myself up without reservation to love Him Who also calmed me, this miserable creature.[214]

There are crooked lines that God makes straight. After her confessor in Pontevedra, Rev. Rodrigues, had ordered her to burn what she had written about the request of the First Saturday's devotion and reparation to the Immaculate Heart of Mary, it was here in Tuy with her confessor, Rev. Aparicio, that she saw the beginning of the spread of this devotion throughout the world, although it was not approved officially until 1939.

---

214 *Ibid*, p. 58 - 59.

2 | Novice

On October 2, 1926, Lucia began her novitiate with the Rite of Vesting, or Taking of the Habit. No family or personal friends were present, although the celebration was announced to her relatives and friends.

I celebrated alone with God and in the company of my friends and co-novices and Superiors. It was a day of great joy, but yes, in intimacy with the Lord. [215]

With questions about her future still remaining in the depths of her soul, she celebrated this day with serenity and peace. Having no family or friends there allowed her to live this day more deeply in silence and prayer. It was the best gift for her—to be able to spend more time with her Hidden Jesus. And would He be there? Doubt always wavered in her heart and the shepherdess could not see a clear answer to this question. She concluded:

The expression of happiness in such cases that I employ refers only to the happiness that is in embracing the cross for the love of God and Our Lady. [216]

The beginning of her novitiate formed the basis of her religious life. It is the time of formation in a life that is dedicated and devoted entirely to God. The schoolmistress, a nun already experienced in this life, is only an instrument, a companion on the path of the novice who begins to walk as a follower of Christ. He is the true educator, acting by His Spirit with the collaboration of a docile novice who feels the call to follow Christ, and His Charisma that attracts her. The future depends on this period, like the stability of a building depends on the strength of its foundation. The schoolmistress can do nothing, however holy she is, if the candidate is not faithful and open to the prompting of the Holy Spirit.

Sister Dores applied in all sincerity to seek the will of God in her life and assimilate the Charism received and transmitted from their holy foundress, St. Paula Frassinetti. Lucia was faithful to this time, absorbing all the teachings that she was taught by Mother Schoolmistress. She liked living in fraternity with the other novices, who at that time were many, for vocations abounded in all congregations. She lived among them without their knowing that she was the Shepherdess of Fatima, always framed by the white veil on the bonnet of a white quilled cotton fabric, symbol of the whiteness of her chosen soul.

The novices at first would talk about Fatima in the presence of Sister Dores during recess. She kept silent and tried to ignore this, because the novices did not know who she was. The only thing Lucia would mention to them was her desire to go to Carmel. The Mother Provincial ordered them not to speak of Fatima in the

---

215 *Ibid*, p. 60.
216 *Ibid*.

presence of Sister Dores. Lucia wrote:

Of course, this mystery that was around me caused many to wonder who I was, not knowing. I soon noticed the curious glances, attentions of sympathy and special devotion. This environment of silence lasted some time, and during it I even assumed that perhaps the devotion to Our Lady of Fatima had ended, never to be known. This assumption made me suffer greatly. Even then I could not convince myself that Our Lady had failed to carry forward the work of His Mercy. It did not take a long time, however, to receive news of what I had confirmed on the contrary. [217]

The news came to her through visits she received from friends and especially the Bishop of Leiria, who spoke at length to her about the future of Fatima. More often news came through Fr. Aparicio, S.J., her confessor and spiritual director, who became an apostle of the devotion of the First Saturdays of Reparation to the Immaculate Heart of Mary. One day Sister Dores was asked a question that subdued her:

One more step, another cross! Unexpectedly, one day after my confession my confessor asked me if I had brought the writings of Pontevedra. I simply answered that I had burned them when His Reverence commanded me.

-You burned them? he exclaimed. Now I was told to write them again. Then I would hand them over to His Reverence for his examination. I stated that I could not do this job without telling the Mother Schoolmistress.

-Well, tell her, His Reverence replied, why not tell her? [218]

With much trepidation and at the first opportunity, Sister Dores courageously told the Mother Schoolmistress about the mandate. She answered several questions from her about the apparitions, in particular those which had been given to her in Pontevedra. After the hearing, the Mother Schoolmistress said she would speak to the Mother Provincial, because having a Sister Helpmate write was something rare. These sisters were there not to write, but to work. Sister Dores waited silently and obediently for the decision of the superior.

Soon she was called to the Mother Provincial's office. She repeated everything that she had told the schoolmistress. Mother Provincial repeated more or less the same thing she had told Sister Dores the first time she met her, adding that she knew the Superior of Pontevedra and had expected to hear this from Sister Dores' mouth. She alerted her to the danger of this being an illusion and was very sorry because if Sister Dores was inclined to take this path she could not stay at the Institute. This started a dialogue, as Lucia wrote:

-Who knows, Mother Provincial, if this is not the path that God wants me to take

---

217 *Ibid,* p. 61.
218 *Ibid,* p. 63.

to Carmel!

-But Sister continues with this idea? Sister does not feel good in the novitiate?

-Yes, in the novitiate I feel good, but I think about the future.

-The future I already promised to be the same as everywhere else; what more do you want?

-But who knows if the successors of His Reverence will be of the same opinion?

-Do not worry about it; you will do things so that it settles. How to write these things now, not ordered by me, but as an act of obedience to your confessor. Write, to propagate this devotion, but do not tell your superiors, that is, the Institute will not take part.[219]

The Mother Provincial gave her some sheets of paper and dismissed her. Sister Dores left before any more objections from her Superior, and waited for the day to confess to the priest. She would ask him for a new opinion and follow his direction. She wrote the request of Our Lady on the First Saturdays devotion using the third person, so that on its disclosure her name would not be presented. Contrary to what she had been told, her Mother Provincial was very enthusiastic about the disclosure of this devotion to the students of their schools. There are many references in the letters from Mother Provincial to Sister Lucia requesting her to send prints of the devotion to Portugal.

3 | Interior Doubts

During her novitiate the Bishop was silent for a long time, leaving his shepherdess in a dark night in which she could see nothing clearly and started to feel that everything might have been a dream. Temptation to doubt entered her soul: *Could I have misled and deceived others? And if so, how many people!* On January 19, 1928, in the second year of her novitiate, Lucia wrote to her spiritual director, Fr. Aparicio, S.J., telling him of her tribulation:

I did not know what to do. I decided since Our Lord had left me for so long, living only the desire to love and suffer for His love and His power to astound me more and more in my misery and my nothingness, to choose a time to visit the chapel when no one was there. After humbly prostrating myself at His feet, I asked for forgiveness for my faults, promising to amend my life. I knocked on the door of the Tabernacle, asking Him to give me the light to know and what to do. If Jesus did not make me see, feel or hear I knew this would prove He was unhappy with me and I had been misleading. If this happened, I was resolved to go around the world telling everyone I had made

---

219 *Ibid*, p. 64.

a mistake and suffer in compensation for the grief I had caused Our Lord. I wanted to submit before God any mistreatment and also say that I did not mislead, since my intention was always to satisfy His holy will. But, O my God, did I do Your will? Now, would it be a mistake? After knocking on the door of the Tabernacle, the six months of silence ended and a good feeling possessed me with a supernatural light. I do not know how but it seemed to me that Jesus was going to take me with Him. After spending just a few moments with Jesus, He left me in a peace and gentleness and I can assure you that I never felt the same again.[220]

This ended a time of immense grief. But it had been like hearing the voice of her mother again, telling her that she was lying and deceiving the world. It was a time of purification in which she would be anchored only in God, having no capacity to hear the authoritative voice of a human mediator. The Bishop, with whom she confided openly, rarely appeared in Tuy, and Father Aparicio was no longer available because he was assigned to the office of Master of Novices in Oya, Brazil. Father Aparicio offered to go through Tuy on his way to continue his guidance in her spiritual life. He understood very well her questions and vocational desire to go to Carmel. Father José Gonçalves, who replaced Fr. Aparicio, thought it was a temptation that she had and advised her to continue on the path where she had set foot. Lucia stated:

The Novitiate passed between doubts and confusion about my perseverance at the Institute... I arrived on September 23, 1928, and made a retreat with the Community in preparation for the profession of temporary vows during these days of greater recollection and prayer. I asked for a lot of light from the Lord, to know His will.

On the 28th, it seemed to me that I was being reckless to profess without hesitation, so I went to talk to the Mother Schoolmistress, expressing again my indecision. Her Reverence told me that it seemed a temptation, but she did not want the responsibility. She said that I should speak to the Mother Provincial. Very soon afterwards the Mother Provincial called me to her office. I repeated to her what I already said on several other occasions. I said it was a temptation, that it was the devil who wanted to trick me with the appearance of a greater good, and that she was right, that after the profession this will pass. But what if during all this time it was possible to transfer? At the moment I was professing by obedience, since it was also the opinion and counsel of my confessor that God would bless. [221]

Lucia surrendered her will to the voice of obedience and made her profession of temporary vows. In her heart she gave herself entirely to the Lord of

---

220 DCF, Volume V, I, Doc. 83.
221 *My Pathway*, I, p. 68.

her life. In her heart there was no division, no stopping: she gave up everything forever. But along the way, the location of her service was the question. Regarding this concern, she asked the Lord for a sign of His will:

In the days of their betrothal, spouses tend to give their loved ones a covenant, a sign of perpetual union. Do not get me wrong, I also ask for a sign of Your will for me. If this is the place that You have chosen for me to serve You until death, if it is so, I feel fortunate to serve You here in perpetual entrustment and consecration, even if this happiness lasts for only the day of my profession. Then if You want, I will drink the cup of sorrow for I want You to accompany me on my journey to Calvary and take with You the Cross of pain. The Lord has heard my supplication. [222]

4 | Signs of God's Preference

On October 2, 1928, the Bishop of Leiria was to preside over the Mass and the ceremony of the vows and the Taking of the Habit. However, there was a small problem with the car that was bringing His Excellency and he had to take the train. They waited all day and the ceremony was not done. It was very troublesome for Sister Dores, seeing how grieved her companions were after the ceremony did not occur. She knew that everyone knew who she was although no one told her, and that the Bishop was coming because she had wanted to entrust her soul to her spiritual father before professing. She felt bad about this burden that wasn't her fault. The next day was the liturgical feast day of St. Therese and the Bishop did not arrive until mid-morning, so the Mass was celebrated by Fr. Cândido Mendes, Provincial of the Portuguese Jesuits.

Saddened, she wondered if this setback was the sign she asked of her Spouse, but more answers would come. At the moment of holy vows, the professed received a crucifix they would wear on their chest. Sometimes because of the work involved the Sisters Helpers received a smaller crucifix. When it was Sister Dores' turn the priest mistakenly gave her a large crucifix. Receiving it with a kiss from her heart, she gazed at Him for a long time and told Him everything that was in her heart, especially her unconditional love. Then she wore it on her chest. After the ceremony, they realized the mistake and a sister came to exchange it for a smaller crucifix. The crucifix large or small represented the same Lord, but what hurt Sister Dores was not being able to keep the crucifix of her profession. Suffering this heartbreak in silence she said to herself:

-*This sign seems to me even clearer than the first, will it not be the symbol of*

---

222 *Ibid*, p. 68 - 69.

change that one day I will make for the Institute for Carmel? [223]

Small thorns can cause greater pain than large ones, for it depends on where they hurt. Our lives are strewn with large and small sufferings, most of which come from people with no intention of hurting us. This inevitably happens in all forms of life. In addition to the joy of her own surrender to the Lord, the young spouse received from her Divine Spouse another sign of predilection—the seal of the cross—and she read it as a more obvious sign that she had asked for in her vocational journey.

In the afternoon, Sister Dores went to the visiting room and greeted the Bishop of Leiria and other persons who came to attend the celebration of her profession, among them Rev. Formigão. He asked her to sign some printed pictures of her memoirs. She refused to do this but the Mother who accompanied her gave her a pen and told her to write. Obeying this order, she signed some pictures. To her surprise when she left the room, she was called to the office of the Mother Provincial, who was very much annoyed. She asked Sister Dores what she was doing in the room without her permission. The shepherdess was speechless. It was established that in the absence of the Superior, she would obey the oldest sister…that's what she did!

In that moment the Superior who had accompanied her went to tell the Mother Provincial of the order that she had given, but the information was only half understood by Mother Provincial. She thought the young professed girl had written of her own initiative, not realizing she had been ordered to write. The misunderstanding was a bitter disappointment, and Sister Dores afterwards humbly kissed the hand of her Superior and went before the tabernacle to pour out her heart and tears to the Heart of Him Who knows and sees everything:

-Your answer is so clear, my God, I no longer doubt, I just lack the knowledge of how and when You want that; with flapping wings, I'll take flight. [224]

On this day some doors opened. Lucia wrote:

Rev. Formigão wanted particularly to talk to me; for this reason, he managed to obtain permission from Rev. Mother Provincial and arrived at 2 o'clock in the afternoon. He spoke to me about several issues related to Fatima, among others the foundation of a new institute, founded in the spirit of the message and dedicated to perpetual adoration of the Blessed Sacrament solemnly exposed.

He wanted to talk to me about adoration of the Blessed Sacrament that was touching the most intimate fiber of my heart, but also to the circumstances in which God had placed me. I wanted seclusion. Confidentially, I did not want to hide from His

---

223 *Ibid*, p. 70.
224 *Ibid*, p. 71 - 72.

Reverence that he had the intention to possibly move me to a Carmel. His Reverence represented the good that I could make becoming part of the new foundation, because of being already a Religious. Since this is not what I wanted, he replied that he would consult with the Bishop of Leiria.

I suppose that this priest has communicated this interview with His Excellency the Archbishop of Evora, Manuel da Conceição Santos, who was soon to arrive in Tuy. Talking distinctly with me, he asked me about my particular vocation. I did not hide the intention of (my) possibly being transferred to Carmel.

His Excellency told me then of my transfer to a new foundation, where he wished me to unite all three new foundations that were there in the beginning and where, in the opinion of His Excellency, I, being already a religious, could give much glory to God and to Our Lady, making me the bond of unity among all.

I replied to His Excellency that this was not my aspiration, but I would pray and consult, then I would do what I thought to be the will of God. His Excellency was very understanding and departing, I received his blessing and while on my knees, I kissed his sacred ring. [225]

Lucia searched for God's will in the night. What difficulty walking a path that seemed not to be hers, but one thing was certain: her joy of knowing she belonged to God! The rest was secondary. She writes of her intimacy with the Hidden Jesus, next to Whom she took refuge at the end of the day of her first profession after having been quite mortified with the taking of a photograph:

Wherever the place is where You desire me to serve, there I will be Yours forever; although officially my profession is temporary, in the intimate contract of our union I will be forever. And whatever is in my path, on the soft or rough stony land that I tread on, I will always be wandering the narrow way before You that You have tread for me. And I feel happy to belong to You, stripped of everything in the Vow of Poverty; I am Yours completely for the indescribable Vow of Chastity with which you deigned to make this poor soul rich and take it to the angelical heights of the celestial court. From now on, I will sing to You in the land this hymn of pure Love, which only the Virgins can sing in a choir with His Heavenly Queen, Regina Virginum, and with her I will tell You each day: Magnificat anima mea Dominum, Et exultavit spiritus meus in Deo Salutaris meo (The Magnificat) [226] *Yes, because you have revealed these things to the humble and the lowly!* [227]

---

225 *Ibid*, p. 73.
226 Lk 1, 46-47.
227 *My Pathway*, I, p. 74.

5 | A Portrait

After the farewell to Rev. Formigão that afternoon of October 3, 1928, the Mother Provincial sent me out to the photographer to take a picture; she wanted to excuse me, but she was ordered to obey. I was accompanied by Sister Alzira Figueiredo. [228] The shepherdess could only imagine how expensive a portrait was and who would pay for it. By request of the Bishop of Leiria and agreed to by Mother Provincial, Mother Monfalim ordered Sister Dores to go to the photographer. It was only for the Fatima newspaper. But the photograph appeared in several newspapers and worse, was made into cards that were for sale. She knew nothing about it until later. At a retreat in 1929 during confession, the priest recognized Sister Dores, having seen her portrait in some newspapers which did not seem right to him. The young nun was unaware that her picture had spread, which caused her much grief. He tried to comfort her but could not stop her tears. Then he spoke to Fr. Aparicio who went to the novitiate and asked to console the shepherdess. To calm her, he reminded her that no one collects newspapers; on the contrary, they are either thrown into the garbage, used under the feet or in other ways. With this vision of the fate of her portrait, she became more serene. [229]

During her entire life she felt repugnance for photography. It was not easy to get a picture of her. She called it "a disease" and only rarely posed with good will. The best photos of her are those obtained without her even realizing it on rare occasions.

6 | Bride of Christ

The profession of the evangelical counsels is a real betrothal of the soul to God. In the temporary profession it is canonically as the word implies, a promise for some time, but in a clearly discerned vocation in the heart, the promise is total and forever. Thus was the inner disposition of Sister Dores:

Though officially my profession is temporary, in the intimate contract of our union, she is now forever. [230]

The engagement lasts several years to better prepare for the total and definitive profession. It is sanctioned by the church, which authenticates the covenant made in the heart. It all starts with God's initiative – *You did not choose*

---

228 *Ibid*, p. 73.
229 Oral Narration of Sister Lucia.
230 *My Pathway*, p. 73.

Me... [231] It is God Who has the last word. Those who feel the call let themselves fall in love with Christ and follow His footsteps. As they walk with Him they understand the greatness of this unspeakable gift of God and feel gratitude that is impossible to express. Then is born the desire to transform this love and gratitude into acts, to be a "fool for Christ" that only love explains. *For love is strong as death.* [232]

At a retreat in preparation for her temporary profession, Sister Dores fervently wrote about this new stage of her consecrated life:

The purposes were twofold: timely assistance to all acts of the community, of which I could only dispense with ill health or obedience. The practice of charity, in which I will never refuse any service requested of me or where I can see that I can be like my sisters, always, of course, that is not against obedience.

Prayer: In addition to the meditation, spiritual reading, assistance at the Holy Mass, Holy Communion, examination of conscience, I will do daily with the Community. I will pray the Rosary every day. For this I must go to the chapel a quarter of an hour before the ringing for Mass and pray the first Rosary, meditating on the joyful mysteries. At four o'clock in the afternoon when I am usually alone, I will make a visit to Jesus present in the Blessed Sacrament and pray the second Rosary, mediating on the sorrowful mysteries. Then if I have time, I will do the Stations of the Cross. If at this time I cannot, I will do it after the examination of the night. The third Rosary I recite with the Community at 6:30 p.m., and I will meditate on the glorious mysteries. I pray the prayers of the Angel five times each day, repeating them three times each: at the first rising prostrate beside the bed. The second when I visit the Blessed Sacrament, at 10 a.m. mid-morning. The third after the examination of the night in the chapel with my arms crossed, as in the morning. The fourth before going to bed, prostrate beside the bed. The fifth when I first wake up, I will get up and recite them prostrate.

On Thursdays, I make a holy hour from 11 to midnight, leaving the chapel in prayers at the end of recreation at night, unless obedience or charity order me to do something else.

Penances: I take the discipline three days a week for a miserere, on Wednesdays, Fridays and Saturdays. I will put on the sackcloth 3 days a week for 3 hours, in union with Our Lord during the 3 hours that He was on the cross, on Mondays, Wednesdays and Fridays. I'll use the rope as a strap and the metal cross on my chest, 3 days, on Tuesdays, Thursdays and Saturdays.

Except for coffee in the morning, I will refrain from drinking three days a week, in union with the thirst that Our Lord suffered in His passion and for His intentions, on

---

231 Jn 15:16.
232 Wis 7:6.

Tuesdays, Fridays and Saturdays; on Mondays and Thursdays I will not eat fruit.

At the table, I will serve and then I will simply take the dish that is presented, not noticing whether it is more or less appetizing, believing that this is what God has intended for me and with which I feed in order to serve Him and love Him.

The usual ejaculations: O Jesus, it is for love of You, for the conversion of sinners, and in reparation for the sins committed against the Immaculate Heart of Mary!

Jesus, meek and humble of heart, make my heart like unto Thine.

Love the Immaculate Heart of Mary and hope in her protection. [233]

This is how she lived concretely with her eyes on Jesus, her Divine Bridegroom, and with a deep desire to give Him and His Mother comfort. In the heart of this young shepherdess a fire crackled continuously and burned intensely with a desire, like Jesus, to see extended to the whole Church the reparation requested at Fatima and more insistently in Pontevedra. On July 13, 1917, the Lady said:

-Jesus wishes to make use of you to make me known and loved. He wants to establish in the world devotion to my Immaculate Heart. [234]

7 | Apostle of the Message

She wanted to shout to everyone the requests of Jesus and Mary, but did her best to deliver them to her superiors and in her letters, without declaring their origin, thus igniting the hearts of that love which she carried within herself. After discussing with her confessor and receiving his approval, it seemed to her that her mother was to have been the first confidant of this desire of Holy Mary. Sister Dores wrote to her mother on July 24, 1927, sharing with her the wish of Our Lady and inviting her to also practice this devotion of reparation. She wrote: *I also wanted that my mother would give me the consolation of embracing a devotion that I know is pleasing to God and our dear Heavenly Mother who had asked for it. As soon as I heard about it, I wanted to hug her, and make everyone else want to embrace her. I hope, therefore, that my mother will answer me to say that she will, and that all the people will embrace her also. You cannot give me greater consolation than this. It is only in doing what is written in this holy picture, Confession may be on another day, and 15 minutes meditation is what seems to me to be confusing. But it is very easy. Who cannot think about a mystery of the Rosary? In the Annunciation of the Angel and in the humility of our dear Mother, that the one to be exalted is to be called a slave? In the passion of Jesus, Who suffered so much for love? And the Blessed Mother with Jesus on*

---

233 *My Pathway*, I, p. 76 ss.
234 MSL I, 4ᵗʰ M, Ch. II, No. 4, p.177.

Calvary? Who cannot like these holy thoughts, spending 15 minutes next to the gentlest Mother of all mothers... [235]

Whenever she could, Sister Dores remained anonymous, in order to not lose time in spreading this devotion. Father Aparicio, her spiritual director, promised to do what he could in this sense, to address her requests from the beginning using his priestly ministry. Everything was done privately, without anything official. Lucia suffered, seeing how slowly this desire of Heaven was put into practice, and hearing the words addressed to her by the Blessed Mother, *You at least console me,* [236] inspired her to make many small gestures of kindness to show great love—love is inventive—and so always kept burning the flame of love given to God and neighbor.

8 | The Love in Service

After temporary professions, the young professed are sent to the various houses of the Province. The Mother Provincial promised Sister Dores she would always remain in the Novitiate House where she could be better protected given her particular situation. Although she lived in the part of the house reserved for novices, she started to relate more with the community. She continued to be in charge of laundering the habits and assisting in various other duties. Being faithful to the purpose of her profession, she always responded to those who asked her help; she gave generously. After her vow of poverty, she did not have much to give. Instead she gave all the love in her heart to those who needed her, and received in return much gratitude from those who benefited from her services.

Sister Dores and the sick had a mutual preference for each other; she liked very much to assist them, and the sick and elderly wanted her company. The sisters in the infirmary adjacent to Sister Dores' place of work asked the Mother Provincial for permission to have her attend to some service for them. This was granted and the occasions were not lacking.

Sister Lucia later wrote a delightful account about this fraternal familiarity in the service of charity:

Among others was the beloved Mother Ordaz. She was the first Portuguese who entered the Institute. Now old and sick, she could only walk supported by a cane and supported by a Sister. She asked me to go to her room; she always had the feeling to hit the pavement with her cane. Sometimes she wanted to see if Mother Provincial was in her office, and if it was possible to receive her, and if so I was there to accompany her.

235 Antonio Maria Martins, *New Documents of Fatima*, p. 118.
236 *My Pathway*, I, p. 50.

Other times she wished to go to the Chapel and I took her there, helping her to sit in the chair and asking at what time should I come back for her. When I received the answer, I asked her to pray for me too. "Oh yes, I will pray much for you, my angel," she answered with an amiable smile. And God knows how many thanks I am indebted for her good prayers!

Due to her age and illness, her health was getting worse until she was confined to bed. So I alternated with a Sister Nurse, night and day, and we never left her alone. One afternoon, I think it was a Sunday, I joined some Mothers who were visiting with her. While we were there, the bell rang to pray the Rosary and Benediction of the Blessed Sacrament; the Sister Nurse said to her:

-Mother rang for the Rosary and Benediction of the Blessed Sacrament for all; I am here to keep you company. When she heard this, Mother took my hand and said:

-They all go; keep Sister Dores here with me.

As the Mothers came out, I knelt down beside her bed to pray the Rosary in a low voice. Mother was responding vaguely to the Hail Mary, the Our Father, Glory Be, Litany, etc.

Singing was heard as well from the Chapel, followed also in a low voice the Tantum Ergo and Panem de Caelo; and Mother listened and smiled sweetly. I said to her:

-Mother, now it is the blessing, we will receive it in spirit.

Leaning against the pillows on the bed, Mother put her hand up. With her rosary between her fingers, she tilted her forehead slightly as a sign of adoration and meditation, and when I waited to see her raise her forehead again, I noticed she no longer lived in this land. While blessing her, the Divine Husband had given her His arm and with Him she had left for Heaven. It was the first death that I witnessed and it is beautiful to see how the saints die!

Sometime later, the Lord gave me the grace to attend another death, no less beautiful. She was the beloved Mother Falcon. This Mother, among other ailments, suffered from loss of sight. She was very pious and since she could not work, she passed the days in the Chapel beside Our Lord. She would not be bothered from the light of the windows, so was always cuddled up in a corner behind the confessional and the wall. When the confessor came to serve the community, it was a problem to convince her to move away. One day she argued with Rev. Barros:

-But Rev. Father, can I confess from this side where I am? I am a little deaf and I cannot hear what you are saying.

Then I remembered to invite her to the sacristy.

-Come Mother, we'll go to the sacristy. I closed all the windows and Mother was there in front of the door to the presbytery, which was better being close to the tabernacle.

She accepted and thanked me, saying:

-I really enjoyed being in the sacristy. Let me go there every time that the confessor comes. Half of the time will be offered by me for the Sister.

Once she went to the chapel, it was during the time when the sun came through the windows across the bottom of the corridor. She entered the linen closet and asked me for the umbrella and (I) put it in her hand. Then I laughed watching her walk down the aisle with the umbrella opened to prevent the sunlight from getting in her eyes, and she said to me:

-Ah! My naughty one, you laugh at me! I will ask Our Lord to pay you very much.

-What a nice pay, my dear Mother. Thank you!

A day later when she returned to the Chapel, she went into the linen closet and asked me to give her a complete change of clothes. It could be that this old sister had worn out her clothes, because she wanted to dress up and be all washed the next day upon rising.

-So Mother will go on a trip? I asked.

-Yes, she replied.

-Ah! But in this case, I do not give you old clothes, I give you the best:

-No, no, give me the old ones. It is a journey where I will never come back.

-Then with even great reason! I will give you better clothes and get you the suitcase.

-No, no. nothing like that. And she told me softly:

-Tomorrow I go to Heaven, and I want to be washed and dressed, so you need not shroud me.

-Was it the Lord Who told you, I asked.

-Yes it was, she replied.

-Ah! Then tell the Lord to take me with you, because I want to go to Heaven too!

-Yes, but Sister, you are still very young, you still have much work to do here on earth, but I will not forget you in Heaven.[237]

Sister Dores told the Mother Provincial about this conversation and asked if she should give her the clothes. With a benevolent smile, the Mother told her to give everything that the elderly sister had requested so that she would have a peaceful sleep. The next morning, the Sister got up as usual, went to Mass and received Communion, staying in the chapel the rest of the morning. Sister Dores did not notice anything special about her, having followed her normal routine.

After the mid-day meal, the sister told the Mother Provincial that she did

---

237 *My Pathway,* I.

not feel well and expressed a desire to confess and receive Holy Viaticum and Anointing. Mother asked if she wanted the doctor. She said it was not necessary and was taken by the shepherdess to her room and laid on the bed. After Sister Dores covered her with the quilt, the elderly sister asked her to go and urge Mother Provincial not to delay in calling a priest. Mother conceded and called the priest who promptly arrived, but not sensing any urgency did not give her the Anointing or the sacred Viaticum, though the Sister insisted.

Sister Dores tended to her after the priest left. While tucking her into bed, she noticed that her face changed with the look of approaching death. They called the priest again, but when he arrived she was already gone. Sister Dores concluded:

I felt a great happiness, believing that it is one more Saint who intercedes for me in Heaven.[238]

The shepherdess felt good about living a life of simplicity and in community with the Sisters whom she loved very much in the Lord. There were times, however, when she realized that she was placed conspicuously to be seen, and did not like it. All of the Sisters were of the opinion that Sister Dores needed to be protected, but they were sometimes distressed upon seeing the insistence with which relatives or friends wanted to see her. And, since "there is no rule without exception," as each person was treated equally, there were many occasions when she was like a celebrity and became the exception to the rule. When the college students came for their annual outing, Sister Dores had to serve them, or when the Mothers were doing their annual retreat, she served them and arranged their rooms. This work she did with love and dedication, but it cost her to see herself 'pursued.' She was tired of it. And the idea of Carmel continued to dance on the horizon...

---

238 *Ibid.*

Lucia with a small image of the Immaculate
Heart of Mary.

Sister Lucia as a Dorothean.

CHAPTER X

REQUEST FOR THE CONSECRATION OF RUSSIA

1 | Vision of the Most Holy Trinity

On July 13, 1917, Our Lady had promised to return to ask for the consecration of Russia to her Immaculate Heart. Twelve years later on June 13, 1929, Sister Dores was worshiping alone before the Blessed Sacrament, lit only by the flickering light of the lamp by the Tabernacle. The Shepherdess of Fatima suddenly noticed that the chapel was illuminated with a light that was familiar to her. She related:

I had requested and obtained permission from my superiors and confessor to make a Holy Hour from 11 p.m.- midnight, from Thursday to Friday. Being alone one night, I knelt between the rail in the middle of the chapel to prostrate and pray the Prayers of the Angel. Feeling tired, I stood up and continued to recite them with arms crossed. The only light was the lamp.

Suddenly the whole chapel lit up with a supernatural light, and above the altar appeared a cross of light reaching to the ceiling. In a brighter light on the upper part of the cross could be seen the face of a man and his body as far as the waist, upon his breast was a dove also of light, and nailed to the cross was the body of another man. A little below the waist, I could see a chalice and a large host suspended in the air. Drops of blood were falling from the face of Jesus Crucified and from the wound in His side. These drops ran down on to the host and fell into the chalice.

Beneath the right arm of the cross was Our Lady. (It was Our Lady of Fatima, with her Immaculate Heart... in her left hand... without sword or roses, but with a crown of thorns and flames...) Under the left arm of the cross were large letters, as if of crystal clear water which ran down upon the altar and formed these words: "Grace and Mercy."

I understood that it was the Mystery of the Most Holy Trinity which was shown to me, and I received insights about this Mystery which I am not permitted to reveal.

Then Our Lady said to me:

-The moment has come in which God asks the Holy Father, in union with all the Bishops of the world, to make the consecration of Russia to my Immaculate Heart, promising to save it by this means. There are so many souls whom the Justice of God condemns for sins committed against me that I have come to ask reparation: sacrifice yourself for this intention and pray.

I have an account of this with my confessor, who ordered me to write down what Our Lady wanted done. [239]

Ever since the apparition of July 13, 1917, Lucia had carried Russia in her

---

239 MSL I, Appendix II, p. 196.

heart, and her love for this country grew exponentially. Her tenderness for this land and its people was present until her death. Just hearing the name Russia was enough to get her notice and attention on what this land meant, and she cherished the dream of going to Russia someday. In 1993, a bishop from Russia stopped by the Carmel of Saint Teresa. At the end of the celebration of the Eucharist with the Community, His Excellency approached the grid of the choir and asked with much commitment for a foundation in Moscow. It was to carry out the Foundation of the Carmel of the Holy Trinity in the Diocese of Guarda in Portugal, but there was no chance it could happen. Sister Lucia's heart beat strongly, although she did not manifest it outwardly. In a letter about this time she said:

We have requests for the founding of several other monasteries, including one in the capital of Russia in Moscow, but for now we cannot commit... [240]

If such a foundation was ever established, Sister Lucia would be its greatest enthusiast. She wanted very much to visit this land that was in her heart since she was 10 years old, and live her final days there. Russia!! How many prayers and sacrifices ascended to Heaven by her for its conversion! How much of her life was sacrificed for this love! Who knows? Someday in Russia there may be a Carmel established in her name resulting from her prayers and supplications. In a letter from July, 1950 written to a lady from Russia who lived in France, Sister Lucia said:

I know that the Russian people are great, noble and cultured, capable of walking the path of justice, truth and goodness. Since I saw the fondness of Our Lady for them, I cherish them as a people and desire nothing more than their salvation. [241]

In 1978 she wrote:

I know that the dear Mother of Heaven and Our Mother love the dear Russian people and wants to help them find a better way. I asked her, therefore, that the Immaculate Mother keep them in her Heart, and lead them to Jesus Christ our Savior! [242]

Returning to the vision that happened during the Holy Hour in the chapel at Tuy, Lucia took advantage of being alone to pray prostrate the prayers taught by the Angel in 1916. After getting tired in this position, she stood and continued to pray them with her arms crossed, no less difficult. These prayers were constant in her life. Everything is included in them: the profession of faith, worship, an act of love, and intercession for those who do not know God, cannot know Him or refuse to know Him. She prayed these prayers in adoration before God, interceding and

---

240 Letter of April 29, 1993.
241 Letter of July 3, 1950, *Irene*.
242 Letter of December 10, 1978, *Liktor Vladimir*.

offering reparation for others.

In this apparition Sister Lucia saw what happens at every Mass in the light of faith. It seemed to relate to the third apparition of the Angel—the Eucharist and the Blood that fell from the Chalice. In the celebration of the Eucharist, the Sacrifice of Calvary becomes present on the altar, in which the Father, Son and Holy Spirit are present. There are two words, **GRACE and MERCY,** which Lucia saw as like crystal clear water running down upon the altar. The GRACE and MERCY of God are fruits of the Sacrifice of the Cross, present at each Mass, which run like a torrential river over all of humanity.

As on Calvary, Mary is present as an intercessor and co-redeemer, that is, she is the Mediatrix of all graces and never tires of pursuing her wayward children. With her maternal love, she warns them of the danger that they are in, placing herself before the Father on their behalf and pleading for mercy. Mary is the personification of the love of the Father Who never gives up on His children and wants to save them. Once again she comes to ask, entrusting the shepherdess to make a request of the Holy Father, on whose accomplishment depends so much good for the world! Once again she asks for reparation, and of her humble confidant, sacrifice and prayer.

2 | I Want My Whole Church to Recognize this Consecration as a Triumph of the Immaculate Heart of Mary

The implementation of the acts that God asks does not depend on Sister Lucia; she simply transmits them obediently and with quiet sacrifice and prayer to the Church. With all of its delays, she does not criticize. In a letter dated June 24, 1987, responding to several questions that hinted of criticism of the Holy Father and the delay in release of the third part of the Secret, Sister Lucia replied:

-*Our respect for the Church and its work on behalf of Christ, Who is its Founder, is always very large.*

And in another paragraph of the same letter, revealing the purity and truth of her position before the Church, she responded: *It is necessary to understand that the Church, before accepting a particular revelation, has to study well and prove the facts, events, and the instruments that God uses to ensure the truth and reality of things before deciding.*[243]

But the Church failed to see the imminent danger that Mary confided to the heart of her young messenger, what Mary feared for the world: *Later, by means of*

---

243 Letter of June 24, 1987, *Araí Daniele.*

an intimate communication, Our Lord told me, complaining:

-If they do not wish to heed my request, as like the king of France, they will repent and do it, but it will be late. Russia will have already spread her errors throughout the world, provoking wars, and persecutions of the Church. The Holy Father will have much to suffer.[244]

In the years between the request and its implementation, and there were many, Sister Lucia did not lose any opportunity for Heaven's message to reach the Holy Father. She worked through those who were closest to her—her spiritual directors in whom she confided, especially the Bishop of Leiria, to get it to the Holy Father. The request of the First Saturdays was easier to implement among the faithful, although officially it was only recognized after the canonical approval of the apparitions. But the request for the Consecration of Russia was directly for the Holy Father and was therefore the greatest difficulty. If Lucia was talking to someone who was going to meet with the Pope, and the person was someone she could trust, she wouldn't miss the chance to send the message.

In 1936 she wrote to her confessor, Father Gonçalves, S.J.:

About the other question whether it would be good to insist in order to obtain the consecration of Russia, I answer in almost the same way as I answered the other times. I am sorry that it has not already been done. However, it is the same God Who requested it Who has permitted this. I am going to say what I feel in this respect, although it is a rather delicate matter to be put in a letter due to the danger of it being lost and read, but I entrust it to the same God, because I am afraid I have not treated the matter with enough clarity. Is it convenient to insist? I do not know. It seems to me that if the Holy Father did it right now, Our Lord would accept and fulfill His promise. There is no doubt that it would please our Lord and the Immaculate Heart of Mary. Intimately I have spoken to Our Lord about the subject, and not too long ago I asked Him why He did not just convert Russia without the Holy Father making the consecration. Our Lord replied:

-Because I want my whole Church to acknowledge this consecration as a triumph of the Immaculate Heart of Mary, in order to later extend its cult and to place the devotion to this Immaculate Heart alongside devotion to My Sacred Heart.

-But, my God, the Holy Father does not believe me, not even if he is influenced by a special inspiration!

-The Holy Father. Pray much for the Holy Father. He will do it, but it will be too late. Nevertheless the Immaculate Heart of Mary will save Russia. It has been entrusted to her.[245]

---

244 MSL I, Appendix II, p. 196.
245 Letter of May 18, 1936.

3 | Lucia's Efforts for the Consecration of the World and Russia

By 1940, sensing the approach of World War II, Sister Lucia was sparing no efforts. Although it pained her, by order of the Bishop of Leiria she wrote to the Holy Father, Pope Pius XII, to relay the request of Our Lady. Some passages follow:

Most Holy Father,

In 1929, Our Lady, through another apparition, asked for the consecration of Russia to her Immaculate Heart, promising by this means to prevent the spread of its errors and its conversion. Sometime later after I gave an account of Our Lady's request to my confessor. His Reverence employed ways to make it known to His Holiness Pope Pius XI so that it could be carried out. In various private communications, Our Lord has not ceased to insist on this request, promising that if Your Holiness deigns to make the consecration of the world to the Immaculate Heart of Mary with a special mention of Russia, and in union with all the Bishops of the world, to shorten the days of tribulation that He has determined to punish the nations for their crimes, by means of war, famine, and various persecutions against the Holy Church and Your Holiness.

Holy Father, I truly feel the sufferings of Your Holiness. And I with my poor prayers and sacrifices can try to lessen them with our good God and the Immaculate Heart of Mary.

Most Holy Father, if in the union of my soul with God I am not mistaken, Our Lord is attentive to the consecration of this country made to the Immaculate Heart of Mary by the Portuguese Bishops, and promised a special protection of our country from this war. And this protection will be the proof of the graces that would be granted to other nations, if they are consecrated to her.[246]

· The promise was fulfilled; Portugal was spared the scourge of war.

Sister Lucia touched on this subject extensively in her correspondence. It was a thorn of mortification in her, knowing how much suffering could be avoided if the request was met in Heaven. During a private meeting with Pope John Paul II on May 13, 1982, in Fatima, she gave His Holiness a letter, which renewed the request of the Mother, saying:

His Holiness John Paul II: I humbly lament and beseech the Consecration of Russia to the Immaculate Heart of Mary in union with all the bishops of the world. So that this consecration is a bond of union of all the members of the Mystical Body of Christ, who with Mary, the Mother of Christ and Our Mother, offer to the Lord to complete the work of the Redemption of the world. And as far as possible, that all

---

246 Letter of December 2, 1940.

Christians and even non-Catholics and non-Christians who want to join in this act of full consecration and surrender to the Lord, be united to the Immaculate Heart of Mary.

This is how I understood that this consecration should be made, in imitation of Christ when He said to His Father: "I consecrate Myself for them, that they also may be consecrated," in truth, justice and love, united in the same faith, the same hope and the same love.

The third part of the secret refers to the words of Our Lady: "If not, she will spread her errors throughout the world, causing wars and persecution of the Church. The good will be martyred, the Holy Father will have much to suffer, various nations will be annihilated" (July 13, 1917).

The third part of the Secret that they are so anxious to know is a symbolic revelation, referring to this part of the Message, conditioned by our yes or no, that we accept or not, what the Message asks of us: "If my requests are heeded, Russia will be converted, and there will be peace; if not, she will spread her errors throughout the world," etc.

Because we have not answered this appeal of the Message, we see that it has been fulfilled. Russia has invaded the world with her errors. And if we haven't seen yet the end of this prophecy accomplished, we see that we are going toward it with great strides if we do not fall back on the path of sin, hatred, revenge, injustice, violating the rights of the human person, immorality and violence, etc. We cannot say that it is God Who punishes us, but rather, that it is men who are preparing themselves for the punishment. God warns us and calls us to the right path, while respecting the freedom that He gave us; therefore, men are responsible.[247]

4 | Was the Consecration Done as Our Lady Asked?

On his pilgrimage to Fatima in 1982, His Holiness Pope John Paul II made the Consecration, but it still did not comply with the request of Our Lady. That same year Sister Lucia was visited by the Apostolic Nuncio Sante Portalupi and told him that the Consecration as Our Lady had requested was still not done. His Excellency conveyed this information to the Holy Father, who then on March 25, 1984, satisfied the request of Our Lady made 55 years earlier, before the image of Our Lady of Fatima that is venerated in the Chapel of Apparitions and that was sent to the Vatican for this Act of Consecration. In August of 1989, Sister Lucia made clear in a letter the question that still exists today:

Was the Consecration of the World made as Our Lady had asked?

---

247 Letter of May 12, 1982.

On October 31, 1942 in a letter (sent to her) from His Holiness Pius XII: They asked me then if it was done as Our Lady had asked; I said no, because it lacked the union with all of the bishops of the world.

After this, Pope Paul VI made it on May 13, 1967. They asked me if it was done as Our Lady requested. I answered no, for the same reason; it lacked the union with all the bishops of the world. It was made again by Pope John Paul II on May 13, 1982. They asked me then if it was done. I said no. It lacked the union with all the bishops of the world. Then, this same Supreme Pontiff John Paul II wrote to all the bishops of the world asking them to unite with him and he gave orders for the image of Our Lady of Fatima to be taken from the Capelinha and brought to Rome, and on March 25, 1984—publicly and in union with all the bishops of the world who wished to unite— made the Consecration as Our Lady requested. They asked me then if it was made as Our Lady had asked for it, and I said yes. Since then it is done.

Why was this demand of God that this consecration be made in union with all the bishops of the world? Because this consecration is a call to unity of all Christians— the Mystical Body of Christ—whose head is the Pope, the only true representative of Christ on earth, whom the Lord has entrusted the Keys of the Kingdom of Heaven. This union depends on the faith in the world, and on love, which is the bond that unites all of us in Christ, as He prayed to the Father: "As you, Father, are in me and I in you, that they also may be in us, so that the world may believe that you sent me… I in them and you in me, that they may become perfected in unity, so that the world may know that you have sent me and have loved them, as you have loved me" (Jn 17: 21-23).[248]

As we see, the union depends on Faith and Charity to be the bond of our union with Christ, whose true representative on earth is the Pope.[249]

Sometime after this Consecration, in a conversation with Father Luis Kondor, to the question of whether the Consecration was done as requested, Sister Lucia replied thus: *"It was done, but it was already too late!"* The priest then asked her what would signal the acceptance of the Consecration by God and the fulfillment of the promise. She said: *"Look to the East."* In her last writing, Sister Lucia showed us how to see the response from Heaven:

This consecration was made by the Holy Father Pope John Paul II in Rome publicly on March 25, 1984, before the image of Our Lady which is venerated in the Chapel of the Apparitions in the Cova da Iria, Fatima, which the Holy Father, after having written to all the bishops of the world asking them to unite with His Holiness in this Act of Consecration that would be led from Rome, to mark well that the Consecration was going to be made before this image, that was requested by Our Lady

---

248 Jn 17: 21-23.
249 Letter of August 29, 1989.

of Fatima.

It is well known to all that this was one of the most critical moments in the history of humanity, when the great powers, hostile to each other, were projecting and preparing for a nuclear atomic war that would destroy the world, if not all, for the most part, with what chances of survival? And who would be able to dissuade these men to change all this to the contrary? Asking for a meeting in order that an embrace of peace may happen? Changing their plans from war into plans of peace? Of injustices aggressive and violent, in aid projects and help, recognizing the right of the human person by abolishing slavery, etc.?

Who but God was able to act on these intellectuals, these wills, these consciences in order to lead them to such an exchange, without fear, without fear of opposing revolts? Of yours and of foreigners? Only the power of God, Who has acted in all, caused them to accept in peace, without riots, or opposition, and without conditions.[250]

Who is like God?

---

250 Irma Lucia, *How I See the Message*, p. 65.

Image of Our Lady of Fatima in Rome.

Pope John Paul II receives the image of Our Lady of Fatima.

Pope John Paul II making the Consecration of the World before the image of Our Lady of Fatima from the chapel, March 25, 1984.

Pope John Paul II with Bishop Alberto Amaral, Bishop of Leiria-Fatima.

Lucia as a Dorothean in Tuy.

CHAPTER XI
DOROTHEAN NUN

1 | To Live with Love and for Love

The young religious in her quest for greater harmony with the will of God, exercised charity and selflessness and increasingly conformed to her delightful model—Mary. She wanted to learn how to be a faithful spouse of Jesus Christ, and looking to Mary Most Holy, continued her walk toward consecrating her whole being and life. The Profession of Perpetual Vows of poverty, chastity and obedience was her final goal, to be achieved six years after professing temporary vows.

During the time between temporary and perpetual professions, Sister Dores faithfully tended to the work that was entrusted to her. She was comfortable being in charge of the black linen clothes because she could sew very well and was efficient in everything she did. In addition to this craft, she was asked to carry out other services, which she did with all her heart. Although weak in health, she did not refuse work that required strength, generously giving with love and for love.

More than weariness and work, what pained her was to be a constant target of people's curious glances. Very often in order to comply with the wishes of people who wanted to visit with the Seer of Fatima, her Superiors arranged any *necessary* task to elicit a chance meeting. God only knows what predicaments this caused, but upon realizing these secondary intentions, Sister Dores would fulfill what was ordered of her quickly, and gracefully tried to avoid these encounters. One time there were two priests who wished to see her. Her Mother Superior told her to bring a chasuble in order that they might see it. She obeyed. Noticing that they were only looking at her and did not care about the chasuble, she said: -*If I am not needed, I will leave.* And she left without ceremony or scruples.

It was not easy for her or her superiors, who often had trouble trying to accommodate the requests while not exposing her. She sometimes could not even be in the chapel before the Tabernacle of her love without the annoying whispers about her, and was mortified to see that because of her, people lacked proper respect before the Blessed Sacrament.

In 1932 black clouds loomed over Spain, threatened by civil war and the establishment of the Republic. Fearing imminent danger, the Mother Provincial decided to bring some of the novices and professed to Portugal, where it was more conducive to religious life. This left the Community in Tuy much reduced. Being in charge of the clothes, Sister Dores collected the wardrobes of the professed, the sacristan and the assistant nurse.

It seemed that the new Republican Government was peace-loving and the novitiate returned to Tuy. But soon outbreaks of communist revolts began to rise in various parts of the country, demonstrating true fury against the Church. For this reason, they had to come up with a new exodus. Mother Provincial gave the Sisters the choice to stay or leave. Sister Lucia was among those who voluntarily stayed, offering the proof of her love of God: *I offered to stay, willingly if God wanted to grant me the grace to give my life for Him again.*[251] By embracing this desire, God would ask of her what would be the slow martyrdom of everyday life. She lived peacefully being very faithful and charitable, leaving every footstep marked with the ruby-red color of her hidden sacrifice, without the glory of a heroic moment. She lived every moment of life heroically.

To save what they had of value, the Dorothean Sisters rented a house in Valença do Minho with the Jesuits, who transported the sisters there before the revolution came to their houses. Due to her knowledge and friendships, Sister Dores placed herself in harm's way to obtain the proper permits for crossing the border between Spain and Portugal.

The border guards all attended me very cordially and granted to me what they usually call 'carte blanche' to everything that I wanted to pass.[252]

She crossed the border many times; then one day the chief representative came and said the borders were closed and it was no longer possible to pass anything. Sister Dores asked if they could cross the loaded truck. The chief representative told her otherwise and advised her to call the border, which she did and was allowed to cross. It was the last opportunity to pass, however. There was a Mother Provincial and a Sister Gomes who was elderly and sick, who followed the truck in a van. Seeing that their van would not be allowed to cross after the truck, Sister Gomes asked for the love of God to let her pass anyway. With no time to think of a solution, Sister Gomes asked if she could sit on top of the bags on the truck. But at the border they said that they could only pass the luggage and not the people. When the Mother Provincial saw the anxiety of the Sister who was not resigning herself to stay, she told them to let her pass. The workers helped Sister to climb to the top and there she was in between the bags under the cover of an umbrella.

Sister Dores followed behind in a car with a lady companion, thinking that they would have to pick up the elderly sister. But upon reaching the border they were amused, and the guards, knowing that she was ill, let her pass, getting a laugh from the odd shaped baggage.

---

251 *My Pathway,* I, p. 93.
252 *Ibid.*

2 | A Providential Support

These six years were exhausting for Sister Dores and she needed to discern her final decision—to make Perpetual Vows or take another course. Inside it was always the same dilemma! She wrote:

However, I had to prepare myself for the perpetual profession or resolve definitely to leave for the Carmel; each time I felt the need for more of a cloistered retreat. The facts of Fatima gradually became known and it progressively increased curiosity about me and my devotion, but also why should I hide it? I think this makes up a great part of my cross, as did the crucial Cross of Jesus Christ. This cannot be escaped anywhere in the world, it is very difficult to live in the spotlight. But when God puts us there, He gives the grace to withstand the blast of fierce windstorms. However, this does not prevent us from seeking shelter.[253]

It was during this period that Lucia had a meeting with His Excellency Antonio Garcia y Garcia, Archbishop of Valladolid, who visited the Novitiate house shortly after taking possession of the diocese. He was for her from that day a providential support with the heart of a father. God never failed to give the necessary help and always at the right moment.

While the Mothers were walking in the garden with His Excellency, they sent Sister Dores to prepare a snack. She was to serve when they sat down at the table. She tells about this first encounter with the one who was going to help her so much in the future:

On the table I had placed several sweets and various kinds of fruits. The Bishop asked me what kind of fruit I liked the most. Fearing that if I said some of what was there, His Excellency would tell me to eat, and being afraid of that invitation, I tried to mention one that was not there and said: cherries. The Bishop looked at the table:

-No las tenemos, pero quizá uvas también le gusten (We do not have them, but maybe you also like grapes), and taking the bunch, tore a branch and told me to eat.

I obeyed and confessed the fault that I had committed:

-Bishop, I haven't been honest, I said cherries to Your Excellency so you would not ask me to eat because I did not deserve anything!

His Excellency smiled and said:

-I am so much embarrassed! In penance, you are going to eat only this. Then taking a muffin he made me eat it.[254]

At the end of lunch the Bishop said to the Mother Provincial that he wished to speak to Sister Dores alone. They talked at length about Fatima, the

253 *Ibid*, p. 95.
254 *Ibid*, p. 96 – 97.

religious life, the Institute, and her personal vocation. Realizing that she was with someone who understood her and wanted to help, the shepherdess answered all the questions he asked her with simplicity and sincerity. She opened her soul and discovered a pleasant relationship with him. In comparison, when the curious-minded asked her questions, she would quickly withdraw and answer with a minimum of words. About her vocation as she had confessed so many times, she stated once again her desire to go to a cloister to avoid being the target of so many glances and meetings. His Excellency agreed with her and approved her desire, but he advised her to profess where she was now, given the political situation in Spain which had been increasingly disturbing and threatening especially for the monasteries. He promised her that as soon as the situation returned to normal, it was his desire to help her to move to a Carmel. He was placed at her disposal and visited her regularly, for he was very much interested in her spiritual life and to see that it continued to grow.

For Sister Dores, the Bishop was a gift from Heaven, as she fondly recalled:

He inspired me with much confidence, helped me a lot, and although sometimes it was difficult for me to say some things, His Excellency always appeared very understanding, and it felt good. Sometimes I would get to go to the Episcopal Palace. He met me when I arrived and drove me to the Chapel to make a little visit to Jesus in the Blessed Sacrament. There was a sister who accompanied me who allowed plenty of time to pray my Rosary.

He went with me to the balcony showing the beautiful sights, and wondering if the Serra de Aire was as beautiful as the mountains ahead.

I answered that for me it was much more beautiful, yet the writers say that it is deceptive. There I was sitting beside him in a large armchair, where I felt so tiny! He asked me about everything that was concerning me, in particular my spiritual life. Having the gift of the word, and a very intense life of intimacy with God, he did not want that to decrease in my spirit. He was very devoted to Saint Teresa and said that he hopes to be able to relocate me to a Carmel. [255]

3 | Perpetual Vows

With the wise counsel she received from him as from the mouth of God, she went to the altar to deliver definitely to God her life and her whole being. On October 3, 1934, the Most Reverend José Alves Correia da Silva, Bishop of Leiria, presided over the ceremony.

---

255 *Ibid,* p. 98.

On the eve of her vows she had a surprise during the evening meal. Sister Dores always sat in the cafeteria next to the preacher, Father Aparicio, S.J., who never missed an opportunity to talk about his affairs to the sister who served. He called attention to the fact that he was on retreat and talked too much. During this meal, the Sister servant told Sister Dores to go to Father Aparicio to give him the news that her nephew, Manuel Pereira, was already in the Apostolic School. After Sister Dores returned to the table, she met Manuel, who had never seen his aunt. They talked for a good while without anyone revealing anything, until finally Father Aparicio asked the young one if he knew to whom he was talking. He replied that she was a religious. When Father told him she was his aunt whom he had never seen, her nephew gave her a huge hug. What a joy! It was Mr. Ferreira de Pico de Regalados who paid for the trip for the family. When crossing the border, they said the children were small, but they passed without a problem.

The day of her Perpetual Vows, the Bridegroom gave Lucia the consolation of the presence of her mother, Maria Rosa. It was also their farewell in this life, the last time they would meet on earth. Lucia, in a moment of intimacy with her mother after the ceremony, asked her if she now believed in the apparitions of Our Lady. Her mother replied:

-*Oh, daughter, I do not know! It seems to me such a great thing!*

Never would her daughter have the consolation of hearing from the mouth of her beloved mother a word of full acceptance. It was not something she would savor and she knew this well! But she repeated in her heart, '*It is for Your sake, Oh my God…*' and no one knew how painful this was for her.

She inserted into the Eucharist her own Ritual of the Ceremony of Profession. The Taking of the Habit was also included in this celebration of Temporary Profession. It is a very significant moment when the Professing of Vows is pronounced.

When she approached for Communion, before the Consecrated Host that the celebrant held up with his hands, she pronounced the formula of the surrender of her life and then received Communion. The formula used by Sister Lucia was as follows:

-*Holy Trinity, Father, Son and Holy Spirit, my God, I, Sister Maria Lucia das Dores, moved with the desire to please You and to contribute with full commitment for the salvation of my neighbor for Your sake, in the presence of the Blessed Virgin Mother of God, of St. Dorothy, the entire Celestial Court and the Institute, and Your Reverend Mother Superior represented here, I do perpetually vow to Your Divine Majesty, Poverty, Chastity, Obedience and Perseverance in our Holy Office, in the manner of the Constitution approved by the Holy See, and I plead therefore, Almighty and Merciful*

God, by the precious Blood of Your Son Jesus, that You deign to accept this sacrifice in the scent of sweetness, and just as You graciously granted me to profess this to You, that by Your infinite mercy You bestow on me the abundant grace to faithfully fulfill this.

Tuy, October 3, 1934

Maria Lucia of Jesus [256]

After lunch, she enjoyed a few moments of free time while waiting for the sisters to gather for recreation. This being the day for her to help with dishes, she instead kept Jesus company near the Tabernacle. He did not delay in giving her a sign of His love and fondness, pouring into the cup of her joyful heart a bitter drop, caused by a mistake. The Mother Provincial spoke to the Sister who was serving, and asked her to call all the newly professed into the recreation room of the school mistresses for a party. The Sister thought that the party was for all who professed that day, so she also called Sister Dores. When the Mother Provincial saw Sister Dores there she became a little upset and said it was just for the teachers, then excused her with an expression that deeply hurt the shepherdess. Mother said to Sister Dores:

-Sister was not called here.

Sister Lucia left the room and went back to the Tabernacle feeling humiliated, but happy to be able to imitate her Spouse to Whom she surrendered with renewed pleasure:

-For You, Oh my Beloved, and with You, I embrace the cross and drink the chalice until the last drop; if it pleases You, reserve it for me. [257]

She interpreted this incident as a sign from God, although this time she did not inquire about her future vocation.

The Bishop of Leiria took leave, promising to return soon. Sister Dores spent the afternoon with her family in the living room. She rejoiced with them, playing with the little ones whom she saw for the first time, and enjoying the cheerful conversation. She was deprived of some moments with her mother, who said, "Goodbye, until we meet in Heaven." They all left happy and she also was happy listening to the will of God. She was in His hands, living faithfully in the place where she was planted, always ready to walk the path of the Divine Will. The next day, through the voice of her Mother Provincial, the Lord said to her again: *Leave... follow me.*

4 | Back in Pontevedra

On October 4, the day following her Profession, the Mother Provincial told

---

256 Sebastião Martins dos Reis, *A Life in the Service of Fatima*, p. 175.

257 *My Pathway*, I, p. 102 – 103.

Sister Dores that she would have to go for some time to Pontevedra, despite the promise of keeping her always in the Novitiate house in Tuy for her protection. Because of the deep spiritual bond they shared Mother Monfalim wanted to keep her there, but it was time for the shepherdess to be transferred.

Having been advised by Bishop Antonio Garcia y Garcia, who promised to visit her in Pontevedra, they had to leave for their new destination the very next day. Sister Dores accompanied by Sister Rose checked every day to see if a coach was available, but would receive the same negative response, not being able to find a means of transportation because of the revolution. Mother Provincial was very concerned about the situation of the Sisters of Pontevedra, not hearing from them and longing to know how they were. Finally on October 9th the sisters found a truck of soldiers who were traveling through. Tired of not getting a coach, Sister Dores scrutinized the soldiers' tempers and the two sisters decided to take their chances and leave with them, who applauded their courage.

There were some stumbling blocks along the way, trees in the road or groups of men forcing them to stop to inspect them for explosives. Everything was resolved peacefully whenever they were stopped (the soldiers had used the two nuns' skirts to hide two suitcases of weapons) but it extended their travels. What should have been a three hour trip to Pontevedra took twelve and a half hours. Sister Dores took advantage of the time with the soldiers, and not wanting to miss the opportunity to do some good for these men, invited them to pray by singing the Rosary while they were traveling. They sang two rosaries! As they were used to singing during travel to pass the time, it was only a difference of words for them, and the shepherdess was very happy to lead these men in prayer to the Blessed Virgin.

Fear reined everywhere and people kept their windows shut tight. Upon hearing the song that rose from that truck and not being a melody typical of soldiers, and even more so in these troubled times, people opened their windows just a bit to see what was happening. Unbelievably in the midst of that sound of men singing loudly, singing with full lungs was the Shepherdess of Fatima!

When they finally arrived in Pontevedra at 8:30 in the evening, they couldn't see anyone in the streets and the commander of the squad sent two soldiers to accompany the sisters to the college, thanking them for the good company that they had enjoyed. It was difficult to open the door when they got there, and as much as they knocked and called, no one ventured to answer. Finally a sister opened the window slightly and peered out, asking who was there. She thought she saw familiar habits, but was surprised to also see soldiers in uniform. Sister Dores with her strong and decisive voice addressed the one in the window to open the door:

-*Sister, open the door!*

The sister replied:

-*Who is it?*

-*I am Sister Dores.*[258]

But it was not easy to convince her of this fact. Finally the door opened and the soldiers went away. Since the soldiers were returning to Tuy on the following day, Sister Dores sent them with the news of their safe arrival to relay to Mother Provincial.

Sister Dores integrated quickly into the life of the Community that she already knew. She was put in charge of the office of the habits, arranging some classrooms, substituting for the caretaker, and serving in the students' cafeteria. She fulfilled her duties diligently and without disturbing others, with promptness, care and joy while living an intense life of intimacy with the Lord. He was her strength. She participated in the Community work without any special favors, doing her chores like everyone else. It was a way for her to "hide" amongst them. But soon the students found out who the hermit *Dolores* was, and thus began the curious glances and "procession" of followers that mortified her and from which she could rarely escape. These were more sacrifices to offer for the conversion of sinners, more flowers to give to the Heart of her Mother. Her love was constant in her heart, and with everything she did she could fulfill the request made by the Angel in the second apparition:

-*From all that you can, offer to God a sacrifice as an act of reparation for sins by which He is offended and in supplication for the conversion of sinners.*[259]

As it was from the beginning when she was with Jacinta and Francisco, she lost no opportunity to offer prayers and sacrifices to the Almighty. And there was no need for her to invent them; just by living a sacrificial life intently she could distinguish them in the ordinary life which offered so many opportunities! In one of her letters to a benefactor she confessed her desire to embrace the cross in life more ardently, and with greater intentions in her heart.

J.M.J.

Pontevedra – November 4, 1934

Isabel of the Cross II, Dorothean Sisters

The Lady Maria Isabel de Vasconcelos,

Pontevedra is where I am now and I recognized with thanks the letter of congratulations from Your Excellency and the Sacred Heart, and in particular your

---

258 Oral Narration of Sister Lucia.

259 MSL I, 2nd M, Ch. II, No. 2, p. 78.

good prayers that I both need and cherish, because it is the only thing that helps me to be able to make myself pleasing to our good God, the only treasure that I seek that makes our happiness, and that I should comfort and love by those who offend and reject to serve. I ask so to keep on asking our good God if He would kindly grant me the grace to sacrifice myself for the love of Him, for the conversion of sinners, for the Priests and in particular for our Holy Father the Pope that both should be specified in the midst of so many current and furious storms.

I am the most humble servant of Your Excellency,
Maria Lucia of Jesus R.S.D

5 | Act of Reparation

One day Sister Dores was walking with the students of Mount Lerez. As she always did when passing by a church, she went in to visit the Blessed Sacrament. Her heart froze with what she saw: the high altar was covered with filthy litter, scattered about were some Hosts, the tabernacle was ajar, giving evidence of a desecration. Some children who had followed them informed her where the pastor of the church lived and she knocked on the door. A very grumpy woman answered and was told of what happened; she replied:

-*Do not worry about it. We are to take care of the Church.*[260]

Without anything more to say, she closed the door in their faces. This saddened Sister Dores even more and she returned to the church to do an act of reparation with the students, then returned home with her heart oppressed. She told the priest who attended the high school about her distress. He volunteered to go collect the hosts. The next day, unsure if they had been consecrated, he consecrated them at Mass and then consumed them.

With her superior's permission, Sister Dores took another sister and some students and cleaned the church, put towels worthy of the altar and left the rags rolled up in the sacristy. Afterwards they sat on the steps of the church and she gave some candy to the children who helped. Sister Dores took the opportunity to question them on their religious education and found that they knew nothing. Some of them were of the age to make their First Communion. She was heartbroken and wanted to help those souls to know and love God. When she returned and told her Mother Superior, she asked permission to go there on Sundays to teach these poor children, but her superior did not see fit for her to go that far and feared that the pastor would not want her. A few days later Sister Dores insisted again on

---

260 *My Pathway,* I, p. 109.

teaching the children, knowing that her superior and the pastor of the church had been thankful for what they did. With much pity and understanding, her superior did not consent, fearing that the long walk Sister Dores would have to make would be too dangerous. Therefore, the students had no catechist and the catechist had no students.

6 | A Grueling Interview

Although Bishop Garcia had promised to visit Sister Dores in Pontevedra, it was not necessary because her Mother Provincial was occasionally called to Tuy to meet with him and they addressed her needs through her Mother Superior.

In early 1936 a writer named Antero de Figueiredo arrived in Pontevedra and wanted to interview Sister Dores to gather material for a book about Fatima. It was not a history book, but a book of art. Lucia informed him that she could only respond with the permission of the Bishop of Leiria. The writer understood and left, returning in the summer with a letter from Mother Provincial. In this letter Mother Monfalim ordered the shepherdess to answer Dr. Antero's questions and asked that the local Mother Superior be present. The shepherdess gave herself to this sacrifice, trusting in the Holy Spirit, but she was torn between the duty to obey and the fear of saying something she should not. It was like a sacrifice with no mercy. She managed to speak by telephone with her Mother Provincial, who reassured her to tell him what she saw but not what she should not reveal. Sister Lucia confessed this interview that lasted several days was one of the worst moments of her life.[261]

7 | At Peace in the Midst of War

What was most feared in Spain happened, and the communist revolution erupted into civil war, flooding the country in a sea of blood and fire, a storm of terror. Russia was spreading its errors, pursuant of the refusal to accept the motherly communication from Our Lady:

-*If what I say to you is done, many souls will be saved and there will be peace… If my requests are heeded, Russia will be converted, and there will be peace, if not, she will spread her errors throughout the world causing wars and persecutions of the Church.*[262]

This "If" of Our Lady is a condition proposed to her children, as stated by Sister Lucia:

261 Cf. MSL I, Introduction, p. 7.
262 MSL I, 4th M, Ch. II, No. 5, p. 178.

This insistent recommendation was not only for the three poor and humble children. No, it is a call for the entire world, all souls, all humanity, believers and unbelievers, because faith is a gift from God and we must ask Him to achieve it: Ask and you shall receive. You have no faith, you ask God for it and He will give it to you, because you that have no faith also have a soul that you need to save so it is not eternally damned.[263]

Lucia faced the dangers with a peaceful heart, even eager to seal her passage through this life with the shedding of blood. She abandoned herself again with heroic love and silent martyrdom through the monotony of each day, as she tells it:

I spent the first few months in Pontevedra during the communist revolution, willing to accept martyrdom if God wanted me to have this grace, but He gave me another martyrdom which at times was not easy, the slow pounding of the hammer of torture and sacrifice of one who refused the pursuer of evil; I continuously lived like the steel file that wears down but I always carried on. Whatever You want, my Lord and my God!

If anyone would come after me, let him deny himself and take up his cross and follow me (Mk 8:34).

Yes! It is the plan outlined by God for my path, renouncing everything of myself. Here there is no greed, illusion, or vanity. I stay here ignored, unknown, forgotten for Love. It is more than being pursued by jealousy, envy, and ambition. It is not to have anything that others might want. It is not to occupy a place to go unnoticed in silence and under cover. It is to follow You Good Jesus in Holy Communion, abandoned in the Tabernacle in the outrage and sacrilege prolonged beyond these times until the end of time. It is the constant renewal of my 'yes.' [264]

8 | Our Lady Asks Again for Prayer and Sacrifice

The humble confidant of Mary redoubled her selfless devotion to prayer and sacrifice, silently being an encouragement to her sisters to seek the sacrificial life. Her eyes were always fixed on God. She invited those who were more intimate with her to take the path of reparation, and she shared with them how to make a Holy Hour.

One day when she was out with a sister, they found a spiny evergreen shrub in bloom with large stems of thorns. Sister Dores began to pick some of the stems, prompting her companion to ask why she wanted them. Sister Dores said:

---

264 *Ibid.* p. 112.

-Our Lord is very offended and seeks reparation.

She invited the sister to also make sacrifices and shared the thorny stems with her. That night the two slept in bed cuddling the stems. But Sister Dores wanted to go further and spread some sugar on the sheet, which aggravated the effect of the thorns and made her whole body raw. She developed a very high fever. Feeling the weight of her conscience for having done penance without permission, she asked her accomplice to hide the stems and to call her confessor before the others found out the reason for her illness. Mother Provincial called the doctor, alarmed at her fever after being so healthy the day before. After making a contrite confession, she asked permission to reveal the reason for her illness to the Mother Provincial, who did not reprimand her. Two days later the shepherdess was healed, to the astonishment of the doctor.[265]

This doctor was a very good friend of the sisters, who offered his services free of charge and he was a communist. When Sister Dores, being an assistant nurse, went to his office to tend the sick sisters the doctor always enjoyed the opportunity to talk with her and promised that he would contemplate her ideas. Later, having been arrested and sentenced to death, he sent a message to Sister Dores to intercede for him before the justices. But that was impossible without her suffering the same sentence. She sent him a crucifix with the assurance of her prayers, and had the consolation of knowing that he turned to God and helped his comrades do the same. There were 30 of them; only one apparently resisted. On the day of their execution, Sister Dores accompanied them in prayer until the last moment of their lives. After confessing and receiving Holy Communion in a Mass celebrated that night in prison by Fr. San Mariano, S.J., they died shouting, "Long live Christ the King."

These executions added to the fear of the communists. One day the pit clogged up and overflowed and the Superior did not know what to do. After fulfilling her other obligations Sister Dores volunteered to do this repulsive work. Two more sisters agreed to help her. At one point one of them became discouraged with that job and fumed:

-This job is so dirty that not even God is here!

Sister Dores, who felt no less disgusted, said with all her soul:

-Oh, Sister, do not say that, because God is everywhere!

While pulling the rake through the deepest part, she noticed something stuck in it. She lifted it and exclaimed:

-Look how God is here!

---

265 Oral Narration of Sister Lucia.

Bishop José Alves Correia da Silva, Bishop of Leiria-Fatima, with Lucia.

Mother Monfalim.

Mother Cunha Matos with Lucia.

It was a rosary. The beads were rotten but not the crucifix. After washing and disinfecting it, with the permission of her Mother Superior, Lucia used this rosary in reparation. Sometime later the communists came to inquire about work for the workers. The Superior and other sisters were filled with fear and did not want to talk to them, so Sister Dores addressed them:

-We have a septic tank that needs to be channeled.

They took note and the work was done. But the Mother Superior did not like that Sister Dores gave the order and scolded her, saying she should not have gotten involved in it. Although she did not like being rebuked she offered it for charity and then said with much grace:

-Mother scolded me, but it's over now![266]

9 | Nothing Would Make Me More Happy Than to Give My Life to God

Sister Dores was in Spain when news of the war in Spain reached the ears of Maria Rosa who was very concerned, not knowing if her daughter had gone to Porto. Maria Rosa wrote to Lucia asking her if she was in Portugal and why she hadn't been informed of it. Sister Dores wrote to reassure her:

JHS

Religious Institute of Saint Dorothy

Pontevedra

June 24, 1936

My dear Mother,

I received your two letters which arrived and I am thankful.

Truly I have neglected to respond to the first. For this reason I hasten to answer this last one to reassure you, thanks to God. I am delighted to tell you that I am well and that it is also good that our family is well, as we have to thank our good God for so many benefits in His Divine mercy that He has given us, that our lives become a continuing act of recognition of the holy Hearts of Jesus and Mary.

I did not know that Maria Lucia had this illness of paralysis. God will cure her if this is His Divine Will, but it seems to me that she would be much happier if God would take her to Heaven; so I ask if someday she will be there. I would be saddened if anyone was with sin, and I ask the same for all my family. As for the benefactors, they have every right to our poor prayers. It is a duty of gratitude to pray and sacrifice for them; therefore, I do not forget them in my poor prayers as this is the will of God. I do not know how they could tell you that I am in Porto; I have not left and I do not know if

---

266 *Ibid.*

my Superiors have the intention to send me out of Pontevedra, due to the situation of the country. It may be that they force us to leave, but in this case I write to you to tell you not to believe what they say to you. Even at the present moment no one has been involved with us and in the future it will be what God wants. Do not be worried; He watches over us, what we want most.

Remember me a lot to the Lady Maria Francisca and to the whole family.

Bless me your daughter who kisses your hand.

Maria Lucia R.S.D.

Because she always trusted in Divine protection and lived with the firm conviction that not a hair of her head would fall out without God allowing it, she remained serene and moved at will. She was happy even in the midst of distress, always looking and wishing for a favorable circumstance to end the problems. She wrote on August 2nd to Father Aparicio:

The Most Rev. Father Aparicio,

Despite being surrounded by so many storms and perils, the good Lord watches over my sisters, so we can say we have gone through fire and water and are left unscathed, thank goodness. Until now we have not had to suffer anything more than a few scares. Actually at the time of greatest danger I did not become frightened, partly because of the trust I had in the Most Holy Hearts of Jesus and Mary and because of the feeling of joy in going to join them in Heaven. But apparently they did not want me there yet. They want me to offer the sacrifice of waiting for the conversion of this nation. I also was not frightened perhaps because of ignoring all the gravity of the danger in which we were. For now, we are in waiting for what will result. We rely on our good God and the protection of the Immaculate Heart of Mary, that soon we will be granted days of peace and quiet. Otherwise I am ready, and I would like nothing more than to give my life for God to somehow repay Him for what He has given to me. However I recognize myself unworthy of such a great favor,

Maria Lucia R.S.D.

10 | Illness and Death of Mother Provincial

The following year in April, 1937, the Mother Provincial, Mother Monfalim, came to Tuy very sick. She immediately gave orders for Sister Dores to return to the Novitiate. In the last hour, she felt that she should not be concerned with her own feelings and decided to move the Shepherdess of Fatima to the place that she promised her and also so she could be next to her. The Mother Superior of

Pontevedra was concerned because Sister Dores was needed at that time of the year and tried to delay this trip to Tuy. But the order was final. Then the Mother Superior wanted to accompany Sister Dores to Tuy with the hope of bringing her back to Pontevedra, which otherwise would not happen.

Mother Monfalim was very ill, worse than previously thought. She had only a few days left on earth. Sister Dores wanted to accompany her in every possible moment, to comfort her with her good humor, which helped distract the sick from their sufferings.

On the 4th day of every month, Sister Dores would pray the novena of Our Lady of Fatima. This May, Mother Monfalim asked her if they could do it together. The novena included the Memorare and three Hail Marys. After the prayer, Mother Monfalim kissed a picture of Our Lady of Fatima, saying:

-*My good Mother, I asked for my healing, but only if that is the will of Our Lord.*

On May 13, rather than improving she worsened, and said:

-*Sister Dores, Our Lady already gave me the answer. I am worse! It is that Our Lord wants to take me to Heaven.*[267]

While sensing the door of eternity opening, her soul was surrounded by a shadow of fear of the moment, and she looked for security in her young confidant. Sister Dores reassured her saying: -*Fear not, Mother Provincial, Our Lady is our Mother! She is here to help you to get to Heaven, her Immaculate Heart throbs with love for us.*

Comforted, Mother Provincial responded: -*You are right and I trust in her protection and her love; she is my Mother!*[268]

With her illness worsening, many of her family members and the Superiors of all the houses in the Province came to visit her. Due to the small number of religious who were left in the house, the Novitiate was again removed to Portugal. Sister Dores had to deal with many of the jobs alone and could no longer stay with Mother Provincial. To accommodate the situation, the Mother Schoolmistress would often replace or help Sister Dores in her work so that she could be free to serve her beloved sick, which she did with great satisfaction.

On the morning of May 31st, the Mother Schoolmistress went looking for Sister Dores to tell her that Mother Monfalim had expressed a desire to eat limes. She wondered where she could get this relatively rare fruit! Sister Dores said she would try to find some, and accompanied by another sister, drove to a farm where she had once seen a lime tree. They soon returned with the desired fruit and peeled some sections to give to her. Mother Monfalim was slowly savoring the

---

267 *Madre Monfalim*, ch. 19, p. 679.
268 Cf. Letter of December 3, 1944, Madre Mariana Cezimbra, *Madre Monfalim*, ch. 91, p. 680.

lime when she received a telegram from the Mother General with a blessing from the Holy Father who was inquiring about her. She asked Sister Dores to go with the same companion to telegraph her answer to Rome. As soon as the two left, Mother Monfalim felt that she was leaving for eternity and began to call:

-Sister Dores! Sister Dores? Where is Sister Dores? I want to see next to me those eyes that saw Our Lady...

But it was not possible. When the two returned from the telegraph, they were surprised to find that Mother Monfalim had died. Sister Dores knelt and prayed silently, crying her eyes out. Then she retired to the chapel and made the Way of the Cross for the eternal rest of her dear Mother Provincial. While immersed in this devotion of suffering, the Mother Schoolmistress came to give her a last message from her Mother. Mother had been:

-... handling a tiny metal image of Our Lady of Fatima, which the Mother Provincial usually had on her bedside table, and realizing that she was dying, took the image, kissed it and handed it to me saying, "give it to Sister Dores, I leave it to Our Lord; do not send her any more to Pontevedra."

This thinking of me by Mother Provincial in her last moment has moved me! And I had desired that Mother die with minimal qualms about me, because God did not give her the grace of my being at her side at the last moment. God's plan! Several times she had said to me: "When I am to die, do not leave me." I had promised it to her, but what are our promises worth when the intentions of God are otherwise![269]

There is a testimony of a sister who said Mother Monfalim died an unhappy death because Sister Dores was not with her, but only God knows her true state at that moment.

Sister Dores helped to shroud the dead body of her Mother and escorted her to the cemetery, reflecting on the words of Jesus: *Be prepared for the Lord will come like a thief in the night, when you least expect* (Mt 24:44), and concluded: *Vanity of vanities, it is not only loving God. Mother Provincial loved God, yes, and this is the only one which is now in the love of God forever!*[270]

According to witnesses, Sister Dores looked as if she was glued to the granite vault where Mother's mortal remains were deposed, seeking the will of God. A sister reminded her of the reality of all that she had gone through, and in silence the seer obeyed. What thoughts and feelings must have occupied her heart and spirit at this time.

A few days after the funeral she wrote to her mother, to whom she had previously requested prayers for Mother Monfalim's improvement. She was still

---

269 *My Pathway*, I, p. 117.
270 *Ibid.*

overcome by the suffering that she saw:

JMJ

Tuy, June 13, 1937

My dear mother,

Just two words to thank you for your letter and to tell you that I am well, thanks to God. Since April 27ᵗʰ I am in Tuy, where I attended to the terrible sickness that led my dearest Mother Provincial to Heaven. I really miss her because Her Reverence was a true mother, a holy superior and a close friend, but our good God wanted to take her to Heaven! May His Holy Will be done.

Please remember me very much to the Lady Maria Francisca and her whole family.

Your daughter will never forget you along with the Hearts of Jesus and Mary.

Maria Lucia of Jesus R.S.D.

The year before, being concerned about the health of Mother Provincial, she had requested of her mother to ask her two nieces to make a novena for her healing:

I ask you to request that Maria Amelia and Etelvina, to my knowledge who are there in the month of September, to pray for 9 days, the Memorare and 3 Hail Marys for the improvement of Mother Provincial, whom Maria Amelia already knows, that they pray fervently at the feet of Our Lady at the Cova da Iria.[271]

Nevertheless, the last wish of Mother Monfalim was that Sister Dores not be sent to Pontevedra anymore. This was not done immediately, so shortly after the funeral Sister Dores departed quietly and obediently to Pontevedra. When the new Mother Provincial, Maria do Carmo Corte Real, visited the house in Tuy, she was surprised that the Seer of Fatima was not there and called Pontevedra to tell her to return to Tuy. The new Mother Provincial also appointed a new Superior of the House of Tuy, Mother Cunha Matos, who assigned Sister Dores in charge of habit clothing and the student dining room, and also named her sacristan. It was the end of the year 1937, which had been the most violent of the war in Spain.

11 | Back in Tuy

In 1939 the war ended, but there was much hunger. It was difficult to find food and it was very expensive. The Dorothean Sisters went frequently to Valença do Minho to get essentials and often they sent Sister Dores on this mission

---

271 Letter written to her mother in the summer of 1936.

because of her relationships near the border. She recalled staying at the home of the Franciscan Hospitable Sisters of the Immaculate Conception at the Asilo Fonseca. According to the testimony of a sister at that time, the first thing Sister Dores did when she arrived was enter the chapel to make a visit to her Jesus. After her visit, they decided what they needed from this hospitable house and loaded the supplies into the car, typically a taxi.

Since the times were so difficult, the sister in charge of their pantry feared they would run out of provisions and would ration them so they would last longer. But sometimes this sacrifice did not achieve what was intended because eventually the supplies got old and ruined, benefitting no one. Sister Dores fell to weakness as did other sisters, because of sickness and hunger.

The food was of very poor quality and there was no bread. For breakfast they would boil for three hours *cascarilla,* which is a bark of cocoa and drink this bitter water with milk and no sugar. There was only enough for some of the sick sisters to have a small amount. They received small quantities of potatoes, lentils and beans from a co-op. Once the sisters in the Community were fasting and when the sisters arrived from Valença with some bread, it was a small treat for them.

Despite their weakness, they accomplished all the work needed. One day Sister Dores seemed to use all of her strength to clean off the wax from the chandelier. Another sister came to call her to the cafeteria where the other sisters had already received a small piece of bread to stave off hunger. Sister Dores, perhaps eager to offer this sacrifice to the Lord, decided not to go. Not being able to convince her, the sister affectionately told her not to be so stubborn. When she reached the door of the dining-hall, she was met by the custodian who saw one more person to feed. Sister Dores, who liked to joke, grabbed the bag of bread and ran away laughing as she said:

-*Oh! Jesus! Here comes another one! I'll eat all the bread and have nothing to put on the table for dinner.*[272]

Everyone laughed and Sister Dores returned to her job with the same hunger, but happy to be able to offer another sacrifice. It is certain that when she reached the chapel, she would have genuflected deeply in front of the Hidden Jesus and repeated with all the fervor of her heart:

-*Oh Jesus, it is for love of You, for the conversion of sinners, and in reparation for the sins committed against the Immaculate Heart of Mary.*[273]

It is very likely she experienced deeply this sacrifice of hunger, but embraced these thorns for what they merited.

---

272 Oral Narration of Sister Lucia.
273 MSL I, 2ndM, Ch. II, No. 6, p. 87–88.

These days were followed by several more years of scarcity, particularly during the Spanish Civil War, which greatly afflicted this nation. World War II came and famine followed everywhere this devastating cyclone hit.

When Mother Cunha Matos came to Tuy as Superior, she saw how difficult it was to get food for the sisters, and asked Sister Dores if she knew someone who could help them find groceries. Sister Dores responded with all honesty:

-I know, Mother Superior, but we are far away from these people and I did not dare to make any requests.

At that Mother said:

-Leave these things, Sister, and do what you can.[274]

She soon returned with the necessary provisions for the pantry.

With her life in full communion with God, Sister Dores felt peace inside and displayed this inner freedom to others. Despite accepting sufferings of all kinds, she did not fail to spread joy and good humor, which lightened the crosses of those around her.

There was a very timid sister who confessed that some things frightened her. Sister Dores remembered that she had played a prank on this sister. It was an hour before bedtime and Sister Dores tied a few bells to the bar of the bed and when the moment came to turn off the lights, she pulled on the wire connected to the bells and began shouting when the bells rang. The poor sister thought it was an alarm. All of this was drowned out by all the sisters laughing underneath their sheets. But then Sister Dores received a talk from Mother Superior, who also was amused, but she had to follow the rules.

One day during their break and before the Holy Hour began, Sister Dores pulled a prank on another sister. This sister confessed that when she finished the Holy Hour, she felt cold and did not want to stay for the Hour of Reparation because this second hour was optional. When the sister went to bed, she found eleven canisters filled with cold water! She patiently removed them from the bed and placed them in a row along the wall, knowing it was Sister Dores who did this. She confirmed her suspicion when she found hidden at the end of the bed a bottle filled with hot water and wrapped in woolen cloths, to repay her for the work she had done for others. The fact is that Sister Dores could be playful without lacking charity.

She once told of finding a purple hat and decided to play a joke. With the hat on her head, she entered the recreation room and told a sister whose last name was Roxo (Purple):

---

274 Oral Narration of Sister Lucia.

-O Sister Purple, look at your father's hat.

The Sister argued that her father was not Purple, but Sister Dores stated:

-It is purple, it is!

All joined in the joke and laughed very much.

12 | At the Beach

Looking back at an earlier time at the end of the school year of 1931, Sister Dores was lacking strength, and not in very robust health. Her doctor advised that she spend a month at the beach every year. The first two years she accompanied Mother Refojo to the home of her sister who lived with a niece on the island of Rianjo. Here, alternating between rest, sea baths, and exercising, Sister Dores would go to the sea early in the morning to avoid meeting others, and accommodate the ladies throughout the rest of the day while not neglecting her life of piety. She continued to fulfill her daily times of prayer, reading and examination of conscience. After attending Mass at the church they would return home to eat breakfast, and Sister Dores helped clean the house and kitchen. She enjoyed their gatherings and was able to rest, free from the curious gazes of others.

Noting that several other sisters needed the sea air, Mother Provincial rented a house in La Toja where they could stay. Some went for eight days; others for fifteen days. Sister Dores went for a month.

One night the tide rose very high and flooded the house. The sisters awoke with the sea inside the house and their beds almost floating away. Soon a party atmosphere broke out. All stood up to clean the house amid great joy. This extraordinary event excused them from the period of silence and Sister Dores being the first at work and full of energy, used this opportunity to enjoy herself and transmit that joy to the others They followed a lighter schedule after this incident but strictly enforced attending Mass, a visit to the Blessed Sacrament, the rosary and plenty of time on the beach. Once the sisters were in the chapel and had a hard time concentrating. They heard a strange and bothersome noise and were shocked at what they saw—the sacristan dusting the altar with something like a horsehair whip. They were so tempted to burst out laughing that they had to leave the chapel out of respect for the Blessed Sacrament. On another afternoon a man arrived and identified himself to a Dorothean Sister. She recognized his Portuguese accent and he asked if it was possible to see Lucia to whom Our Lady had appeared. The sister that he was speaking to was Lucia but he wasn't aware of it. She responded that it was possible if allowed by the superiors. The man asked again if she was in Tuy. Lucia responded with the whole truth:

-Not now!

-Would you go to see if she is here?

-It's not worth it. She is a sister just like the others….

-This is not quite so, because she always saw Our Lady.

-This is true, however, she looks at her the same as I …

-So that's it; if you cannot see her, you cannot see. Patience! [275]

After some time conversing about other matters, he departed. Sister Lucia felt fortunate to have escaped being identified. In these circumstances, the other sisters did not intervene in the conversation, lest they slip and unwittingly identify what she wanted to hide. But sometimes she went through a lot of trouble to remain serious. As soon as they were alone, they exploded with laughter, as it was difficult to contain themselves during the conversation.

13 | Saving Young Children

One year while at the beach, Sister Dores became ill with an acute colitis. She was attended by Dr. Peña from the Grand Hotel at the beach, who despite his communist ideology, treated her with respect and provided the drugs needed for her recovery. However, the merciful hand of God was at work during this illness, also recovering some lost sheep. When Sister Dores was better, the doctor asked permission to introduce his wife to her. After assessing his good intentions she agreed to meet with them that afternoon on the sidewalk near the pine forest. She was surprised when she saw the doctor accompanied by two young ladies. Being a mature person, he withdrew after their greeting leaving only the ladies. His 'wife' revealed her identity and Sister Dores learned that she had been educated in a college of Dorothean Sisters in Sintra. Leaving a young son in the care of her parents, she abandoned her husband and left for Madrid with a maid who had also abandoned a husband, and there found the doctor whom she began living with as if married.

Soon the doctor rejoined them, and Sister Dores wasted no time in targeting the truth and working to save these souls. Her words fell like lightning in the dark of night and illuminated their consciences, which soon opened to the light of grace. The doctor told Sister Dores that he was not happy with the weight that he carried. She proposed that he change his life and he found that echoed in his soul, which was thirsting for peace. She procured a meeting for the doctor with a priest and hoped it would not be a problem for him. To her surprise, it was not a

---

275 *Ibid.*

problem.   He agreed to a separation and offered to take them to Tuy and Valença, where the parents of the lady came to get them. With some regret, Sister Dores was not able to follow up and stay in touch with them, but these souls were very present in her prayers.

She spent some time on the beaches in Marin and Placeres. One morning on the beach she saved the lives of two children who almost drowned. Sister Dores told the story:

-*There were some women there collecting seaweed that the waves were dragging out. With them were two children playing in the sand. The sea here is ordinarily gentle, but on this day, the sea was a bit strong. I braced myself for the bath and waited for calmer moments. I climbed to the top of some rocks to harvest shellfish (limpets). Soon I heard some distressing screams. I looked and saw the poor women calling out as a strong wave dragged the little ones away.*

I threw off the mariner dress that was hindering me and jumped into the water. I managed to grab one of the children and bring her out. At first I didn't see the other, but soon discovered her leaning on a rock where, fortunately, she was trapped, wedged between rocks. I pulled her out with the help of Our Lady to whom I called, and managed to save those two lives. After a few agonizing moments during which the children vomited up the sea water they had swallowed, the poor women did not know how to thank me. "You have to thank the Virgin that was here and not me," I told them, to instill in them devotion to Our Lady. In fact, I believed that it was she who helped me because although swimming was easy for me, the affliction was enough to stop me.[276]

This event was sweetness throughout her life. She always had an indescribable brightness in her eyes when talking about it.

In the hours she spent alone sitting on a rock sunbathing, Sister Dores was occupied by praying, reading or writing, and enjoying the time away from all the probing eyes that secretly tried to see what she was writing. In the summer of 1932, she wrote a long poem entitled "The Cross." Several stanzas show the serene but constant groan deep in her soul on fire with love of souls:

> O Cross in blessings so flowering,
> With enchanting love this soul praises You;
> I sat in Your shadow, I found peace, life.
> I fell in Your arms and I am happy.

> Calls to me the soul of the poor sinner,

---

276 *My Pathway*, I, p. 86 – 87.

Next to the black abyss where it goes down.
I am a victim offered in the arms of the Lord,
My life in blood for Him until death.
La Toja, 1932[277]

14 | Tireless Messenger

In the latter years when she lived in Spain, Sister Dores devoted herself with all her heart to an additional role that filled her soul—teaching catechism and guiding the children of the Churches of St. Bartholomew, St. Francis, and two chapels in the vicinity of Tuy. She loved doing this. It was a dream that was within her apostolic heart. There are testimonies in which she took great care in preparing the children with much love. The Prior of St. Francis said the children who were prepared by Sister Dores stood out among all the others, and could also confess much better. She also took care of their physical needs, asking the aid of friends and supporters for this purpose. In a letter to a friend in October, 1941, she expressed her gratitude for the alms received on behalf of the young children who were so poorly dressed:

Dear Friend,

... I thank you for such a generous donation that you deigned to send to me for the poor children of my catechesis. May our good God and our dear Mother in Heaven reward you for so much charity. The box with everything in it arrived here without any problems. I ask that you thank your good brother and sister for me. I am sincerely grateful to them and I will have these children pray for their intentions. In particular we will offer up the rosary at Christmas and all Sundays when we pray at 5 p.m.[278]

Many girls during this postwar period were poor and had difficulties in their families. For their Solemn Communion, she made dresses for them with permission from her Superiors, adapting little white gowns from the habits of the sisters. She wanted this special day to be very memorable for them, and its value meaningful.

Sister Dores was happy to be able to give these children clothes made by her own hands. Some were dressed so scarcely and miserably. She was so fond of giving. Besides helping with their physical necessities, she offered the treasure in her heart—her love for God and Our Lady, which opened their innocent hearts. She prepared them well for the love of God and taught them the love of reparation for the salvation of souls.

---

277 *Archives- Carmel of Coimbra.*
278 Letter of October 24, 1941, Rita Lucia Neves.

Sister Dores had a special way of telling the story of Fatima; they were mesmerized by her words, and full of enthusiasm afterwards to imitate the shepherds. She carried a burning fire within her. Whenever she encountered an opportunity to ignite that flame in some other heart, she did not miss it. In children especially, the fire spread generously in the fertile soil of their pure hearts. But the Shepherdess was not only available for children. At home, she taught catechism to a group of servants and the result of this was so well-known that the ladies whom they served also asked to attend lessons.

Dorothean Sisters.

Lucia writing.

Bishop José Alves Correia da Silva
with Lucia as a Dorothean Sister.

Hands of Sister Lucia with a few volumes of her writings.

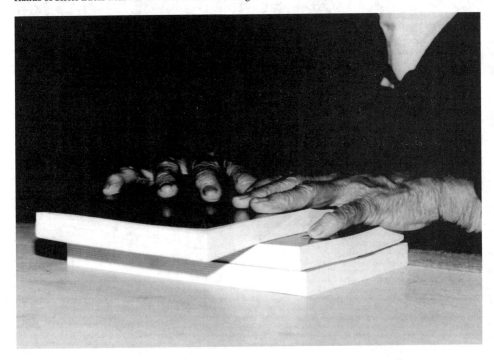

CHAPTER XII
WRITING UNDER OBEDIENCE

1 | Obeying - She Wrote

In 1935 the Bishop of Leiria ordered Sister Dores to write down the memories she had of Jacinta. This request came after His Excellency read a letter from the shepherdess thanking him for the photos of Jacinta taken when she was transferred from the cemetery of Ourem to Fatima. Noting the enthusiasm about her cousin in the letter, the Bishop thought that one should not lose this memory so rich. And so Lucia's First Memoir was written. Later, after being subjected to the interrogation of Dr. Antero de Figueiredo, the Bishop told Sister Dores to write down everything that related to the story of Fatima. She provided Rev. José Galamba with the elements to write the book of Jacinta. Like the first time, she had difficulty getting permission from her Superior because it was rare for a Sister helpmate to write and it would invite attention and curious inquiries as to what she was writing.

She did not have a room to herself and could only write at night because she had to perform her duties during the day. Also the lights had to be off at a certain time, so she could not write in her bedroom. She would have to conceal her writing in the classroom and then go to bed with a thousand cares not to disturb the sisters. When she could write during the day, she went to a corner in the attic where she would not be discovered, writing under the light of a glass tile.

-Those moments were still frequently interrupted by the ringing of the bell that called me. Often it happened to be the Vice Superior that asked:

-Where have you been, daughter, no one can find you?

I answered:

-I was up in the cupboard of the sacristy. I have a lot to do there.

-But I was looking for you and opened the door and I did not see you.

The reason was that inside there is a smaller door where it was perforated on the loft of the roof where I was concealed.[279]

It was with much repugnance that Sister Dores fulfilled this obedience, because she did not understand the paternal guidance of the Bishop. She confessed:

-The Bishop of Tuy, Antonio Garcia y Garcia, was still guiding my steps as he had been long ago. I feel that God fulfills me in what the Psalmist tells us:

"He ordered His Angels to guard you and lead you in all your ways. And taking you by the hand, lead you lest you dash your foot against the stone." So I also understand the phrase of the same prophet: "When you look for God, He is radiant with joy." In

---

279 *My Pathway*, I, p. 144.

this way, suffering becomes a joy because as St. Augustine said: "If you have not or if you suffer, that suffering is Love!"

To achieve this, it is humility that is the strength, because grace falls to the souls who are humble, and then everything sings in their heart the hymn of Love! In the abyss of my nothingness, I felt elevated to the heights of the Infinite! The mystery of pain and love![280]

Before its publishing the Bishop of Leiria sent Sister Dores the book about Jacinta, asking her to fix what was not correct. She responded quickly from the heart. She wrote as if *"obeying an inspiration,"* and moved by the Spirit of God she almost did not even realize what she wrote:

Most Reverend Bishop,

I was very impressed with "Jacinta" with some of the things revealed in secret, and in her love for the Holy Father and for sinners. She said to me many times: 'Poor Holy Father! I feel sorry for sinners!' If she was living now when these things are so close at hand, how much more it is evident! If the world only knew that moment when grace is still granted if they do penance!

Time passes, the souls do not die, and eternity remains!

I see in the Immense Light that is God, the earth is shaken and trembles before the breath of His voice: cities and villages buried, destroyed, defenseless people swallowed by the hills; I see the falls amid thunder and lightning, rivers and seas overflowing (and) floods, and souls sleeping in the sleep of death! Men still keep on plotting wars, ambitions, destruction and death...

I feel myself in a mystery of Light—this mystery that comes from faith in God, God in me and I am nothing, lost in the Light as a small drop of alcohol thrown in the flame, and I was within the flame. It gave me another appearance, a faint reflection, and I found in her strength, grace, life, peace and love.

It is the mystery of faith, of hope, of certainty, of justice, of compassion and of love! Eternal God, God the immense, uncreated Light, a mirror where everything passes, where everything reflects, that penetrates everything, where nothing escapes! Mirror of the Eternal wisdom, of the Eternal power, the wanting of the Immense, the Infinite Kindness, Patience and Love!

Yes, God is patient, waiting, God is good, forgiving, God is love and He loves us! But, either way, it demands our correspondence, our allegiance and our faithfulness! God is the Lord and I His humble servant.[281]

This explosion of intimate confidence must have been the origin of the

---

280 *Ibid.* p. 123 – 124.
281 *Ibid.* p. 124 – 125.

order given by Bishop José Alves Correia da Silva a few years later for Sister Dores to write the third part of the Secret. Sometime later, Rev. Galamba needed some clarification and with the permission from the Bishop, scheduled an interview with the seer in Tuy. But there was some difficulty with his passport and Sister Dores had to travel to Valença, where they were able to talk. A Mother Superior accompanied her as usual and was present during the interview, which was a great suffering for the poor shepherdess, who had spent so much time writing without being discovered and now had to answer everything with great reserve. Sister Dores knew that these things always aroused curiosity, even without malicious intent.

2 | The First Letter to the Pope

In 1940, she was called upon by the Bishop of Leiria, the Bishop of Gurza, and her Superior to write her first letter to the Holy Father, Pius XII, requesting the Consecration of Russia to the Immaculate Heart of Mary. Much evil had already taken place, but if the request could be fulfilled, much more evil would be avoided. It is a great mystery where God submits to the will of men! But He does so for the sake of the Church that its members practice humility received from the light from Heaven through a humble, brilliant, almost invisible person. The poor souls chosen to convey these messages also have to practice deep humility to even dare to communicate the messages from Heaven.

With her tenderhearted charm, Sister Lucia could talk about God to little children and this was for her the sweetest honey. But it was difficult for her to talk to the Princes of the Church. It was a sacrifice offered through obedience. Humbly, she asked for help to carefully word the letter, which follows:

Holy Father,

Humbly lying prostrate at the feet of Your Holiness, I come as the last sheep of the flock entrusted to the custody of your Holiness, to faithfully open my heart at the order of my spiritual director. I am the only survivor of the children to whom Our Lady deigned to appear in Fatima (Portugal) on the 13th of May to October, 1917. The Blessed Virgin has granted me many graces, the largest being my admission to the Institute of Saint Dorothy.

I ask you, Holy Father, to review my requests that I have already sent several times to Your Holiness.

The request, Most Holy Father, is from Our Lord and our good Mother in Heaven.

In 1917, in part of the apparitions that we have designated as the secret, the Blessed Virgin revealed the end of the war which then afflicted Europe and announced another in the future, saying to prevent this, she would ask for the consecration of Russia to her Immaculate Heart and the Communion of Reparation on the First Saturday, promising conversion of that nation and peace if her requests were met.

Otherwise she announced that Russia would spread her errors throughout the world, causing wars and persecutions of the Holy Church, martyrdom of many Christians, several persecutions and sufferings destined for Your Holiness and the annihilation of various nations.

Most Holy Father, until 1926, I was silent, according to the expressed order of Our Mother. Then after a revelation I was asked to propagate throughout the world, a Communion of Reparation on the First Saturdays of five consecutive months, to confess, to meditate on the mysteries of the Rosary for 15 minutes, and pray a rosary in reparation for the outrages, sacrileges and indifferences committed against Her Immaculate Heart. Those who practice this devotion our kind heavenly Mother will assist at the hour of death with all the graces necessary for salvation.

I have explained the request of Our Lady to my confessor who employed some means that it would be made known. But only on September 13, 1939, His Excellency the Bishop of Leiria, deigned in Fatima to make public this request of Our Lady.

I, Holy Father, at this time ask Your Holiness to bless and extend this devotion throughout the world. In 1929, Our Lady through another apparition, asked for the consecration of Russia to Her Immaculate Heart, promising to hereby prevent the spread of their errors and for their conversion.

Sometime later, I gave this consideration to my confessor at the request of Our Lady. His Reverence employed some means to implement and make it reach the knowledge of His Holiness Pope Pius XI.

In several intimate communications with Our Lord, He has not stopped insisting on this request, promising lately, if Your Holiness deigns to make the consecration of the world to the Immaculate Heart of Mary with a special mention for Russia, and order that in union with Your Holiness at the same time with all the Bishops of the world, He would shorten the days of tribulation with which He has determined to punish the nations for their crimes by means of war, famine, and several persecutions against the Holy Church and Your Holiness.

I truly feel, Most Holy Father, the suffering of Your Holiness, and as is possible for me, with my poor prayers and sacrifices, I try to lessen them from Our Good Lord and the Immaculate Heart of Mary.

Most Holy Father, if I am not mistaken, it is in the union of my soul with God that Our Lord promised to be attentive to the consecration made by the Bishops of our *nation to the Immaculate Heart of Mary, that a special protection would be granted to our country in this war and this protection will be the proof of graces that would be granted to other nations if they are consecrated to her.*

Now, Most Holy Father, allow me only one more request that is a burning desire in my poor heart, that the devotion in honor of the Immaculate Heart of Mary be extended to the world as an important action in the Holy Church.

With the greatest respect and reverence I beseech Your Apostolic Blessing.

God keep Your Holiness.

Tuy, Spain, December 2, 1940

Sr. Maria Lucia

3 | Our Lord Makes a Request to the Bishops of Spain

Sister Lucia had a Holy Hour every Thursday from 11:00 p.m. to midnight. Sometimes she would ask permission to be in the chapel from the start of the evening recreation. She loved to spend these hours alone before the Blessed Sacrament. During these times of intimacy with the Lord of her life, exposed to His light she could see in His truth.

During the recreation time at night I was alone with the Blessed Sacrament in the chapel, which was only lit up by a pale glow of the lamp. Kneeling in the middle of the Holy Communion rail, meditating on the mystery of the Divine Presence in the august Sacrament, the good God communicated Himself to my soul so deeply that I felt crushed by the force of love, the humiliation, and the abatement of my own nothingness. But love, when it annihilates, purifies and gives life; when it is slaughtered, it gives strength; when it humiliates, it gives light and raises the intimate union.

It is the heart that He consumes and purifies of its own miseries; it is the pride which He destroys with the strength of humiliation in His presence; it is the nature that He slaughters by lifting it to the regions of sacrifice, renunciation, immolation through Him and for Him.

For You my God, I wait for the grace to follow faithfully in what You want of me and I give everything to You! I will sing to the Lord a new song, resound my praises at the meeting of the Saints.

I will accompany my song with the psaltery and the sound of the zither, because You have delighted me Lord, with Your mercy. [282]

There were nights in which she struggled with sleep. After a day of work, her body was often weakened from lack of rest or by penance that she practiced

---

282 *My Pathway,* I, p. 139.

139

A sós com Jesus Sacramentado

29-5-1941 - Fiquei só com Jesus Sacramentado na capela, desde o fim do recreio da noite até à meia noite, alumiada apenas pelo pálido clarão da lâmpada.

Ajoelhada no meio junto ao degrau da mesa da Sag. Comunhão, meditava no mistério da Divina presença no augusto Sacramento, e o Bom Deus comunicou-se tão intensamente à minha alma que me senti aniquilada com a força do Amor, na humilhação, no abatimento do próprio nada. Mas o Amor quando aniquila purifica e dá vida, quando abate dá força, quando humilha dá luz e levanta à íntima união.

É o coração que Ele consome e purifica das próprias misérias, é o orgulho que Ele aniquila com a força da humilhação na sua presença, é a natureza que Ele abate levantando-a às regiões do sacrifício, da renúncia, da imolação por Ele e para Ele.

De Ti meu Deus, espero a graça de seguir com fidelidade o que de mim quereis, dar-Te tudo, dar-me toda!

«Cantarei ao Senhor, um cântico novo e ressoarão os meus louvores na reunião dos Santos.

Acompanharei o meu cântico com o saltério e com o sonido da cítara. Porque me havereis deleitado Senhor, com a Vossa misericórdia...

Avé-Maria!

Original manuscript by Sister Lucia, My Pathway, p. 139.

discreetly. But she was thirsty to repair the Heart of God and to intercede for the Holy Father, for the Holy Church, for the conversion of sinners and for the sanctification of priests, and for Spain and Russia that she carried always in her heart. She prayed, implored, offered up, and sometimes asked the Lord for more suffering.

In these hours of greatest recollection, usually the good Lord communicated so intensely to my poor soul that I do not have any doubt of His real presence. Ordinarily, after being absorbed in my own nothingness and misery, feeling what displeases Him in me, I continue to pray and lament certain situations and pray for other events in the poor world, both so much disliked.[283]

On the evenings of the 12th and 13th of the month, she was spiritually united to Fatima, praying in the midst of the crowd of pilgrims, with them and for them. These dates were so ingrained in her that nothing could erase them. Sometimes she obtained permission to stay in prayer all night. This happened on June 12, 1941, a Thursday, the day of Corpus Christi. It was a special vigil. That night Our Lord asked her to give a message to the Archbishop of Valladolid, who wanted to do something to restore the fervor in the Church in Spain. Her letter of 1943 confirmed this request:

If the Bishops of Spain were brought together in a house for the intention of making a retreat and agreed on ways to lead the souls entrusted to them, they would receive the light of the Holy Spirit and special graces. I convey this message to the Archbishop that He ardently wishes that the Bishops gather in retreat and agree to reform the ways of Christian people and to remedy the weaknesses of the clergy and a large portion of Religious men and women. The number of those who serve Him in the practice of sacrifice is very limited. He desires souls and priests who serve Him and sacrifice for Him and for all souls.[284]

She prayed:

-Oh, my good Jesus, I feel the bitterness of Your Heart in feeling the loss of souls. I feel I cannot do anything more for You and for them, the souls of Your people. I also, as You know, have great difficulty in saying to this Bishop that You wish him to remedy these evils. Otherwise, if this is Your desire I am here, I will wait for the opportune time, and I hope that You will help me here and always! Oh how sad and painful is the retreat of consecrated souls. Lord, I am afraid of myself, help my extreme weakness.[285]

At this time she had not managed to be faithful to the first opportunity of informing the Bishop and she felt that the Lord was upset with her. It was a very

283   Letter of January 31, 1943, Bishop Garcia.

284   *Ibid.*

285   *My Pathway,* I, p. 140.

heavy cross for her. She wrote to her spiritual director, the Bishop of Gurza, asking if he would communicate this request to the Archbishop of Valladolid, without saying where it came from. She received a response to this request in a letter from the Bishop of Gurza, who ordered her to send the letter to the Archbishop of Valladolid. She had no choice, and with the pain of obeying she did so in the month of January 1943. She received a fatherly rebuke for not being more open.

4 | Silver Anniversary of the Apparitions

In the meantime, on May 13, 1942, two Silver Anniversaries would take place: the Silver Anniversary of the First Apparition of Fatima and the Silver Anniversary of His Holiness Pope Pius XII, who was actually consecrated a Bishop on May 13, 1917. Some days before, the Bishop of Leiria, while in Valença do Minho, asked Sister Lucia if she thought it would be a good idea if the Bishops of Portugal asked the Holy Father to make the Consecration of the World to the Immaculate Heart of Mary on this anniversary. Sister Lucia said yes because the consecration had been made before but not in the way Our Lady requested.

The Consecration was made on October 31, 1942, but as Sister Lucia explained, this was also not valid because it was not done in union with all the Bishops of the world, a condition requested by Our Lady.

Every effort to respond to the request of Heaven, though incomplete, is received with love by the Heart of the Father, who knows His children are weak and always needing more impetus. In a letter to the Bishop of Leiria, Sister Lucia confessed some of her intimacies with Our Lord and His Mother:

The good Lord has already shown me His delight by this act. Even though it was incomplete "according to His desire" with the Holy Father and several bishops, in exchange He promises to bring an end soon to the war, and the conversion of Russia will not be now. The good Lord Himself will be pacified, but bitterly and painfully complains about the extremely limited number of souls in grace who are willing to resign themselves to what is required of them in observance of His Law.

This is now the penance that our good Lord asks: "The sacrifice that all people have to impose on themselves is to lead a life of righteousness in the observance of His Law, and to do this to make clear the way for souls, because many judge the meaning of the word penance in great austerity, they do not feel the strength and pleasure to do it and are discouraged in a life of weakness and sin."

Being in the chapel on the 5th to the 6th with permission of my Mother Superiors, at midnight Our Lord told me: "The sacrifice of each one required is the fulfilment of their own duty and observance of My Law; it is penance that is now demanded and asked."[286]

It was 25 years earlier, May 13, 1917, that the little Shepherdess was experiencing indescribable emotion while keeping silent. On May 10, 1942, she wrote to the Bishop of Leiria, promising her spiritual presence on this occasion and confessing her deep gratitude for all the Bishops had already done to satisfy the desires of the Mother of Heaven:

On the days of the 12th and 13th, I will be there spiritually, joining all the prayers and sacrifices to give thanks to God and the Immaculate Heart of Mary, for so many people and so many great graces thay have deigned to grant us. And the 10 days that follow, I will offer up for the Bishops who are doing the retreat, all my poor prayers and sacrifices, and there is no doubt that in a special way I will offer them for His Excellency. I will ask in particular on these days that the most Sacred Hearts of Jesus and Mary grant a reward to everyone with abundant graces for so much work and sacrifices undertaken for His glory.[287]

On the anniversary of the 13th, she suffered alone in her heart the silence that surrounded her. To protect her and as a measure of prudence, her Mother Superiors did not speak to her about Fatima, though their devotion to Our Lady of Fatima was alive in their hearts. The shepherdess suffered the pangs of separation from Fatima, imagining what it would be like if she was there. She experienced all these feelings and sufferings as part of her human nature, but she did not stop there. She used it as a springboard to deliver to the Lady of her life new roses stripped of leaves and dyed with the blood of her heart, and scented with a love never contradicted and always self-sacrificing, to be accepted by Mary *as a rough hidden stone in the foundation of her Triumph!*[288]

She looked at Portugal as she did many times, casting her gaze on the horizon that was so close by. From Tuy she could see her homeland! And the longing in her heart rose like a high tide, but she learned to master her feelings, suffering internally and without any awareness of those near her. She once lamented:

-It seems that it is with nostalgia that Our Lord wants to make me win Heaven... Thankfully, He is so great and so beautiful... I am not surprised that the pain is so costly...[289]

She lived in Spain, but her heart was in the Serra de Aire, and her spirit was in Fatima during the months of the jubilee and the celebration of the apparitions. She was informed of the celebrations that followed especially through Bishop de

---

286 Letter of April 20, 1942.
287 Letter of May 10, 1942.
288 *My Pathway*, I, p. 146.
289 Letter of May 26, 1946, Madre Cunha Matos.

Silva, and she participated in them with her prayers which she wrote about in a letter to him:

Thank you for the news of the great celebration that will be held at Fatima on the 13th. There in spirit I will pass this great day by joining with my poor and humble prayers of consecration to many souls gathered there, and especially to the Bishops, asking especially for the intentions and need of Your Excellency.[290]

In November, feeling the need to reiterate her deep gratitude for everything that had been done in honor of God through His Mother, she wrote one more time to the Bishop of Leiria, acknowledging that her soul was especially grateful for the act of consecration made by the Holy Father on October 31, 1942.

I feel confused with the distinguished grace that our good Lord has just granted us. It is my great sense of gratitude to Him, with the Heart of Our Immaculate Mother and with the Holy Father, that Your Excellency had reason to tell me in your last letter that there were many graces Heaven had given me and little time to thank Him. So it is, and will be multiplied in such great numbers that the same eternity will be little to show my thanks to God, so I ask you willingly to also thank Him for me.[291]

5 | Death of Lucia's Mother

During the year of the Silver Jubilee of the apparitions, the Lady more brilliant than the sun came to take home to eternity the one who bore the pain and cross of the heavenly revelations next to the shepherdess—Maria Rosa. She died on July 16, 1942, the day the Church celebrates Our Lady of Mount Carmel, in whose image Our Lady appeared in Fatima on October 13, 1917. Maria Rosa never dared to confess that she was a true believer in the apparitions because she thought it was too great a thing to happen in her family. Perhaps like the Virgin of Nazareth chosen to be the Mother of God, she thought it could have been any other person, but God chooses the lowly, poor and humble. When Maria Rosa entered into the eternal Light and saw the truth, she no doubt offered her praise without end to the two Hearts.

Sister Lucia noted that death is always painful for those who remain on this side. Though faith sheds light in these moments and gives meaning to the passage to the other side, human nature suffers. The ties that weave life together are broken, and the closer the person is the more it hurts. She wrote of this time:

The flight of my mother to Heaven:

It was on July 16, 1942, when around 4 p.m. my sister Gloria called and gave me

---

290 Letter of October 9, 1942.
291 Ibid.

the news of the departure of our dear mother to Heaven.

It was the Feast Day of Our Lady of Mount Carmel, and I hoped that she was welcomed by her motherly arms to carry her to Heaven.

But despite all this hope, with faith that enlightens my spirit, natural death always comes wrapped up in the cause of sin and therefore feels the weight of the punishment and the darkness of the grave, besides the nostalgia which brings the separation and makes us shed tears of pain.

Our Lady also wept at the death of her beloved Son, and knew within 3 days He would be resurrected again.

I know that I am going to see my mother in Heaven and this certainty mitigates in me the bitterness and alleviates the nostalgia.

I feel more for her than for me.

Days before having taken to her bed foreseeing her end was near, it was impossible to place a phone call to say goodbye to her poor daughter who was so far away. God allowed this small consolation to be denied – Hail Mary! I love You, my Jesus! [292]

Always alive and well in her heart was a burning love for the salvation of souls, and everything was transformed into an offering for those who wait for help to return to God. In a letter written to a friend in August 1942, she confessed:

Dear Friend,

I have here your two cards of condolence and the latest I received three days ago. I thank you and I am appreciative of them, in particular for your prayers for my late mother. I actually feel strongly the natural yearning and the sacrifice of not having been able to give her a final farewell in this life, but for the sake of our good Lord and for the conversion of so many miserable sinners, all the sacrifices are few and I feel happy to give all for our good Lord and the Immaculate Heart of our good Mother in Heaven if asked of me. As for my dear mother, I fully trust in the protection of the Immaculate Heart of Mary who loved her with fondness. I must thank Heaven for her virtue that I have received and that led her immediately to enjoy and be happy in the company of Heaven. She will look after those left here on earth waiting for that happy moment of joining her in the eternal possession of Our God. [293]

A few months before her mother died, she envisioned how painful this was going to be for her and was fearful of denying God the entirety of her heart. She wrote to a priest friend:

... I do not know why death brings something of pity and sorrow for the poor human nature. Is this piece of flesh that we have in our chest not just to love God only? Patience; after all I want what God wants and I did not ask Him anything other than

292 *My Pathway,* I, p. 146 – 147.
293 Letter of August 23, 1942, Rita Lucia Neves.

to do His Most Holy Will.[294]

6 | New Message from Our Lord to the Bishops of Spain

In June of the following year, the Archbishop of Valladolid, wanting to respond to the request that the Lord had asked of him through his humble servant, decided to consecrate his diocese to the Immaculate Heart of Mary. This solemn ceremony was held in Tuy. Sister Dores chose to stay with the Hidden Jesus, to live this great emotion with Him.

On June 13, 1943, the Archbishop of Valladolid, Tuy, came to consecrate the diocese to the Immaculate Heart of Mary. This act was clothed with great solemnity within the presence of religious and civil authorities. Almost everyone was watching in the Community, but I preferred to unite myself spiritually during those hours with my beloved Jesus in the Tabernacle alone. These moments are always very emotional for me and so I prefer as much as possible to pass them alone with God in the intimacy of His presence and the feeling of nothingness. It is then that Jesus speaks, and makes me feel, and communicates His requests insisting: Tell the Archbishop who works to achieve the union of Bishops in Spain and by his union of the clergy, that without a union they will not have peace in the Church or even in the nation. If they do not meet my desires, communism will continue to spread its errors, to promote wars and bloodshed. In the union, they will find the Light, strength and peace.[295]

This was one more message to convey and she would do it the next day. She felt ill, already stricken with a serious illness that was still in its infancy. After taking some medication, she was able to converse with Archbishop Antonio Garcia for a long time, from 6 to 11 p.m. They talked about many subjects related to messages she had received and the steps toward compliance. The Archbishop reassured the seer, who at this time was suffering with some doubts about the communications she received, telling her that they were from God and that she was in the hands of God for everything He wanted. She asked if everything was resolved for her to enter the Carmel. The Archbishop affirmed this and promised to return soon to address this issue, which had been pending for so long. Once the political atmosphere allowed he would take her to the Carmel of Valladolid.

This was not possible at this time, however, because the next day the Archbishop returned to find the shepherdess sick with a high fever. During the short visit he had with her in the infirmary, he concluded:

---

294 Letter of October 26, 1941, Humberto Pascoal.
295 *My Pathway,* I, p. 152.

-We have to wait until you are better, my daughter and recovered.[296]

It was going to take a long time to become better. Regretfully, seeing her so weak, the Archbishop knew it would have been a great effort to take her to the Carmel.

---

296 *Ibid.* p. 154.

Image of Our Lady of Fatima, venerated in the
Chapel of the Apparitions.

Lucia 38 years old.

CHAPTER XIII
THE SECRET WRITING

1 | At the Gates of Heaven

Sister Dores' fever worsened and she was diagnosed with pleurisy. On the morning of September 15, 1943, she suffered several setbacks with her high and prolonged temperature, and there was concern for her life. The Bishop of Leiria came to Tuy and they spoke at length. It was a great comfort for her to open her soul with one she knew so well and who understood her. At the end of the visit, she suffered a further decline as her fever rose.

Considering the possibility that she could die, the Bishop ordered her to write the third part of the Secret. Opposing this, as was her usual custom, she resisted, saying:

-*Reverend Bishop, I cannot do it!*

-*But then, did not Our Lady tell you to follow the path that I indicated to you?*

-*Yes.*

-*So now this is it. I ask for the glory of God and Our Lady. She does not get angry. If she is disappointed it will be me. She will bless your humility and obedience.*[297]

Concluding their visit, Sister Dores visited briefly with those who came with him: Rev. Galamba and Rev. Correia, nephew of the Bishop and acting Bishop of Valença do Minho. The poor sick one was so worried about the order she received that she did not engage much in this visit, wishing to be alone as soon as possible.

She was very apprehensive about writing the third part of the Secret—still hidden—because she had not received orders to do so from Heaven. This created a dilemma in her conscience: whom to obey? For now, she was not obliged to do this work due to her state of health, which would continue for some time.

After several months, alternating between high temperatures and improvements, she also suffered an infection in her leg due to an injection. Dr. José Abraldes advised that she have an operation to clear the pus that had formed along the bone. For this she was to be sent to the hospital in Pontevedra and placed under the care of Dr. Henry Marescot. She left Tuy after the Community Mass and having earlier received communion in the infirmary, arrived in Pontevedra at 10:30 a.m. The Sisters who brought her left her in the care of the Mother Superior. Mother Superior and Sister Dores met with the doctors at the hospital and some nurses who were Franciscan Sisters. They immediately transported her on a stretcher into the operating room. Dr. Marescot examined her and said:

-*Sister, we're going to have to cut.*[298]

She gave her okay, but asked them not to give her general anesthesia. The

---

297 *Ibid.* p. 4.
298 *Ibid*, p. 156.

doctor only smiled at her and shortly after that Dr. Pinto, who was standing behind her, placed a mask on her. She resisted, but the doctor laughed and said to her:

-*Speak, speak, the more the better!*

She relaxed then, placing herself in the hands of God and the doctors. Sister Lucia explained her concern:

-*I did not want general anesthesia because I was worried about the last order of the Bishop, and that being unconscious I would reveal something. So when I woke up, my first care was to ask my Mother Superior what I had said. Her Reverence responded:*

-*Nothing, this is the first thing that you have said.*

-*Thank God! And I was at peace.*[299]

Against the wishes of Dr. Marescot and the Sisters, Sister Dores wanted to go as soon as possible to the house at Pontevedra where a nurse could come daily and care for her. On October 10th she returned to Tuy where she continued her care with the house doctor. It was a very slow and long convalescence. After several months with high temperatures, she was very weak, but slowly regained her strength.

2 | Difficulty Writing the Secret

The order by the Bishop to write the Secret was not forgotten and it was still a burden on her heart. Just as the Blessed Mother asked at the Annunciation, Sister Lucia wanted clarification, but always with the firm determination to obey:

If only my strength allowed me to, I wanted to write what the Bishop had ordered me but I cannot explain what was happening to me as my hand shook and I could not form the words. This may have been caused by my impression that I had to write something against the orders of Our Lady, but still by obedience.

I attempted several times without getting any results. Because of this conflict, I wrote to the Bishop of Leiria, telling him what was happening to me. His Excellency replied by renewing the order he had already given me, perhaps in more expressive terms, in a letter dated October 16, 1943. After receiving this letter, I wanted to write again, but I still did not succeed.[300]

In December, she wrote to the Archbishop of Valladolid, asking him for advice about this problem. She opened her soul to him, tormented by doubt and the desire to act.

This order made me shudder. The Good Lord gave me orders not to tell anyone; His representative told me to write it. A real struggle raged within me and this is why I

---

299 *Ibid.* p. 156 – 157.
300 *Ibid.* p. 158.

wanted advice and direction before writing it. Being guided by faith, I want to obey and to that I am resolved. It seems to me that it is the same God Who, through His minister, gave me this order, but a doubt remains in my spirit. I do not know if I believe it is good and am fearful to go against an order from God that makes me set aside writing. Three times I already began to write and I do not know what passes in me because I begin to tremble and I am not able to write anything. I am also afraid that delaying the execution of this order is a lack of obedience. And now the Good God keeps silence; it seems that I am to Him a soul unknown. Patience. He knows well that my sole desire is not to be displeasing.[301]

On the advice of the Bishop of Valladolid, on December 19 she wrote again to Bishop Correia Da Silva, confessing her inability:

I have still not written what Your Excellency has ordered me. I have tried five times and I was not able. I do not know what it is but every time I place the pen on the paper my hand trembles and I am not able to write a letter. I think it is an unnatural nervousness because at the same time when I write something different, I have a steady hand. It also seems to me that it is not any moral fear because I have formed my conscience according to faith, believing that it is God through His Excellency Who orders me. So, I do not know what to do. But in fact this caused such an impression on me that it seems I am afraid to pick up the pen for that purpose. But who knows, it may be the devil who wants to prevent me from this act of obedience. But I want to obey. I do not want to displease Our Lord and therefore I wait to see if He wants to give me the grace for this one day.[302]

For Sister Lucia the time leading up to Christmas and the days that followed were enveloped by a thick cloud of doubt, anguish and fear. In her sincere search for God's will, she was met with heavy silence and a dark night.

Sister Lucia certainly sang the merry tunes of Christmas as always to the eyes of those who saw her; however, what a great disquiet in her interior! On Christmas Day she wrote a letter to her spiritual director, Archbishop Antonio Garcia y Garcia, giving thanks for a letter she received from him that brought her some comfort:

Most Reverend Archbishop of Valladolid, Antonio Garcia y Garcia,
I received and thank you for Your Excellency's letter.

With what Your Excellency told me, I was a little more at peace. I've done what you told me, that is, I wrote to His Excellency, the Bishop of Leiria, telling him what's wrong with me. I still have no answer. It may be what God wants, not to write any more all that has made such an impression on me. It seems that I am afraid to pick up the pen

---

301 Letter of December 1, 1943.
302 Letter of December 19, 1943.

for this purpose.

I would like very much that the heart of Our Good Lord grant to Your Excellency and to all the souls that are entrusted to Him, the greatest graces and blessings of His Divine Heart for the new year.

I would be grateful if you would bless me.

Your inferior servant of Your Excellency,

Maria Lucia of Jesus R.S.D.

December 25, 1943 [303]

3 | Our Lady Gives Her Enlightenment

The answer from the Bishop of Leiria was long in arriving, and she felt obligated to try to execute the order she received. With repugnance and some fear, she tried again and could not do it! This truly perplexed her. She wrote about this dilemma:

While I was waiting for an answer, on January 3, 1944, I knelt beside the bed which sometimes served as a writing table, and again I experienced the same without success. What most impressed me was that at the same moment I could write anything else without difficulty. I then asked Our Lady to let me know if it was the Will of God. I went to the chapel at 4 p.m. in the afternoon, the hour that I always made a visit to the Blessed Sacrament because I was ordinarily alone. I do not know why, but I liked being alone with Jesus in the Tabernacle.

Then I knelt in the middle, next to the rung of the Communion rail and asked Jesus to make known to me what was His Will. Accustomed as I was to believe that the order of the Superiors was the expression of the Will of God, I couldn't believe that this wasn't. Feeling puzzled and half absorbed under the weight of a dark cloud that seemed to hang over me, with my face between my hands, I hoped without knowing how for a response. I then felt a friendly, affectionate and motherly hand touch me on the shoulder and I looked up and saw the beloved Mother from Heaven. "Do not be afraid, God wanted to prove your obedience, faith and humility. Be at peace and write what they order you, but not what has been given you to understand its meaning. After writing it, place it in an envelope, close and seal it and write on the outside that this can be opened in 1960 by the Cardinal Patriarch of Lisbon or by the Bishop of Leiria." [304]

---

303 Letter of December 25, 1943.

304 Publishers Note: In her conversation with Cardinal Tarcisio Bertone 56 years later on April 27, 2000, Sister Lucia said the date of 1960 for the opening of the envelope was her own initiative (Cf. Congregation for the Doctrine of the Faith, The Message of Fatima). The information published here is from her diary and is completely consistent with the information she recorded on each of the two envelopes that, one inside the other, kept the contents of the third part of the Secret.

I felt my spirit flooded by a mystery of light that is God and in Him saw and heard:

-The tip of the spear as a flame unlatches and touches the axis of the earth. It shudders. Mountains, cities, towns and villages with their inhabitants are buried. The sea, the rivers, and the clouds emerge from their limits, overflowing and bringing with them in a whirlwind houses and people in numbers that are not possible to count. It is the purification of the world because of sin as it plunges. Hatred and ambition cause the destructive war!

Then I felt the rapid beating of my heart and in my mind the echo of a gentle voice saying:

-In time, one faith, one baptism, one Church, Holy, Catholic and Apostolic. In eternity, Heaven! This word Heaven filled my soul with peace and happiness, so that almost without realizing it, I was repeating for a long time:

-Heaven! Heaven! As soon as the full force of the supernatural passed, I went to write, without difficulty on January 3, 1944, on my knees, resting on the bed that served me as a table.[305]

4 | Lucia Writes What She Saw Leaving the Interpretation to the Church

She wrote what they ordered, but not her understanding of its meaning.[306]

This part of the Secret was kept in the silence of her heart, and only later revealed in her intimate notes, which she called, "My Pathway." Without appearing as someone in contact with the invisible, it seems that it was usual for her to see in God, as in a mirror, a film of the life of humanity. Some years earlier in a letter to the Bishop of Leiria and moved by the Spirit of God, as mentioned above, she reported a scenario very similar to this one when speaking of Blessed Jacinta.

She never gave a word of personal opinion as to the meaning of these visions, affirming always -*the interpretation belongs to the Church.*

The Secret was fully revealed in 2000, just as Sister Lucia wrote it and sent enclosed in a sealed envelope to Bishop José Correia da Silva. She herself attested to its authenticity several times before its revelation to the public on May 13, 2000, in Fatima. She confirmed her writing several times in front of witnesses after receiving news that its authenticity was questioned. Then, in December of 2003, His Eminence Cardinal Tarcisio Bertone visited her and she again gave him the same answer: -*the Secret has been fully revealed.* She then added with some sorrow:

---

305 *My Pathway*, I, p. 158 – 160.
306 *Ibid*, p. 159.

-Some people are never happy! It is no matter.

5 | A New Call to Conversion

There is in the description of the vision of Tuy, when Our Lady allowed her to write the third part of the Secret, a sentence which can be used as a meditation and light, a new invitation to conversion. In the vision of July 13, 1917, *flames came off the flaming sword wielded by the Angel, and the flame was extinguished when it came in contact with the light radiated from the right hand of Our Lady.*[307] Now, however, on January 3, 1944, Lucia sees *a flame given off from the tip of the spear touches the axis of the earth...* Why? Would Our Lady drop her arms and stop interceding and pleading?

The only word that was spoken by the Angel in the third part of the Secret and repeated three times was *Penance! Penance! Penance!*

This cry was often repeated during several apparitions. When Sister Lucia heard the insistence by some to reveal the third part of the Secret, she sighed with pain: *-If only they live what is the most important thing, which has already been said... They only concern themselves with what is left to be said, instead of complying with the request that was prayer and penance!*[308]

The flaming sword of the Angel and his cry of warning wounded the heart of the shepherdess in such a way that it kindled in her an intense flame of love for the salvation of her brethren, wanting at any cost to pull them out of the chains of sin. One of her intimate notes states:

I must show the souls the way to Heaven by the gentle path of prayer and penance; for the well-being of these souls He has already left us a description in the Holy Gospel: "My yoke is easy, and my burden is light. Learn from me for I am meek and humble of heart and you shall find rest for your souls." [309]

Toward this end she wrote "Calls from the Message of Fatima," desiring to bring light amidst the darkness of ignorance of God's Law. In one passage she confessed with sorrow:

It is therefore alarming to see in today's world the disorder which prevails in this respect, and the ease with which people plunge into immorality. To remedy the situation, there is only one solution: that people should repent, reform their lives and do penance.[310]

And she entrusted to us what Our Lord confided in her heart, pointing the

---

307 Cf. *The Message of Fatima (the Secret)*, Congregation for the Doctrine of the Faith, or MSL I, Appendix III, Part III of 'The Secret' p. 215.
308 *Irma Lucia – A Memory that We Have of Her*, p. 24.
309 *My Pathway*, I, p. 157.
310 *Calls from the Message of Fatima*, 29, p. 239.

aí ajoelhei-me no meio, junto ao degrau da mesa da Comunhão e pedia a Jesus que me fizesse conhecer qual era a Sua Vontade. Habituada como estava, a crer que as ordens dos superiores são a expressão certa da Vontade de Deus, não podia crer que esta o não fosse. E preplexa, meio absorta, sob o peso duma nuvem escura que parecia pairar sobre mim, com o rosto entre as mãos, esperava sem saber como, uma resposta. Senti então, que uma mão, amiga, carinhosa e maternal me toca no ombro, levanto o olhar e vejo a querida Mãe do céu. «Não temas, quis Deus provar a tua obediência, Fé e humildade, está em paz e escreve o que te mandam, não porém o que te é dado entender do seu significado. Depois de escrito encerra-o num envelope, fecha-o e lacra-o e escreve por fora, «que só pode ser aberto em 1960, pelo Sr. Cardeal Patriarca de Lisboa ou pelo Sr. Bispo de Leiria».

E senti o espírito inundado por um mistério de luz que é Deus e N'Ele vi e ouvi, - A ponta da lança como chama que se desprende, toca o eixo da terra, - Ela estremece, montanhas, cidades, Vilas e aldeias com os seus moradores são sepultados. - O mar, os rios e as nuvens, saem dos seus limites, transbordam, inundam e arrastam consigo num redemoinho, moradias e gente em número que se não pode contar, é a purificação do mundo pelo pecado em que se mergulha. - O ódio, a ambição provocam a guerra destruidora! - Depois senti no palpitar acelerado do coração e no meu espírito o eco duma voz suave que dizia: - No tempo, uma só Fé, um só Batismo, uma só Igreja, Santa, Católica, Apostólica: - Na eternidade, o Céu»!

Esta palavra «Céu» encheu a minha alma de paz, felicidade, de tal forma que, quase sem me dar conta, fiquei repetindo por muito tempo, - O céu! O céu!

Apenas passou a maior força do sobrenatural, fui escrever e fi-lo sem dificuldade, no dia 3 de Janeiro de 1944, de joelhos apoiada sobre a cama que me serviu de mesa.

Avé-Maria!

Original manuscript by Sister Lucia, My Pathway, p. 158 and 159.

way forward:

This is the penance and prayer that the Lord now asks and demands: prayer and penance, public and collective, together with abstaining from sins. These do more to enliven the Faith in souls, give confidence to souls, and light the flame of charity in their hearts. Our Lord moves those who are indifferent, giving light to the blind and attracting the unbelievers. It is for this that the Lord waits to send His Angel with the flaming sword and dispel the evil armies invading the world. They are blind men and destroy peace: the peace of the Church, the peace of the nations, the peace of the families in the homes, the peace of the conscience in the souls. People lack peace because they lack faith, lack penance, and lack public and collective prayer.

"Pray the Rosary every day to achieve peace for the world and the end of the war," said Our Lady on May 13, 1917. *This insistent recommendation was not only for the three poor and humble children; it is a call to the whole world, to all souls, to all humanity, believers and unbelievers, because Faith is a gift from God and we are to ask Him for it: 'ask and you shall receive.' You who have no Faith, ask it of God and He will grant it, because you who have no Faith have a soul that you need to save so that you will not be eternally miserable.*[311]

6 | It is a Purification of the World from Sin as It Plunges

Sister Lucia said: *God does not punish man. It is man himself who with his intemperance causes punishments.* [312]

And this happens at all levels. Freedom, this ineffable gift of God to humanity, does not mean being able to do everything one desires, but knowing how to choose between good and evil. However, people often use this gift erroneously: confusing freedom with debauchery, causing disturbances in their personal lives and the community, and then everyone suffers the consequences.

God created everything perfectly and entrusted everything to humanity with authority over all. But *the hatred and ambition* taking possession of the human heart reduces it to the worst form of slavery: detachment from God. And without God everyone is capable of all atrocities and aberrances. Then like a sorrowful mother who presents a wounded son to a surgeon for the saving scalpel, despite the painful procedure, so does God, in His infinite love for humanity that is unable to hear His voice and is in danger, bring the Grace of suffering so that mankind will reconsider his errant ways and be open to God's way, able to love again.

The cause of all evil in the world is sin, and only humanity is capable of

311 *My Pathway,* I, p. 398.
312 Oral Narration of Sister Lucia.

sinning! But until the last moment God waits with open arms for the return of the child who has never left His Heart, [313] because God is Love [314] and always loves.

Sister Lucia responded, through correspondence, to help those who were under the weight of sin, imploring them to follow the right path and to trust in Him as the Good Shepherd Who does not banish the wayward sheep. She helped them with the Master's firmness and the Mother's affection, taking the sin upon herself with humility, transforming the consequences of the sin through penance and reparation. As an example, here is an excerpt from one letter, among many:

> *Dear X,*
>
> *I received your letter and I respond.*
>
> *As to your request, it implies much about the Law of God that we all have an obligation to observe.*
>
> *Your infidelity does not consist of the pregnancy, but yes, in the life of sin that you led before, in which pregnancy was the fruit. And this fruit, although the fruit of sin, you cannot now annihilate or destroy, because it would be committing a new sin, killing your own child. On the contrary, you are obliged to accept it as a new creation that is entitled to life, and to do your part to do everything possible to have this child in good health and be perfect. This is a duty that cannot be lacking, because it would go against the commandment of the Law of God that tells us: "Do not kill" (Ex. 20-13). You should accept it with love and an open heart, in the spirit of sacrifice in reparation for your sin, that this sad experience will serve you not to return to sin any more [...] search for a start of a new, young, serious and honorable life...*
>
> *There is nothing to pay for the honorable life of a young person which makes them worthy of the grace of God in their soul, the purity of their body and their heart. This is the best way that you must now embrace with pleasure, fidelity and sacrifice in reparation for the past and that will make you happier in the future—leading a better life with which you merit from God the grace to be happier, because unhappiness comes from sin. No one has ever been happy in a life of sin.*
>
> *I am praying for you, hoping that you will understand what I say here and will follow the path that I suggest, to lead a better life on earth and to be more happy in heaven.*
>
> *In union of prayers*
>
> *Coimbra, June 11, 1983*
>
> *Sister Lucia*

In her constant prayer to God, she spread out her arms pleading for

---

313   Lk 15:11-32.

314   1 Jn 4:8.

humanity thus:

Spiritually united to the Vicar of Christ on earth, I want to become a host immolated on the altar of sacrifice in union with the Victim of Calvary, offered to the Father in an act of reparation, of adoration and supplication for my Mother Church, the members of His Mystical Body so that they live the life of Christ, united in the same faith, the same hope and in the same charity.[315]

7 | The Sealed Envelope

After Our Lady told Sister Lucia to write the third part of the Secret and keep it in a closed and sealed envelope, it is interesting how she managed to obey this order. After writing it she closed the envelope and the next day asked her Mother Superior to seal and stamp it. The Superior was surprised by the request and asked her why she wanted that. Sister Dores, unsure how to respond, said she wanted to guard the enclosed letter.

-*But how important is this letter?* Mother Superior asked.

Sister Dores could not tell her what it was and just shrugged her shoulders. Lowering her eyes and smiling slightly she went away helpless, but confident she would be helped. She went before the Tabernacle and entrusted the problem to the Hidden Jesus, then went about her work.

Shortly thereafter, the Vice-Superior asked her to go to the kitchen and burn the paper in the wastepaper basket. Sister Dores was always available to help anyone who asked, despite her other work obligations. She soon left what she was doing and went to the kitchen to burn the papers. While throwing the papers on the fire she discovered at the bottom of the wastebasket a small piece of wax. She could not believe her eyes. Then in her heart she exclaimed:

-*How good You are my Jesus, how good You are! I already have Your answer, thank you Lord, thank you!*[316]

True to the spirit of poverty, after replacing the empty basket she showed the Vice-Superior the piece of the seal that she had found and asked permission to use it. Mother laughed. Being such a small crumb in her opinion, she asked why she wanted it. Sister Dores replied that she wanted to paste it to a paper. Smiling, Mother told her to keep it for what it was worth.

I took it with me and I sealed the letter. In fact, the piece was so small that to melt it I had to hold it with the tips of the pliers, but blessed be the poor in spirit for theirs is the kingdom of Heaven. I renewed my vow of poverty and thanked the Lord for giving

---

315 *My Pathway,* II, p. 224.
316 *My Pathway,* I, p. 161.

me the opportunity to perform this.[317]

Having carried out the order, she was in a hurry to bring the envelope to its destination and be relieved of this burden. Being allowed to write letters only on Sundays, she waited for January 9th and on that day she wrote another letter to Bishop da Silva to give him the news, also dating this letter January 9th. The letter included a message from Heaven for him. Because he was sick, Sister Lucia had spoken about him to Our Lady and was glad to tell him the Mother's response:

> *Tuy, January 9, 1944*
>
> *Most Reverend Bishop,*
>
> *As it is nearing the 15th, I write now so that it arrives in time with my humble congratulations and poor prayers. I am worried about the health of Your Excellency. God wants you to be better and not be burdened with more illness, and the good Lord will have compassion on you. A few days ago, (supposing that Your Excellency likes what I send, I will say this) I had the opportunity to ask our good Mother of Heaven for health and life for Your Excellency and she responded to me (life yes, but in Heaven). The Bishop likes the promise? I was so happy. Heaven dictates to us eternal happiness. That is good, in Heaven forever with God, in His love and in His grace. I have written what was ordered of me. God wanted me to prove myself a bit but finally this was indeed His will. This is sealed inside an envelope and this within a loose-leaf book. If Your Excellency desires that I send it, I will deliver it to the first reliable carrier that arrives here, or if Your Excellency wants to seek it in Valencia, I'll take it there. I'm afraid to mail it for fear that it may become lost.*
>
> *Again, my sincere congratulations and I ask for your blessing.*
>
> *Inferior servant of Your Excellency,*
>
> *Maria Lucia of Jesus R.S.D.*

8 | Why the Date 1960 on the Envelope?

The Secret was given to the Church in June through a reliable carrier, Archbishop Manuel Maria, Bishop of Gurza, who hand-carried it to its destination. It was, as she wrote in a letter to Bishop da Silva in March:

> *One more fiber of the heart and at last I do not know why! Often I hear the Sisters and even some Superiors say: so many writings, so much to write, I do not know why! And here in the depths of my poor heart I say also: they are right, I do not know why. But soon I found the answer: it is to obey, it is to show to the world the Divine Mercy and attract souls to God.* [318]

---

317 *Ibid.*
318 Letter of March 12, 1944.

Why was 1960 the date given to open the envelope containing the Secret? In a letter written to Pope Pius XII on June 6, 1958, Sister Lucia explained it this way:

Holy Father,

It is with the greatest respect and veneration for the august person of Your Holiness, and under the direction and knowledge of His Excellency the Rev. Apostolic Nuncio and the Archbishop of Coimbra, who come to expose what I believe to be the will of God.

Your Holiness knows of the existence of the so-called secret of Fatima, enclosed in a sealed envelope that can be opened in 1960. Although I cannot speak of the text and because the time is approaching, I must say that in 1960, communism will reach its maximum height, which can be decreased in intensity and duration, and to which it must comply with the triumph of the Immaculate Heart of Mary and the Reign of Christ.

To achieve this purpose, God wants to intensify all apostolic works, beyond which He wants to be heard in the world. Like an echo of His, my voice exposes what was and what is the message of Fatima in relation to God and souls, for time and eternity, in order to elucidate for souls on the road of Christian life that must be followed, and the errors which must be removed so that they are not fooled by false doctrines.[319]

When asked about the reason for this date, Sister Lucia, not wanting to reveal the new encounter with Our Lady who appeared to her in Spain, said she thought she would already be dead by this time. This was not a lie; she was almost certain and had hoped her death would happen very soon because of her condition.

Heaven…but when? With the health problems she suffered during the previous decade and still feeling very weak, it seemed to her that this was going to be very soon and so desired as she expressed in a short letter to the Bishop of Leiria on July 1, 1943:

Most Reverend Bishop,

I write in bed where I am now 17 days with a very high fever… Maybe all of this is the beginning of the end and I am glad. It is well that my mission on earth is finishing; the good God is preparing me for the paths to Heaven.[320]

After a slight improvement, she had a relapse of which she referred to in a letter to the Bishop on July 26:

I am in bed again, but it seems to me that there will be nothing of greater importance. However, I still did not want to leave coughing up blood, which the doctor

---

319 Author's note: following this letter of June 6, 1958, the book, *Calls from the Message of Fatima*, was published.
320 Letter of July 1, 1943.

said was not important. But what caused the external abscesses in my lungs was pneumonia. I do not know if this will be, that is, what God will want: Heaven is much more attractive than earth. For now, I do not write any more, I am a little tired.[321]

The complications that arose from the pulmonary disease nourished some hope in her that she would soon enjoy the eternal homeland. She lived courageously during this time, offering all the sufferings from the illness and treatments that she underwent, including the surgery noted earlier. As always, she offered everything with love and always with her eyes on Heaven. In another letter to Bishop da Silva in December, she gave news of her state of health and expressed this intimate hope again:

As for me I am getting much better, even though I doubt that the improvements are very durable, but which God wills. My left side was very weak and therefore it seems to me that it will not be much longer, I get tired with almost everything, but I do not feel sorry! To get to Heaven you must walk the path; and I wish it! I have missed that! But it is necessary that I wait with a little more patience…[322]

I need to wait a little more… I will stay here for some time…

So resigned, she continued on, never missing a second of life that could be spent in the humble delivery of her daily duty for love and with love, always waiting to see that heavenly door open. The Lady more brilliant than the sun occasionally sprinkled some reflections of light from Heaven in the life of her shepherdess, but these were but flashes that further intensified her homesickness for Heaven. On her 39th birthday, the last birthday she celebrated in Spain, she told Mother Superior Maria do Carmo Cunha Matos, with whom she had a great affinity, that Mother Monfalim had told her she would not be on earth for a long time, since her mission seemed to be already finished. She concluded with some tearing in her eyes:

-*After all I'm still here!*

If only she knew that she was not even halfway through her pilgrimage!

---

321 Letter of July 26, 1943.
322 Letter of December 19, 1943.

Lucia in the streets of Vigo with a lady friend.

CHAPTER XIV
LAST YEARS IN SPAIN

1 | Lucia Reveals a Great Love for Missions

Still convalescing but gaining in strength, Sister Dores occupied her time making rosaries for the missions during recess between prayer and light work and Sundays. Her letters reference this work on Sunday, the day of the Lord, as dedicated to the service of charity. To a family who asked her for a rosary, she answered:

The rosary, I do not know when I will be able to do it for lack of time. For the missions, I'm making some on Sundays; for you I cannot work on a Sunday, and during the week I do not have enough time to make rosaries. Let us see if the work changes.[323]

To make the rosaries and other liturgical items, she begged for materials from her friends and benefactors in Porto, who were very glad to provide these to her. If they wanted to offer something to her personally, she replied as in this letter to the Bishop:

I appreciate the offer of Your Excellency, but I do not want anything for me. I send this brochure about the mission that I received; if Your Excellency would like to contribute with some alms for the founding of the Mission of Zambezia, I would be very thankful instead of sending something to me. I would like very much to have at least ($10.00) to be sent there for a goddaughter with my name if Your Excellency wanted to make this handout with this order and send them to the Rev. Father José Bernardo Gonçalves.[324]

And this other:

J.M.J.

Tuy, January 12, 1942

Miss Maria Isabel de Vasconcelos,

I acknowledge and I am thankful for the letter from the Bishop, as well as for the alms I received from Mother Cabral from many people. I thank you on behalf of the Community where, because of my vow of poverty, I cannot keep anything that is given exclusively to me. I ask that they are not sacrificing for me, and while it is true there is now a shortage of everything here, it is also true that with more or less difficulty Our Lord did not leave us lacking the necessary. The donations I always receive with much pleasure are crucifixes, wire, medals, and beads to make rosaries for the missions. I have here a letter that I received recently from a missionary of Alta Zambezia Lite, asking me to send him rosaries. He says Christians are distinguished there from those who are not wearing the rosary on their neck. He tells me that the rosary is imposed on them after the baptism with a similar ceremony to which we have here for the imposition of

---

323 Letter of July 12, 1946, Maria Carolina.
324 Letter of January 5, 1941, Senhora D. Virgilia Martins Ferreira de Brito.

the scapular. He regrets that there are approximately 97 adults to be baptized, but not enough rosaries to impose on them, and presently he does not want to sell things that are donated. For this reason, he appreciated this handout the most with pleasure to extend the cult of our kind heavenly Mother among these poor souls. Maybe they prefer the beads to be in colors, glass or stone. I say this not to ask for them a new donation, but as Your Excellency would like to give me happiness, to know that this is what I like, or something for the poor of my catechesis. Helping the missionaries is a donation which God will not fail to reward widely in Heaven. Excuse me for speaking to you so frankly, but as Your Excellency likes to send me something from time to time, this is what always gives me pleasure.

A small servant of His Excellency,
Maria Lucia of Jesus R.S.D.

To be a missionary! It was another dream that lit up her thoughts. She even offered to go in 1941 when the Mother Provincial asked for volunteers for the missions. In her private notes, she confessed:

I volunteered, wanting to be accepted, as the Lord did not open the doors of the cloister. But, for me to go to the land of Africa alongside the missionaries to lead souls to the love that burns and strengthens, the hope and faith that guides and rises from the earth to Heaven—to go with the Divine Shepherd to lead the sheep to the verdant pastures, where there runs the crystal clear water of the eternal fountain!

But this does not explain myself, I feel in me aspiration so opposite! How happy I would be to fly away to the backwoods of Africa in conquest of the souls of my dear distant brethren, and I come to envy those who have such luck. How happy I would be to sacrifice myself in the hospitals next to the suffering members of Christ, offering my services and providing them with all kinds of relief. I would be happier to be buried in leprosy reaping the groans of humanity in decay, offering them to God as reparation for the sins of the world.

I would like to obtain all the knowledge and transmit it to these souls as a reflection of eternal Wisdom, the source which pours out all the light of intelligence and knowledge, to be able to raise them from their path on earth to the light of the Supernatural! But poor me; I am nothing and I have nothing! And in the union of my soul with Jesus I encounter everything, because it is from the depths of the despicable that God lifts me up to the heights of the supernatural. It is from the humility that descends to the ocean floor that there is the light, the strength, the joy and where God grants the grace of reaching the peak of love! Hence, it is my ardent desire to stay alone with Him in the silence of a cloister, where I can give Him everything in a more perfect union, a meeting more intimate by the Church, my Mother, and the souls of my dear brethren.

So I will be in my union with Christ—the Love that burns, the Hope that strengthens, and the Faith that illuminates the path to eternal life!   And to become like this, everyone has to be united in the same Faith, Hope and Love, believing in the existence of the eternal God, one God in Three Persons; in His Son Jesus Christ and life everlasting, in the Redemption and to complement the Trinity in His Church—One, Holy, Catholic and Apostolic! [325] She sought to live her consecration fully and for love, and to her sisters she conveyed an outpouring of joy that flowed from her heart entirely in God, the source of true joy. However, she still felt the desire of Carmel—that longing for solitude. The Bishop of Valladolid who was close to her had a keen interest in helping her realize her dream. When he visited her on January 10, 1944, he intended to find a way to send her soon to the Carmel of Valladolid, and to do so before returning to the diocese of Tuy. But seeing her still so weak and feverish, concluded: we have to wait. Three times he wanted to help the Shepherdess of Fatima take this step, but whenever he proposed it she got sick. God's plans were different. Sister Lucia continued to walk in darkness, guided only by human mediations and the light of faith, which in the words of St. John of the Cross is the light that we have to stow in this life.[326]

2 | Lucia Feels the Need to Pray for Priests

Sometime later she had the joy of helping bring the Good Shepherd to two sheep that had gone astray. This time it was a priest who had left the ministry and was living in an improper situation. He felt the touch of grace through the Bishop of Gurza who asked him to meet with Sister Dores, hoping with her help he could get back on track. It would require leaving the lady with whom he lived and who already had a child. They met in Valencia, and after five hours of conversation guided by the firm words of Sister Dores, the lady who had been caught by surprise, although painful, consented to the separation. Sister Dores was not one to postpone things, knowing that if you wait for "someday" to put into practice what is agreed, the wills would weaken. It was soon established that the priest in question would go to the house, get his belongings, and live with his sister. The lady, accompanied by two friends who were present, would go to the house and help get his belongings together.

With everything decided they departed and Sister Dores returned to Tuy,

---

325 My Pathway, I, p. 137 – 138.
326 St. John of the Cross, Ascent of Mount Carmel, 2, XVI, 15.

happy to have been able to help these two souls leave the life of sin.

But the devil is furious when you steal his prey! A week later, Sister Dores was surprised by the storm heaped upon her: she was not to have any more contact with these people because they had gone to tell her Provincial Superior that this conversion had been a farce. Furthermore, all correspondence would have to pass through the hands of the Mother Provincial and the Bishop of Leiria. Lucia suffered greatly knowing she was also concerned about the confidence of her local Superior, who had authorized this meeting. In the depths of her soul, however, she felt peace and confidence that God would reveal the truth; of that she was convinced.

Shortly thereafter she was able to see the good arrangements of the lady, now recovered in the grace of God, having gone through this with the support of some friends, participating in a retreat that was held in the house of the Dorothean Sisters in Tuy. Sister Dores was responsible for serving this group and observed closely her devotion and willpower to start a new life. Later, knowing about the ban of the aforementioned priest, the lady asked Sister Dores to communicate with him in Tuy. Her Mother Superior agreed, stating the ban only referred to correspondence. She also attended the visit, which was consoling knowing that the arrangements made for the priest had been for the good. It was not until 1946 in Porto when she was visited by the Bishop of the diocese to which the priest belonged that Sister Dores was told what had happened. The same person who had informed the Provincial Mother Superior and who had provoked so much suffering in Sister Dores, went also to the Bishop. Noting that this person was moved by passion and not by charity, the Bishop dismissed him without giving credit to the information he gave, and advised him to take care of his duties.[327] As Saint Teresa said: *the truth suffers but does not perish.*

The priests! Sister Lucia loved and feared for them. From her experiences with those who looked to her for help, she would exclaim personally or by letter:

-*Oh! It is necessary to pray and help the Priests!*[328]

She took them into her heart and wrapped them with her prayers, knowing well the need for them to have strong armor to live in the world and not be of the world, to wade through the marshlands with a light that never dims, never causing harm or injury while passing through the thorns.

---

327 Cf. *My Pathway*, I, p. 174.
328 *My Pathway*, I, p. 174.

3 | Charity Toward Her Sisters

On April 7, 1945, Sister Dores participated with great emotion in the exhumation of the remains of Mother Monfalim, which were to be transferred to Portugal. She ordered the remains to be put in a small funeral urn, and while doing so, *meditated, not on death, but on the reality of life,* and remembered the words from the Gospel: *Store up treasure that thieves cannot steal, rust cannot destroy, and that is not subject to decay in the grave.*[329]

She carried in the car to Valença the urn with the ashes to facilitate the transition, making sure no problems occurred, and then returned to the house in Tuy. Accompanying her on the trip in another car was the Superior, Mother Maria do Carmo Cunha Matos, with whom she maintained very close correspondence. In a letter to her dated April 14, she gives a beautiful interpretation of the words of Our Lady, which applies to everyone:

J.M.J.

Nobis quoque peccatoribus…

Very dear Reverend Mother Superior,

I do not send this to remind Her Reverence of the contract, but to tell you that I did not forget.

I do not know if this will reach Your Reverence when still in Lisbon or if you have already flown to Fatima. I hope you won't forget me there at the feet of our Heavenly Mother, and that I miss Jacinta without end… I do not think I am sad for not going. I like to offer this sacrifice because Our Lady is the one saving souls and I always remember the great promise that filled me with joy: "I will never leave you, My Immaculate Heart will be your refuge and the way that leads you to God."[330] I believe that this promise is not only for me, but for all the souls who wish to take refuge in the Heart of the Heavenly Mother, and let themselves be led by the way she designs… It seems to me that these also would be the intentions of the Immaculate Heart of Mary, to shine forth on more souls this ray of light, showing them the door of salvation, always ready to welcome all the castaways of this world… As for me, I am savoring the delicious fruits of this beautiful garden and desire to let the souls go to Fatima to ease their hunger and thirst for grace, comfort and support.

When I started to write, I did not think to say any of this; let's see if I will tear it up instead of sending it because I do not know how I let this pen write here with all the nonsense that is dictated from my heart. This is not my usual way but it was a day for exposing my heart.

---

329 *Ibid.* p. 182.
330 MSL I, 4th M, Ch. II, No. 4, p. 177.

Yesterday the postcard arrived from Your Reverence. Now they say that Your Reverence had just phoned and I did not have the good fortune to be there. They say that Your Reverence does not know when you will come. Watch what you do, remember us; I am going to ask Our Lord to give you a great gift to give us much time alone… Do not forget to be careful because last time you became very ill… [331]

Faced with Mother Superior's long delay in returning, Sister Dores confessed on everyone's behalf that they missed her. Each day that passed seemed like a year. She wrote to her the daily news about community life, always reporting the nostalgia of all due to her absence. She revealed tenderly that they missed the flowers for the Child Jesus in the Tabernacle:

-I made two visits to the Child Jesus and gave Him some kisses: it is very sad without Your Reverence, who says that one who stays away too long, dies from nostalgia… See if He helps you… Our Tabernacle is full of requests. Every time I go there I ask about you: when is Mother Superior coming? And I reply with repetition: tomorrow… tomorrow…

Sister Marinho said Your Reverence gave her two embraces at your farewell and gave me none: I count that you will give me four when you return unless you give them to me from Our Lady of Fatima… [332]

She said in another letter, always joking:

Very dear Reverend Mother Superior,

It seems to me now that half a year has already passed and the next half will pass without you, making it an entire year, and please God that it does not exceed this. May these longings be cured when you come our way…

I make this novena alone and remember well Your Reverence and at the end, pray one more Hail Mary so that you come soon and in good health, with much strength to carry the Cross.

Two days later while congratulating her in the name of all, she signed: '*The abandoned daughters in Tuy.*'[333]

Then, confessing a small suffering, she asked her for a remedy. She had placed on a windowsill in the bright sun a statue of Our Lady of Fatima. As luck would have it, the wind blew it down and it broke. Entrusting this to her Superior she asked her to buy another one in Fatima, which certainly happened.

---

331 Letter of April 14, 1945.

332 *Ibid.*

333 Letter of October 2, 1945.

4 | First Contact with Carmel

In the summer of 1945, Sister Dores went on a pilgrimage to Santiago de Compostela accompanied by her niece, who spent a few days of vacation in Tuy with Mrs. Lucia Neves. Mrs. Neves wanted to receive the graces from the Jubilee of St. James the Apostle, and asked the Mother Superior for permission for Sister Dores to accompany her on this trip with another sister. Lucia tells about this pilgrimage:

On the morning of the 24th, we left Tuy on the 8 a.m. train after Mass and Holy Communion. We arrived in Santiago at about 2 p.m. We stayed in our house and after lunch went to visit the Cathedral; the priests were singing the Divine Office, which we witnessed.

The next day the 25th, after having attended Mass and receiving Holy Communion in the college, we went to watch the Solemn Pontifical Mass in the Cathedral. When this ended, we kissed the foot of the Apostle from behind the high altar, then visited the exposed sepulcher and climbed up to the gazebos and tower. In the middle of the staircase, we came upon the residence of the sacristan's family, a man, woman and some children, and they informed us that to get to the top we had to climb much further, but from there the views were precious. They wished to accompany us and when we got there we enjoyed everything very much! When I found that we were so high, it seemed to be close to Heaven!

What surprised me after Holy Mass were the traditional huge groups that entered the Cathedral playing castanets and tambourines, dancing in the chapel before the Blessed Sacrament. There were two bishops who were present, the Archbishop of Santiago and the Bishop of Tuy, José Ortiz, the priests and more clergy who were seated in armchairs to the sides. When the dancing finished, it was followed by the ceremony that is called "Botafumeiro," which is the incensing of the relics that follows the procession.[334]

In the afternoon, they visited some churches. Sister Dores first entered a Carmelite place—Carmel of Santiago. Her companions did not notice, but she shivered inside and confessed that she had a great temptation to go talk to the person in charge about her secret desire, but she contained herself knowing that nothing would be resolved there.

---

334 *My Pathway*, I, p. 172 – 173.

5 | The Shepherdess Leads Souls to the Pastor

Toward the end of 1945, Sister Dores had the joy of reconciling two more souls with God. Having obtained permission for the visit, the Ambassador of Brazil came to Tuy for this purpose. The chief consulate of Portugal at Tuy, at the request of the Portuguese government, was waiting at the border to accompany her on this visit. He did this with great diplomacy, but with little desire—he disliked the nuns and everything associated with the Church. It appears that in these cases, he did not know how to be a polite diplomat.

Forced by duty of his profession he accompanied the Lady Ambassador Irascena. It was admirable to see this lady make such a long trip to visit a sister so humble. While the Lady Ambassador spoke alone with Sister Dores, the entourage visited the garden in the company of Mother Superior and during this time the chief consulate's heart softened. He departed from Sister Dores with a gentle handshake and offered his services again, asking if he could return with his wife. The Mother Superior agreed and gave him a new date to meet soon.

The second meeting was spent sitting in the afternoon shade of the garden. The chief consulate gave Sister Dores a summary of his life. He spoke of his communist ideas and about his diplomatic assignments in several countries where these ideas had become more deep-rooted, including as a messenger for Spain, which was not to his liking. Sister Lucia described to us the topic of this conversation:

Exercising his career, he traveled through various nations to clarify his communist ideas, and he made some trips to Russia. Now he was regretting if he had the misfortune to be sent to a nation where communism is not understood, and he was still regretting the situation of the poor, subject to be created from the rich without the possibility to rise and be equal in society, etc. After hearing this, I interrupted and asked:

-Is the chief consulate willing to distribute all his goods to the poor so that they may rise equal to you?

After a moment of silence, he replied:

-I see that Sister is opposing.

-Yes, Mr. Consulate, and not worth discussing. [335]

Without wasting any time, she took advantage of the moment, always with her eyes on the well-being of those who approached her. She asked the consulate if he had faith. He confessed not to have lost all of it, but he had already forgotten everything he learned from his First Communion. His godmother, being in Braga,

---

335 *Ibid.* p. 177.

had a great devotion to Our Lady of Sameiro. With the permission of her Mother Superior, Sister Dores looked for a catechism and offered it to her distinguished visitor, asking him to remember the Lord's Prayer and the Hail Mary.

She would pray two rosaries for him, and she asked that he and his wife promise to say the prayers as well. He told her he sometimes listened to the broadcasts of the ceremonies in Fatima and confessed that he was moved when he heard the crowd praying.

The visit ended with them having great joy and peace in their hearts. Then they asked Sister Dores to promise to make them rosaries and send them soon. She herself delivered them the next time she had to go to the Consulate, because from this meeting she had formed a good relationship with them. The Mother Superior was besieged with requests to resolve issues at the Consulate, and so Sister Dores would come with another request, always very well-received with her companion, often Mother Superior. They had to schedule extra time to visit because as soon as they came, they were asked to go to the consulate's office where he and his wife conversed a long time with Sister Lucia who led them in the spiritual life. After about five months of this, she had a joyful surprise. She tells of this day, April 8, 1946:

We went to the Consulate on this day because of certain documentation, and as usual the Consulate received us with a singular satisfaction and led us to his office where he said:

-You know Sister, we are resolved to confess and receive Communion, but with the provision that Sister arranges this with a Portuguese confessor.

-This would not be difficult; right here in Carvalhinho is a Portuguese priest who comes to Tuy very frequently. He is Franciscan, Fr. Luis. I'll see if he can do this on the next 13th, the anniversary of your marriage, and don't you think it would be a beautiful way to celebrate this day?

-Oh! And how was it that Sister remembered that date?

I noted they were moved.[336]

Back home she contacted the priest who was not only willing to hear the couple's confessions, but to have them make a good preparation for three days to recommence their Christian life. On the morning of the 13th, Sister Dores had the consolation of seeing them at the Communion Table after having confessed in the house chapel of Tuy. What a joy for her heart to be able to help bring these souls to God!

---

336 *Ibid*, p. 179.

6 | Coronation of Our Lady

Previously, on October 13, 1942, at the close of the Silver Jubilee of the Apparitions, a magnificent crown of jewels was given to Our Lady of Fatima by the Portuguese women. There were numerous pieces of gold and precious stones, gifts from many hands that wanted to honor the Queen. Like the many grains of wheat that form a large loaf of bread to nourish the whole house, so these jewels from all over Portugal were brought together to form on this day that wonderful jewel that shines on the head of the image of Our Lady of the Rosary at Fatima.

Likewise, Pope Pius XII wanted to present to the Queen of Peace a gesture of gratitude when he saw the end of the Second World War in 1945. He appointed as his legate to the solemn coronation on May 13, 1946, Cardinal Cento Aloisi Masalla, telling him, as told by the Portuguese Cardinal Manuel Gonçalves Cerejeira:

-*Go Your Eminence and crown at Fatima the Queen of Heaven and earth, Regina Mundi.*

Fatima had become the Altar of the world.

The Coronation was enshrined with supreme authority, and a splendor rarely seen took place in the sky (in the pouring rain at the precise moment of the coronation, the sun appeared and covered the Image with its gilded rays), the saving Message from the Immaculate Heart of the Mother of Mercy sent to the world about to drown in a sea of blood and mud (blood of war and mud of afflictions). [337]

Sister Lucia participated in this event from a distance in Spain, her heart celebrating with great joy. It was another step toward the Triumph of the Mother and all that concerned the Lady more brilliant than the sun. Many Mothers from the Institute of Saint Dorothy went to Fatima to participate in the ceremony, but the shepherdess, although the Bishop of Leiria had spoken about it, found it more prudent to be absent. Her letters to Mother Superior Maria do Carmo Cunha Matos in Tuy during these days are full of tenderness. It is worth sharing some of the passages from this collection to show how her heart was on the other side of the river Minho, cherishing each stone on those paths that she knew so well. She wrote at the end of a letter from April 11 after sharing the little events of the day with a child's heart:

Please, God, that everything goes very well and that our dear Mother in Heaven will grant many graces and communicate to me some little thing. If I am to be there on these days, to go to the Loca do Cabeço and pray the prayers of the Angel for me; to go to

---

337 Words of His Eminence the Cardinal Patriarch of Lisbon, *Fatima Altar of the World*, Introduction.

▶ Pilgrims at the Basilica for the Coronation of Our Lady of Fatima.

▼ Lucia as a Dorothean.

▶ Cardinal Aloisi Masella Benedict at Fatima for the Coronation of Our Lady.

▲ Coronation of the image of
Our Lady of Fatima by
Cardinal Aloisi Masella Benedict,
on October 13, 1942.

▶ Image just crowned.

the well and bring a little bottle of water to drink; I miss her so. At the feet of our beloved
Mother, my longings are endless... it is with them that I form the crown that is offered.
Kiss for me the ring of the Bishop and ask for a blessing for me. I long for the Reverend
Mother Provincial, Reverend Mother Teacher and for all.

To Your Reverence whom I really miss - I respectfully kiss the hand of Your Reverence

  Sister Maria Lucia of Jesus R.S.D.

  Tuy, April 24, 1946

Two days later she wrote again to her Mother Superior, chronicling in detail
her community life with enchanting simplicity. Reading her letter, who would
know that she lived a life so touched by the supernatural; she was always so natural
and simple. As the most humble of the earth, she communicated so well with the
highest of Heaven!

  My very dear Mother Superior,

  Recently I heard the voice of Your Reverence on the phone. Thanks be to God
that I heard the sound of a voice speaking from Fatima. I am content for now, that you
gave me this pleasure one more time: Our Lady gave me this from the generosity of her
Heart.

  Here at home, what happens? There is not much to write or tell you about. We
have visits from people going to Santiago. They were expected to arrive in the afternoon
in the rain and cold, preferably without thunder and lightning; and to when and which
hour will they arrive? It is already 10 p.m. at night, and I am writing in the hope that
they all came. Lately do you know what time we have been going to bed? Some of us
go to bed around midnight and others at 1a.m. The pilgrimages usually end at 11 or
11:30 p.m. [Pilgrims on foot would stop at the convent on the way, arriving at all hours,
especially at night.]

  When they arrived, Mother Assis was very happy and told me that they brought
great gifts to Her Reverence, 5k of almonds, a hundred oranges, boxes of cakes, etc.
Naturally, in the absence of Her Reverence the gifts were handed to Mother Pereira, but
enough of this until I see more... I only saw some oranges and thanked God... they were
packed in a large solid box and nothing leaked, like our kitchen pans leak from poor
work by the tinsmith...

  The good news: Since Your Reverence was here we have abundant water in the
faucets upstairs in the sisters' bedroom and do not have to cut the water off because there
are no leaks, except for hot water. It is our beloved Mother in Heaven who watches over
her orphans and with her love came to help us: There is no one like Her!...(I will never
abandon you). Did you receive my other letter? Please God that you did! Do not forget
to ask for the holy picture for me from the representative of the Holy Father. I already
sent a message to Mr. Chantre.

… Do you know? The girls cut the tips of their veils and gave them to me… I had asked the Schoolmistress that they give me the tips from the new veils and they agreed and were very happy, but they want to keep the rest of the veils. It is difficult to finish the relics because the girls stole the pieces of the veils. Mother Pereira and the police officer found them in the girls' possession. It is now 11:00 p.m. and the girls still do not admit the theft. [Sister Lucia is describing an incident involving some girls from Lisbon who were staying at the home of the Dorotheans while on their pilgrimage to Santiago. They stole the pieces after they found out that it was Sister Lucia who asked for them. The tips of the new veils were to be used in the making of relics.]

Pray very much for us because we suffer from homesickness but still desire to make it here.

Enjoy the Heavenly Mother of Heaven, her graces and blessings, the tenderness of her Immaculate Heart and rest a lot.

… As I finish this paper, I miss and I long without end for Our Lady, Jacinta, Francisco, the cave, the well, the old threshing floor, etc., etc. Finally I miss everyone and everything… even the stones on the paths and hills of hay where I made the cord, the lilies and peonies of the hill and the Angel's well, without forgetting the flowers of the fields and the blooms of the wheat… for the Mother Provincial, Mother Schoolmistress and for Your Reverence whom I miss without end…

I humbly and respectfully request to kiss the hand of Your Reverence.

A more humble daughter,

Sister Maria Lucia of Holy Jesus R.S.D.

Tuy, April 26, 1946

P.S. I had closed the letter but opened it to tell Your Reverence that midnight passed without the appearance of the weekenders.[338] *They finally arrived! It is 2:30 a.m.; let us go to bed…*

Two days later she wrote another letter to her Mother Superior in Fatima, sharing numerous details as if she was sitting next to her in the community at Tuy. At the end of this letter, she added an explanation of how she gracefully escaped an incident:

More to this letter: today a Dominican priest came to celebrate Mass here. In the morning they told me to prepare a table for him for lunch. I understood… but I preferred him to stay in the house of the Seminary so he could not talk to me. In spite of all the efforts put to Mother del Rocio, I put everything on the table and walked away before he came. If he wanted to ask for permission to meet me, he should go to the

---

338 Author's note: It concerns the girls of the College of Lisbon on a tour of Spain.

Bishop.[339]

The letter continued, always with her mind transported to the land of her birth where the Virgin Mary captured her heart.

On May 4, finishing what she began the evening before, she gave an account of an intention she suggested to the Sisters in preparation for the May 13 anniversary: *Today on the 4th we begin the Novena and we will do it to the end! We are united in the Sacred Hearts of Jesus and Mary and I will not forget such a consecration.*[340]

Sisters, we thank God fervently. On the eve of the month of May, we have combined our recreation to offer to Our Lady the flower of silence, the need to speak softly, and if anyone forgets, to not respond while one speaks loudly; with the particular examination to account for any faults, and for each fault to pray a Hail Mary in the evening prayer with arms crossed. Those who spend the day without committing any fault pray three Hail Marys in thanksgiving. In our room we place flowers near Our Lady with two oil lamps on blue paper. During our recreation at night in the month of Mary, we pray, we sing etc.

It is the month of the Portuguese: Our Lady is beautiful: Yesterday we sang the Salve Noble Patroness (Hail Noble Patroness) and when we were singing the line, 'as long as there are Portuguese,' others sang 'as long as there are Spaniards,' but these poor ones, it does not suit them in verse. For now we kept silence about it and it was very effective because some of the Sisters say it gave them the impression of being on retreat...

I was offered two radios from Lopes and D. Concha to listen to the ceremonies on the 13th in Fatima. I also bought the ribbon to use with the bouquet of roses from our garden that I will send with the pilgrims. The bouquet will be delivered to Mr. Roca (Xucia) and he will deliver it to His Excellency. I do not know if Mother Pereira will leave today until midnight, we'll see... [341]

After Mr. Roca mentioned to the Bishops who the flowers were from they took some, but the gentleman managed to save some for the Heavenly Mother.

Before sending the bouquet, Sister Lucia wrote the following verses to the Heavenly Mother on the white ribbon that bound the roses. Though the poem is not of high literary quality, it is from the tenderness of her heart in flames, presented at the feet of Mary:

---

339 Letter of April 26, 1946.

340 Author's note: Consecration of the Monfort Fathers who were heard on the radio and processed in Fatima on May 13, 1946, the day of the coronation of Our Lady.

341 Letter of May 4, 1946.

I miss you, dear Mother.
I offer with love
To see this longing in
Every flower of this bouquet…

I do not offer you a gold crown
Because I am poor.
I offer you this crown of love
O Heavenly Queen…

How would your heart tremble in condition so unique and solemn?!
Sister Maria Lucia of Jesus
Tuy, May 13, 1946 [342]

Earlier on May 8, after sharing many issues, her letter ends thus:
For three days we had not received a reply from His Reverence… and would I be
able to overcome a temptation?...To write something!... [343]

On May 12 and 13th, she was with the Community and followed the ceremonies of Fatima on the radio. More than anyone else, she lived the first moment of the ceremony with great solemnity, depositing her heart again and entirely at the feet, or rather, in the heart of her Queen. In a letter she wrote later, she said she renewed the consecration which she had made at the time of her First Communion while in the office of her Mother Superior. As they had two radio sets, she opted to listen on one of the radios alone in the office to experience in private the abundant emotions of that day. How could her heart not shudder in such a unique and solemn circumstance? She was very careful not to show it, however.

Shortly before being advised of the order to return to Portugal, she wrote for the last time to her Mother Superior in Tuy, describing in detail how this day was lived in the Community.

---

342 Cf. Father Lucian Cristino, *Journal of the Voice of Fatima,* No. 780, September 13, 1987, p. 3.
343 Letter of May 8, 1946.

Pilgrims in the Cova da Iria waving at the passing Image of Our Lady of Fatima.

Lucia in Aljustrel 1946.

CHAPTER XV
RETURN TO PORTUGAL

1 | Leave and Follow Me - Third Time

On May 15 at 10 a.m. the Vice Superior called Sister Dores and told her that the chief consulate wanted to speak to her. She tells how she experienced this moment of surprise with a spirit of faith and unquestionable obedience:

I went to the room with Her Reverence and when the chief consulate saw us, he said:

-Sister just called me from Porto; your superior asked me to give you a passport to go to the College of Sardão to talk with Mother Vicar, but you must go today and sleep at Valença to be on the train at 5:30 in the morning. There is not enough time to give you an official document because Sister is registered in Vigo, but I'll give you a provisional document that affirms your return by your Mother Superior. Your Mother said for you to go with Sister Maria Augusta Marinho.

-Mr. Consulate, it seems to me a very strange thing! Such an order without saying anything here and so urgently!

-Well, Sister, don't let me down. Your Superior asked me for this favor very dearly and I promised that I would do it for her.

At this time there was a phone call for me from Mother Superior from Sardão and she told me the same.

In the rush, I gathered what I needed to take with me and went to the home of Mr. Jesus Varela to say goodbye to him. For what he had done for me, I gave him as a remembrance a rosary I made which had the crucifix that I found in the pit, and then I departed because I thought he had another commitment. I also asked Mr. Varela the favor of presenting my farewell to the Bishop since there was not time for me to do it personally, and to communicate the same to the Bishop of Valladolid, for although my superiors at the moment affirmed that I would return I did not feel this would likely happen.

I returned home and said goodbye to the community, my beloved Tabernacle and chapel, and passed by the consulate to collect the documents. I took leave of Mrs. Elvira and the chief consulate who proved too optimistic in reference to my return, and I went to Valença, which was necessary to cross the border before 6 p.m.

Sister Marinho and I arrived at Asilo Fonseca around 7 p.m.; Mother Dilecta, the Mother Superior, hosted us very well and provided a feast for supper: chicken soup, rice, roasted chicken with fried potatoes, jam, cakes and fruit. The community had their recreation with us, and for rest they prepared us a beautiful room with 2 beds adorned with loops of blue and white silk, as if it were for the Immaculate, to whom, thanks to God, these sisters and I and the entire Franciscan Order are devoted.

In the morning we got up early and at 5:30 departed Porto on the train. We had made our farewells at night, but in the morning the Mother Superior still got up to give us one more hug.

-I do not know, but I have the impression that Sister will not come back here, Mother told me.

-I also think so, I answered.

-Mother Vicar is capable and wants to take you to Rome. If so, ask a blessing for me from the Holy Father.

-Oh! I have no such luck! I wish I could see and talk to the Holy Father. But I do not think so. My fate is not for this world!

We arrived at Porto around 10:30 a.m. The chauffer was waiting at the station for us and we reached the College of Sardão around 11 a.m. The chaplain, Rev. Luis, was waiting for us to give us Holy Communion. We thanked him and he led us to the cafeteria to have some coffee and then we went upstairs to greet Reverend Mother. We spoke in the recreation room and this made me full of joy. After our greeting, the Reverend Mother Vicar led me to her office to speak privately with me. In spite of Her Reverence being Italian and not knowing Portuguese, we understood each other very well. She spoke to me about Our Lady and Mother Monfalim, and at the end of our conversation she asked me if I had something of Mother Monfalim's that I could give her as a keepsake. As there was only a tiny image of Our Lady that Mother Monfalim had left me at the time of her death and I always carried it with me, I took it off and gave it to her. [344]

She spent the rest of the day talking with the Mother Vicar who needed some information about the apparitions for a book she was writing with Mother Provincial. They said nothing to her about the future. The next day the Mother Superior of Tuy, Mother Maria do Carmo Cunha Matos, was there and spoke at length with Sister Lucia while they walked along the garden and pine forest. Lucia was very comfortable with Mother Maria who had been her Schoolmistress while she lived in Tuy.

As soon as the students discovered who the Sister was that arrived, they began to wait in all corners of the house to see her. Some passed the news to others whose families then came. The Sisters, each one wanting the favor of introducing her, asked to have a word with her. Poor Shepherdess! There she was again besieged by the crowds. She said no to the many requests, especially when asked to give autographs, noting that they were not happy and could not be otherwise.

---

344 *My Pathway*, I, p. 195 – 198.

2 | Lucia Visits Fatima

On the afternoon of May 19 having a little time left, the Mother Provincial told her that the next day she would go to Fatima with Mother Vicar.

She added that the Bishop had asked me to go on the 13th, but that did not seem prudent due to the large crowd that day.

-And now I don't know, Mother Provincial; I believe that there are always many people there, I replied, while seeking to conceal the enthusiasm at the thought I was going to see again that place I had departed 25 years ago.

I give the following account with Mother Provincial:

Mother said: -The Bishop asks for Sister to go there. Mother Vicar wanted to take you with her so that we do not have to think about it anymore. Of course, if I were consulted, I would say that I prefer not to go, not because I do not want to, but to avoid problems. Since now obedience is in charge, I speak as Mother Provincial: no more 'food for thought.' [345]

One can imagine what it was like for Sister Lucia that night. She was once again going to the land of her birth and childhood. She would visit again those places sanctified by the presence of Mary and the Angel. And this is precisely what the Bishop wanted—for her to identify the locations of the apparitions of the Angel. The next day Sister Lucia, accompanied by Mother Vicar, the Mother's Assistant, and Mother Provincial, went to Fatima, stopping for lunch in Coimbra. They left Coimbra at 4 p.m. in the college car with Mother Brito. As they passed Leiria, the shepherdess did not mention her desire to go to the Episcopal Palace to receive a blessing from her spiritual guide, and they continued on their way. Sister Lucia tells the story of her arrival in Fatima, dictated when she was alive:

We arrived at Fatima by 6:30 in the afternoon. There were drops of drizzling rain. The car brought us to the Chapel of the Apparitions. We went down, and staying a few steps behind the Mothers while they went inside to pray I was able to be alone to kneel at the place where I had stood before at the tiny holm oak tree on which Our Lady rested Her Immaculate feet, and the grid (now in place where the holm oak tree once grew). While kneeling down there after so many years, I felt a strong impression, such as that of a shiver, but managed to control myself without the Mothers knowing. Then with an inner energy I was filled with the memory of events that took place, and then the Mother touched me on the shoulder to go home and I was completely serene. Everything had happened fortunately only between God and me. [346]

She said nothing to the Mothers, but briefly relived the path she traveled on

345 *Ibid*, p. 199.
346 *Ibid*, p. 200.

that distant day of June 15, 1921, offering again along this path her faithful 'yes' that was so painful at the time. Deep in her heart like a serene lake, she may have felt the presence of her Mother telling her again: *God is pleased,* [347] and she wanted nothing more.

Deciding to wait until the next day to visit all the important places of Fatima, the Mothers went to their house to rest. Sister Dores, in her capacity as a Sister Helpmate, joined the other Sister Helpmates in their state, taking a meal with them and helping them with housekeeping and cleaning the kitchen. Before retiring, she received a call from the Bishop of Leiria, José Alves Correia da Silva, saying that the next morning he would celebrate Mass in the Chapel of the Apparitions and wanted Sister Dores there. The Mothers consented and promised to accompany her. But it was the will of God to do otherwise. Some moments later they received a phone call from Lisbon advising them that they would have to go very early to catch a plane for a trip scheduled for Italy. For the Mothers, Fatima was reserved for another time.

The next morning before Mass, Sister Dores and Mother Brito went to the Chapel of the Apparitions to wait for the Bishop. He greeted them when he arrived. Sister Dores had a feeling that this was to be the first and last time she would receive Holy Communion here, and it was the only time she ever did.

The Bishop asked me to go to the retreat house to have lunch with His Excellency. Mother Brito said yes and we went. At the table, as if once more in Formigueira, the Bishop wanted me to sit next to him and serve him. Seeing what I took to eat, he said:

-Oh, my daughter, if you do not eat more than that it is not enough to hear the cuckoo sing!

To which I replied that we should walk around.

Then he showed me the house, the chapel, and the throne room still decorated as it had been for His Excellency the Cardinal Legate. Then the Bishop made me sit in a large chair beside him as in the days before and we talked particularly about various subjects. [348]

She returned with Mother Brito to the house of the Dorothean Sisters. At 2 p.m. they began the pilgrimage led by the shepherdess to identify the places of the apparitions. Sister Lucia described this trip:

As ordered by the Bishop, I left with Mother Brito, Rev. José Galamba and Rev. Carlos to go to the Cabeço, Valinhos and the well. I proposed that we go by the open area to avoid people. Rev. Galamba asked if I still remembered the way so I would not get lost. I replied, yes, and that we were on the same pathway that I went with Jacinta

---

and Francisco 29 years ago to the Cova da Iria.

On the way we found a woman with a little girl who reminded me of Jacinta. They had two sheep. Fr. Carlos took a picture of them, and at this time they did not know me or I them. Later I came to know that it was Olympia, one of many friends at the time I was a child.

We arrived at Barreiro, a path between the bushes, and climbed the slope of the hill and went to sit on the rocks where for years I had gone with my first companions in my time as a shepherdess and which manifested a figure we could not define. The Rev. Carlos took a picture and we continued to go back to the mountain, passing a little below the windmills towards the Loca.

I do not know if it was on purpose that those who accompanied me were no longer standing behind me without my realizing it. When I arrived at the Loca, I found myself alone. I was glad and climbed the plateau of the rock and land. I knelt down tilting my forehead to the ground and prayed the prayers of the Angel; so I was able to gain this first impression alone. I got up and took a few steps backwards, and saw people talking with a group of Dominican Sisters. I signaled them and they came to me and were surprised when I told them that the Loca was there; I think they assumed that it would be further down where I could not see. Rev. Galamba found this was more consistent with my information.

The Dominican Sisters joined us, knelt and prayed the prayers of the Angel, and we continued our journey toward Valinhos. We crossed the Pregueira, an olive grove that belonged to my parents and where each stone reminded me of my conversations with Jacinta and Francisco... When we reached Valinhos, already the news had spread and a group of people was waiting for us. Among them were Ti Marto and Rev. John DeMarchi holding hands with two little first grade students who were my nieces.[349]

While greeting Ti Marto, I said to him:

-What beautiful girls they are! It is worth my trip to see you come into this world! You remind me of Jacinta and Francisco. So uncle, do you not remember me?...

-If they were alive they would be like you...

-Oh! They would be better than me! Our Lord this time made a mistake. He should have left one of them here and taken me.[350]

Then we prayed the Rosary and continued the journey to the house of my parents and I went to the well. There I knelt and prayed with the people who followed me. I wanted to drink some water, so I excused myself to the Mother and placed the bucket at the bottom. I lifted the water and in the manner of peasants, picked a cabbage leaf, formed a shell and drank. People followed my example and enjoyed the freshness and

---

349 *Ibid*, P. 203 – 204.
350 Oral Narration of Sister Lucia.

taste of the water. On our return, my sisters wanted to offer us a snack, which Mother Brito and the Fathers accepted. For that reason we entered the house and that impression made me see myself there again!

Everything was pretty much the same. I wanted to be alone but I was surrounded by a crowd that filled every corner. Outside was crowded also. Rev. Galamba disappeared and soon came with the parish priest and a car to drive us, which otherwise was too difficult to walk.

I went down for a few moments to the house of Ti Marto, but the crowd soon joined.[351]

Aunt Olympia was at the fireplace and we spoke to each other:

-So Aunt! You don't know me?

-Ah! It is true that you are Lucia? They told me that you were walking around, but as many times they have lied, so now I also did want to believe...

-As it is, it is to die the same as Thomas.

-Who is this?

-It is true! It is a subject that my aunt does not know... In my time here there was a cellar; who lives there now?

-The other who lives with me is John. Do you remember my Jacinta and my Francisco?

-Yes, I remember, and the sermons preached to us by my aunt.

-Yes, but your mother was more close to you; she was worse than I.

-Why, she was not: a thousand times better! Don't you know the proverb that says: The one who gives the bread gives the creation?

-So it is...[352]

I said goodbye, hugging Aunt Olympia. With difficulty, I managed to get into the car surrounded by people, and we went to the parish church for a short visit to the Blessed Sacrament, my dear Lady of the Rosary, the cemetery where the graves of my dear parents are, and Jacinta and Francisco. It was then necessary to get into the car and leave because the crowd was already overflowing.[353]

The pilgrimage with the shepherdess to whom the Message of Fatima was given was finished. The evangelical message, once as small as a mustard seed, was now a tree that branched out to the whole world. It was a day of intense emotions for Sister Lucia, who repressed and stored them in the reserve of her heart, well-accustomed to storing secrets. If she could have done this journey alone with God... well one can only imagine this was in her heart, but it was not possible.

---

351 *My Pathway,* I, p. 204 – 205.
352 Oral Narration of Sister Lucia.
353 *My Pathway,* I, p. 205.

▲ Meeting of Lucia with Ti Marto,
    father of Francisco and Jacinta,
    1946.

▶ Lucia visiting Aljustrel, drinking water
    from the well at the house of her parents.

▼ Lucia with a herd and a child in Aljustrel.

▲ Lucia with a group of people that followed her to identify the place of the Apparitions of the Angel.

▶ Lucia during her visit to the places of her childhood.

Identification of the site of the Apparitions
of the Angel.

► Lucia in the Chapel
  of the Apparitions.

Lucia, Mother Manuela Brito and Father José Galamba de Oliveira.

Already nighttime, they gathered at the house. Shortly afterward the Bishop came to invite Sister Dores and the Sisters of the community to go to the retreat house and watch a movie of some festivals celebrated at the shrine, and to see the magnificent crown of Our Lady. Several sisters went with her and they returned at 11 p.m. Sister Lucia said nothing to them, but was greatly fatigued and experiencing unceasing emotions from visiting the paths of her childhood and reliving the stored memories that she could only share with God and Our Lady. Would she even sleep? Surely she rested her weary forehead on the lap of Our Lady and abandoned all, grateful for all she received, and slept like an angel.

The next day, May 22, she participated in the Eucharist at the house chapel and received several visitors authorized by the Bishop. In the afternoon she returned to the shrine to say goodbye, visiting the Basilica still under construction and her sister Gloria's house. After saying goodbye to the Community of Dorothean Sisters of Fatima, she began the return trip with Mother Brito, this time in the car of the governor who had asked Bishop José for this honor in the company of his wife. They brought them to the Episcopal Palace in Leiria. Sister Dores talked for some time with the Bishop, then visited the Blessed Sacrament in his private chapel. After greeting some people who were waiting for her in the street, she left in the college car to stay overnight in Coimbra. On the evening of the 23rd she returned to Porto in the company of another Mother.

3 | Praising the Wonders of God

Sister Lucia wrote a personal reflection of her pilgrimage:

I made this pilgrimage singing in my heart a hymn of thanksgiving, though I noticed once more that the crowds run after me in search of the supernatural that they do not find in the world. I want my steps to leave a trail of light to show them by faith the path to Heaven, the encounter with the living God, the reality of His Infinite Being, Immense, Eternal! Surely this is the mission that He wanted for me. Looking at the universe, I feel the responsibility of pointing souls to the true Light. 'Do not light a lamp and hide it... so your light shines...' Through prayer, silence, recollection, humility, penance, the retreat and charity! It is what the world is deficient in, and it is in the virtues that the light of the supernatural shines. She is showing God to these souls, like St. John in the wilderness pointing to the Lamb of God, far from the ambitions of the earth, of indecency and of pleasures! 'I have come into the world, but I am not of the world.' Because the world for me is just the path to God![354]

---

354 *Ibid*, p. 207.

On the morning of May 24 after Holy Mass, she was invited by her Superior of Tuy, Mother Cunha Matos, to take a stroll in the residence at Porto. She soon realized that Mother had something painful to tell her and she noticed her suffering even to tears. The Mother Vicar and Mother Provincial had decided that she was not to return to Tuy! After 21 years, she had deep roots and friendships that were painful for her to leave. Once again the Lord was inviting her to open her heart and look to Him alone. She prayed in her sorrowful heart: *it is for love of You, O my God, for the conversion of sinners, for the Holy Father and in reparation for sins committed against the Immaculate Heart of Mary.*[355]

It was painful to have yet another obstacle in her dream of entering Carmel, especially since she had hoped to announce to the Bishop of Valladolid that she was in good health. She abandoned herself entirely into the hands of God, and like Our Lady, said in her heart: *Behold the handmaid of the Lord, let it be done to me according to Your will.*[356]

Mother Cunha Matos wept inconsolably with the prospect of having to go back to Spain without her, knowing how people would react, namely the chief consulate, the Bishop of the diocese and the personnel at the border where Sister Dores was very well known and loved. To let them down easier, it was decided to tell them that she was taking some time to rest, and meanwhile, everyone would become accustomed to her absence.

Mother Cunha Matos returned to Tuy, her heart plunged in sadness. Now the roles were reversed and she wrote to Sister Dores from Tuy a few days later, full of nostalgia and longing for her return. The child had missed her Superior; now the Superior missed her shepherdess who was in Portugal. Mother Cunha Matos made excuses to one after another who asked about Sister Dores, telling them she stayed some time to rest and for a change of scenery. On the other end Sister Dores prayed with a spirit of faith:

-*Grant me, O good Jesus, that always in everything I follow the path of Your steps and the light of Your examples. Like the star that shines before me guiding my path, I will follow the echo of Your voice. Help me to climb with a firm step the rustic slope of the mountain that rises in front of me, so that everything gives You glory as You say: 'The things, therefore, that I say, I say them as My Father has said them to me'...* [357]

355 MSL I, 2nd M, Ch. II, No. 16, p. 98.
356 Lk 1:38.
357 *My Pathway*, I, p. 209.

4 | Our Lady, Pilgrim of the World

Our Lady of Fatima was already very much known around the world, and a desire began to germinate in some hearts to bring her image to the world. She wanted to be a pilgrim and visit all of her children.

In September 1943, when the world was still groaning under the lash of a fierce war, the National Council of Catholic Youth Women gathered in Fatima and vowed to organize an international pilgrimage of thanksgiving to the Cova da Iria as soon as this plague ended. The heart of Maria Teresa Pereira da Cunha was inspired to mentor this promise and see it through. That same year a Belgian priest, Father Demoutiez, Oblate of the Immaculate Heart, began to feel the desire to make a pilgrimage to Fatima with a group of scouts as soon as the war ended. Not being able to see clearly what this was about, the same seed began to grow in his heart. These two souls were unknowingly chosen to be united in the same bold adventure by the authorities of the Church to promote the Pilgrimage of Our Lady of Fatima throughout the war-weary world.

In May 1945, the scourge of war ended. In April the following year, the Portuguese Catholic Youth Women were invited to take part in the international meeting in the city of Gand. There a Russian representative spoke passionately about Fatima, and the young person representing Portugal was thankful for these words and took the opportunity to invite all the young people present to take part in the first International Pilgrimage to the Cova da Iria in May of 1947. It was then that the Holy Spirit spoke through the mouth of the representative of Luxembourg saying:

-If an image of Our Lady of Fatima went out of the Cova da Iria, it would bring to devastated Europe the message of peace.[358]

At that same time, Father Demoutiez wrote to Rome asking that an image of Our Lady of Fatima leave the Cova da Iria and travel between the capitals of Europe. It was the Heart of the Mother eager to find and comfort her children, who would see the light and desire this in their hearts. Through this pilgrimage and other acts that had already occurred, the necessary steps were put in place for the fulfillment of the words of Our Lady on July 13th:

-In the end, my Immaculate Heart will triumph.[359]

Maria Teresa, affectionately acquainted with Sister Dores, was strengthened by her who embraced this idea with much joy and prayed for its intention fervently.

---

358 Maria Teresa Pereira da Cunha, *Our Lady of Fatima Pilgrimage of the World*, first journey: beginning of the pilgrimage in Europe.

359 MSL I, 4th M, Ch. II, No. 5, p. 179.

Images of Our Lady's Pilgrimage trip around the world.

There are many letters from her to Maria Teresa on this subject, sometimes giving advice and other times encouraging her with absolute trust in Divine Providence, especially in relation to the enormous expense of the trip. In this regard, when Maria Teresa brought the daring project to the Bishop of Leiria, His Excellency replied:

-This pilgrimage requires huge expenses. Where will the money come from?

Moved by the Holy Spirit, Maria Teresa said:

-Bishop, if Our Lady wants that the Pilgrimage be done, the money will come. If it doesn't, it is because she does not want it, in which case we will give up. [360]

Our Lady blessed the blind trust of this intrepid and sacrificial apostle. Maria Teresa knew God's work always carries the seal of the cross, which authenticates the origin of the undertaking. She threw herself into the journey empty-handed, knowing that if enough money was given to fund the enterprise, it would not be missed.

Father Demoutiez was also given the cross. When he presented himself to his Provincial to make the pilgrimage to Fatima, the response to him was a firm negative.

He humbly abandoned the idea to the Heart of Mary, and when least expected, it was the Provincial himself who, at the request of his superior, sent him to Fatima with the task of organizing a pilgrimage of penance and prayer between Fatima and Maastricht in Holland. The Provincial wrote to the National Directorate of J.C.F. of Portugal asking for support, a request that was accepted as a light from Heaven because it opened the door for the growth of the project.

The image of Our Lady of Fatima that departed on this first journey was sculpted by Mr. Dom José Thedim in 1947, who had been told to replicate the one that was in the Capelinha when he journeyed there as a pilgrim. It was made with the precise instructions of Sister Lucia. Her desire was that the pilgrim image represent Our Lady's position when she revealed herself as the Immaculate Heart to the Shepherds in 1917.

In a letter written to Sister Lucia, Maria Teresa lamented that at the beginning of the pilgrimage to Spain, Our Lady was delivered to a foreign priest, and she and other members of the entourage could not be present. To console her, Sister Lucia replied with her magnanimous vision not to worry about it, because with Our Lady there were no foreigners—all are her children. The Lady of the holm oak was accompanied by the man chosen by her, Father Demoutiez, who did not know a word of Portuguese or Spanish, but who spoke the language of

---

360 Maria Teresa Pereira da Cunha, *Our Lady of Fatima Pilgrimage of the World*, first journey: beginning of the pilgrimage in Europe.

Mary, which is the Gospel.

5 | A Smile from Heaven in the World

The Pilgrim Statue left Portugal in 1947 and traveled for two years, visiting 33 countries. Fr. Demoutiez, O.M.I., organized the tour and Msgr. Marques Dos Santos, vicar-general of the Diocese of Leiria-Fatima, was in charge of it. On foot, by car, plane or boat, the image Our Lady of Fatima was brought throughout the world, named the "Pilgrim Virgin Statue," spreading in the hearts of people her maternal love and peace.

It is delightful to read the story of the whole Pilgrimage by the tireless companion of the Pilgrim Lady! What joy she brought to hearts, how much peace and grace. How many wayward sheep were brought back to the Good Shepherd just through the sweet motherly look of that beautiful image, though far short of reality? She followed the prayer of the people, who sang:

> O Lady of the holm-oak
> Go through the entire earth
> Follow your ways.
> Go through the entire earth
> O Mother of our desires,
> Lady of gentle doves,
> Lady of the Shepherds.[361]

Behind this pilgrimage and all of its fruits was the silent confidant of Our Lady of Fatima. In her seclusion, Sister Dores occupied herself humbly with sacrificial prayers, obeying what was asked or commanded of her. She constantly interceded with her arms raised before God on behalf of the people. The entourage—the priests, Maria Teresa and others who accompanied the Lady in white—knew they could count on the support promised to Maria Teresa, which often was repeated in letters from Sister Dores. Sister Dores was thrilled with the news that came to her from distant lands where the pilgrimage was made. Truly, the glory of the shepherdess was her surrender to her Lady, *The White Shepherdess of the New Times.*[362] Later when the shepherdess was a Carmelite, the Celestial Pilgrim also visited her community. On October 12, 1950, the Pilgrim Virgin came to the cloister to stay a few hours with the Carmelite Sisters of Saint Teresa.

361 *Sing To The Lord,* editorial L.I.A.M., 6th Edition, 1972.
362 Hymn of the Fiftieth Anniversary of the Apparitions.

During the visit, two sisters at a time would take turns each hour praying the Rosary with the image. The image returned again in 1954 for 24 hours to the great delight of the entire community.

At the end of the National Pilgrimage, members of the entourage of the White Lady wanted to offer to Sister Lucia the doves that accompanied the image in the hills and valleys. She received them with immense affection and cared for them in the loft that was made for them near the garden.

6 | In Sardão

Sister Dores continued to have minor fevers and weakness, and settled in an upstairs room with a window opening to Heaven to get some needed rest. She walked in the garden and forest, and helped with the linens as much as she could, but without the responsibility. She especially enjoyed walking alone so she could pray the Rosary and visit the grottos of the Sacred Heart of Jesus and Our Lady. She often sacrificed this time alone to receive visitors who came with the Superior's permission. It was impossible to escape this and it was not infrequent, to her great mortification. With her eyes on God, she silently offered these sacrifices with love, repeating each time with more fervor: *O Jesus, it is for love of You...* [363]

She lived her life thus, always lifting her eyes to God and her heavenly Mother, imploring mercy for the people. Now she had a room alone, a treasure which offered her more privacy. Being a convalescent, she had more free time to visit the Blessed Sacrament, but it was not so easy to obtain permission to make Holy Hours on Thursdays. The superiors thought she needed rest and didn't think it was appropriate.

One day, however, she asked Mother Provincial if she could make the Holy Hour that night. Mother told her she could only make a visit to the Blessed Sacrament and then go rest. She thanked her and obeyed. When she entered the chapel, the superior of the house came and a cat jumped inside. The superior recommended to Sister Dores not to leave the cat there alone, so she kept company with her Lord while the cat nestled. Only at midnight did the cat resolve to leave, so Sister Dores shut the door and took the key to the Mother Provincial, who was surprised and asked:

-*Sister, you have only just come!*

-*Yes, I made the visit as you told me. But when I got to the chapel, the superior ordered me not to leave the cat that entered the chapel. And it just came out now.* [364]

---

363 MSL I, 4th M, Ch. II, No. 5, p. 178.
364 Oral Narration of Sister Lucia.

The Mother Provincial smiled and so did the shepherdess.

7 | The Carmel on the Horizon

In late July 1946 she received a visit from a great friend, Mrs. Olympia Pereira Coutinho. She offered Sister Dores the possibility of going to Rome, and would pay for her and another sister designated to monitor her if permission was granted. It was a joy in her heart to go to Rome to see the Pope and be able to talk to him. At first permission was granted, but some time later it was withdrawn. She was told she was not going to be sister's helpmate, but the real reason was revealed to her later by a sick sister whom she took by wheelchair to the garden.

She told me that the Mothers would not let me go to Rome because they suspected that I wanted to ask the Holy Father to let me relocate to Carmel. I kept silent, but actually, they were not wrong. [365]

Carmel! Her heart screamed louder its desire to be away from so many visitors from whom she could not escape. As the Fatima apparitions became known, more and more people wanted to see her and she did not lack the friends of friends who sought the opportunity to meet her. There was discontent with the spirituality of the Institute in which she had been dedicated to the Lord, Whom she loved very much, as well as the sisters with whom she lived. But the desire for Carmel was constant in her life, since the day of her departure from Fatima on June 15, 1921; how distant in time that was, but so close at heart.

It is possible the desire for Carmel would have become less imperative if the environment around her were less exposed to the outside world, but despite the efforts of her superiors to protect her, she was sought after and there was no other remedy to satisfy the wishes of others. God only knows how many bitter moments the Mother Superiors spent trying to remove her from the requested meetings.

While in Spain, the shepherdess saw most of the doors open and the Bishop of Valladolid was very interested in helping her, but now she felt more alone. She received some visits from the Bishop of Gurza and opened her heart to him, who understood. His Excellency was of the opinion that Reverend Mother should move her to a Carmel, but how? She had some hope with the trip to Rome, but that door also closed. Walking alone at night she did not lose heart; Our Lady was going to open her path unexpectedly.

On February 6, 1947, on the recommendation of the Bishop of Leiria, two Dominican priests spoke with Sister Dores. One of them was Fr. Thomas McGlynn,

---

365 *My Pathway*, I, p. 219.

O.P. who wanted information for making an exact image of the Immaculate Heart of Mary. For three days Sister Dores gave directions for making the model that would serve as a model for the image. As some issues arose that needed attention, the Mother designated to accompany her left her alone on a few occasions. During one of these occasions Fr. McGlynn said he would be going to Rome and was going to have an audience with the Holy Father. The heart of the shepherdess jumped and she exclaimed:

-*What luck!*

Then Father asked,

-*Why? Would Sister like to speak with the Holy Father?*

She responded:

-*Oh, I would like that! But this is not for me, I have no such luck!* [366]

Promptly the priest offered to do everything that she wanted. Reflecting in her heart, it seemed to her that God was revealing the only opportunity and it was because of Our Lady that this door opened. She was not disobeying because there were no restrictions on her to communicate with the Pope; he is the Holy Father. Concealing her emotions, she asked:

-*If I give you a sealed letter for the Pope, will Your Reverence deliver it personally without anyone else knowing?* [367]

Having received an affirmative answer to guarantee absolute confidentiality, Sister Dores left and went to the chapel to pray. She was always near the Tabernacle when she received the light needed for decisive moments. She describes this moment:

I retired and went to the Chapel in the outer classroom where I was more alone with the Lord. I knelt near the tabernacle, asking for the light of the Lord.

-*Is this the way You want me to go? The door is open, should I enter? If I attempt to arrange things through my Superiors, I will never be able to! If the Holy Father tells me yes, then no one would dare say no. If the Holy Father tells me no, it is because this is the Will of God. I will not think any more about such a thing. If the Holy Father ignores me and does not answer me, which is perhaps a most certain thing, I will intend to arrange things then through my Superiors.*

It seems to me that I felt the light of God. I went upstairs, walked into my room and wrote. I did not keep a copy so I would not expose myself to being found out. The next day just before parting I gave the letter to Father McGlynn, asking once again for his absolute secrecy.

---

366 *Ibid*, I, p. 220.
367 *Ibid.*

-Be calm, Sister, no one else will know. [368]

On the 19th of the following April, Sister Dores was surprised by the proposal of the Bishop of Leiria. He who had always been opposed to her going to a Carmel, now proposed for her to go for a season to the Carmel in Fatima to experience it. If she did not feel good there, she could return to the Institute. Sister Dores left it up to the Bishop to talk to her Superior, who refused this solution. She concluded:

I did not want to go to Fatima because it seemed to me that this very convent would be disturbed because of me, but I did not dare say it to the Bishop. [369]

Two days later, she was called to the Episcopal Palace in Porto and was accompanied by Mother Provincial. The Bishop spoke first with Mother and then privately with Sister Dores. He reported that he had received a letter from the Holy Father in response to what she had written to His Holiness. The Holy Father ordered him to facilitate her entry into Carmel. The Bishop asked her to think about it for eight days and then give an answer. Sister Dores replied that she felt it was unnecessary to think anymore because she had decided, but the Bishop demanded that she think about it. Sister Lucia described the following scene:

The Bishop again sent for the Mother Provincial, which proved to be very stressful. His Excellency sought to cheer her up and look at these things as a sign of God's Will, and willingly to accept with pleasure whatever the end was. The Bishop gave us his blessing and we kissed his sacred ring and said goodbye. In the car Mother Provincial cried the whole time to me until we arrived home. It flowed through my heart and I wanted to console her and could not, because the only thing that could console her was if I were to tell her that I stopped the idea of going to Carmel, and so I could not say this because I felt it was something from the Will of God. [370]

Thus began a time she described as a painful ordeal. Many influential people from Sardão tried to change her mind, among them Mother Maria José Martins with whom she shared a great friendship. They strolled through the garden every day and conversed on this subject, especially how much suffering it caused. Although Sister Lucia's heart bled, she would not be moved and answered:

-It is not that I intend to find in Carmel a life of roses. No. I think that if anything it will perhaps reap more painful thorns... Yes, but what I try to find in Carmel and what I do not have here, or cannot have, are the enclosed walls that protect me from the large stream of curious and indiscreet views in order to achieve a life of gathering and

---

368 *Ibid,* p. 220–221.
369 *Ibid,* p. 241.
370 *Ibid,* p. 254.

intimacy more intense with the Lord, and I hope that He gives me this grace.[371]

8 | A Sign from Heaven

Father Guerra, S.J. arrived, asking her to make a list of standards for a possible missionary foundation. Although she felt unable to do so, she followed the order of her Superior, and doing the best she could gave it to him. After looking over this outline, he asked her to go there for a time to orientate the candidates' first steps. She declined, saying that she was going to Carmel.

At the beginning of May, she received a balm from the Bishop of Gurza who visited and encouraged her to continue with her desire. On May 12 she talked with the Bishop of Porto, confessing her decision to join a Carmel as soon as possible. The Bishop of Porto, in turn, spoke to Father Guerra and told him she could go a couple of times to the new Institute because the Holy Father's permission had no dates, and then she would go to Carmel. But the shepherdess remained steadfast and did not yield to this suggestion.

The visits continued and increased. When the Mother Provincial returned from Rome, Mother suspected that Sister Dores had gone there incognito. When questioned about it, Mother requested that Sister Dores ask the Sisters what reason they had given for her absence. It became known that Sister Dores wanted to go to a Carmel and invitations arrived for her to join other contemplative orders. This made her days doubly bitter because it was causing other sufferings and it also caused her to leave her birthplace of religious life. It was not in vain that she lived there in the wholesome years of her youth, where she had consecrated her heart to the Lord forever. This was followed by strong words from some Bishops who visited her, which she described:

They resorted also to the intercession of some Bishops who exerted their influence, each in his own way: the Archbishop of Evora, Bishop Manuel Mendes da Conceição, the Archbishop of Mitilene, Bishop Manuel da Trindade Salgueiro, the Bishop of Leiria, who went back on his word of support for me, and the Bishop of Porto, who told me that the permission sent by the Holy Father was not valid, that we had to ask another of the Sacred Congregation, etc. But in the middle of everything, I felt the grace of God give me the strength and confidence that it had come to an end. [372]

On August 12, 1947, she had a new interview with Bishop Agostinho, the Bishop of Porto. He asked Sister Dores which Carmel she wanted to join. She suggested the Viana do Castelo where she could be more cloistered. In addition,

---

371 *Ibid*, p. 225.
372 *Ibid*, p. 237.

the Prioress there was well-known to her. But the Bishop wanted her to stay in Porto and he thought it was prudent to wait until the Community in Viana do Castelo adjusted to normal operation, since it was a new foundation and the Community had to strengthen its organization. Sister Dores agreed to the proposal because she also knew the Prioress of Porto. She just wanted these things to be settled quickly.

The Bishop, however, said again that the permission she had from the Holy Father was not enough. The statement in his letter was not valid for her transfer to Carmel. It was an enormous question mark for Sister Dores, who came to doubt and asked for a sign of guidance in the middle of the night:

I went to the Tabernacle asking for light and strength.

-I know, my Good Jesus, that we should not abuse Your goodness asking for signs, but do not take me wrong that in the circumstances in which I find myself I ask You for one. You know how the Mother Provincial has forbidden them to send me to talk to any person outside. Well, on the 15th, the feast of the Assumption of Our Blessed Mother into Heaven, a Carmelite priest arrived and told me to speak to You. I will take this as a sure sign that You desire me to go to Carmel. If this fails, then I do not know, perhaps for the sake of my Superior to give up, I do not know! Give me light and strength! [373]

The response from Heaven was one she did not expect. Mid-morning on the following day, Sister Dores was called to the visiting room where Fr. Humberto Maria Pasquale, S.D.B., confessor of the College, was waiting for her along with two Carmelite priests. They were Friar Isidoro da Virgem do Carmo, who was Provincial Vicar of the Portuguese Carmel that was being revived under the terms of the Province of St. Joaquim of Navarra, and Friar Gonzalo da Virgem do Carmo, both Spaniards. She could not believe what she saw. Father Pasquale, who had accepted the role of confessor of the College with the condition that he could visit and talk with Sister Lucia when he wanted, introduced the two priests, friends of his, and let them talk to her while he fulfilled his ministry. Sister Dores spoke of various subjects with the two priests, and without revealing anything of her desires, asked the state of the Carmelites, to which Father Isidoro responded in detail, volunteering what she needed.

Did he know the desires of the shepherdess? That is possible, because the matter was already widely known, but nothing transpired in the conversation.

She bid farewell to the visitors and thanked them for answering her with so much clarity:

I went to the chapel to thank Our Lord for such a rapid response, which on this

---

373 *Ibid,* p. 238 - 239.

occasion and circumstances was almost a miracle.

-Already there is nothing to make me give up, no! Now I am sure that this is Your desire, my Good Jesus; thank you very much! [374]

She entrusted herself to the protection of the Immaculate Heart of Mary and spent the time with God in peace. She was on the cross but was in peace because she sought with truth the will of God. She stayed in this atmosphere of peace and participated in the Community's annual retreat from August 30 to September 8, during which she made her general confession for the third time, feeling the peace that He left in her heart.

9 | The Choice of Carmel

A few days later she received a visit from her close friend, the Bishop of Leiria, but this time she was left in a sea of tears following their conversation:

-You need to give up these ideas to relocate to Carmel; you just stay where you are as well.

Upon hearing this, the tears ran down my face and I said:

-Now, I cannot ever give up.

-How can you not? Did not Our Lady say to you that you should follow the way that I indicate to you?

-Yes, but now the Holy Father approves that I go and I think I should go. Because if this is so, I am not thinking of the Carmel in Fatima, I would not accept to go there. It doesn't matter, I also do not desire to go there. I would be very exposed and the monastery would be very disturbed because of me. I prefer going to one that is far away.[375]

After this visit she was steeped in great pain. Her heart, although accustomed to much suffering, had not known this level. She shared a faithful relationship with the Bishop of Leiria, and felt loved and understood, always finding in him wise and paternal advice and unparalleled support for the dark curves along her path. This day she felt rejected:

I was reminded of parents who are disgusted with their children when they behave badly or persist in lying. It made me cry during several days and nights, but it also made me well, because I was detached so much from these people. It is in the Tabernacle where I always find comfort.

-O my Good Jesus, You still had reserved in the bottom of the chalice this bitter drop for me! I want to savor all the bitterness for You! I trust, and with the Psalmist I repeat:

374 *Ibid,* p. 240.
375 *Ibid,* p. 241.

-The righteous cried and the Lord heard them, and He delivered them from all their troubles. Close is the Lord to all the afflicted who have a heart and a humble spirit. He will save them (Ps.33: 18-19). [376]

A week later she was called to the Episcopal Palace of Porto, accompanied by Mother. The Bishop asked her if she had changed her mind. She had not and asked permission to deal directly with the prioress of Carmel to end all the suffering for her and the Community. Again she was told that it was necessary to wait for permission from the Sacred Congregation for Religious because the Holy Father's letter was not enough. She questioned this answer, and seeing that this matter had dragged on interminably and the atmosphere around her was getting heavier, she decided to write again to the Holy Father, this time by mail, and asked the chaplain to please send the letter, which he did so secretly. This was at the end of October, 1947.

In January the following year, the Bishop of Porto visited the Community and she spoke with him again. He told her she had to wait, and he had not yet delivered to the Prioress of Carmel the letter that he had ordered her to write in October, asking for her admission to the Monastery.

Anchored in prayer, where she drew the strength to remain serene in the midst of the storm, she continued her normal life, fulfilling her duties as if nothing happened and remaining attentive to those needing her help. One day during recess she saw a postulant who was very sad because she desired to stay at the Institute, but being of very weak health she was sure she would have to leave. Sister Dores approached her and comforted her, urging her to trust. Then she invited her to make a novena with her to Our Lady, and so the two stayed together in the chapel at the end of the visit to the Blessed Sacrament. A sister who witnessed the scene admired it very much and was edified. She told the Mother Superior that at last Sister Dores liked the Institute, since she had offered to help the postulant seek the grace of perseverance. The postulant recovered her health and remained.

During an exhibition held over several days at the College of Sardão, there was a lot of activity, and therefore, more work. Typically when visitors came to stay and needed a room, some of the sisters would give up their rooms for those who came from the outside. It so happened that Sister Dores was asked to give up her room. She settled in a little room where they used to fix the dustbins and brooms. This room had a window shaped like a trapdoor that opened onto the roof. The window was rarely used because it was difficult to close. On one of the nights there was a storm and it was drafty and the rain came in. She went to the

376 *Ibid,* p. 242.

corner for more shelter, but contracted a severe flu, with fever and hoarseness. She also got a sore throat and began to have strong toothaches. When her temperature came down she went to the dentist. The diagnosis of Dr. Alcino Magalhães was severe: he had to remove all her teeth and put in false teeth. The doctor offered to do all the treatment for free. He removed two of her teeth and asked her to return in three days to continue the work.

On February 29, 1948, the Pilgrim Statue of Our Lady of Fatima arrived at Leixões, a small village in Porto, returning from its first journey around the world, and bringing the response that the shepherdess desired.

Bishop José Alves Correia da Silva traveled to Porto to wait for the statue, and passed by Sardão to talk with his 'pupil' whom he had left hurting the last time he saw her. He asked her if her thoughts were the same and before she could answer yes, he told her that he had already written to the Prioress of Porto. He told her that she was going to go to the Carmel in Fatima and with humility, but firmness, Sister Dores replied:

-Bishop, I thought least of all to go to Fatima since Your Excellency told me at the last visit that this would not be allowed.

-Oh! Well, that does not mean anything if it is to be there.

-That I do not know. Bishop Agostinho wants me to stay here in the Carmel of Porto and this also sounds better to me. [377]

The Bishop took his leave, saying he would meet with Bishop Agostinho and solve everything. He asked her if she still had a dowry. A dowry was asked of the postulants at this time, but was not a firm requirement. There were benefactors who made donations to any postulant who did not have a dowry. Sister Dores responded that she had an inheritance from her parents which she could sell or retain, but left this decision to her Superiors. The Bishop concluded saying that if she were to sell it, he would buy it for the Shrine. (Her inheritance from her parents was the property and house, and the Shrine did purchase it).

Sister Dores was left to her duties and to the maternal protection of the Mother Superior. She did not know ahead of time that the Pilgrim Statue would be in Leixões because of being concealed in the Convent, but she was able to greet the Image with all the affection of her heart. A few days later, she received a response from the Pope who gave her the permission to follow the path that she so long desired.

On March 5 after having two more teeth removed, she was called to the Bishop's Palace. She left immediately and this time the Bishop was not happy with

---

377 *Ibid,* p. 249.

her. Sister Lucia tells how the meeting was:

When I arrived the Bishop received me in the room and told me, scolding:

-So you were writing again to Rome!

-Yes, I wrote, because Your Excellency said it was necessary for the other permission that never came here.

-Okay, it was Our Lady who gave me the answer through you as you passed through Porto, she continued. *-Msgr. Montini wrote and said that the Holy Father told you to facilitate my transfer to Carmel. Not the Carmel in Porto as I desired, not even for me to go to Fatima as the Bishop of Leiria wanted, but to go to the Carmel of Coimbra.*

-It seems to me that it was Our Lady who prepared things. As you know, the Bishop of Leiria came here to wait for the Image of Our Lady on the 29th of last month, and I was to accompany it to Fatima. While passing through Coimbra, the Bishop was sick and we stopped and took the Image to his bedroom. We spoke casually about my transfer to the Carmel. Then Bishop Antonio asked Sister about my going to Coimbra. Since he was very sick this was his will, and because Sister was midway between Fatima and Porto. Was this okay?

-Yes, Bishop, I did what His Excellency asked. In Coimbra I do not know anyone and I had never thought of that monastery, but there I also will have a Tabernacle, and that is enough. As it is, I cannot go now because of a cold that suddenly overtook me with an infection in my mouth, and the doctor says that he will pull out all my teeth. He took some already, but there is still plenty more to complete the treatment before entering. However, we can deal with the Carmel and arrange the things I will need to take.

-Very well. I still have the letter that Sister wrote to the Mother Prioress of Porto. It will serve Coimbra. I'll send it to the Bishop to be delivered and we will wait for the answer.

I said goodbye and kissed the Sacred Ring of His Excellency, who then blessed me, and I returned home accompanied by the general schoolmistress, Mother Pignatelli.[378]

Thus, in two strokes it was decided what course to take. Again, she would be going into the unknown; as Abraham was told from the Lord:

-Leave your country and go to the land that I will show you. [379]

The shepherdess renewed once again her 'yes' of May 13, 1917, and consented to follow this new path. She was attracted to other Carmels—Viano do Castelo, Porto and Fatima—because she got to know people and their land, but Coimbra was a stranger and unknown. Her consolation was the certainty

---

378 *Ibid*, p. 250 - 251.
379 Gn 12:1.

that *'there, too, she will have a Tabernacle, and that is enough.'* The Tabernacle, her Hidden Jesus, was her refuge and solace for her difficult hours, her dark nights. Could the whole world miss her? She knew that *one who has God lacks nothing, because God alone suffices!* [380]

She quietly lived with her secret, not getting excited or shedding a spotlight on her news, knowing however that it would spread like oil, especially in the closest environments. And the news spread. The shepherdess gave *all to God, to His Holy Will, lived inside, ignoring what was happening outside.*[381]

She had the strength of mind not to reveal any expression of regret. She was anchored only in her Lord and took refuge in the Immaculate Heart of her Mother with the certainty of the promise heard 31 years ago in 1917, and whose words were more than a memory. They were etched in her heart:

-I will never leave you. My Immaculate Heart will be your refuge and the way that will lead you to God. [382]

When she could, she gave the news only to her chaplain and confessor, who advised her to finish the treatment of her mouth before entering Carmel. The law of enclosure was so much more demanding in the matter of making exits. Even for health care, permission is needed from the Holy See through the Apostolic Enunciator. It was therefore appropriate that the treatment was completed before her entrance into her new life. But God's ways are not ours; just the opposite. God performs an exquisite work in our lives underneath the full picture that is given in the end. He weaves a marvelous work which we only see when our human loom is done, and we are in the hands of God and can say, 'This is His work!' Then we will say, 'How wonderful!' But in the meantime…the cross will plow our land.

10 | Leave and Follow Me - Fourth Time

Monday of Holy Week, March 22, the official day of her birthday, Sister Dores was suffering, but was going to receive a long overdue gift. After returning from the dentist, she was given the news that her entry into the Carmel of Coimbra was scheduled for March 25, Holy Thursday. This left her in a panic—so quickly and in the middle of her dental treatments?

As Christ had *long desired to eat this Passover with His disciples,*[383] which was enveloped in the supreme pain of His Passion, Sister Lucia also had a great

---

380 St. Teresa of Avila, Poetry 7.
381 Luis Perroy S. J., *Ascent to Calvary,* 2nd Edition, Part 1, Ch. 5, p. 30.
382 MSL I, 4th M, Ch. II, No. 4. p. 177.
383 Lk 22:15.

yearning to carry the cross. She had followed this path since childhood without any pleasure, but offered to the Lord *the consolation of not having any.*[384]

God does not ask too much or too little; He asks EVERYTHING even if it is only a few poor nets, such as the first Apostles. She wanted to immediately and unconditionally bond to His invitation of love, and without looking back, never perceived anything as too much suffering for Him, for *those who love Him too, will see that they can suffer very much for Him.*[385] The shepherdess kept saying 'yes' to all the surprises and rough times in life with an ever greater love, renewing her 'Yes' of May 13, 1917, the constant song of her life.

Because of who she was and to protect her, the Bishops handled everything with the Carmel. Sister Dores did not know the Community and the Community did not know her, a very rare occurrence. When this happens, there is a least an exchange of correspondence, but with Sister Dores even this was not done. The Bishop of Coimbra, Bishop Antonio Antunes, wrote to the Prioress on March 12 asking if she had a vacant cell to receive a new candidate who had *large gifts of humility, self-sacrifice, devotion to Our Lady, etc.* At first he did not tell her who the candidate was; only some days later did he reveal her identity. Sister Dores' admission was an exceptional case. There was no note of the Chapter and no minutes to account for it, simply information from the Bishop of the diocese who at that time was in charge of the Carmel of St. Teresa, which was under his jurisdiction by express permission of the Holy Father.

If the Prioress had known that Lucia was being treated for an infection that required the extraction of all her teeth, she would have been the first to reject the candidate. This information, however, did not reach the Carmel, so March 25, Holy Thursday, was a beautiful day to enter. In addition, on the morning of this great day, she would make her Solemn Profession of Vows to Sister Mary of the Cross. At this time, the ceremony of profession took place in the chapter room of the Community at 6 a.m., so Sister Dores was asked to be ready to participate at 5:30am. The Carmel thought this invitation would give Sister Dores great pleasure, but the thorns were sharp in this path to a new life; the lack of information brought about sufferings of which no one was guilty.

Sister Dores asked the Mother Provincial to defer entry until her dental work was finished, but as the Bishop had been in charge she should obey and not be worried about her health. This being a well-known exceptional case, it was natural that the Community bonded together, not wanting Sister Dores to leave, but for her it was more beneficial to offer the sacrifice as before. It was very

---

384 St. Teresa of Avila, *Complete Works*, Manuscript B.
385 St. Teresa of Avila, *The Way of Perfection*, Ch. 32, 7.

difficult for the Community to see a member leave, even if they only had a few years of life in common together, but this member was very special. It ached all the more. It hurt the poor shepherdess to see so much suffering around her. She tried another solution. Since her presence in the Community was too uncomfortable and at every step she was asked to give up her quest for Carmel, she proposed to spend the remaining time before leaving at the home of the Vasconcelos family, where she would be welcomed with open arms. But this solution was not feasible.

Before the Tabernacle she asked for strength to continue her path, which was shrouded in darkness. In the confessional, she asked advice from her confessor. He told her to leave it in the hands of God, which she followed faithfully. She then prepared the little that she had to take with her, including some of her writings, and burned a great many of them, especially letters.

11 | Farewell

Aware that Sister Dores' departure was imminent, the Sisters, some with whom she had shared many years and who had helped strengthen her faith life, would cry along with Sister Dores. Over the years Sister Dores had sacrificed the tasks that were entrusted to her. She was so simply alive and so happy. She often laughed to the point of crying during recreations and was moved to devotion when praying in the chapel; it seemed that she did not know anything else. She was totally absorbed, attracted by her God. Oh, how painful it was for them to see her leave. The chaplain, a great friend, wanted to say goodbye to Sister Dores. She described the conversation:

On the 23rd Rev. Cabral came to say goodbye. His Reverence advised me to go without taking anything, or only what I would need to take, or for health or illness:

-God will not fail you!

-Yes, God will not fail me, nor with His Cross. I will always be led by His Love, renewing each day my "yes" of May 13, 1917, but I trust! 'My Immaculate Heart will be your refuge and the way that will lead you to God!'

'O Jesus, it is for love of You, for the conversion of sinners and in reparation for the sins committed against the Immaculate Heart of Mary!'

'Then you are going to have much to suffer, but the grace of God will be your comfort.'

Yes, it is there that I hope! [386]

March 24 arrived, the day she was to leave the house. She was to leave at

---

[386] *My Pathway,* I, p. 256 – 257.

noon, at which time the sisters would be in the chapel. She wanted to say goodbye to the Community, but the Mother Provincial found it prudent not to consent to this to prevent further suffering. Therefore, the sisters went to her, arriving in the corridors and embracing her in a sea of tears. She had a last request: to give an image of the Child Jesus that was given to her by her Superior in Tuy to the Mother Provincial. But Mother Provincial did not want to release her and let her go. Conditions demanded it, however, and she offered everything with a greater love, repeating:

-O Jesus, it is for love of You, for the conversion of sinners and in reparation for sins committed against the Immaculate Heart of Mary! [387] At the appointed time, she relates:

In a quick turn, I went back to the Quinta to say goodbye to the beautiful statue of Our Lady of Lourdes, the Grotto of the Sacred Heart of Jesus, the image of the Immaculate in the garden outside the classroom, my dear Tabernacle in the Chapel of the college and outside. It was almost time, and I went up to my room to put on a shawl to go out and give my last kisses to the image of my dear Child Jesus:

-Do not allow my Baby to be treated this way again! I carry You in my heart although I leave You in the image. And with these last kisses I also leave You some of my tears of nostalgia. [388]

At the door she conversed with some sisters, among them was one who had been her novice schoolmistress. She was crying and could not manage to speak, but her tears spoke eloquently. Waiting for her by the car door was Mother Provincial who hugged her, sobbing.

I asked forgiveness from Her Reverence and asked her for the same from the Community since I could not do so. Her Reverence crying, told me:

-Go, and if you are not well, return, knowing that all the doors of the Institute are open to you.

Thanking her, I got into the car and we left. [389]

Two hours later they were at Coimbra University, which was then at Filipe Simões Street where Sister Dores would stay overnight. She said goodbye to her Mother Superior who returned to Porto, leaving her with the Superior of the Home, Mother Brito, who accompanied her to the Bishop's Palace to speak to Bishop Antunes. While Sister Dores spoke to him, Mother Brito spoke with the Prioress of the Carmelite convent in Coimbra, Mother Maria do Carmo, and then Sister Dores went to the Carmel with her. Here conversation was different

---

387 MSL I, 4th M, Ch. II, No. 5, p. 178.
388 *My Pathway*, I, p. 259 – 260.
389 *Ibid*, p. 260.

from the information they had received from the Palace. Sister Dores would not wear the habit after all on the day of her entry, because it was necessary to get the fabric and make it. The Carmel was in the process of being restored and was very poor; as such, it did not have reserves. The Prioress spoke again with the Bishop, who made available to her what was needed. He was surprised to learn that Sister Dores did not have a habit and that Mother Maria had not said anything to him. It was one more miscommunication given in ignorance, one more cause of sorrow, a few more drops in the cup already so full of suffering.

The Bishop was ill at this time and either communicated with the Prioress by letter or by someone who would be going to the Carmel since the Carmel still had no telephone. Being Spanish, the Prioress Mother Maria do Carmo had some difficulty understanding the questions and requests that were given to her. She would answer them as she understood them. As Sister Dores was not able to be dressed like other postulants at the moment of her entry, she wore the habit as soon as she received it because it represented being a Religious of Perpetual Vows. However, it was well understood that it was the Bishop who sent it to her.

At the Carmel, the sisters went out to see what was in the suitcases that came with Sister Dores in the car and discovered a black dress and veil from the time when Sister Dores was a student in Vilar. Thus, stripped of everything, she passed through the doors of the cloister in absolute poverty.

Sister Lucia identifying the location of the apparition of the Angel in 1916.

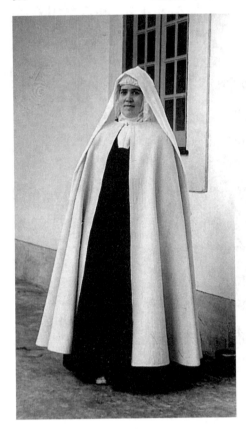

**Sister Lucia on the day of the Taking of the Habit
in the Carmel of Coimbra, May 13, 1948.**

CHAPTER XVI

RELIGIOUS CARMELITE

1 | Finally in Carmel

Sister Dores arose at 4:30 on the morning of March 25, 1948. Did she sleep? We don't know for certain, but she knew very well how to live every hour of her time in the presence of the Lord. For her overnight accommodations, the Superior asked a girl at the home in Coimbra University to give up her room for a sister who needed to spend the night and would leave early. The "thin one," as they called her, kindly gave up her room so the sister could have some privacy and time alone. Little did she know who the guest was, or that three years later she would join the shepherdess in the same Carmel with the name Sister Maria das Mercês de Jesus!

Upon leaving the home, Sister Dores asked Mother Brito if she could take the rosary that she used at the waist while a Religious. Mother allowed her to take only the crucifix of the rosary, so she detached it and they walked to the Carmel of Saint Teresa. Sister Dores offered these words about those first moments, turning the page of her new life:

Accompanied by Mother Brito, we arrived at Carmel a few minutes before 5:30a.m. I knelt in the front pew before the Blessed Sacrament. The Rev. Rocha arrived and gave me a blessing and led us to the lobby, then opened the door and embraced Mother Brito, and I entered like the Israelites, very early in the morning before sunrise to gather the manna in the desert [an expression of Lucia]. In front of the regular door, the Community was in absolute silence. Each one in turn embraced me with a lovely smile. Then we headed to the choir where I took part in the ceremony of offering of significant merits of the newly professed and then attended the Ceremony of Profession.

The day of Holy Thursday in the Carmel is celebrated with great solemnity, as well as all Holy Week, but especially the last 3 days. The most enchanting thing is the rigorous silence next to all the liturgical ceremonies, singing the Divine Office, and hours of adoration of the Blessed Sacrament on this admirable day that overflowed the Love of His Sacred Heart towards humanity. How sweet it was, especially on these days, the solitude, the gathering and silence at the foot of the Tabernacle! A wonderful mystery in which I forgot all the suffering, all the pain and all the bitterness because there is nothing that can compare to the pains and sorrows of Our God! What I had wanted then was to be able to take upon me a part of these anxieties and suffer them for Him so that He would not suffer so much for me. Oh! I love you my Jesus! [390]

Sister Lucia entered the Carmelite convent on the same liturgical day that she was born—Holy Thursday. It was also the Feast of the Annunciation,

---

390 *Ibid*, p. 264 – 265.

and now also the Solemn Profession of a sister entering as a new member in the Community, all of which was absorbed by the Solemnity of the day. In the Easter Triduum, the silence is more profound, making it more desirable to adore and contemplate the mystery of the Passion, Death and Resurrection of Our Lord, Who for our sake became man and suffered death to save us from sin and death.

After Mass, Sister Lucia, in the company of Mother Prioress, was given her cell dedicated to the Immaculate Heart of Mary. Centered on top of the door was a small frame which read: *'Immaculate Heart of Mary'*, and then a sentence addressed to the inhabitant *'My Immaculate Heart will be your refuge.'* This sentence was at eye level and she read it every time she entered her cell. It would be a heavenly melody in her heart during the 57 years she lived in Carmel.

Her cell had a large window that opened to a balcony overlooking the cloister where there was a lot of sun. The bed, the footstool, a small shelf to store books, and a detachable board to place on her knees to write was all the furniture in her cell. On the wall was a picture of devotion and a large wooden empty cross reminding her that the Carmelite should always live with arms raised like Christ in continual oblation. The shepherdess understood this very well and was always thirsting to offer to the Lord all that she could to save souls and for the sanctification of priests.

The bed was covered with a brown fabric, the same as the habits, perfumed by holy poverty, and a poem that was a welcome greeting which she saved all her life:

To our dear little sister on the day of her entry into the Holy Carmel: March 25, 1948, Holy Thursday

The Carmel of Mary
Ark of love and light,
Sought on this day
A dove of Jesus…

Here, the world is hidden,
And more close to the Heavens
Will be her entire life
"Hidden with Christ in God."

Here, for He was immolated,
Sacrificed to want to live
In continual self-denial…

Like a little host,
Joined to the divine Host,
In the most intimate union.

Uniting the divine Sorrows,
Her Holocaust of love,
Wanting to help the Lord
To save sinners.

And as the Virgin Mary,
She also each day
Is to say with truth:
"I am the handmaid of the Lord!
Let it be done to me, for love of
Your divine Will."
And this blessed Will,
Accepted so fully,
Will make you eternally
A Carmelite saint!

2 | First Impressions of Carmel

The next day, responding to a postcard from the Bishop, she expressed:

I thank God for the shelter where they welcomed me, removing me from so many curious views of the poor world. I pity the souls that are there struggling with many difficulties. It is here where I can help them better in a more complete sacrifice and a more intimate life of prayer and union with God. Their confidences are so sad, which hinder the good that God could do with them, taking time from me and filling my mind of things that I should disregard.

She later expressed a common desire to all beginners:

I am pleased and very happy. It is from here that I hope to go to Heaven, that God will give me mercy. I desire to wear the holy habit and make solemn vows, but God knows when it will be. Now here I am, ignorant; I need to learn many things to be a good Carmelite and if it is His Will, a saint. To conquer this honor that I want to put forth, I hope for the grace of Heaven. [391]

On Easter Monday, March 29, she wrote to her Superior in Tuy, Mother

---

391 Letter of March 26, 1948, Bishop Antonio Antunes.

Cunha Matos, telling her of her joy:

As of right now you know that on Holy Thursday morning at 5:30 a.m. I entered the Carmel of Coimbra, by the arrangements of the Bishop here, who came on this day and at that hour to assist in the Solemn Profession of a Sister. I enjoyed it very much and I am very well and extremely happy. My name is Sister Mary of the Immaculate Heart, what a beautiful name, is it not? Far more beautiful than Sr. Dores, don't you think? Here I found a small group of lovely sisters; whenever I encounter them I have the impression of meeting St. Teresa. The name was chosen here by the Bishop.

Later she confessed the friendship with the family that was hers for so many years and only left to follow the Divine call, which continued to nourish her:

But look, despite being so happy, I did not forget Your Reverence, or the Mothers and Sisters. I pray and I ask always for all and hopefully that they will not fail to ask the same for me. [392]

In those early days, she also wrote to Pope Pius XII, to thank him for the permission he granted and to let him know her new address. She wrote with her characteristic simplicity as if she were addressing her own parents, on April 10, 1948:

I humbly lay prostrate at the feet of Your Holiness; I acknowledge this distinguished grace that you so graciously deigned to grant to me, this favor of my humble plea to move to a Carmel.

By virtue of this permission granted by Your Holiness and by the arrangements of the Bishops of Porto and Coimbra, on March 25ᵗʰ I entered the Carmel of Coimbra at 5:30 in the morning to attend the solemn profession of a Sister.

By the merciful grace of the Good God, I find myself very well and happy, protected much more from the curious eyes of the world.

I found in this convent a group of lovely souls, which with an unspeakable joy are sacrificed for the love of the Good God…

Joining with me, the whole Community humbly and respectfully kisses the feet of Your Holiness and pleads for Your Apostolic Blessing.

Sister Mary of the Immaculate Heart (Lucia of Jesus)

Shortly thereafter she responded to her niece Sister Maria Amelia, who also asked the Dorotheans for entry into the Carmel, and warned her to think well about it:

The life here is much more austere in the whole sense, count on it, but Our Lord softens it so you almost do not feel it. It is the complement of perfection on earth that a

---

392 Letter of March 29, 1948, Madre Cunha Matos.

poor soul can attain self-sacrifice and mystical union... and I like it so much! Not one hour has changed from the happiness that I feel for the greater good of the world.[393]

After a while her niece joined her at the Carmel, taking the name Sister Agnes of the Eucharist. In the first eight days, the newly professed are followed discretely by an "Angel," a novice designated to guide the first steps of the newcomer, to orient her to the home, in time to manage the Breviary and the initial requirements of protocol, which are extremely detailed small things, but they are great when lived with love. During this time, the "Angel" who is called Rafael, can enter the cell of her "Tobias" to answer any questions and teach her the customs and daily procedures, because for new arrivals everything is new and can sometimes be confusing. The "Angel's" mission is to facilitate the integration of the new candidate. She discreetly leaves her to move about with more freedom, only intervening if she sees that she needs help, so that at the end of eight days she will be acclimated.

Mother Maria do Carmo of the Blessed Sacrament, the prioress of this thriving Community, still in its infancy, also held the office of Mistress of Novices. Sister Lucia understood her very well and vice versa. They spoke with ease in Spanish and Portuguese, which for Lucia was a return for a few moments to her native land, which she graciously left after 14 years to rise again as this little dove of Our Lady of Mount Carmel. The original Carmel of Saint Teresa had been forced out in the deployment of the Republic in 1910 and transformed into a barracks until 1945, at which time it was returned to its previous state. The Community relocated here on March 7, 1946—'*The day of the keys.*' The first Carmelites reached Coimbra in 1934, coming with their Mother Maria do Carmo, courageously sacrificing themselves and their Carmel of Loeches. They were housed in the seminary, then in Calhabe, and then in a little house in Cedral, and finally in the Carmel building, which was left in appalling conditions by the soldiers. When Sister Lucia entered it still had a lot of damage and the Community was very poor.

On April 20, Sister Lucia participated in the Prioress's birthday party. She had overseen the preparation of the "theater" with her companions who were all young, as she expressed in a letter written in August to her friend Mother Maria José Martins:

I found here a small group of lovely souls; fresh as the dew of the morning, smiling to the first rays of the rising sun. [394]

Although in age she was not so young, her spirit always retained the freshness of youth and she lived among the young people as if she were one of

---

393 Letter written after March 25, 1948, Holy Thursday.
394 Letter of August 21, 1948.

them. In the afternoon of that day, she had a pleasant surprise—they put a habit on her which left her mouth watering:

> Yesterday afternoon, they wanted to see how I looked and dressed me in the Holy Habit, and that made me feel good inside! But the punishment was that it was only for a few hours. They said that I looked pretty good. [395]

Soon it would be forever.

3 | Carmelite Novice

The Taking of the Habit was scheduled for May 13 in that same year of 1948. It was a joy for the shepherdess, the time to make her 'outfit' all new. They purchased a fabric that was very strong, but too warm. Having compassion on her and because they were able, they arranged something less expensive and lighter. The sisters used to wear these in summer instead of the expensive habits that at the time were made of woolen cloth. When a new one was made, everything together—tunic, habit and cape—weighed around five pounds! Poor novice! With the joy of being a Carmelite and the fervor of surrender, however, Sister Lucia did not remember and everything was easy, as she expressed in a May 4th letter to the Bishop of Coimbra, Antonio Antunes:

> People in the world do not realize the intimate happiness that God communicates to the good souls who are consecrated to Him and serve Him faithfully. There is only a moment in which we are not in the act of sacrifice for Him and for souls until we retreat and bear the stamp of penance. But oh! Instead of the comfort of chairs which we left in the poor world, I sit on the floor and offer it to God; I say poor world, because the world is very far from feeling our happiness on the ground sitting among beautiful objects. And so, in all the moments of our humble life, we are so glad that even in times of greater austerity and penance, the only thing we see on everyone's lips is a cheerful smile. I am quite certain that this joy belongs to the children of God. [396]

On May 9 it was announced that a retreat would begin in preparation for the Taking of the Habit. Sister Lucia wrote to Bishop Antunes:

> Tomorrow will be increasingly content and happy for me, God willing, to gather myself to do this three-day retreat to better prepare myself for the 13th to wear the Holy Habit, the only habit that our beloved Mother of Heaven has deigned me to wear... it is such a great grace that I do not feel worthy, but it is one more excess of the Divine Goodness to me. The good Lord knows how much I want to meet Him and be faithful to Him all the days of my poor life. In this sense, I too recommend the prayers of Your

---

395 Letter of April 21, 1948, Bishop Antonio Antunes.
396 Letter of May 4, 1948.

Excellency.[397]

On the afternoon of the 12th the novices invaded her cell. It is always a joyful surprise, because in the Taking of the Habit the customs are not known to the novice.

Sister Lucia's bed was adorned with flowers and gifts, and the greatest gift—the Holy Habit that she would wear the next day. A poem would be proclaimed the next day in the cafeteria, replacing the usual reading. In the evening, all the sisters would gather in the recreation room. Mother would then call the novice from her retreat and all would go to a party in the cell of the novice.

The ceremony, which is typically a great solemnity, was held in private at the request of Sister Lucia.

I preferred the ceremony to be performed without assistance from any outsiders. And not even with my family who did not join us. It took place only in the presence of the Community, presided by Rev. Rocha, the Chaplain of the Carmel.[398]

Since it was a private ceremony, it was celebrated in a closed chapel at the same hour that the ceremonies in Fatima took place. The chaplain, vested with a chasuble and stole, waited outside the grid while the community entered in procession singing: Ó *Gloriosa Virginum*. A novice processed in front carrying the cross, followed by the community. Last to process in was the Prioress and Sister Lucia dressed in a brown tunic and cap. Sister Lucia moved to the center and knelt on a carpet that was placed there. The celebrant asked:

-*Sister Mary of the Immaculate Heart, what do you ask?*

Sister Lucia's voice choked with emotion, but with her characteristic firmness, she responded:

-*The Mercy of God, the Poverty of the Order in this company of Sisters in this Monastery of Saint Teresa.* [399]

After a talk by the celebrant, the Prioress and another sister approached to place the remaining parts of the habit on her. While this was happening, the celebrant declared the significance of each part with an evangelical phrase and his blessing. These parts included the belt, scapular, white cape, and the veil of ceremony with a crown of white roses. After the vesting, Sister Lucia prostrated while the community sang the hymn *Veni Creator Spiritus*. This is a prayer asking the Holy Spirit to light this new stage of life—light for the candidate and light for the community, which jointly shall discern the will of God for her path. Then the Prioress embraced the novice, followed by each one of the sisters, who sang: *Ecce*

---

397   Letter of May 9, 1948.

398   *My Pathway*, I, p. 271.

399   Rite of the Taking of the Habit.

quam bonum. With the blessing of the celebrant, the procession formed again and they processed out of the choir. It was a very special day, a day of celebration for everyone; as such, the community was exempt from silence in the cafeteria. The new novice made her first appearance, sitting at the head of the table between the Mother Prioress and Mother Vice-Prioress. The menu, although better than usual, is not that important, because joy is always the best condiment of any meal. With the heart of God, one does not even think about refined food, but everything is received with gratitude and joy. [400]

The next day Sister Lucia wrote to the Bishop of Coimbra:

Thank God, thank you for your letter, Excellency; I already assumed the Holy Habit. That our beloved Mother in Heaven should take me one more time for her daughter, although unworthy, and grant me the grace of her maternal protection.

A small party was held and it was very intimate, being very close to the prayers and ceremonies of Fatima without worldly noise that often serves only to disrupt.[401]

It was a year for the novice to assimilate the spirituality of Carmel. Sister Mary of the Immaculate Heart was already a religious; as such, there were no differences, but as a Carmelite she needed training. It is in experiencing the Carmelite way that one learns to live.

Amid the festivities and joy of finally becoming a Carmelite, she bore a cross without complaining, the infection in her mouth. As promised by the Bishop, after the Taking of the Habit she met with a very good specialist. Seeing the conditions in which the prior work was done and seeing it so bad, the doctor refused to deal with it in-house and was dismissed. The Lord, however, is attentive to those who trust in Him, and He saw to it that she did not lack what was needed at the right time.

Dr. Alcino Magalhães, who had begun her treatment in Porto, found it strange that she did not return for surgery. It did not take long for him to find out why. From the newspaper he knew why and hastened to write to her, offering to come to Coimbra and finish the extraction of her teeth, treat the infection and implant the false teeth. With grateful hearts, the Prioress and Sister Lucia accepted the generous offer. To avoid him having to make multiple trips, Sister Lucia asked him to take three teeth each time, which caused her great suffering. She endured everything in a spirit of mortification, not complaining. No one thought to give her relief, either to rest or to retrieve some medication for the pain. She suffered everything with love, repeating every step of offering taught by the Lady of the holm oak:

---

400 *Constitutions of the Discalced Sisters of the Order of the Blessed Virgin Mary of Mount Carmel, No. 93.*
401 Letter to Bishop Antonio Antunes, written on May 14, 1948.

Between the pain I still had, the wounds of the pulled out teeth, and the bad effect being produced from the injections, I felt so bad and I was not able to rest. In this state it was necessary to follow all the acts of the Community, to go to the choir in the mornings for reading lessons, to make the offices of the Psalmist and Bible… to get up with Community for spiritual prayer and canonical hours. God forgive me for any wrong that I may have done, but He knows I was not capable of doing better. I did not know what I was thinking and dared not to complain, because I did not want to deny Him anything He wanted to ask of me.[402]

Finally the dental treatment was completed and the shepherdess was even more beautiful!

4 | A Dream Realized - The Image of the Immaculate Heart of Mary

Sister Lucia wanted very much to have an image depicting Our Lady when she showed her Immaculate Heart. With due diligence, she had twice given instructions to a girl who was dressed as the apparition and served as a model to be photographed, but it never happened. When the statue went on the World Pilgrimage in 1948, it was Sister Lucia's desire that the image be of the Immaculate Heart of Mary, but it was not. Everything was resolved with great consolation to her, when on her first anniversary as a Carmelite, March 25, 1949, she saw upon entering the cloister a statue that bore the image of the Lady in white who appeared to her in the Cova da Iria. The Mother came to visit the daughter of her Heart. She gave this news in a letter to Maria Teresa Pereira da Cunha:

The image of the Immaculate Heart of Mary I could not do until after my coming to Carmel. All difficulties vanished as if by magic when I saw the image just after the sculptor finished it and it was blessed by the Bishop of Leiria, and observed by the Bishop of Cordoba and several priests. It was put up for public veneration in our church by His Excellency Archbishop Conde of Coimbra on March 25, 1949.[403]

The sculptor, José Ferreira Thedim, had presented an image to Sister Lucia, but she did not approve it because the right hand was too high. After this assessment, Thedim offered this image to the Carmel of Bom Jesus in Braga, and made a new sculpture. The second one had the hands in the right position. Sister Lucia interpreted the maternal gesture of the hands: *with the left hand lifting the son who fell and with the right hand sustains him and blesses him. This son is each one of us.* The sculptor, however, great as he was, could not until now please the one who saw the invisible. There was always a 'but' or an 'if.' On the day of Sister Lucia's

---

402 My Pathway, I, p. 273.
403 Letter of August 11, 1949.

Sister Lucia on the day of her Solemn Profession in Carmel.

Sister Lucia in the Carmel of St. Teresa, Coimbra.

▲ Sister Lucia with the first image of the
  Immaculate Heart of Mary, made to her instructions.

▶ Image of the Immaculate Heart of Mary
  is venerated in the church of the Carmel of Coimbra.

Solemn Profession photographs were taken of the Image to serve as a reminder.

5 | Solemn Profession

When the first year of the novitiate passed, Sister Lucia was admitted to the Chapter of Solemn Profession. Being a Religious of Perpetual Vows already, she did not have to make temporary vows. Solemn Profession and the Taking of the Veil was celebrated on May 31, 1949, the Feast of Our Lady, Mediatrix of all Graces, at the convenience of Archbishop Ernesto Sena de Oliveira who wished to preside at the ceremony. Otherwise it would have been scheduled on May 13, the day she completed the canonical year of her novitiate.

On the eve before, her confessor Rev. Manuel dos Santos Rocha, knew the provisions of absolute surrender of the novice who was walking a common path with her heart on fire, and said to her:

-Tomorrow my Mass is for you; I will set your soul on the paten together with the Host to offer it to the Lord as a sacrifice to please Him. You already know that the first intention of Jesus Christ in the Eucharist is to become a victim of expiation for souls, and in the quality as supreme Priest, for the priestly souls. Do you accept?

She replied:

-Yes. Once again it is my 'yes' of May 13, 1917, given to Our Lady. I believe it is God Who asked this of me and I cannot deny Him.

The confessor concluded:

-Well then, you give yourself fully and live the prayer of Jesus: 'They are not of the world, even as I am not of the world. Sanctify them in the truth. As Thou hast sent Me into the world, I also send them into the world. For them I consecrate Myself that they may also be consecrated in truth (John 17:16-19).' [404]

In the evening during recess, the novice left the silence and austerity of the retreat that began May 20 and joined the community in recreation. Kneeling, she asked the sisters for their spiritual blessings. Each one passed by offering her the merits of some good works for a given time. Afterward, she was accompanied to her cell to see the gifts. The novices adorned her with flowers, a black veil and the crucifix, which were the insignia of her profession, and gave her some souvenirs to offer friends and family: scapulars, photos, some with dedications—small items, but full of love and affection—and a card offered by the Community with a poem dedicated to this day:

---

404 *My Pathway*, I, p. 284 – 285.

Greetings May 31, 1949

Sister and daughter of ours,
Very much the favorite of Mary,
Ask the Virgin for us
Torrents of love and joy.

Of His beloved Son
She is a very beloved wife.[405]
With Jesus you have everything
Even possessing nothing!

Maria a name more beautiful
Full of charm and light,
Brings captive to the whole world
The sweet Mother of Jesus.

Immaculate mystic Spouse,
Virgin of the soul, first love,
In perpetual immolation You came
In a true sacrifice!

Lucia is a source of light,
Of fortitude and of love.
In slow martyrdom she offered
Herself to her King, God and Lord.

Heart burning flame
Consuming in love
Before the throne of the Almighty,
In eternal and everlasting praise!

The radiant morning of the big day arrived. Since the days of St. Teresa of Avila until Vatican Council II, the profession in Carmel, either simple or solemn, was always celebrated in the chapter room and only in the presence of the Community. Only the imposition of the black veil was public. Thus, on the morning of May 31, 1949, in the intimacy of the Community and according to the ritual of the Order of Validity, Sister Maria Lucia of Jesus and the Immaculate Heart professed once more the sacred bonds, which now united her forever to her Lord through the solemn vows of poverty, chastity and obedience. She felt weak physically, but was full of fervor.

At 9:30 a.m., Archbishop Ernesto Sena de Oliveira came and celebrated the Mass. Also attending the celebration were the Bishop of Gurza, Rev. Vernocchi, and the chaplain, who at that time were not yet allowed to con-celebrate.

At the end of the Mass, with an exhortation to this purpose, and the theme 'My First and Last Love,' the Archbishop imposed the black veil on the newly professed.

On the chest of Sister Lucia, she had a note with the intentions that filled her heart:

J.M. + J.T.[406]

---

405 Note of the translator – In the above poem it is translated: She is a very beloved wife... because when Sister Lucia consecrated herself to Jesus, she became a bride of Jesus.

406 Initials used in Carmel that signify: Jesus, Mary + Joseph and Teresa.

Lord, accept the love that I have for you in my poor soul. I offer You the holocaust in my Solemn Profession in the scent of sweetness and victim immolated in love for You, and for Your Blessed Mother, a perennial eternal song of praise and thanksgiving. For me only do I beseech You, to live and die in an act of pure love in the time of my abyss in You in eternity.

I also ask this of You for Your Church, for Your Vicar on earth, for all the Priestly hierarchy, for which I renew to You my poor and humble offering, and for the conversion of sinners and of poor Russia and for the union of my dear brethren separated to hasten the moment in which Your Church is one, holy, catholic and apostolic. For the order in which You, Who are so dear, received me, for this Community and for each one of my sisters so that they are sanctified and so that they give You glory, and for my family, to be good in the world so that they are sanctified and saved for eternity. Finally for this multitude of needs and intentions that You know well, that was, is and will be recommended by my poor prayers. For all those who have been, are and will be my confessors to try to guide me by the straight ways of Your Law.

Coimbra, May 31, 1949

Sister Maria Lucia of Jesus and the Immaculate Heart. i.c.d. [407]

Then she entrusted to the Lord her generous heart. Fearing her weakness as a helpless child, she abandoned herself fully into the arms of the One in Whom she trusted:

Today is resumed, O Jesus, the ties of our oneness, our love, our encounter forever! Only in eternity will there be the consummated fulfillment and the ecstasy of infinity! Remain with me on earth and lead my steps by the straight path of Love, and if You see that I hesitate, support my weakness so that I do not fall.

You know the aspiration that You Yourself gave to me: To love you and sacrifice myself for Your love! On this day, as always, I pray You take that which is written on my heart, which You satisfy in me, a hunger for Your Love!

That in this love I offer myself to Your beautiful pleasure, for this I renew my offer to sacrifice, if You accept it for souls, especially for priestly souls. Lord behold me! Our Blessed Mother has guided me for this, which I propose to imitate and follow. She will help me, and with my gaze on her Immaculate Heart, I will search my faltering steps, my life obscured from the eyes of the world. That is why I am here to hide myself from the observance of the common life, without anything that I perceive. I will only try to attract Your eyes, so that they increasingly light my way. Lord, it makes me feel increasingly the abyss of my nothingness, the helplessness, the weakness of my deeper self, the misery that I have graduated, to strengthen me in the greatness of the firm hope in You! Always

---

407 *My Pathway,* I, p. 282 – 283.

staring at the star to guide me through this – Maria! [408]

In the act which describes the ceremony of Profession and the Taking of the Veil, it is signed by the professed, the Prioress and the Council. After transcribing the text of the formula of Profession she had this note:

Upon receiving the Holy Habit, she took the name of the Immaculate Heart of Mary, but the profession of her desire and so to be known around the world, it was determined that Sister Mary of the Immaculate Heart be called Maria Lucia of Jesus and the Immaculate Heart. [409]

Lucia stayed in the novitiate cell for one year to complete her Carmelite training. There is a custom or tradition in the Community that Our Lady will come to visit the cell of any novice on the eve of the Taking of the Habit or Profession. Her presence is felt in a special way and she says to the novice: "Treat well this cell…There are Secrets that lead to Heaven."

6 | Bishop Ernesto Sena de Oliveira, Chosen by Our Lady

Bishop Antonio Antunes died in the summer of 1948 and Archbishop Ernesto Sena de Oliveira was named the new Bishop of Coimbra. He was responsible mainly for any correspondence that related to the Seer of Fatima and the works at the monastery. Sister Lucia soon discovered that she could open her soul to this pastor of the Church and found him to be the answer for her spiritual needs. She did not want to step out of obedience.

Sister Lucia believed that Our Lady chose him to lead her. She offered the Bishop a photo with the image of the Immaculate Heart of Mary with a written message:

Tell him it was I who chose him and want to help him.

(August 22, 1949)

Sister Lucia i.c.d.

The explanation for this is found in a letter written to the Bishop on November 24 the following year:

From my letter written on the 31ˢᵗ the last day of the month, I saw that Your Excellency became suspicious of a further visit of the beloved Mother of Heaven. I haven't had this grace. What I wrote was referring to my words of August 22, 1949: "It was I who chose him and want to help him." In my humble experience, these words say a lot and mean having great preference. They are of Heaven!

Knowing the source she trusted was safe, the shepherdess unconditionally

408 *Ibid,* I, p. 283 – 284.
409 Archives of the Carmel of Coimbra, *Book of Professions.*

surrendered to the guidance of the Bishop and pastor, who was unparalleled in his dedication to her. He was to Sister Lucia a very important support and spiritual guide in the early years of Carmelite life. He was her confessor and traveled frequently to Carmel to talk with her. In addition, they exchanged letters, wherein she communicated with the simplicity and confidence of a child.

To gather these respectively:

Honorable and most Reverend Archbishop,

On the 20ᵗʰ at night beginning with the annual Community retreat for 8 days to finish on the 29ᵗʰ in the morning, I beg to use daily during this time the rope and to be prostrate in prayer with my arms crossed, praying the prayers of the Angel, during the time we have to rest between the hours we awake and finish 8 to 9 p.m. After early mornings we stand in the choir until 11am in prayer. This addition of penance was established by the laws and customs that are practiced in common and of the individuals who are excused for another day by Your Excellency.

I know that the principle of the exercises is not a penance, but I feel that the Lord wants penance; He needs souls who sacrifice themselves and I feel confused by doing so little, but my weakness is not capable of more. I wanted to give Him a lot and I find myself without anything. And even the little that I have, I want to give generously.[410]

At the end of the retreat, she wrote again:

Thank God I finished my retreat. This time it was very difficult, but it has passed. Inwardly it was also a little painful, I'd even say, extremely painful... Our Lord made me feel that He was unhappy! He is right; I was bad during this year. I was not humble or obedient. It is already one year that my confessor and Superior told me to write to Your Excellency, and I still thought to find some means of escape. Archbishop, forgive me? I already promised Our Lord to correct myself and now I obey, but it is with so much difficulty... Furthermore, Our Lord discovers in me, it seems to me, how many sins and miseries there are in the world: He is right, I have them all. I am particularly proud. Forgive me Most Honorable Archbishop, I have already asked Our Lord for forgiveness; it is so hard, I felt Him so unhappy... But even so I still like the feel of this. It is good, that this is happening.

It was a retreat so humiliating at the feet of Our Lord, but it made me well, and was needed. It is one of the crosses most bitter that Our Lord usually gives me every once in a while.[411]

In the following year, April 29, 1951, after some time of silence, Sister Lucia opened her heart:

Your Excellency is perhaps surprised with my silence, so unusual? Two reasons led

---

410 Letter of March 18, 1950.

411 Letter of March 29, 1950.

me: the fear of being bothersome and taking away too much time with such an intimate correspondence and continuous movement to silence. This is not a new movement; by contrast, it is very old, I would say ancient, but it is renewed once in a while with more intensity and it is now one of these practices.

I feel good alone with God in the depths of my soul, and I find in Him everything; and how much further away from the better things of the Earth the more I dive in Him alone. I don't know if it's an illusion, but I believe as well that, no, because it is the faith I know and I am a small drop of water lost in Him and this gives me enough. Sometimes I do not know that externally He comes to want to disturb me, to say to me that I am wrong. Therefore I would like Your Excellency from time to time around here to guide my steps. When you are unable to be here, I remain in peace. I trust in love as I know God has in me and I am certain it will not let me go out from the path that has been outlined for me. I abandon myself more and more to live His life in me and to disappear in His Immense, Infinite and Eternal being… that He will help me and make me do what you please.

There! I don't know how I wrote this letter, I wanted to tear it up and write another, but I do not have time because our mother is in a hurry to send it in the mail. I hope Your Excellency will excuse all the nonsense that I say. I let my heart speak a little bit and nothing else.

With the utmost respect and faithful dedication, Your Excellency, I kiss your sacred ring and ask for your blessing.

Your tiny servant,

Maria Lucia i.c.d. [412]

With the same simplicity, she would deal with matters of her soul, the works of the Community, or asking the company of the Archbishop in his important visits, which she desired to receive. After one of these visits, she wrote:

I am thankful that you have deigned to come here with the Cardinal, seeming to me there was not a great justification, but before a Superior it is more restrained. I was very worried about the fall that Your Excellency had on the stairs. I asked and I prayed to Our Lady that Your Excellency was not harmed, and as a good Mother she will grant this grace. After all the intentions which I brought to Your Excellency, they could not be resolved due to the company that was with us. Patience… it is for when you return here. I'm not saying here what it is, because I do not trust anything on paper. The blessed man served as a disadvantage. [413]

At that time, when a Cardinal visited the Carmel or another person with permission to enter the cloister, that person entered with all companions and

---

412 Initials that signify Unworthy Discalced Carmelite.
413 Letter of August 30, 1949.

roamed throughout the house and garden. This blessed man, referred to by Sister Lucia, took much advantage of being in the house, giving free rein to his curiosity, so she felt unable to talk freely in the presence of her Pastor.

7 | First Farewell from the Carmel

On the morning of February 6, 1950, the Bishop came to meet with Mother Maria do Carmo of the Blessed Sacrament. However, Mother had died during the night after a short illness. Her sudden death came as a painful surprise to all her daughters and they were like a brood of chicks without their mother. That evening, the Bishop wanted to talk alone with the shepherdess to tell her about his concern for the future of the Community, which was growing with the blessing of God, but was very young, and the few older ones were no longer able to steer the boat to a good port. There was a Spanish Mother who was very holy, but she did not have many skills to govern. Sister Lucia promised to help her in everything she could.

Even though Sister Lucia was still in the novitiate and did not have an active voice in the Chapter, Mother Maria do Carmo had placed her in charge of the restoration of the monastery, taking advantage of the many skills and relationships she had with families that could help monetarily or with the licenses that were difficult to obtain. One donor who had recently visited benefitted dear Mother Maria by being able to get the license to use the cloister cemetery again. Sister Lucia also had the joy of giving her the news that the government had granted the funds for the construction of the walls of the cloister, thus giving Mother Maria some peace. She did not, however, know how to get the money for the construction which was needed for the cloister, which at that time was an Episcopal home where Bishops once lived.

One month after Mother Maria's death, the Chapter met for new elections and Mother Madeleine Sofia of the Heart of Jesus, also from the Carmel of Loeches, was elected. A new page opened in Community life, which was still in training. Certainly it troubled Mother Sofia to accept this position with so much responsibility, but in the spirit of obedience to the will of God, expressed by the Community who asked her, she said yes. Each person has the gifts that God gave them and is not to blame for lacking others. God alone knows the fruits that can bloom in the painful moments of life. After Mother Sofia's first year of being Prioress, the Bishop noticed how the Community was suffering; he spoke to the Superior and found a solution. Rev. Friar Hipolito, O.C.D. made an Apostolic visitation and accepted the resignation of Mother Madeleine Sofia of the Heart of

Jesus as Prioress. At that time there was a sister in the Community who was able to replace her. This Mother was from the Carmel of Echazacoiz, Mother Mary of Christ. She was from the Portuguese family Freitas Branco, and had entered the Carmel of Spain when the Portuguese cloisters were shut down. She was very much loved by all the sisters and is still remembered with great gratitude and veneration. She was a pillar and a cornerstone in the structure of the monastery. [414]

8 | A Promise

Meanwhile, by order of the Archbishop, Sister Lucia continued to take the necessary steps for the reconstruction of the convent, especially the chapel and the walls. During the military occupation the chapel had been turned into stables and had completely bare walls. There was only a very small altar for the celebration of the Eucharist. Sister Lucia, who did not like to wait for anyone, perfected her patience waiting for the fulfilment of a promise. She wrote and spoke to influential people, but the situation dragged on. Then she turned to Our Lady. With all her faithfulness she asked for help and promised that in thanksgiving after the walls were completed she would place in the garden an image of the Immaculate Heart of Mary. The response was immediate. All restoration was able to be done with money given by the state and donations provided by benefactors. And the promise? Sister Lucia was reprimanded by her confessor and the Provincial Vicar, Friar Isidoro O.C.D.:

-*You should not have made this promise without permission from Superiors.* [415]

God would provide, however. On July 25, 1956, a marble image 6-3/4 feet high was placed at the end of the garden and was blessed by the Apostolic Nuncio, Archbishop Fernando Cento, later a Cardinal. The image, made by the sculptor Guilherme Thedim, (not the same as Jose Thedim, the sculptor for the Fatima statue) was offered by Mrs. Olga Maria Nicolis di Robilant Alvares Pereira de Melo, Marquesa de Cadaval.

How did this lady arrive in the life of Sister Lucia? She was born in Turin, Italy, of the family Robilant. She came to Portugal and married Mr. Antonio Alvares Pereira de Melo, Marquis of Cadaval.

When Sister Lucia entered the Carmel of Saint Teresa in Coimbra, the Marquesa told Pope Pius XII that it was such a poor monastery and the shepherdess would endure hardships that could be a risk to her weak health. The Holy Father asked her to visit his spiritual daughter and see what was needed. He gave her permission to enter the cloistered cell and visit the seer.

---

414 Cf. Ps 143:12.
415 *Oral Narration of Sister Lucia.*

Sister Lucia with the first image of
Our Lady of Fatima that was given to her.

Bishop Ernesto Sena de Oliveira,
Bishop of Coimbra.

Mother Prioress Sister Maria de Cristo, Bishop
Ernesto, and Sister Lucia.

▲ The Apostolic Nuncio, Archbishop Fernando Cento, blessing the image of the Immaculate Heart of Mary placed in the garden of Carmel on July 25, 1956.

◄ Sister Lucia at the image of the Immaculate Heart of Mary, with the pigeons that were offered to her that accompanied the image of Our Lady of the Rosary.

The Marquesa once visited discreetly and was able to tell the Holy Father how she found the conditions. Thus began a great and sincere friendship that lasted her whole life. Every month on the 13th, except in Advent and Lent, after serving the pilgrims at Fatima, she would go to Coimbra to visit, bringing flowers which Sister Lucia enjoyed as a very sweet gift. She inhaled the scent of these flowers containing the perfumes of Fatima.

9 | In Community Life

On May 31, 1950, Sister Lucia completed her time in the novitiate, as provided by the constitution. In the small chapel reserved only for novices she took leave of her companions who were still in training, giving each a hug. Sister Lucia was moving to a new cell within the Community and was given a lovely image of the Child Jesus. In the company of Mother Prioress she went from cell to cell receiving a welcome embrace from each Sister, a unique opportunity, except in the case of a prolonged illness. While Sister Lucia was making this *pilgrimage,* the novices quickly carried her limited furniture to her new cell and decorated her bed with a symbolic motif made with flowers. Then they waited cheerfully for one more hug and returned to their silence, only to speak on feast days. It is an education to become accustomed to and remain silent in this atmosphere, which is necessary to a life of prayer, *for the love of silence leads to the silence of love.* [416]

The new cell was in the middle of a hallway and faced south so that Sister Lucia received a lot of sun from a window that overlooked the garden. She lived here for 55 years before the Lady brighter than the sun came to seek her on the afternoon of February 13, 2005. Between these two dates, how many things passed this small room where she was alone with her Bridegroom?

Sister Lucia worked very hard in her new cell or in the workshop that was nearby in the same corridor. She worked while praying, and prayed while working. She was very orderly and gave time for everything. At the first sound of the bell, she left what was in her hands, and with her steps now and then difficult, went to meet the Lord where obedience called her, *because the works of Religious are not their own but of obedience.* [417] Everything is God.

Faithful to the common schedule, she did not have the freedom to change from one task to another without asking permission from the Prioress. With great care she lived in the spirit of obedience and would not take a single step that was not marked by the seal of God. Sometimes it was not easy for her to combine

---

416 M.M. Philipon, *Spiritual Doctrine of Sister Elizabeth of the Trinity.*
417 St. John of the Cross, *Warnings,* 11.

being a religious and the seer of Fatima. She did not lack the light of God and the maternal protection of Our Lady, however, which helped her discern the right path, always faithfully guided by obedience.

She lived in Community with simplicity, without being obvious. She very naturally followed their motto "on the outside as all, inside as none." This allowed her to be close to the Sisters with the naturalness of her manner of life. She wanted to be like the Foundress of Carmel: *Here all will be friends, everyone must love.*[418] Behind her very small stature and youthful countenance, her open smile and easy humor which she faithfully kept for the hour of recreation, concealed an intense fire, keen to burn in love for the world and all humanity which she embraced like the Son. Lucia carried with and for love the huge burden that she voluntarily accepted under the banner of Fatima and never regretted the 'yes' and never had the temptation to give it up. It was etched in her heart with fire and a sword, and no one or anything could ever blur that mark. As little Jacinta might say:

-*I seem to have a fire in my chest, but it does not burn me.* [419]

In the monotony of everyday life, she always found the freshness of a renewed love in the generous and total gift of her whole being, powered by a solid and profound prayer life, the force of all her strength and strength of her life. Whenever news reached her of the evils of the world, when she received letters with accounts of lives sunk in the mire of sin, she intensified her prayer. With arms raised in prayer and suffering, she was powerless to remedy such damage, but she entrusted everyone and everything to the maternal love of the Immaculate Mother of all people.

While her strength allowed and whenever other duties did not prevent her, she attended all common work. It was beautiful to see her in her 70s and 80s, actively assisting at the sink, taking advantage of this shared work after leisure activities, inclined to remember some songs of her childhood. In those circumstances when it was easy to stop work and talk on some subject, she gave an example and drew attention saying: -*Oh girls, hands do not speak!* She smiled or participated while continuing to work or sing:

> It is true, it is true,
> Heaven is my home!
>
> Heaven is my home,
> I long to be there,
> And it will be mine, never fear,

---

418 St. Teresa of Avila, *The Way of Perfection*, Ch. 4, p. 7.
419 MSL I, 1ˢᵗ M, Ch. II, No. 3, p. 56.

Close to the Mother of God, the beloved.

Heaven is my home,
Home of eternal bliss,
There I shall always be happy,
Close to the Mother of God, the beloved. [420]

Sister Lucia was responsible for several tasks and was always available for whatever was required of her obedience, never refusing anything, even when feeling the lack of strength. She always strived to perform her work well to avoid any problems for the Prioress.

When she entered the Carmel, the sisters received tasks in a solemn act from the Chapter during the canonical visit, after the election of the prioress which is renewed every three years. In the parlor when all the Sisters were brought together, the visitor named the task and the sister responsible for it made a short, authentic exhortation on how to sanctify this function. Later the ritual became less formal, but no longer had the same supernatural significance. It is always in the spirit of the sacred bond of obedience that any work is executed, and it is only so that what is done is consecrated. For many years Sister Lucia took the same position as the Prioress with unparalleled expertise: the direction of the work of the restoration of the house, giving her valuable opinions about repairs to be done, meeting with the Chief Architects and Engineers of National Monuments to solve problems, and she was very careful to inspect the work to see that everything was done correctly

On one occasion she accompanied one of these gentlemen and drew his attention to the need to repair the main staircase. The limestone had become very worn and slippery from the shoes of the soldiers during the years of occupation. This led to frequent falls of the sisters. She described the scene thus:

When we walked down the main staircase, I pointed out to the chief that the stairs were very worn and slippery and made him see that it was one of the works that was most necessary and urgent, because very often there the sisters slid and fell.

-Sister, this staircase is not good, if you walk this way it is better. But just as he said these words, I slipped and fell in such a way that I tumbled to the bottom of the steps. He ran panicking to help lift me because he thought I had hurt myself very much. As soon as I stood up, he turned to me and said:

-Sister, you are right, this staircase needs to be fixed. [421]

420 MSL II, 6th M, No. 75, p. 190-191.
421 Oral Narration of Sister Lucia.

So when we fall, we get up and we understand the falls of others, they apologize and we forgive them and that is how God makes the good from evil.[422]

During their recreation break Sister Lucia related that she had enormous difficulty containing her laughter when she told of this episode to Our Lord, and that He must not have found this to be a great grace.

She was informed about people who knew the chapel before the expulsion of the Community and sought their help. Very soon they were captivated by her friendliness and clarity of thought, and she had managed to restore the chapel to approximately its previous appearance. Like Mother St. Teresa of Avila, she never thought this was too much for the Lord. It was her great joy to see her work crowned with success. While doing these works of restoration of the chapel, the grid of the lower choir was enlarged and the wall was torn down opening the gallery of the Novitiate. Here the novices can spend quiet moments of intimacy and worship the Lord beside the Tabernacle.

Along with this task, she was the steward in charge of the Office of Clothing, and was responsible for the works in the vegetable garden and the Office of Sacristan, which she greatly enjoyed. She was the first sacristan when the chapter hall was transformed into a chapel with the Blessed Sacrament. She liked very much having the Tabernacle close and taking care of the arrangement of this sacred space! She prepared everything that was related to the Divine worship with much love.

She worked alone, but was always diligent and put into practice a teaching received in the past when she was a student in Vilar. One day while she was taking care of arranging the high altar, Monsignor Parvin was near the back of the chapel watching her. He called her and said:

-When you come to arrange the chapel, make a well-done genuflection as reverence to the Lord for Whom you will be working. Then each time you pass in front of the Tabernacle, just make a nod; genuflection is not needed, the fulfillment is already done. [423]

Grateful, she observed this lesson all her life and proceeded with spiritual freedom. Once in a while, she gazed at length at the Tabernacle; that look said everything and her Bridegroom totally understood. Her soul was bowed down before Him and in that she presented all humanity and each one of the people who asked her to pray. Her heart was absorbed in union with the Heart of her Lord in redemption for the world, for the Pope, priests, and for Russia.

It was lovely to see her in the garden in search of flowers to put in vases.

---

422 *My Pathway,* III, p. 385.
423 Oral Narration of Sister Lucia.

She did it with joy. In the winter time, when the flowers were rare, she found a solution. She placed some potted cyclamen on the altars, which she preferred to artificial flowers. She was always very happy with gifts of flowers. Later, when she no longer had this task and when people sent her flowers, she asked to place them next to Our Lord. Her heart was always turned to Him.

She was friendly to any sister who asked her for help, especially if the job was overwhelming for the person in charge. For several years, Sister Lucia was the steward who assigned the sister cooks what should be served to the Community. Within these duties, it was required that the food be well-prepared, as the Holy Mother asked for this in the original Constitution. While the sisters prepared the meals, Sister Lucia would go into the kitchen to taste the food and sometimes would rectify the meal so that the sisters stayed well fed. She taught them competently with joy and patience, and without pretention. As it says in the book of Wisdom: *I learned with loyalty, communicate without envy...* [424]

She knew how to teach and she did so with pleasure, but was demanding. The newly arrived she started in the technique of making rosaries. This was the first work that the postulants learned to do during recreation. After explaining how to handle the pliers, she had her disciples work alone to practice any difficulties. When someone made a decade of the Rosary, Sister Lucia would comment on the work and was usually negative at the beginning. Then they would disassemble it and do it again. She liked everything to be perfect. Finally there came the *'very good'* and title of *'master in the craft'* which was celebrated with joy by all.

With the same joy and attention as rosary-making, she taught them how to treat the beehives, make the meals, care for the plants, do the delicate work of embroidery or darning of old clothing. She taught them to clean and care for the things used in common, where there could be some sloppiness because no one was directly responsible. For Sister Lucia everything had importance because it was the house of the Lord and was a requirement of the vow of poverty.

Do not keep for yourselves what could be useful to others; always apply the gift of nature and grace. The same detachment is requested in the Rule of Carmel in relation to material goods:

No one shall consider anything as their own. [425] For this reason Sister Lucia did not use the possessive *my* but *ours.* With an open heart she *placed at the service of the sisters her energies and qualities.* [426]

During community meetings, participating in the care of the common good,

---

424 Wis. 7:13.

425 *Rule of the Order of the Blessed Virgin Mary of Mount Carmel, No. 10.*

426 *Constitutions of the Discalced Sisters of the Order of the Blessed Virgin Mary of Mount Carmel, No. 37.*

her words were venerated and respected by all the sisters. From her wise teachings that flowed toward a virtuous life, she was like a fountain that flows quickly, able to speak about all subjects. She gently drew attention while not wasting time on trivial matters, which are part of community life and should be discussed, but without taking the place of what is truly important—the experience of virtue.

She had a special care to preserve the unity of the Community, knowing how easy it is for small missteps to cause disturbances in the water of common life. A family needs to collaborate and renounce all, so the devil does not find loopholes in which to get through. It is through the unconditional surrender of each and all in the pursuit of the common good that community life becomes a Heaven, as stated by our Mother St. Teresa: *This home is a Heaven for those who are content to settle only to God.* [427]

With her experience of life and knowing that God does not ask of everyone the same, she wrote as many times as she said:

-*To maintain unity in community life, we need to know to pass, understand the shortcomings, to apologize, to appreciate the values, to take them into account. Our life of Community union should be a witness of faith, hope and love, as Christ prayed to the Father: "That they may be one as You and I are One."* [428]

She humbly asked forgiveness for the faults she saw in her delicate conscience, but not scrupulously, and with sincerity promised to be ever more faithful. She felt a great desire for perfection and to grow in love, so that her prayer had more power in the Heart of God. Her sisters were seeing her fragility, the tendencies of her independent nature claiming her rights—a very marked trait in her personality—and she labored with remorse:

-*I am sorry for everything that contradicts my way of seeing and feeling. I must die so that others may live. Christ died to give life to me.* [429]

And she had to mortify! How much she had to suffer! But with her eyes fixed on Christ, she moved on without looking too much for the marks that the thorns left in her feet, giving everything a spiritual sense, as she writes:

...*we, as children abandoned ourselves in the arms of the Father, Who wants to lead us to the flat paths or through tortuous paths, stepping on thorns, thorns and thistles, putting our feet in the footprints that Christ going ahead of us left marked in the soil of the earth; it is to rise with You up the steep mountain of Mount Calvary; it is to drink with You even to the last drop of the cup which the Father presented to You; it*

---

427 St. Teresa of Avila, *The Way of Perfection*, Ch. 13, 7.

428 *My Pathway*, 4, p. 3.

429 *Ibid*, p, 5 – 6.

**Community of the Carmel
of Coimbra.**

▲ Community of the Carmel of Coimbra.

▼ Community of the Carmel of Coimbra with the Image of the Pilgrim Virgin.

▲ Sister Lucia in the garden of the Carmel of Coimbra.

▼ Community of the Carmelite Sisters in recreation.

◄ Sister Lucia in the Cloister
with some Sisters of Carmel.

is to be one with You in the breaking of the bread and drinking. [430]

She had much to suffer, as the Lady had promised her on May 13, 1917. She always knew suffering, offering generously her pain for the redemption of the world, the great intentions of the Holy Father, always united to Christ her Bridegroom.

10 | One Like All and Always Unique

Sister Lucia was cheerful, spontaneous, genuine, and simple, but prudently reserved. Her natural spontaneity from her early years as a child, and the purity of her trust in those with whom she lived retreated to her interior as if frightened from the time of the Apparitions. Early on with her family where she was once the center of attention, little 10-year-old Lucia felt abandoned while constantly running up against all the doubts and false accusations. It was an enormous cross! She felt she had lost her mother and that opened a huge wound in her heart. She endured tense meetings with the parish priest at a time when religious authority was very much revered. In the village, she was hounded by endless interrogations of so many priests who arrived at Fatima seeking explanations. Finally, there was the endless procession of people from all walks of life with whom she had to meet alone, always repeating the same answers to their questions. The parade never ended. Wherever she went she was always discovered, and there would arrive the well-intentioned seeking help to collaborate in spreading the message, but also the curious seeking her out for other intentions.

In Carmel she was protected by the strict confinement, and it was not long after she arrived that she savored the absence of such visits. Like any Carmelite she could receive visitors—family members and intimate friends—during normal times, except Lent and Advent.

She wanted to be like everyone else, but as the shepherdess she was unique. As a religious she was equal, and as a Carmelite she had a distinct lifestyle exemplified by love that she strove to live faithfully. At the same time she was the Seer of Fatima, increasingly requested by people from all corners of the earth, which caused her no small amount of suffering.

Those who sought her knocked on the doors of the monastery, and being unsuccessful, they would appeal to Archbishop Ernesto Sene de Oliveira to arrange the favor they wanted.

It was necessary for her to give in sacrificially, and also to the Prioress,

---

430 Sister Lucia, *How I See the Message*, p. 38.

who sometimes found it very difficult to protect her. The Archbishop, in spite of himself, had to sign one more permission slip and present the visitor. Each visitor thought an exception should be made especially for him and that it would not affect the life of Sister Lucia or the Community life. They did not consider what it meant for her to receive so many exceptions.

She asked Archbishop Ernesto for help in a letter, confessing how difficult it was to receive so many visits. At the same time she offered this sacrifice, not wanting to lose anything that could be of benefit to the people:

These visits form a small portion of my cross, but they are also a part of the Mission which God entrusted to me. Not even in Heaven will they leave me alone, but there I will meet them with great pleasure, because there will be no danger of disturbing the union of my soul with God. [431]

Seeing he could not avoid so many requests and to prevent multiple visits, the Archbishop, during a trip to Rome, asked for an authorized standard under the Constitution prescribing that all visitors who were not of her family or more intimate friendships could only be received with permission from the Holy See. With this protection the visits became very rare, since it was more difficult to reach Rome.

As for visits with the Community, it was to her discretion to participate or not. Without contradicting her spirit she was committed to the sisters when she went to the parlor, but using the freedom she had for this, often decided not to go. If she did go, she did so with great simplicity and naturalness, always looking to be friendly with people. With their presence, the visits were enjoyable for her. Since she had already lived a long life with many experiences that required immense grace, it made time pass without notice.

11 | Correspondence from All Over the World

Besides the many tasks assigned to her, Sister Lucia was always occupied with correspondence that came from all over the world, which increased each year. There were letters from people that implored her prayers for problems and pains that plagued them. Some were confessions from those with troubled consciences who desired to be free from sin. After she read and answered these letters Sister Lucia burned them out of respect for their confidentiality. She would not leave the fire until everything was gray ash. When she could not do this, she would ask in good conscience for help ensuring that everything went into the fire. She

---

431 Letter of August 30, 1949.

generally responded to everyone, and in the majority of cases sent a card printed in several languages, ensuring her prayers and always including some photos. In special cases she answered more fully, having at her service a machine that made a carbon copy so she could keep one out of prudence. Later a friend and benefactor of the Community offered her an Olivetti. This machine had memory, which for her was a very nice gift because it could delete without erasing and make as many copies as she wanted. Tenaciously, she learned how to use it despite already being in her seventies, and she did it!

Sister Lucia occupied herself personally with this work until the year 2000. After the beatification of her two cousins, the revelation of the third part of the Secret, and the publication of her book, "Calls from the Message of Fatima," it seemed Sister Lucia felt her mission was accomplished and she rarely responded to letters that arrived. She opened them, read them, and then decided whether they should be answered by placing a sign on the envelope—R for answered or S.R. for not answered—and gave them to the Prioress. By now she felt that she had essentially answered everyone in "Calls." It was a collective response to the fundamental problems of the human person, a catechism to understand the law of God and the primary penance He asked, as she wrote:

This is now the penance that the Good Lord asks: The sacrifice each person has to impose on himself is to lead a life of righteousness in observance of His law and desire this to make clear the way for souls, since many people judge the meaning of the word penance as great austerity, but not feeling the strength or pleasure to do it, they lose heart in a life of weakness and sin. [432]

12 | The Foundation of New Carmels

In the 1960s, she began to ponder the idea of founding a new monastery. A foundation in the Diocese of Lamego had previously been requested, but at that time the Community did not meet the conditions and the idea was abandoned. On April 27, 1963, her good friend Maria Eugenia Pestana visited her. She talked to her about her aunt, Maria José Vasconcelos, now an elderly woman and a close friend of Sister Lucia since the days at the Institute of Vilar. She spoke of the Quinta da Fonte Pedrinha, which belonged to the lady, and Sister Lucia was thrilled remembering the past when she was a little girl. Noting this emotion, Maria Eugenia asked her if this house mattered to her and the shepherdess responded:

-*Personally not for me, because by the Vow of Poverty I cannot have anything,*

---

432 *Ibid.*

but for the Foundation of a new Carmel. It would be good if her aunt could leave it.[433]

The visitor was filled with enthusiasm about the idea and promised to talk to her aunt, who would also be very happy with the fate of her property. With her Superiors' permission, Sister Lucia wrote to several members of the Pestana family, asking for the Quinta da Fonte Pedrinha for this purpose. Maria José Vasconcelos was still living and was pleased to offer the Quinta with her nephews' blessing since they were the heirs.

Sister Lucia gave her heart and soul to this project, contacting Superiors, asking permission on behalf of the Prioress who delegated to her the responsibility for many issues, preparing the plan for adapting the house with the minimum requirements for a monastery, planning and preparing a "trousseau" and furnishings for the new Community, and helping remove any obstacles in the course of the work. Seven times she went to Braga to see and guide the construction of what would become known as the Carmel of the Immaculate Conception that was completed on April 29, 1970, and to finalize preparations for the inauguration that would take place on May 2. Four Sisters would already be there on that day, two of them from the Carmel of Porto, which was the co-founder. After spending two days at the new Foundation, Sister Lucia expressed in a letter to the Countess of Riba D'Ave:

I was able to help prepare everything, and this Foundation was appealing to me because I believe that it is for the glory of God and for the good of souls. Another Carmel is another light shining through the darkness of the world to indicate Heaven, as an ascent to the supernatural, to the Living God, Creator and Supreme Lord of all things, the beginning and end of our own existence, the source of life and grace by which we are saved. It is a silent preaching to those who pass by and observe it, a center of pure souls who pray and are occupied with their brethren who live and struggle in the midst of the world.

It was a day of great joy and consolation, a day to savor the joy that once filled their Mother, St. Teresa, when she opened a new monastery because it was another shrine to welcome Our Lord. Sister Lucia wrote of the feelings that inundated her:

It was for me an immense joy that Our Lord wanted this poor Soul to serve to open again the Tabernacle and put it on that same altar! I thank the Lord for so much love! [434]

Sister Lucia always nurtured a motherly affection for the Carmel of Braga, which is situated on the hill of Bom Jesus, located in northern Portugal. At first

---

433 *My Pathway,* II, p. 90.
434 *Ibid,* p. 359.

she was serious about integrating with the founding Community, but for various reasons it did not happen. She was always interested in these sisters who had a loyal observance of the regular Carmelite life, but who also took pains to prepare for the birth of a new Carmel. Later it was not possible to fulfill Sister Lucia's desire to make the monastery permanent because the building needed to be enlarged. The sisters built from scratch a new home with the help of a group of friends from Germany called "friends of Fatima." Sister Lucia had felt this was something worthwhile.

After nearly 20 years, Bishop Antonio dos Santos, Bishop of Guarda, asked the Community for a foundation in his diocese. For this foundation, Sister Lucia, being more advanced in years, was still very interested and informative, and was involved in choosing the location for the Monastery. She was 87 years old, yet made the long journey without a problem. On August 24, 1994, she saw the new 'Virgin's House of Peace,' and seven Sisters left the Carmel in Coimbra for the Carmel of the Holy Trinity on the anniversary of the first Teresian Foundation.

Sister Lucia in the garden of the Carmel of Coimbra.

◄ Entrance to Sister Lucia's cell at the Carmel.

▼ Rosary made with pieces of the Berlin Wall that Sister Lucia placed on the cross on the wall in her cell.

▲ Sister Lucia's cell.

CHAPTER XVII

VISITS FROM HEAVEN IN HER CELL

1 | I Will Never Forsake You

It was uplifting to see Sister Lucia in her daily occupations following the actions of the community as her age and health allowed. Seeing her so simple, natural and industrious, one had no idea of the intense inner life the walls of her fragile body supported! As Moses kept his arms raised in prayer for the world she adopted a life of continuous prayer for the world. She prayed and loved, offering her life constantly for the Church, the Holy Father and for all humanity. She liked to remain before the small shrine in her cell and open her soul, entrusting the necessities of the world to the Heart of her Mother, and through her to the Heart of Jesus.

Her cell was a place to indulge in prayer, reading or working. She also received some visits from Heaven, perhaps many. These visits had a single goal: to help her carry out her mission to make known and loved the Sacred Heart of Jesus and the Immaculate Heart of Mary.[435] Here she received the answers to her anxieties, her prayers, and new requests.

When somewhat seriously we would say to her, -*Sister Lucia, when Our Lady comes around, call for us,* she would quickly reply with a giggle:

-*Yeah right! While I'm going to call you, she goes away...*

Other times she would say:

-*Open your eyes...* [436]

If only the walls of her cell could talk! As it was, she remained silent. Many marvelous pages the shepherdess never wrote down; they remained a secret from God, because as she stated more than once, she had no confidence in writing on paper because she was worried it would get in the wrong hands. She confessed in a letter:

I am not like the world. If you can, imagine the number of happy souls in Heaven that can see and speak personally with Our Lord all the days. These graces have been granted to me from Heaven. Many years sometimes separate visits from Heaven and I remain during these times, treading my poor way by the light of faith and grace that these favors have in my spirit. But I am not alone; I feel the presence of God absorbing me in His Infinite Being, communicating to me light, grace and strength to carry the cross that is left to me. He knows well all my weaknesses and misery and does not abandon me, because He knows that I am not capable of more.[437]

These mystical graces did not exempt her from the dark nights and

---

435 Cf. MSL I, 4ᵗʰ M, Ch. II, No. 4, p. 177.
436 Oral Narration of Sister Lucia.
437 Letter of December 2, 1949.

doubts, but prompted her to totally abandon herself into the hands of God. Like any Christian, Sister Lucia had to walk by faith, in hope and charity, enduring the suffering inherent to her human condition, and overcoming problems and obstacles in favor of the Message that the Lady had entrusted to her. God intended her for a special mission and knew that she, a mere creature, needed the help of her Creator. She was not without support and help from her Creator who "communicated to her light, grace and strength," in crucial moments and kept her in an intimate communion with Him, the only Love of her life.

On June 13, 1917, Our Lady said she would take Francisco and Jacinta to Heaven soon and Lucia would remain here some time longer, telling her, -*I will never forsake you.*[438] This was a consolation to Sister Lucia, assuring her the best company she could have, the Virgin Mary herself. Our Lady was true to her promise. Sister Lucia always felt the faithful companionship of the Lady of the Rosary throughout her life, especially in the most difficult moments.

She never thought the sweetness of the face and voice of the Lady more brilliant than the sun would ever leave her, and how grateful she was after each new visit from the Mother of Heaven. With much courage, she was ever attentive and faithful to the will of God, which was printed in her soul. Although these visits were few and brief, they gave light and strength to fulfill her mission from Heaven.

2 | Visits of Our Lady to Sister Lucia

There is no doubt that during the Virgin Mary's visits to Sister Lucia, she would have expressed that her shepherdess stay "more time" on earth. Unfortunately Sister Lucia did not record in writing everything that happened in these apparitions, as her wish was always to go unnoticed. She guarded the secret given to her from the Mother of Heaven, because perfume that is exposed to air loses its odor (a Portuguese expression meaning if the secret is told then everything is exposed). When Our Lady gave her a "message" to convey, even though she felt an inner repulsiveness to do so, she faithfully delivered the message entrusted to her.

We believe the apparitions of Our Lady to Sister Lucia in the Carmel of Coimbra over the 57 years she lived there were made in her cell, the gathering place of intimacy and prayer for the Carmelite. These visits happened with great secrecy and no one guessed when or where they might occur. Sister Lucia was always very poised and lived in times of prayer as in times of work, very cheerful

---

438 MSL I, 4th M, Ch. II, No. 4, p. 177.

and communicative in the time devoted to community life. Everything about her exuded the calmness and normalcy of a person living a quiet and happy life, completely abandoned to the will of God, without seeking anything extraordinary or outside the life of a Carmelite. She gratefully received what Heaven gave her as a gift of God, of which she did not feel worthy.

We note then that the visits of Our Lady, so far as we know, are from the very words of Sister Lucia.

We have already told of the message that Our Lady gave her for the Archbishop of Coimbra, Ernesto Sena de Oliveira, on August 22, 1949. It would definitely have been the first time Our Lady visited her in Carmel showing her the path she should follow, that obedience to the Bishop was the will of God, as she did in Fatima in the seventh apparition. On December 31, 1979, she revealed another meeting that she recorded. It was the Community retreat on the last day of the year. In her prayer she interceded for the Holy Church, seeing it as a fragile boat tossed in the waves of the world's revolt, but with the solemn promise of Christ: *The gates of hell will not prevail against her!* [439] Sister Lucia described that moment of intense intercessory prayer in this meeting:

In my soul, everything was darkness and bitterness! As the Lord said, His Church will not perish! Did He not promise to be with her (the Church) until the end of time? Did He not give this to His own Mother, my Mother, to be her Protector and Advocate from many enemies and assist in the tortuous and difficult path of life? Did He not promise her the assistance of the Holy Spirit, Light and source of grace, strength and wisdom that enlightens the mind and guides along the paths of truth, justice and love? If need be, Lord, accept my life; I would rather die than fail to serve and love You each day at every moment. Turn me into You, so that the Father takes pleasure in seeing You in me!

So I prayed with my forehead tilted in my cell in the dark with the window closed, when I felt a gentle hand on my left shoulder. I looked and saw, it was my sweet Mother who had listened to my humble prayer:

-God has heard your prayer and sent me to tell you that it is necessary to intensify your prayer and your work for the union of the Church, of the bishops with the Holy Father and of the priests with the bishops to lead the people of God on the paths of truth, faith, hope and love, united in Christ our Savior.

Although I felt happy after this meeting and inundated with peace, light and grace, I also felt the difficulty of such a mission. It's so difficult to move the hardness of human hearts that only God can do, such as the stones, the children of Abraham! But I

---

439 Mt 16:18.

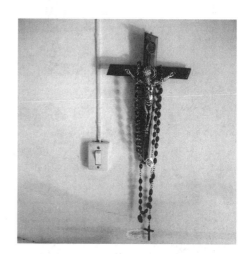

◄ The Image of Our Lady given to Sister Lucia by Pope John Paul II that she kept in her cell.

▼ Rosary on which Sister Lucia prayed with the crucifix on the wall next to her bed.

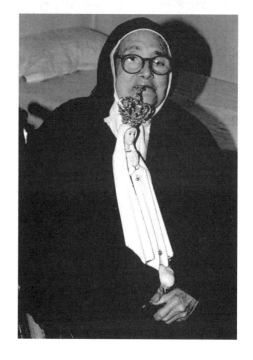

▲ Holy water font in the cell of Sister Lucia.

► Sister Lucia with the Image of Our Lady given to her by the Pope.

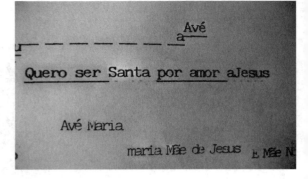

 Avé

a

Quero ser Santa por amor aJesus

Avé Maria

maria Mãe de Jesus   E Mãe N

▲ Sister Lucia working at the
typewriter where she responded to
innumerable correspondence
for which it was intended.

▶ The last item that Sister Lucia wrote
on the typewriter.

trust in God. If God wills it He is there to do it, because nothing is impossible with Him.

I trust in the protection of His Mother. I know that she is the Messenger of the Lord to give me His word; it is He who fulfills this although serving this humble and poor instrument. [440]

The following year on March 15, 1980, there was another meeting: this time a visit of maternal affection to comfort her in a time of darkness, perhaps listening to her moan because of such a delay for her departure to Heaven. She saw herself with less strength and it seemed to her that she was doing nothing.

It hovered over me one very dark night, things that God allows; the dense shadows that only God knows and can dissipate. So I trusted Him and He gave me happiness. When I least expected it, the Mother of God entered my cell, a brief visit. Even though it was short, I would have liked it longer! Thank you dear Lady for the help you gave to this poor daughter. You go to a lot of trouble.

-God is your comfort and I am here to help you. It is to serve Him that you are still here. [441]

In gratitude, these verses left her heart spontaneously to a song she already knew:

O Mother the more I see you,
You are more beautiful to me!
I desire to come and place
My heart at your feet!

And if one day a madness
Again requests, do not
Return me, Mother pure,
Because I can lose!

You are the Queen of Heaven,
The earth's loving Mother!
Welcome into your bosom
This loving daughter.

You are the dawn of Heaven,
Your radiance covers the earth!
Reflection of the light of God,
You are the Mother of eternal love!

---

440 *My Pathway,* IV, p. 132 – 133.
441 *My Pathway,* December 15, 1980.

Raise my hymns to Heaven,
That of the earth's charm!
To devout pilgrims
Extend the tip of your mantle! [442]

In October, 1984 during the Community retreat, she again received a visit from Our Lady in her cell. This time she only said that she received the heavenly visit without recording the contents of the message.

3 | Through Mary to Jesus

Beyond these sporadic encounters which Sister Lucia received with a poor, humble and grateful heart, her life being one of deep prayer, she may have asked questions showing some anguish or affliction because she was interceding for matters on behalf of some subject. These questions were answered through responses that she heard in the intimacy of her heart, where she lived in the presence of the Invisible, as noted on April 6, 1951:

On the First Friday of the month while on retreat, I felt the presence of God. I feel that I am alive in His Tabernacle where He lives with Infinite Mercy, One God in Three Persons. He owns me and I am from Him. I repeat to you in the depths of my soul: 'O, Most Holy Trinity, I love You! My God, my God, I love You in the Most Blessed Sacrament' and I feel the echo of those distant words: "The grace that is given to you today will always remain alive in your heart, producing fruits of eternal life." [443]

And on October 16, 1971:

I felt the presence of God in me. I did not hear the sound of His voice vibrating in my natural ears. I cannot see Him with my eyes in the flesh, but I feel His presence as if I see Him naturally and I am immersed in His light and His love. He is not only in my prayer; I feel Him in my work, in the day-to-day occupation when I sometimes have less hope. It is thus that my love for Him and for His Mother the Virgin Mary increases and grows, leading me to the practice of virtue that sanctifies and cleanses me in His love. [444]

In March, 1987 at the end of the Community retreat in which she participated with great fervor despite not being in good health and on the eve of completing 80 years, she noted:

With the Community I finished the spiritual exercises that were wonderful, which were about the experience of liturgical prayer. I felt the presence of God and immersed

---

442 Archives of the Carmel of Coimbra, *Poems*.
443 *My Pathway*, I, p. 321 – 322.
444 *Ibid, III*, p. 146.

myself in His immensity. I lost myself in the ocean of His love; I love You with Your Love that You gave to me. You are my Heaven! I found in You all that I wished and nothing more do I want from You. I love the Trinity. [445]

Since Sister Lucia met the Lady brighter than the sun and saw the Light which is God, she never took her eyes off her face, which was etched forever in her heart. Her eyes brightened by that unmistakable light, never strayed from this Star, which led sometimes into the midst of thick darkness, lit only by the certainty of the Mother's promise:

-I will never leave you. My Immaculate Heart will be your refuge and the way that will lead you to God. [446]

Mary is always the way, the guide and light that leads to God, Trinity of Love.

Sister Lucia lived with this certainty anchored in faith, feeling the longing for Heaven that delayed so long opening its doors for her. She lived intensely her vocation, immersed in and delivered to her Love, as she confessed in a letter written to Bishop Ernesto Sena de Oliveira, Bishop of Coimbra on April 29, 1952:

J. + M.
Carmel of S. Teresa
Coimbra, April 29, 1952
Most Reverend Archbishop,
The main purpose of this letter is to send you my poor and humble congratulations. I also thank you for your visit on the 26th; Our Lord rewards Your Excellency for this act of charity. I was spiritually well-prepared and felt understood to see myself formed for love… it is my vocation since childhood. The words of Our Lady: "Tell Jesus many times and in particular that you always make everything a sacrifice: O my Jesus, it is for love of You, for the conversion of sinners and in reparation for the sins committed against the Immaculate Heart of Mary," are indelibly impressed in my heart, so that this prayer sprouts by itself without effort. I do this by one of the greatest graces that the beloved Mother of Heaven left in me. I call it my vocation to love, supplemented by the other "Pray, pray very much and make sacrifices for sinners; many souls go to hell because there is no one to sacrifice and pray for them." This is my mission, the apostolate of prayer, sacrifice and love.

I don't know how many silly things I say, but it is what I feel and more and more each day I can confirm. It seems that Your Excellency guessed when without knowing in my Solemn Profession that I did practice and never forgot about "my first and last

---

445 *Ibid*, 1987.
446 MSL I, 4th M, Ch. II, No. 4, p. 177.

love." I say what my heart dictates and I send this without studying the words as I quit writing. I ask Your Excellency to correct the errors of my way.

With the greatest respect and dedication I faithfully kiss the sacred ring of Your Excellency and ask for your blessing.

Sister Lucia i.c.d.

Although she had to climb the steep path from nothing, her living faith was face-to-face in the midst of the darkness, the true light that illuminated her path.

Sister Lucia kisses the ring of Pope John Paul II and he kisses her head, Fatima 1991.

CHAPTER XVIII

ENCOUNTERS WITH THE BISHOP
DRESSED IN WHITE

1 | Pope Paul VI - 1965

May 13, 1965. The shepherdess of the Serra de Aire experienced great joy when Pope Paul VI sent a Golden Rose to Our Lady of Fatima. It was a gesture of affection from the Church in the person of its supreme head towards the Lady brighter than the sun, and a sign of authenticity of the Message of Our Lady. That same day Sister Lucia wrote a letter to the Pope expressing her deep gratitude, and also for having proclaimed Mary as Mother of the Church:

-Thank you very much, Your Holiness, for the devotion with which you deigned to distinguish Our Lady of Fatima, offering her the Golden Rose, symbol of faithful affection of Your Holiness with such a good Mother. Thank you Holy Father for the Declaration of Our Lady, 'Mother of the Church,' in a moment so precise! As a little member of this Mystical Body of Christ, I feel deeply moved by this gesture of faithful devotion by Your Holiness to the sweet Mother of Heaven!

Two years later, on May 4, 1967, Sister Lucia's heart jumped for joy when she received news that Pope Paul VI would be going as a pilgrim to Fatima on May 13 to celebrate the 50th anniversary of the Apparitions. This was a dream she had for 50 years—to see the Holy Father! She did not dare utter a word, however:

-They gave us the news that the Holy Father will come to Fatima on the 13th. I felt a great joy by this honor given to Our Lady! And who knows, does Our Lady want to give me this great grace? But I do not deserve it, I am very happy with His glory. [447]

Two days later new information arrived that was disappointing:

-They say that the Holy Father will come to Fatima for certain hours and minutes and then return on the same day. I lost hope, but I offer this wonderful sacrifice to Our Lady so that everything goes well and for the glory of God, the Holy Church, peace in the world, and for those people who are separated from the Church. [448]

Two more days passed and a ray of sunshine pierced her heart when word from Archbishop Ernesto of Coimbra gave her hope of the desired meeting. She was incredulous:

-Is it true? I do not know! But I know that God is good, very good! [449]

Finally on May 9, almost at the last minute, the same bishop confirmed what he had implied—the shepherdess would go to Fatima to meet the Supreme Pastor; she would see in person the "Bishop dressed in white."[450]

In a private conversation the previous year with Cardinal Ferreto, who

---

447 *My Pathway*, II, p. 127.
448 *Ibid.*
449 *Ibid.*
450 MSL I, Appendix III, Third part of the "Secret", p. 215.

visited her after presiding at the May 13 celebrations in Fatima, she confessed how much she wanted to speak with the Holy Father. She had written to the Pope in April that year expressing her desire to see His Holiness in Fatima, and asking for a private meeting, which did not happen.

Sister Lucia went to Fatima in the car of Dr. Miguel Barata, a good friend and doctor of the Community, accompanied by the Prioress Mother Maria of Christ, and her niece, Sister Agnes of the Eucharist. They left on the afternoon of May 10, arriving at the Carmel of St. Joseph in Fatima at 8:30 p.m. As they approached Fatima, Sister Lucia tried to hide her emotions, seeing the endless lines of pilgrims who were walking in the torrential rain. She experienced a strong desire to get out of the car and make her way with them, praying and singing. Even from the car her heart was walking on the muddy land with them, since she typically celebrated these days in spirit from the silence of her cell. No matter where she was or how she felt, her heart was like a compass, never deviating from her path—to Mary, Fatima. Now she was in Fatima! What a whirlwind of feelings invaded her:

Everything impresses me and makes me feel in my heart a shiver going down my spine that I want to conceal so that no one notices what is in my soul. I feel I am offering a prayer to God for this crowd, in the middle of which if it were possible I would hide as a stranger, unknown among them, joining my voice to theirs, spending the night outside in the cold and offering to God this penance in reparation, adoration and supplication, as 50 years ago here we were asked: "Are you willing to offer yourselves to God and bear all the sufferings He wills to send you, as an act of reparation for the sins by which He is offended, and in supplication for the conversion of sinners? –Yes, we do." [451]

On the night of the 12th she wanted to stay the whole night in adoration in the chapel, but having a very bad cold, was not permitted and obediently went to bed. She hardly slept. That night was not for sleeping! She went to pray and quickly prostrated herself in adoration before the Blessed Sacrament.

She waited the next morning for the Monsignor to give her instructions about the much-desired audience with the Holy Father, but he never came. She knew the Bishop of Leiria was to attend the Mass with the Pope, and being at the pulpit, she was puzzled and concluded there was some confusion. She waited a little longer for the Monsignor to talk to her, but that never happened. She called the Papal Nuncio who confirmed that it was the decision of the Holy Father not to see her privately. She did not want this, but if His Holiness ordered it, she obeyed. Then she asked the Papal Nuncio for permission to accompany some other Carmelite Sisters. She wanted to be in the midst of the sisters to better conceal

---

451 *My Pathway*, II, p. 129 – 130.

her presence. She was given permission to accompany the Prioress and the first counselor of the Carmel of St. Joseph, along with the Prioress of Coimbra and Sister Agnes, her niece.

At 9 a.m. they went to the Shrine. As soon as they were settled in their seats, a line of people formed who wanted to greet her. She could not escape it. Soon the Bishop dressed in white entered the Shrine. She related that the Holy Father passed through the gallery like lightning. She hardly saw him, but when he appeared vested for Mass, he passed before her and smiling, he blessed her. What an emotion!

The Mass followed, which she prayed with great intensity; then came time to receive Holy Communion. She expressed her feelings:

I cannot describe what I felt when I had the joy of receiving the bread of Angels from the fatherly hands of the Pope! Only God can show us in Heaven the excellence of grace that is given to us on earth!

The thanksgiving was not short, because it still lingers in the silence of my soul, grateful for so many gifts from the good God, the dear Heavenly Mother to whom I refer with all glory and honor, and the Vicar of Christ on earth whom I revere, obey and cherish as the representative of the same God.[452]

At the end of the Eucharist, the shepherdess was invited to approach the Holy Father, who extended his arms saying in Italian:

-*Viene figliola mia, viene.* [453] *(Come my daughter, come.)*

Sister Lucia was alive with excitement and kissed the feet of the Holy Father and then his ring. His Holiness said that he had received her letter from April and without further explanation told her to speak with her bishop on the subject matter and to obey him. When she asked to speak with him privately, she only heard a 'No' and accepted it without insisting. Beside her the Bishop of Leiria thought Sister Lucia did not understand the Holy Father's words and said to her:

-*The Holy Father would like you to tell me what you wish to say to His Holiness and I will convey it to him.*

To which the Pope replied:

-*Eso és.* [454]*(That's it.)*

Sister Lucia offered to the Holy Father a corporal, which is a linen cloth on which elements are placed for the celebration of the Eucharist, and a visor embroidered with gold by her gifted hands, and a parchment in which she wrote:

Blessed Father,

---

452 *Ibid*, p. 138.
453 *Ibid*, p. 139.
454 *Ibid*.

The message of Our Lady of peace, mercy and supplication:

In May 1917, Our Lady said: "Pray the rosary every day to obtain peace for the world and for the end of the war." That is why I beg Your Holiness be obliged to intensify the prayer of the Rosary and if it is possible to arrange that on Sundays and Holy Days, in all the Churches and chapels, public and semi-public where there is no evening Mass, to pray the Rosary before the exposed Blessed Sacrament, ending with a blessing in a spirit of reparation, adoration and supplication.

Imploring your Apostolic Blessing,

Maria Lucia of the Immaculate Heart [455]

From His Holiness she received a rosary and a beautiful white case for it. She ended the meeting with the Pope faithful and grateful, yet she felt a certain bitterness in her heart because when she was finally next to the Pope she could she not freely open her soul! Only with the Pope could she be an open book and talk about certain matters pertaining to the apparitions. She had a great respect for and faith in human mediation, but if she only could speak directly to the Pope. So many years she had desired this moment and now when she was in the presence of the Supreme Pastor, she was not allowed to speak.

Despite the immense pleasure she derived from her encounter with the Holy Father, this bitter drop tempered the happiness of the moment. It was an opportunity, however, to prove her humility and accept peacefully that the Pope had not granted her the desired audience. In the silence of her heart, that place where 50 years ago she had given her 'yes' to any suffering God wanted to send her, she accepted this and kissed the thorn with profound love.

She went out to her place in the gallery while the Holy Father received and blessed some members of her family. He then placed a Rosary on the image of Our Lady and gathered a few moments in prayer before her. About this time a crowd filled the sanctuary and hailed the Pope with vibrant enthusiasm to which His Holiness responded by opening his arms in a gesture meant to hug everyone. Suddenly an echo of a request came from the crowd:

-Lucia! Lucia! Most Holy Father, show us Lucia!

Having been informed what they were asking, the Holy Father sent for Sister Lucia. She tells of this moment:

-By order of His Holiness came a Monsignor next to me and motioned to me the way to go forward. As I approached the Pope, he came to meet me, stretching out his fatherly arms. Since I did not know what His Holiness wanted, when I arrived next to the Holy Father I knelt down. Then His Holiness, leaning paternally, helped me up while

---

455 *Ibid*, p. 134.

I kissed his holy ring, and taking me by the hand, led me to the front of the Rostrum, placing my hand in his and with a gesture of submission, said to the pilgrims: 'Here she is!' Naturally, the enthusiasm of the crowd doubled, applauding His Holiness.

After a few moments, the Holy Father solemnly gave once more the sign of the cross over the excited people and blessed them. He then withdrew a little backwards and with a simple gesture said goodbye to the pilgrims, and I retreated together with the Holy Father. His Holiness paused there for a few moments contemplating the wonderful aspect of the crowd, united in the same spirit of faith, love and devotion to Our Lady, whom the Vicar of Christ on earth loves, respects and obeys with faithful devotion.

Then the Holy Father gave me another blessing that I received on my knees and I respectfully kissed the sacred ring of His Holiness and retired to the Basilica.

I could then greet the beautiful image of Our Lady, who stood beside me on a litter, and at the foot of which the Holy Father left me in the company of two doves that were released by him. They were not frightened and did not take off even with the sounds of the crowd who were praying and singing, or the airplanes that crossed the sky, not even with the great Rosary which the Holy Father had touched them, or with the grandeur of pontifical vestments! Taking them into my hands, I also wanted to caress them, certain of the presence they represented. But I'm still on earth where I have to comply with the requirements of the circumstances in which God has placed me, and sacrificing for His love the most innocent and pure as acts of praise and gratitude for so many benefits and countless graces that He is pleased to grant me and why I hope to forever sing the hymn of eternal praise! [456]

She received greetings from all the cardinals, bishops, priests and officials who were present, along with the other Carmelite Sisters who accompanied her. Then she went into the Basilica to pray at the tombs of her beloved cousins, Francisco and Jacinta.

The return to the Carmel of St. Joseph was chaotic. Although the car taking her was preceded by the police, as soon as people realized the Shepherdess was in the car, the police, who normally brought order in five minutes, took four hours to accomplish it! Sister Lucia saw this as a reward from Our Lady for all those pilgrims and for the extreme patience of her close friend Dr. Miguel Barata and the powerless police.

To avoid any further mishaps, she stayed two days at the Carmel in Fatima, returning to Coimbra on the afternoon of the 15th, singing the *Magnificat* in her heart in union with the Immaculate Heart of Mary. On the 17th she wrote to the Holy Father to express all the gratitude that filled her heart:

---

456 *Ibid*, p. 141 – 142.

▲ Sister Lucia with Pope Paul VI in
Fatima, May 13, 1967.

▶ Sister Lucia in the Shrine of Fatima.

▼ The Sanctuary of Fatima during the
visit of Paul VI.

▲◄ Sister Lucia meeting with Pope Paul VI.

▼   Bishop João Venâncio, Pope Paul VI and Sister Lucia.

Paul VI presents Sister Lucia to the multitude in the Cova da Iria.

Paul VI prays before the image of Our Lady of Fátima.

Sister Lucia beside her Mother Prioress, Sister Mary of Christ, greeting people present in the Sanctuary.

Albino Luciani, Pope John Paul I.

Autograph of Cardinal Luciani during his visit
with Sister Lucia, July 11, 1977.

Cardinal Albino Luciani celebrates the Eucharist
in the Church of the Carmel of Coimbra, 1977.

My gratitude will last forever. Although God did not grant me the grace that I desired to speak particularly to the Holy Father, He has granted me other ways of which I had never thought. He is the One who knows me and chooses for us and for His Glory. His Cross is the Bearer of all our victories. Everything is grace! Hail Mary! [457]

Sister Lucia could always discern the meaning of God's messages to her through her circumstances in life, no matter how adverse they were. She stood firm in any event, but her interior gaze always discovered the path God wanted in her life. Light always came through the darkness.

2 | Cardinal Albino Luciani - Pope John Paul I – 1977

July 11, 1977. Cardinal Albino Luciano, the Archbishop of Venice, visited the monastery. He concelebrated with 12 priests in our Church, and then entered into our cloister with Ms. Marquisa de Cadaval, who was serving as interpreter. He spoke to me in our parlor, and not wanting to sit in a chair, he sat on a small bench next to me. [458]

Thus Sister Lucia noted this visit of the future Pope John Paul I. As always, nothing transpired of this conversation. Had she 'prophesied' that he would be Pope?

His Eminence was a simple and unceremonious person. Sister Lucia could have told him with simplicity that being cardinal, he could become Pope. After the visits of cardinals whom she had received, she said that any one of them could be Pope. All would ask for her signature on a print of the Immaculate Heart of Mary, which they kept as a souvenir, and she would say:

-*If you are Pope, you already have my signature.* [459]

In the case of Cardinal Luciani, she was right.

She received with sadness, but with a spirit of faith, the news of his death. This Pope was like a meteor, leaving behind a trail of light, a smile of God on earth which was his character. The smiling Pope! In the 33 days of his Pontificate, he won the hearts of all by his simplicity.

3 | Pope John Paul II - A Deep Friendship

October 16, 1978. During the afternoon, two tolls of the household bell broke the silence. It was the signal of a phone call and the Prioress came out. All thought it would be someone to announce the name of the new Pope that

---

457 *Ibid,p. 146.*
458 *My Pathway,* 1977.
459 Oral Narration of Sister Lucia.

was expected, an important time in the Church. But the Prioress returned and said nothing. A few minutes later there was a new call and she came back with a grin articulating with some difficulty the name of the new Pope—Karol Wojtyla. Although unknown, he was received with a spirit of faith, love and reverence, being immediately in the prayers of all and particularly in Sister Lucia—John Paul II.

The sisters followed the ceremonies commemorating his Pontificate on the radio. Sister Lucia was withdrawn while being attentive to all that was said about His Holiness, particularly his words. The coming forth of this Pope from the East was pondered very deeply in her heart, as Our Lady came from the East when she appeared in Fatima. Sister Lucia felt immediately that this new Pope was going to be a Pope of Our Lady. There was something very special about him coming from a land that was under the power of Russia behind the iron curtain and she must have felt a blossom of new hope that the requests of Our Lady might finally be fulfilled. She did not say anything, however, always concealing her emotions and *anything meditating in her heart.* [460]

She did not go around the hand of God, and the hand of Our Lady.

On the Feast Day of the Immaculate Conception, December 8, 1978, she wrote a letter to the Holy Father which began:

Most Holy Father John Paul II,

I thank God for the choice that He deigned to make Your Holiness His Representative and Head of His Church. Praise the Holy Spirit for the actions of His Light.

She could not hear very well, so naturally she missed much of what was said in the cafeteria. But, through the media, she was aware of all events happening. She would read carefully *L'Osservatore Romano*, the Vatican City newspaper, in her cell, savoring the words of the Supreme Pontiff, being always in tune with the voice of the Church and very interested in anything referencing the Holy Father.

The news of the May 13, 1981, attack on Pope John Paul II shook her deeply. This news opened a wound in everyone's heart, creating a greater love for the Pope. In the heart of Sister Lucia, it produced an enormous tear and awareness that this was the BISHOP DRESSED IN WHITE seen in 1917. It is true, she wrote, that the *Bishop dressed in white* is not the personification of *a Pope, but the Pope, because each one carries the weight of a large cross and walks afflicted with pain and sorrow,* [461] having not only the care of all the churches as St. Paul, but concern for all humanity. The Pope, being the Representative of Christ on earth, is not

---

460 Lk 2:19.
461 MSL I, Appendix III, p. 215.

only concerned about the sheep in the Church's fold, but of everyone. He is the universal Shepherd with a heart open to all people of good will, like Christ on the Cross Who opened His arms and let His Heart be torn open and made visible to all. As in the vision of Blessed Jacinta, the Pope is the one constantly standing before God interceding for His children, and does escape attacks of which he is a victim, from both outside and inside the Church. He is the Shepherd who does not run away from danger.[462]

Sister Lucia was reserved and rarely commented, but she was very focused. She wrote a short record of the event that said it all in just a few words:

We were surprised by the sad news of the attack on the Holy Father John Paul II, which was greatly felt and we prayed asking for the health and life of His Holiness. We also prayed for the assassins, that God would convert and bring them on the good path.[463]

She followed the critical state of the Holy Father and begged with her prayers for his recovery. In her view of the "Secret," the Pope fell dead. But as once before in the beginning, the Church returned freedom to the first Pope, St. Peter, who awaited death in prison, so now the tremendous outpouring of prayer for the Holy Father returned him to life, a life that became a great gift from God. Mary was there, diverting the trajectory of the assassin's bullet, and what was predicted did not happen. When John Paul II visited the prison of Rebibbia on December 27, 1983, during the Holy Year of the Redemption, Mehmet Ali Agca, the assassin, anxiously asked the Pope:

-Why didn't you die? I'm sure that I had you well in my sight. I know that the bullet was devastating and deadly. Why is it you did not die? [464]

For him, a professional gunman, this fact was amazing! He knew his aim was accurate and he shot to kill, but with God everything is in the Present and the power of all the prayers for the Holy Father was a protective armor, not allowing the wounds to be fatal. Sister Lucia prayed confidently in the silence of her life as a Carmelite. While recovering in the Gemelli clinic, Pope John Paul II reflected on the significance of what happened to him, and seeing the coincidence of the day, May 13, something was illuminated and he wanted to know more about Fatima and the text of the third part of the secret.

462 Cf. Jn 10:11-12.
463 *My Pathway*, 1978.
464 Stanislao Dziwisz, *A Life with Karol.*

Meeting of Pope John Paul II with Sister Lucia,
Fatima 1982.

Meeting of Pope John Paul II with
Sister Lucia, Fatima 1982.

John Paul II praying in the Chapel
of the Apparitions, 1982.

4 | Pope John Paul II - The First Meeting in 1982

The following year after the attack in the Piazza of St. Peter, Pope John Paul II went to Fatima as a pilgrim to thank the Blessed Virgin for her maternal protection.

He was invited to come to Portugal by the hierarchy of the Portuguese Church and the government, but his purpose was to thank the Mother for her protection, and he wanted to meet the Shepherdess in Fatima.

Sister Lucia and the Prioress Mother Maria das Merces left the Carmel at 7:00 a.m. on May 7th in the car of Dr. Miguel Barata. They arrived at the Carmel of St. Joseph two hours later. Sister Lucia had spent 15 days there in 1980 giving instructions for the painting of some scenes of the Apparitions at Fatima. At that time she wrote a letter to the Pope, fearing she would not have the time to open her soul to His Holiness. This time she would speak face to face with him. When she met with Pope John Paul II, they spent much of the time in quick conversation, but she gave him the letter, which the eyes of all journalists were on, and it later served as *guidance for the interpretation of the third part of the "secret."* [465]

This extensive letter contained the major desires carried in the heart of Sister Lucia who wanted to see them satisfied. This was the desire of Our Lady, the fruit of Sister Lucia's meditations on the Message that was delivered to her to convey to the world.

On the morning of May 13th, the planned meeting between the Holy Father and the Shepherdess took place in the house of Our Lady of Mount Carmel. The Holy Father was waiting for her at the door of the office. They dismissed the interpreter as they understood each other very well. Sister Lucia describes this meeting:

The Holy Father, holding my right hand in his, told me:

-We have to talk fast because the time is short.

There was much that I wanted for this meeting, but it had to be for the Pope! He smiled and asked me two questions to which I replied with simplicity and truth, feeling much at ease as if I was alone with God, to Whom nothing is hidden and everything is said. Faith led me to see the Holy Father, whoever he is, as a living image of Christ Who said: 'Whatever you bind on earth shall be bound in Heaven, and whatever you loose on earth shall be loosed in Heaven' (Mt 16-19).

Then I explained what I wanted to say to His Holiness. We talked about the secret and agreed that it was more prudent to keep it silent as before.

---

465 Congregation for the Doctrine of the Faith, *The Message of Fatima.* p. 14.

We then talked about the consecration of Russia in union with all the bishops of the world. There are many difficulties; however, the Holy Father was favorable to this being possible and said:

-We will do whatever is in our hands. [466]

Sister Lucia continued to relay verbally the contents of the letter: She asked that the Rosary be declared a liturgical prayer and shared a broad meditation on the prayer of the Hail Mary and the Our Father, to which the Holy Father responded:

-It is so, it is so, and it is beautiful. [467]

She asked for the Beatification of the Shepherds, and finally, the publication of her book "Calls from the Message of Fatima." It is what Sister Lucia called a *transmission of the message* written to provide a general answer to all the questions and concerns she received in numerous correspondences, and the original was sent to Paul VI. The Pope promised to take care of it and expressed his desire also to see that soon the Little Shepherds would be beatified.

Time ran out and Msgr. Silveira knocked on the door to warn that it was necessary to be prepared for his next meeting. The Holy Father got up and agreed to go to another room where the Mother Prioress and Father Provincial, Friar Jeremias Carlos Vechina, O.C.D., were waiting. Sister Lucia presented to the Pope gifts she had prepared: a white styrofoam lamb full of rosaries made by her, a framed picture of Our Lady, and a box with some pounds in gold. She offered these with the permission of the Community; they had been left to Sister Lucia in a will by a friend. Having signed a few prints that she presented to him, the Holy Father said goodbye and went to the meeting with the Bishops of Portugal.

Afterwards, there was the great Eucharistic Celebration at the end of which the Holy Father pronounced the Consecration of the World to the Immaculate Heart of Mary while kneeling at the feet of Our Lady on the litter. Sister Lucia watched with her impassioned heart. While this was accomplished, however, it still was not with the conditions requested by Our Lady.

Was Sister Lucia demanding of the consecration? Well, she deferred to the efforts being made and she saw the difficulties, but the issue was not personal. The consecration had to be done as Our Lady had requested. She was just serving a mission, humbly, faithful and obedient, but if a point was lacking she would not be silent. The well-accomplished Giuseppe De Carli (Vatican reporter) called her an *awkward Carmelite, who was a thorn that pierced the throat of all the Popes of the*

---

466 *My Pathway*, 1982.
467 *Ibid.*

Meeting of Pope John Paul II with Sister Lucia, Fatima 1991.

From left to right: Mother Prioress Sister Maria do Carmo, Pope John Paul II,
Sister Lucia and Bishop Alberto, Bishop of Leiria-Fatima.

Meeting of Pope John Paul II with Sister Lucia,
Fatima 1991.

John Paul II thanks and kisses the rosary that Sister
Lucia offered to him.

▲ Sister Lucia receives communion from
Pope John Paul II during the Mass in
the Sanctuary of Fatima.

▶ Pope John Paul II, May 13, 1991.

twentieth century. [468]

Pope John Paul II completed the visit that left her heart full of happiness. She then met the Pope in the Basilica:

We passed the tombs of Francisco and Jacinta. Then again we met with the Holy Father and he gave me his blessing and kissed me on the head. His kiss was as if it were the kiss of Christ, whom I thanked feeling my own unworthiness and understanding that it is the most poor to whom Christ leans. [469]

She stayed a few more days in the Carmel in Fatima, hoping that everything would return to normal with no more meetings, and returned to Coimbra on the 19th, her soul filled with happy memories.

5 | Pope John Paul II - The Second Meeting in 1991

In 1991, Pope John Paul II returned to Fatima on May 12 and 13. This time Sister Lucia was not called to attend. She would remain with the Community and follow the journey of His Holiness in Portugal on television. But a surprise phone call to the Prioress on the morning of the 12th came from the Bishops of Leiria and Coimbra, delivering an order from the Holy Father for Sister Lucia to be in Fatima the next day.

It is also an exception for a Carmelite to leave the Carmel, but it is also no problem because it does not require much preparation. By late afternoon, Sister Lucia and the Mother Prioress left in the car of Dr. Miguel Barata and his wife. He asked for a police escort and they arrived in Fatima with haste.

The meeting with the Pope was to take place on the morning of the 13th before Mass in the house of Our Lady of Mount Carmel. Sister Lucia and the Mother Prioress arrived before the Pope and were invited to go to the Blessed Sacrament chapel. They prayed briefly before being told the Pope was coming. He came in and prayed for a short time before the Blessed Sacrament, and with joy and simplicity greeted Mother Prioress and Sister Lucia before heading to the meeting room. In the corridor, several journalists and photographers came forward and delicately asked if they could take some photographs. The Holy Father, noticing how the Shepherdess withdrew—she did not like being photographed—took her by the hand and with a gentle smile said:

-*We have to oblige.* [470]

There was no other remedy! Another sacrifice, but this time she also offered

---

468 Cardinal Tarcisio Bertone with Giuseppe De Carli, *The Last Secret of Fatima,* Introduction.
469 *My Pathway,* 1982.
470 Oral Narration of Sister Lucia.

obedience to the Holy Father.

They proceeded down the hall to the room where they could talk alone. Sister Lucia was still immersed in the joy of participating in the Eucharist presided by the "Bishop dressed in white" at the place where Our Lady had first shown her this figure. Nothing was recorded at this meeting, but she had the *pleasure once again of speaking privately with the Holy Father.* [471]

She returned in the same car to the Carmel of St. Teresa on May 17. Until next time! Certainly she would be back because she asked the Holy Father for the Beatification of her cousins. Both wanted to see them on the altar (Beatified). And they did see, but they had to wait a few more years.

6 | Pope John Paul II - The Third Meeting in 2000

On February 10, 1999, Father Luis Kondor visited Sister Lucia and told her the miracle had been approved that opened the door for the Beatification of the Servants of God, Francisco and Jacinta Marto. It was a joy to her heart. When would it be and where? It was clear that Sister Lucia was vigorous in her prayers for the Holy Father to come to Fatima for the Beatification, which seemed impossible because in 2000 the Pope would be leaving Rome to go on a pilgrimage to the Holy Land, and nothing more. But the unexpected happened. When the Beatification was scheduled to be celebrated in Rome in April, the Pope decided to make an exception to his program for the year and return to Fatima. What jubilation for the Shepherdess!

The news of the coming of the Holy Father to Fatima filled me with joy. I don't know how to thank God and the maternal protection of Our Lady! I want to continue to be a tiny wafer of praise to the Lord, sacrificed on the altar of love! [472]

Looking tenderly to her cousins, she continued:

The two little shepherds, Francisco and Jacinta Marto, were two Angels who passed through the land without a spot of dust from the roads, thanks to the designs of God and the maternal protection of Our Lady. How good it is to let ourselves be driven in the arms of the Father and Mother in Heaven! [473]

Sister Lucia was now 92 years old and still had her eyes on the center of her love, willing to please Him forever. She was never found in a position to sit back. With the wisdom of 90 years, she lived with the simplicity of a two-year-old and the boldness of an 18-year-old, always desiring more of the love of God

---

471 *Ibid.*

472 *My Pathway*, 2000.

473 *Ibid.*

in response to His grace, seeking the highest peak to achieve this, not for glory, but for the ardor of this love: more holiness to be more pleasing to the eyes of the Father and to be more influential in her prayer of intercession on behalf of her brothers and sisters. Her heart beat with the freshness of the first time, applying the requests in the apparition of Our Lady in August of 1917:

-Pray, pray very much and make sacrifices for sinners, for many souls go to hell because there is no one to make sacrifices and pray for them. [474]

7 | Cousins Beatified

With news of the beatification of Francisco and Jacinta, Sister Lucia had a new energy. She wanted this so much that she asked the Holy Father and collaborated with him for this with her writings, testimonies and evidence. She cherished the hope of seeing them on the altar before her departure to Heaven, and to this she added a new joy—to be able to meet with the Holy Father again.

It was a very happy time of recreation in the parlor when she told the Community of the event on the day she received a visit from Bishop Alberto Cosme do Amaral, retired bishop of Leiria-Fatima, and Father Luis Kondor. In Fatima the year before, they had questioned whether she would be able to withstand another trip to Fatima on May 13 the following year. But when Sister Lucia opened the curtains in the parlor to greet them—they did not see or hear her coming—she heard them say very happily to each other, seeing her in good health:

-She can! She can!

Looking at Sister Lucia, they repeated:

-You can! You can!

She, dying of laughter, asked:

-I can what?

The two visitors then told her the reason for their joy: they were very happy to see that she was still able to go to Fatima and participate in the Rite of Beatification, and she was delighted.

The Holy Father had also decided to make public the third part of the Secret. To do so, he wanted Sister Lucia to testify that the text stored in the Holy Office was really written by her hand on January 3, 1944, and was the same text that she delivered to Bishop da Silva. To confirm this, the Sacred Congregation for the Doctrine of the Faith sent Msgr. Tarcisio Bertone, later Cardinal Secretary of

---

474 MSL I, 4th M, Ch. II, No. 6, p.180.

State, with a letter from the Holy Father asking Sister Lucia to speak openly and honestly with the renowned Vatican figure and to clarify anything she was asked.

In the presence of Bishop Serafim, Bishop of Leiria-Fatima, Cardinal Bertone handed her the envelope from 1960, and feeling the paper, she said:

-Yes, this is my letter, this text is mine.

She had a very frank conversation with the envoy of the Holy Father, as if speaking personally with the Pope, and she was glad to know the text would be published. It had already given her so many headaches, having to deal with all the speculation about its contents. She used to say:

-If they live most importantly what has already been said… Just deal with what was said and comply with what was requested: Prayer and Penance![475]

And we see that the only word spoken three times in this part of the secret is: *Penance! Penance! Penance!*[476]

May 11th arrived. This time she traveled to Fatima in the car of her nephew, Mr. José Maria Vieira, accompanied by his wife, the Mother Prioress, and Dr. Branca Paul, doctor of the Community. They traveled with more security, escorted by two cars from the Portuguese Security Police. At 93 years old, Sister Lucia endured very well the 70km ride from Coimbra to Fatima. Again they were warmly received by the Carmelite Sisters of St. Joseph in Fatima.

Like the other times, she was thrilled with the spectacle of pilgrims on foot. With her heart united to God, she prayed with them and for them, presenting to the Blessed Virgin Mary the aspirations of all those hearts.

A few days before, she sent to Fatima the gift that she wished to offer to the Holy Father. It was a consignment of 300 rosaries made by her hands. They were divided into three acrylic boxes and wrapped with white lace, to be given during the offertory of the Mass on the 13th. No one asked for publicity, and the media was not asked not to publicize the rosaries that Sister Lucia was giving to the Pope, but requests poured in for 'a rosary made by Sister Lucia!' The rosaries made by Sister Lucia, however, were very rare and only given as gifts from her.

She watched on television with the Community of the Carmel of Fatima the Holy Father's arrival in Portugal and then Fatima on May 12. On the morning of the 13th she was driven by police car to meet the Holy Father in the sacristy of the Sanctuary. Here the little Shepherdess of Fatima met the Supreme Pastor of the Church whom she revered. She was before His Holiness who was bent over from illness. It was a meeting of friends. Although their meetings were very rare, there was a special bond between Sister Lucia and the Holy Father. God only

---

475 Oral Narration of Sister Lucia.
476 MSL I, Appendix III, p. 215.

knows what was in their hearts, so in love with Mary!

There was a great celebration on May 13, during which the Rite of Beatification of the Little Shepherds was included. How their cousin Lucia rejoiced! There she was in front of the entire terrace and a sea of people. In her mind must have passed a movie of her life captured by those who were now proclaimed Blessed. There again she saw herself between them playing with the gentle lambs, picking the flowers that abounded on this slope, and she sang with deep emotion:

Let us sing cheerfully with one voice: Francisco and Jacinta, pray for us. [477]

A dream! An ecstasy! Eighty-three years separated that day when only the three of them were in this place, and at the invitation of Mary gave their 'Yes' to God and to all that He wanted to ask of them, and who walked that long way, *stepping on thorns, thorns and thistles, putting their feet in the footprints of Christ, going forward in the marks left in the soil of the earth!* [478]

Her cousins went very fast to Heaven, as they had been promised, and she was to be here for some time...how long would it be? Like the old man Simeon with the Infant Jesus in his arms in the Temple of Jerusalem, she could now sing *Nunc dimittis. (Now dismiss.)* [479] The Message of the Lady was already given to the Church and had spread to all four corners of the world. The Consecration of the World was already made as Our Lady had requested and now her cousins were beatified, and the third part of the Secret would be made public within moments. Was her mission carried out? Yes, at whatever time the Lord wanted. She was, in the eyes of those who were with her on the 13th, a girl with a nostalgia, a longing for Heaven, who saw the real beauty, as nothing on earth could fill her soul.

At the end of the Eucharist, His Eminence Cardinal Sodano, Secretary of State, read the text of the third part of the Secret to the crowd that filled the Sanctuary of Fatima, and all those around the world who were following this solemn celebration on television. It was a page-turner in the history of Fatima; a thick curtain raised and delivered to the world eager to know that Secret, hidden for so many years.

Although Sister Lucia was surrounded by a group of people who were protecting her at the end of the celebration, it seemed they forgot about her. In the moment they were all concentrating on the Holy Father, the situation around Sister Lucia and their exit from the Basilica became chaotic. As soon as the people found her unprotected, they almost crushed her, all wanting to touch her or talk

---

477 Hymn of the Beatification of Francisco and Jacinta Marto.
478 Sister Lucia, *How I See the Message*, p. 38.
479 Lk 2:29–32.

**Meeting of Pope John Paul II with Sister Lucia,
Fatima 2000.**

▲◀ Sister Lucia was present at the Mass in which John Paul II beatified Francisco and Jacinta Marto, Shrine of Fatima 2000.

◀ Sister Lucia observing the crown of the statue of Our Lady of Fatima Chapel, where the bullet is located that was extracted from Pope John Paul II.

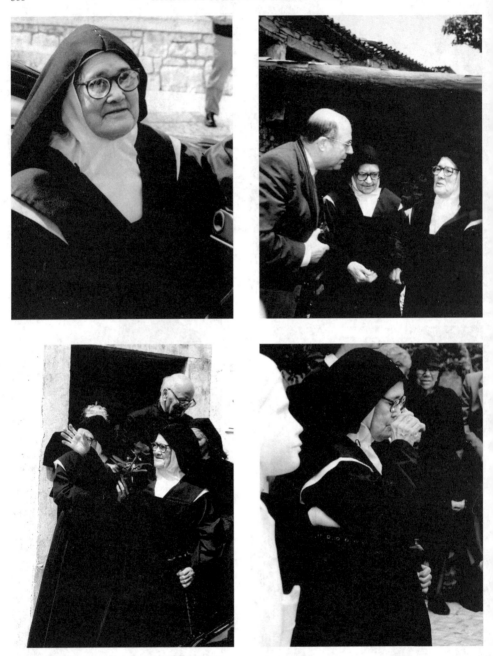

Sister Lucia visiting the places of her childhood, May 2000.

Sister Lucia visiting the places of her childhood, May 2000.

Sister Lucia with Father Luis Kondor, Postulator of the Cause of Beatification of Francisco and Jacinta Marto.

Visit to the Fatima parish church.

Visit to the Fatima
parish church,
beside the baptismal
font where she was
baptized.

to her. It was like the days on the 13th of the last months of 1917. As soon as the security guards noticed they restored order, and she and her companions were able to return to Carmel with hearts full of joy.

8 | Pilgrimage of the Heart

Knowing that it would be a great joy for Sister Lucia, Mother Maria do Carmo of St. John of the Cross, the Prioress who accompanied her to Fatima, also met with the Holy Father and asked for permission before returning to Coimbra to visit the places related to the Apparitions and her family life. The Pope replied with much emphasis:

-*Yes, yes! And the entire Community!*

Who would have thought that the whole Community would accompany Sister Lucia!

The Rector of the Shrine, Msgr. Luciano Guerra, wanted to let the Shepherdess place her hands on the crown of Our Lady, which now contained the bullet that wounded the Pope set in its center. Sister Lucia appreciated this special favor; it touched her heart greatly. A feeling of excitement went through her soul to be able to touch that object that was both a sign of sin and grace!

After three days when the environment was quieter, they bade farewell to the loving community of the Carmel of Fatima. Then the Shepherdess of the Serra de Aire, accompanied by the Mother Prioress, some nephews and nieces, the Rev. Father Luis Kondor and some police officers revisited those places where she had met with Heaven. It was filmed by Rev. Father Antonio to document her journey that day.

As always Sister Lucia hid the intimate emotions that filled her heart as she walked to all the places related to her life at the time of the Apparitions. She visited Valinhos and Loca do Cabeço, drank water at the well, touched the wall of her home and her room, sat on her bed, sat at the fireplace, and in the parish church she kissed the baptismal font where she became a Christian.

She was enchanted by all the signs of nature in that springtime celebration, finding among the bushes the freshness of her heart that she left there almost 90 years ago!

Everything was speaking to her! Oh, that she could drop the walking stick and go alone on these many paths that she trod in those first years as a girl! Now the heavy pace would not allow her this lightness, but her spirit was still walking lightly, going through the early years of her history written in the book of life by the hand of Our Lady. She was the Shepherdess, the fragile feather that the Mother used.

Sister Lucia began this "pilgrimage" with a few companions who had promised to keep it a secret, but when they arrived at the parish church it was already full! Patience! Sister Lucia had a smile for everyone, a caress. It was her farewell to the people of her land, with whom she always felt an affinity—like they were her family.

This church had many memories for her, joyful and painful, but always with hours of grace by which she would be grateful and kiss the Lord. Here she worshiped the "Hidden Jesus" available for all, and welcomed the image of the Lady of the Rosary who smiled at her at her First Communion. Her last stop was at the Chapel of the Apparitions where it was not possible for her to leave the car. There were so many people! Inside the car, Sister Lucia with folded hands prayed a Hail Mary to Our Lady and everyone joined her, trusting again in the promise given to her to be sheltered in her Immaculate Heart!

Goodbye, O Fatima!

They returned with her nephew and his wife to the Carmel of Coimbra, arriving in the evening. Sister Lucia was tired, but happy. She was so happy that she did not realize she was tired. Her heart sang a joyful Magnificat for everything that the Lord had done in and through her. She looked back at the long trip and now she could rest. With a thankful heart, on the 20th day she participated in the Mass of Thanksgiving for the Beatification of the Little Shepherds, which Bishop Albino Mamede Cleto and several priests concelebrated. She sang again with all her soul the Hymn of the Beatification and repeated with tenderness those names so dear to her heart! The glory of her cousins was a crown and once again she repeated:

-It is all because of Our Lady.

9 | Cardinal Joseph Ratzinger - Pope Benedict XVI - 1996

October 13, 1996. Cardinal Joseph Ratzinger, Prefect of the Congregation for the Doctrine of Faith, presided at the Pilgrimage Anniversary of the Apparitions of Fatima and the next day he visited the Carmel of Coimbra to speak with the Shepherdess. After a solemn celebration of the Mass, His Eminence entered the cloister with his entourage. Sister Lucia thus noted this visit:

These gentlemen visited our Carmel:

Cardinal Joseph Ratzinger, Prefect of the Sacred Congregation for the Doctrine of the Faith

Bishop Thadeusz Kondrusiewicz, Archbishop of Moscow

Cardinal Joseph Ratzinger, the future Benedict XVI in Fatima 1996.

Cardinal Joseph Ratzinger, the future Benedict XVI, with Sister Lucia in the Carmel of Coimbra, 1996.

Bishop Edmund Piszz, Archbishop of Olsztyn (Poland), President of the
   Episcopal Commission for Polish Marian Subject

Msgr. Amândio Tomas, Rector of the Pontifical Portuguese College (Rome)

Bishop Serafim de Sousa Ferreira e Silva, Bishop of Leiria-Fatima

Bishop João Alves, Bishop of Coimbra

Bishop José Werth, Apostolic Administrator of Siberia

Bishop Jan Pawel Lenga, Bishop of Cazaquistão

There was also the Rev. Father Luis Kondor and I do not remember anymore.

I went to the parlor with the Community.

By order of His Eminence Cardinal Ratzinger, each (in turn) gave their testimony about Fatima. I felt grateful to God for His immense mercy and great protection that He has granted to the world through Our Lady and I felt confused by the appreciation that I received from the Cardinal of Germany. I deserve nothing. It is God Who does everything, Who is using Our Lady. Finally Cardinal Ratzinger wanted me to say a few words. I felt confused and I wanted to refuse and with a humble gesture, I indicated that I had nothing to say, but the Bishop of Coimbra, João Alves, approached me and told me to say something. In obedience, I said as the basis of the entire message, rooted in faith, hope and love: 'My God, I believe, I adore, I hope and I love You. I ask pardon for those who do not believe, do not adore, do not hope and do not love You.'

Then Cardinal Ratzinger wanted particularly to talk to me.

I took the opportunity to ask what I should do when the Cardinals were present with numerous people. His Eminence replied: -Do not worry about that, the responsibility belongs to the Cardinals.

Thanks be to God!

I also asked Cardinal Ratzinger if the answer that I had given to the Russian Orthodox team who had visited was good. The Cardinal responded:

-Well, it was very good, very good!

I was happy giving thanks to God and the maternal protection of Our Lady.
October 14, 1996. [480]

At the same time, there was also a group of Polish pilgrims that carried the image of Our Lady to Poland. At the end of the celebration when the Cardinal was moving toward the entrance of the cloister, some people from the group approached the railing of the choir and asked to enter the cloister with the image for a moment. They went by the grid of Communion and Sister Lucia, who had already left the choir, was advised and returned to kiss the image. When they realized she was there, all the pilgrims rushed to the presbytery. Our Lady

---

480 My Pathway, 1996.

must have found favor in such devotion! There were no chairs available and they climbed on anything that was high in order to view the Shepherdess. Everything that was available served as a pedestal!

When Sister Lucia left, they returned outside with the image. The pilgrims were very happy because Our Lady showed them her confidant!

The ones that did not notice anything were the numerous journalists who were following the Cardinal very closely to the door of the cloister.

Sister Lucia.

CHAPTER XIX

ONLY SOME MORE TIME

1 | Golden Jubilee of the Religious Carmelite

Every step she took was already marked by much difficulty and pain. It was one more offering in her soul during this celebration, knowing she was giving life and light to many people who were unknowingly stretching their hands to her from the chains of sin.

May 31, 1999, had arrived—the Golden Jubilee of Lucia's Profession in Carmel. She accepted with great humility everything that was done for her throughout the feast. On the evening before we organized a procession to Our Lady, singing along to the music of the Fatima Avé with some verses made for the occasion.

As soon as everyone arrived, two sisters came forward and removed the cloth covering the statue. They revealed a ceramic tile of the three shepherds. According to Sister Lucia, it was the first photograph taken of them. She was touched and very thankful for this surprise. At the Carmel she agreed to sit in a chair covered with a gold fabric and listen to a song created for the celebration:

WE PRAISE GOD!
What cloud of perfumed incense
Rises to Heaven, pure and mild,
The Yes by her today renewed,
At once God receives!
WE PRAISE GOD!

Sister, by this Jubilee
What a triumph, what a triumph of love,
WE PRAISE GOD!

For that luminous trail that you left
In the path, the path that you walked,
WE PRAISE GOD!

For these years that are already an eternity
And for all who live,
WE PRAISE GOD!

For all the thorns that you kissed,
Pain and the cross, which generated roses,

WE PRAISE GOD!

To your Thanksgiving with Mary
We are joined in one heart.
WE PRAISE GOD!

Then all the sisters embraced her and gave her gifts, including a parchment with a blessing from the Holy Father.

For Sister Lucia, the 31st was a day of celebration, but a little tiring at her age. Everything was accomplished with simplicity; she even joked in the cafeteria, taking the apron from the sister who was serving, something she had not done in many years. She received several visits from relatives and friends who came for the Holy Mass in the afternoon with the celebrant Bishop João Alves, Bishop of Coimbra. On this day she wrote a brief note:

In addition to the Bishop of the Diocese, his coadjutor and I do not know how many concelebrants there were, Rev. José Valinho, Rev. Manuel Pereira, Rev. Luis Kondor, the Rector of the Shrine and the Bishop of Leiria-Fatima, etc., and among them were my nephews and nieces, that God and Our Lady repay them and that Our Lady send her Motherly Blessing. [481]

At night in the intimacy of the Community she was offered a spiritual bouquet and some chocolates which she joyfully shared with all.

2 | Last Years

In 2000, when Sister Lucia arrived at the Carmel after the trip to Fatima she had much joy in her heart, but soon she began to feel a sharp pain in one leg, and especially her foot. She was used to having pain, but this seemed different, more acute. Her devoted doctor tried to treat it, but nothing would relieve the violent pains. Seeing that her suffering continued without respite, they sought the help of an orthopedic doctor who was a friend of the Community. Being very experienced, Dr. Joaquim Rodrigues could see what was happening and took her for an X-ray.

The problem was in her spine. The 'pilgrimage' to her childhood home required much walking, which placed a lot of strain on her spine, already very deformed, and the pain was diverted to her foot. The doctor said it would take about six months to heal and advised the use of a brace to help relieve the pain.

---

481 *My Pathway, 1999.*

When they presented her with the strap, she exclaimed:

-*So, I complained about my foot and the doctor tells me to tighten the belly?*

Even in suffering she would joke about the situation.

To save her a lot of effort, she used a wheelchair for long distances. It was beautiful to see her enter the recreation room, first with a cane in hand, then taken by wheelchair, and with her arms and hands open and raised to Heaven, she sang the song of her childhood and family who sang at night asking the blessing of Our Lady:

My Mother, my Lady
Among these daughters cast
Your affectionate blessing.
Give us this grace from Heaven.

In the name of the Father,
Of the Son and the Holy Spirit.
Your Motherly blessing! Amen.

After this most pressing and painful period, she resumed her daily visits to the memorial of the Immaculate Heart of Mary at the end of the garden. She would take the elevator down for a small lunch of tea and bread or some toast, and if weather permitted she went out in the sun with her straw hat and walked slowly while praying the Rosary, supported by her cane, which she chided:

-*It's not worth much because if I take my hand off it, it falls! After all I do have to hold it!* [482]

She would stop for a while and pray before the image and then return to the Convent through the oratory where she could visit the Blessed Sacrament.

On the Feast of Christ the King in 2000, she made for the last time this *pilgrimage* alone to the garden that she enjoyed so much. On her return after her conversation with Our Lady, she felt dizzy and fell on the cement floor. She did not suffer injury but it was very painful. Without any support to get up and being alone, she crawled up next to an iron support and holding the branches of a rose bush was able to stand up. Moments later a Sister saw her from a distance having difficulty walking and went to her aid. It was a pity; she was trembling all over. Thank God she was only bruised, but never again was she left alone. She offered to the Lord this sacrifice of freedom and proceeded to go in a wheelchair, pushed by a Sister.

---

482 Oral Narration of Sister Lucia.

A daily schedule was organized and a sister was assigned to take her where she needed to go. In the summertime in the evening, she would be in prayer for an hour. Sometimes the sisters prayed the Rosary with her and they would also bring her in her wheelchair and place her in front of the statue of the Immaculate Heart of Mary, close enough so it would be comfortable for her in her faithful conversations with the Mother. There she would stay without ever getting tired of looking at the image of the Lady. She would raise her hands, her fingers no longer straight because of arthritis, and present to the Lady all the requests she received through countless letters and also those not made directly to her but to God, Who knew what was in the hearts of His people. Every day she prayed the full Rosary, including one five-decade rosary for the intentions entrusted to her. She always said "hello" to her cousins represented in the tile at the feet of Our Lady.

She gave food to the fish in the pond—scraps of communion wafers—calling them 'beautiful, beautiful' while stirring the water with the tip of her cane. She liked to see them come to the surface in search of the morsels she offered. Because of this habit, they could sense when she was coming to greet them, and she said they already knew her voice!

In her daily routine, she would take her medical prescriptions in her cell in the morning, and then stand for the Community Mass at 8:00 a.m., to which she listened through a public address system that the Prioress bought for the Community. This obedience was painful for her, but once again she said 'Yes' to the will of God, knowing how to give back and not showing the sacrifice she made. We always joked with her, saying:

-So, you are lazy that you do not go to Mass!

Immediately she would have the answer:

-But the Mass comes to me.

That waiver did not apply to the Midnight Mass at Christmas and the Easter Vigil, but the Christmas of 2000 was the first time she did not attend the Mass. After Mass we brought the Child Jesus to her cell. So it was like this for her last Christmas. She was very sad, because every year we would go to her cell and usually spent the time singing with her after the Mass of the Nativity. What a lot of gifts she made to the image of the Little Child. She also had some treats for her Sisters because she would ask the Prioress in advance to offer them sweets or chocolates. She would distribute them with much joy. When she was kept in bed because of a flu or illness, she would later visit the Sisters in the passageway to the recreation room, which was next to her cell, and she always offered them a sweet.

The memory of her last ten years was engraved in the hearts of all the Sisters who had the privilege of accompanying her in the final phase of life. The more the years passed, the more light was seen in this woman of God. She radiated a visible joy that was very noticeable, which came from her intimate union with the Lord. It was truly a swan song at the end of her life, the melodious song of the worker at the end of the journey, who lived with love and fidelity *the entire weight of the day and the scorching heat.*[483] She felt the longing of Heaven, but she was happy in the will of God Who wanted her here *some more time.* [484]

During recreations, she was the center of attention where everyone gathered. With her plentiful works during so many years, she had plenty of stories to tell, stories of her life in which there was humor attached. She relived the mischief of her childhood, the time that she was a pupil in the Van Zeller Institute, her holidays with the Pestana family, and in Braga at the Quinta da Formigueira. She told of her memories as a Dorothean religious and her difficulties with the Spanish language, recalling these times with tears and laughter. She enjoyed reliving these moments so distant, yet so alive in her memory. Even when she would repeat them, it was as interesting as hearing them the first time because she would always add something new.

Despite her age, she never seemed to be a little old lady and became increasingly beautiful and attractive. In her later years it seemed like *she turned back into the girl she was when she saw Our Lady.*[485] There are days when the sunset has the same beauty as the aurora. In the life of the Shepherdess of Fatima, the same happened: in the twilight of her life, she was enveloped in the lightness of her innocent childhood. Detached from everything, her heart sang with St. John of the Cross:

-*You are the only love of my life.* [486]

After the year 2000, she became more stressed by the changes in her life, a turn of the page. Her body needed more rest and she no longer fought it. When we told her in recreation that she had to do penance, she responded smiling:

-*Now I do it with the Sisters, I've already done a lot.*

In fact she continued to do much penance now that she was no longer active, put passive. She suffered serenely without complaining about the limitations of her age and weight, offering them with the formula Our Lady taught her on July 13, 1917. The Sisters empathized with the sufferings she felt, and she sometimes confessed:

-*No one wants to die young, but it is very painful to be old!*

---

483 Mt 20:12.
484 MSL I, 4ᵗʰ M, Ch. II, No. 4, p. 177.
485 Sister Lucia, *A Memory that We Have of Her,* p. 45.
486 St. John of the Cross, *Spiritual Canticle,* Song 28.

▲ Sister Lucia together with the image of the Immaculate Heart of Mary and the tile panel with the three shepherd children placed in the garden of the Carmel of Coimbra on the occasion of her Golden Jubilee of Religious Consecration.

▲ Sister Lucia showing the book that she wrote, "Calls From the Message of Fatima," signed by Pope John Paul II.

◀ Sister Lucia, center, with the community of the Carmelite Sisters, 1997.

◀ Commemoration of the 96th birthday anniversary of Sister Lucia, with the group of Carmelite Fathers who celebrated the Eucharist 2003.

Sister Lucia in the garden of the
Carmel of Coimbra, 2004.

Sister Lucia with Cardinal Eduardo
Pironio, their companions and
some Sisters during their entry into
the cloister, 1983.

Sister Lucia with Cardinal Maisner,
Monsignor Michael and
Fr Luis Kondor, 1998.

Cardinal Maisner delivering to
Sister Lucia, on behalf of Pope
John Paul II, the cassock worn by
him in 2002.

Father Drozdeke handing the
rosary sent by Pope John Paul II,
in the parlor of the
Carmel of Coimbra, 2003.

◀ Sister Lucia with Cardinal
Saraiva Martins in one of his
visits to the Carmel of Coimbra,
2003.

◀ Cardinal Erdo greeting
Sister Lucia, 2003.

▲ Journalist Aura Miguel with Sister
Lucia, 2003.

▶ Cardinal Tarcisio Bertone with
Sister Lucia in the cloister of
Carmel, 2003.

Four months before her departure:

-Our Lady said I was here for some time more... but it is already so much! [487]

In October 2003, we celebrated 75 years since her first consecration to the Lord as a Religious Dorothean. The celebration was held in the intimacy of the Community, because she had just celebrated her Golden Jubilee as a Carmelite, which was public.

The newly-elected Superior General, Father Luis Arostegui Gamboa, was present. He was coming to Portugal in October and accepted the invitation to come to the monastery on the 22nd to celebrate the Mass of Thanksgiving for her life given completely to the Lord. Sister Lucia was very happy and touched by his presence, a rare occurrence.

3 | Serenity and Good Humor Until the End

March 2004. The hourglass of Sister Lucia's life began the countdown of her final days, dropping the last grains of sands of her time in this world. The Mass was scheduled for 11:30 a.m. on the 22nd when her birthday was celebrated. The chapel was crowded as was the case for many years. Although the people could not see her, they had the joy of knowing they were participating at Mass near her. This year was not her time to leave us. There was a week during this time in which she suffered severe pain in her legs and could not get up. After 11 hours what was she to do? The doctor gave her a strong injection and she managed to go to Mass during the day and receive a few visits from some friends. It was a gift from her Bridegroom, a day free of pain.

The pain stemmed from her deformed spine, which also caused her hands and feet to be noticeably deformed. Even in this suffering, however, she remained cheerful to any Sister who visited and appreciated the visits of the Community on the days when she could not go to the recreation room.

Easter 2004 was a day of relief. During the noon recreation she spent time with the whole Community in the garden with the image of the Immaculate Heart of Mary. She communicated joyfully and was delighted to recount the numerous stories of her life, especially to the younger Sisters who surrounded her. She did dream this would be the last time she celebrated the feast of Easter!

In her cell she had a bell to summon help when needed. She was not to work, however, because her legs were already so fragile, and if she ventured to stand up and fall she would bruise easily. The bruising was not important; what

---

487   Sister Lucia, *A Memory that We Have of Her*, p. 27.

was worse, she thought, was the decision that a Sister would always accompany her now, and she was not pleased that she was given no work. Sister Lucia finally could have a good night's rest, however, because a comfortable bed was placed in her cell. She asked what it was for, saying it was not necessary, but once the decision was made she accepted it with humility. Each night she would ask:

-*Who is it today?*

And invariably concluded:

-*I am poorly served!*

Without complaint or remorse, her limitations were always graced by a sense of humor. Two sisters divided each night into two parts—one staying until 2 a.m. and another until morning—so they could have some rest and not be too tired to participate in Community life. While a sacrifice, it was a pleasure for them to be with someone who suffered so gracefully. When the younger sisters were with her, she would laugh that the Mother Prioress had to tell them to be quiet. If she needed help, she would call out with her little hoarse voice, longing to know:

-*Is anyone there!*

And then would pronounce the phrase from Revelation:

-*Neither cold nor hot, I will vomit you out of my mouth.*[488]

She had her ups and downs until the month of November when she began the most difficult and final period. She still went down to the cafeteria in her wheelchair, but was not eating enough and no one realized it. Her tired body rejected food and longed for rest.

She was impatient to finish the Community retreat conducted by Bishop João Bosco, who was the Bishop of Patos de Minas in Brazil. It was very rare to invite a preacher from Brazil to lead the retreat, and when it was over she closed her fist and patted her forehead, asking the Prioress:

-*What's gotten into your head to call a Bishop from Brazil to preach the retreat?*

Every day she wondered when it would finish; it seems that she foresaw the beginning of her Calvary.

The retreat ended on November 20. It was the last time she went to the choir to attend Mass.

During the recreation at night, she enjoyed giving the news to every sister who came into the room:

-*Have you heard the news? The retreat has ended!!!*

With each one, she clapped her hands. It seems she sensed something special was coming. Sunday the 21st, the Feast of Christ the King, was the first

---

488 Rev 3:16

warning sign. During Mass, the Sister who was to take her down for Communion noticed she was in great distress. She looked so bad the Sister didn't know whether to even leave her to call for help. She ran to the door of the choir and called for the Mother who immediately called the doctor. The Sisters in the choir were distracted by the activity, but did not know what happened until the end of Mass, and thanked God the crisis had passed. They noted, however, that their beloved sick Shepherdess looked pale and was less lively and talkative. Feeding her became more difficult. She never felt like eating anything, only lupine seeds! The lupines were a childhood favorite. She said her father used to bring lupines in his pockets and the children, knowing that, accompanied him when they met him. Sometimes they asked him for them but at other times they just helped themselves. She was so familiar with lupines that it felt good to eat them now when nothing else felt good. At the end of the year, she went three days without eating anything. When presented with a list of foods, she only said yes to lupines, but there were none in the house. Sister Lucia said with grace:

-Now, you offer what you do not have!

The Prioress phoned the doctor, asking if this 'delicacy' could even be given to her. After three days without food, how would her stomach react to lupines? The doctor looked for some at a brewery. The doctor told the dealer who they were for and he offered them with pleasure. Sister Lucia ate them with great enjoyment. We only gave her a few, however, a precaution she did not understand, and when the nurse said to her:

-You ate a bowl of lupines!

Sister Lucia corrected her:

-The bowl came, but there were only a half dozen at the bottom.

Although very fragile, she had to laugh. When we told her she should make an effort to eat something else because she was too thin, she responded with a naughty face:

-You give me less food than you give to animals.

Even before this sharp decline, Sister Lucia was weak. After Mass, the nurse sister served her breakfast and she was still resting. By 11:00 a.m. she helped her get up and said:

-You're lucky not to have your mother here, so you can sleep as long as you want. To me, you do not have to stay in bed.

The nurse sister told her that the doctor had given an order to get up, to which she responded:

-Ah! When the doctor is my age, I shall see!

If the Prioress arrived, Sister Lucia would say:

-Our Mother, take this girl away from me, who does not leave me in peace!

The Prioress would tell her the nurse knew what to do, and Sister Lucia would conclude:

-It is not worth it to be a Superior! What can we do!

Here was one raised by the love of God, always joking with the situation, making light of the work of those who served. Someone had spread a rumor that Sister Lucia spent her days and nights praying and crying, which was very wrong— praying, yes; she was always praying for the requests that Our Lady asked for, and as a Carmelite she lived the Rule that says *always to be concealed in prayer.*[489]

As for crying, her heart cried out for the sins of the world, but she lived without being depressed, knowing that *God loves a cheerful giver.* [490]   This was recommended by our Mother St. Teresa, who knew that virtue should be captivating.[491]

When Sister Lucia heard what was said, she exclaimed:

-My God! How many things they say I do! If I spent the night crying, how could I pray during the day? [492]

4 | Finishing Touches

Going back, let us follow her during this exhausting 'more time' that Heaven allowed.

On November 27 after Vespers, she received the anointing of the sick from our chaplain, the Rev. João Lavrador, who today is Auxiliary Bishop of Porto, with the entire Community present. She was well enough to participate. The next evening around 8:30 p.m., we were alarmed to see her so weak and called the doctor who came promptly. Sister Lucia stated:

-When I feel bad, the doctor is always here... When I improve, I did not think of the suffering or what it may have been. I never asked anyone about my health.

If the doctor listened to Sister Lucia's heart and told her that everything was fine, she would respond:

-I always had a good heart!

With her good mood, she reduced the tension which everyone felt. In that cell, where the Shepherdess of Fatima was preparing for the eternal meeting with the Lady more brilliant than the sun, she lived in holy joy and spoke of death as a

---

489 Rule, No. 8.
490 2 Cor 9:7.
491 St. Teresa of Avila, *The Way of Perfection*, ch. 41, p. 7.
492 Oral Narration of Sister Lucia.

◄ Sister Lucia.

▼ The hands of Sister Lucia.

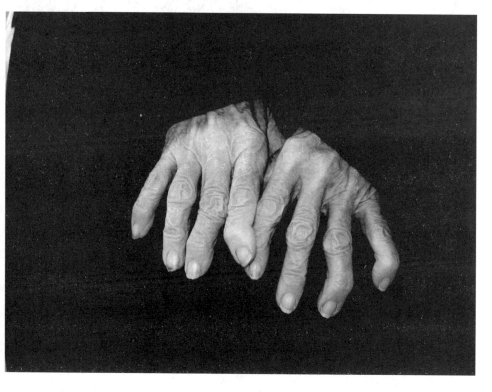

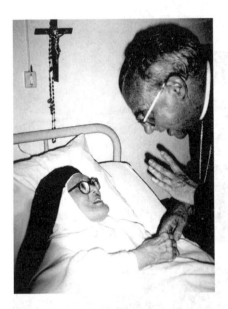

◄ Visit of Bishop Albino Cleto, the Bishop of Coimbra, with Sister Lucia already confined to bed, June 15, 2004.

▼ Sister Lucia in her cell, February 2005.

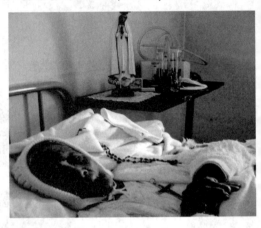

◄ The hands of Sister Lucia holding the rosary that was given to her by Pope John Paul II.

◄ The hands of Sister Lucia holding the crucifix of her Religious Profession.

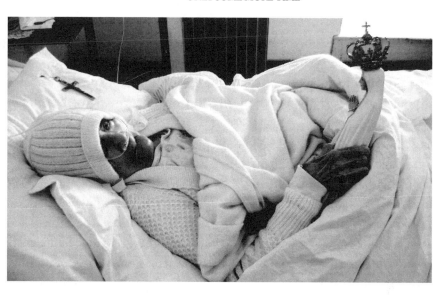

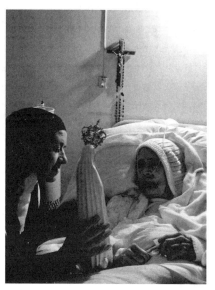

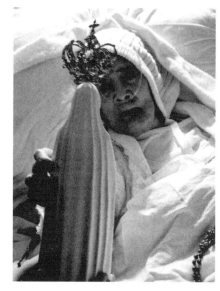

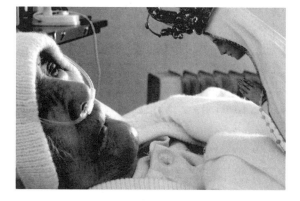

Sister Lucia with the image of Our Lady given to her by Pope John Paul II, January 2005.

feast much desired.

On the morning of the 29th she had a slight fainting spell. The sisters accompanying her also stayed through the night, which passed quietly, but she did not sleep any longer. The following evening, the same thing happened. The doctor came and once again everything went well. But on the evening of December 1st, everything made us believe that the end would be soon. It was impossible to contact the chaplain, so they phoned the Episcopal Palace and Bishop Albino Cleto came immediately. While the doctor assisted the beloved Shepherdess, the Bishop prayed with the Community until she was calm.

It was the last and most serious crisis. Our Lady was alerting us that soon she would come to seek her Shepherdess. The Community suffered emptiness and pain when she briefly discussed what to do with her mortal remains. Some years before, Sister Lucia said she wanted to be like the other sisters in the Community and be buried in the monastery cemetery, but after listening to her Superiors, she admitted that she would like to go to Fatima and granted that her body be buried at the Shrine of Fatima. As it was easy to talk to Sister Lucia about her death, a matter she spoke of naturally, the Prioress, Sister Maria Celina, told her how painful it would be for everyone once she passed away. To this she replied:

-*After I die, the Sisters can do what they want.*

However, when she was reminded that she had already made a document, she objected:

-*I have already written…*

Without undoing what had been written, the Prioress suggested writing a little note, stating that she would remain in the cemetery of the monastery for at least one year, to which she nodded in agreement. She wrote a short text that Sister Lucia would copy and sign. But Sister Lucia copied only the first word and started writing her own personal text, before appearing tired and abandoning the pen. What was written by her and signed was accepted. It was the last thing she wrote.

On December 6, 2004, she began again to go to recreation with the Community on the days she was less fatigued. On the Feast of the Immaculate Conception she was unable to attend the ceremony of the Taking of the Habit by a Novice, but embraced her with great affection and joy, telling her to stay and take her place, as she saw the signs of her imminent departure. In the afternoon, she had a CT scan to see if anything could be done for her, but it was always the same conclusion—her old age.

On the 13th, the feast of St. Luzia, she received some letters from foreign countries where the name of Luzia and Lucia are the same, sending her good wishes. One gift that really pleased her was a gorgeous Icon of St. Luzia from Russia, brought by the son of the lady who sent it to her. The reverse side of the icon is covered with small icons of Our Lady under many invocations. She liked it very much because it was beautiful and it came from Russia. Russia was always in her heart!

Christmas came, her last on earth. She was not able to be visited after Midnight Mass because of her weakness. But on Christmas Day we went to her to give the Child Jesus a Merry Christmas embrace and enjoy the chocolates she had to offer.

With that, she gladly did! In the early afternoon while preparing to eat lunch, the Bishop visited her and she had the honor of eating with him, which gave her much joy. It was a novelty that she told each Sister who visited her that afternoon:

-*You know, today I had the honor to eat lunch with the Bishop.*

The subsequent days were like the trickle of the last grains of sand in an hourglass, counting down her life. Each day we saw her weaker and more pale, but still joking with her helpers. She lived this period of total dependence with abandonment, not showing any opposition. Until the end she artfully hid her pains from the outside world. She always felt very cold. There was an oven to warm her cell, but it did not do enough. Some years earlier a friend had given her an electric blanket, which finally warmed her up.

At the end of January she was extremely weak and after the 28th did not resume eating. She sipped some liquids, but very little. On February 1, she began to receive intravenous feeding, but this sometimes was blocked and caused more suffering. When it was no longer possible to insert a needle into her hand and arms the nurse had to poke at her feet, which was very painful. Throughout all this she was silent as a lamb. In her heart she offered everything, and everything already offered and delivered beforehand. Two teachers from the University of Coimbra Hospital visited to assess whether it would be better for her to be in the hospital. But they concluded that nothing more could be done and in the hospital she would not have the affectionate care and love that surrounded her at home. Her doctor, with tremendous concern, visited her every day and some days more than once.

5 | Ascent to Calvary with Jesus and Mary

On February 3, she received the anointing of the sick again, but this time she lay prostrate and alert and did not participate. Increasingly, all eyes were fixed on her impending death. On February 5, a first Saturday, it was thought she would not make it through the day after a very painful and restless night. She spent the morning with much suffering. The Bishop visited that afternoon. With her eyes drooping, she kissed his pectoral cross, but did not speak. When His Excellency gave his blessing, she crossed herself, a gesture she repeated often at this stage.

She improved in the evening. The whole community spent their recreation with her. She gave many hugs to the image of Our Lady of Fatima that Pope John Paul II sent to her in December of 2003. She always kept the image in her cell and repeatedly crossed herself, staring at it with tenderness.

We challenged her to eat some lupines and she nodded that she wanted to eat. She tried repeatedly to put her teeth in her mouth but was unable to do so and she could not talk. We asked her to try again on another day and she consented and tried a lupine. It was the only thing she wanted to eat. The days and nights that followed were very difficult. She suffered unceasingly and those who stayed with her were not able to relieve her suffering. Still, she conveyed a serene countenance to everyone tending her. Sometimes she would stare at the sister nurse with a gaze that although not as brilliant, was so full of tenderness, expressing all her gratitude for their services.

We noticed that she was suffering from shortness of breath and she was administered oxygen. Throughout the night of February 7-8, she wanted to see the sister who was keeping her company. When she would lean back for a moment to rest, she could not see her and would lament:

-*They left me!!!*

The sister stood up to show herself and the Shepherdess smiled and shook her hand with great force. Afterwards she said haltingly:

-*Our Lady!...Our Lady!...Angels!...Angels!...Heart of Jesus!...Heart of Jesus!...*

Her confessor, Rev. Father Pedro Ferreira, O.C.D. visited her on February 8th. Smiling and with folded hands she received absolution and crossed herself, almost unable to speak. He proposed to take a "message" to the Lady of the Chapel of the Apparitions for her, and she consented with a nod.

That night she fainted again. The whole Community gathered in her cell where she consummated her last days in sacrifice, a girl who offered to suffer everything that God wanted to send her. She was a ripe fruit that the Divine Farmer was about to reap, but still her hour had not come. Her suffering decreased and the Community withdrew for the night. Opening her eyes and seeing the Sisters leaving, she enveloped them with a beautiful smile, which was seen as friendship, tenderness and gratitude.

She spent the whole night without sleeping and looked constantly for her companion, who also did not sleep, but patted her forehead gently. On February 9 she received her last Holy Communion. Shortly after this she could not swallow anything, not even water. From then on, the Prioress, when taking Communion to another sick patient would spend a few minutes in Sister Lucia's cell and place the reliquary with the Hidden Jesus on her chest for a few moments of adoration. The Shepherdess now was taking communion on the Cross!

6 | Last Words

At this same time we watched the declining health of the Holy Father who was hospitalized. We remembered Sister Lucia lifting her hands, repeating:

-*For the Holy Father! For the Holy Father!*

She continued her offering in the silent sanctuary of her heart. We always noticed her great love for the Holy Father, a love that was imprinted in her heart from the revelation of the Secret. This love grew along with her because at the beginning she did not even know the name of the Pope, but now had a name and face. In addition to the faithful love that harbored them, they shared a mutual friendship. With great affection she grasped in her hands until the time of her departure for Heaven the Rosary that the Pope had given her on her birthday the year before. God had joined the two—the Shepherdess and the Shepherd—in the last climb to Calvary! On the morning of February 10, she said her last words and they were again an offering for the Holy Father. When the sister nurse asked her if she suffered much, she replied:

-*I suffer!*

-*Do you offer this suffering for the Holy Father?*

-*I offer for the Holy Father… for the Holy Father… for the Holy Father!…*[493]

From that moment, she did not say another word. She generously and heroically surrendered to the will of God, patiently accepting her great suffering in these last remaining hours in her body, already so worn and tired. Her spirit, however, was as firm in its 'yes' as the first time. She had a three-day 'retreat' which was the next preparation to *enter into the joy of the Lord.*[494]

The next day she alternated between moments of bad coughing spells and much peace and gentleness with her crucifix, which she kissed several times and gazed at length. She wanted to put it on her heart where she placed it on the day of her Profession. She wanted Him to receive the palpitations of her heart that throbbed only for Him, under the gaze of Mary.

---

493 Oral Narration of Sister Lucia.

494 Mt 25:21.

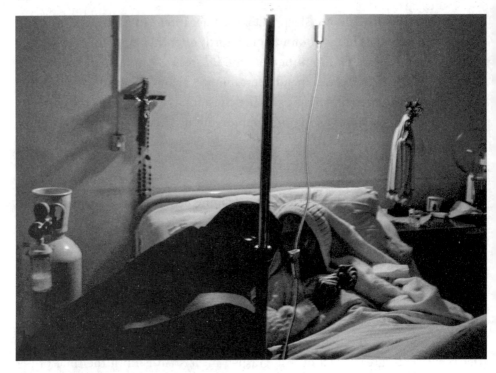

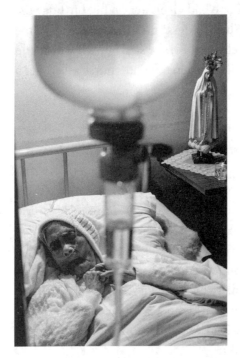

Sister Lucia in the last days of her earthly life.

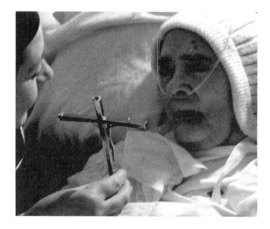

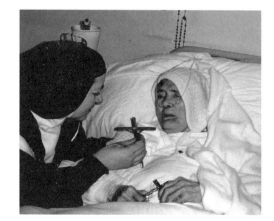

▲ Sister Lucia reading the fax that was sent by Pope John Paul II on the morning of February 13, 2005.

▶ Mother Prioress Sister Maria Celina giving the crucifix to Sister Lucia to kiss at the end of her walk among us.

In the afternoon she received a present: a woolen lamb brought from Italy by a Carmelite Father. How many memories were linked to these lambs!

The nights were always the hardest, but her last nights were very difficult. She could not rest. She had violent attacks of coughing and it seemed that she wanted to break out of her chest. With each new attack the sisters helped her to rise slightly, a position that gave her relief. Afterward, she would thank them with a very sweet look, which also mirrored immense suffering. The sisters, united in her suffering, were unable to relieve her. Everything was an offering to the Lord for her and with her.

On day 12, Saturday, we noticed that she was exhausted and greatly depressed. We were always thinking that the Mother would come for her on a Saturday. Her heart began to show serious signs of stopping; a strong irregular heart beat began. In the afternoon, Sister Lucia presented her Prioress with a significant gift of her love; the rosary that was always in her hand or spread out on her chest, she cupped in her hand and put it into hers, staring at her intently as if to say:

-*You take it and pray it now, I no longer can.*

Seeing her cry, Sister Lucia raised her arms and pulled the Prioress to her, gave her a kiss on the forehead and smiled. It was a touching thank you and farewell. She could barely make these gestures! Still, she had to suffer through the insertion of another intravenous tube. She did not have the veins to support the needles except in her feet where it was extremely painful. This was done without a moan from her mouth; it was an ordeal that would not be repeated, however. The Sisters were crying when Sister Lucia said goodbye to her doctor and nurse with a slight but significant nodding of her head. The Virgin had lit the lamp to enter the room of the banquet, to which the opening of the door was imminent.[495]

7 | It is Finished

This was followed by the last night of much suffering, but in peace. Around midnight, the sister assisting her pressed to Sister Lucia's lips the image of Our Lady of Fatima, as she silently offered her sacrifice. She kissed it, her last kiss, a greeting to the Lady brighter than the sun. It was the start of the last day the Shepherdess would have sunsets—February 13, the day of her natural death. During the night while her companion prayed the Rosary, Sister Lucia moved her fingers as if to pass the rosary beads, faithful to the request of Our Lady of the

---

495 Mt 25:10.

holm oak until the end.

At dawn, we noticed she had a great light about her. She opened her eyes after so many days of them almost always closed, and did not show any signs of distress. Was Our Lady there to remove her pains as she did with Jacinta? It is a question, but something happened. The face of the Shepherdess which was so contracted with pain during the evening was now fresh and joyful, radiating happiness and having a beautiful smile for all. The Prioress pointed her index finger to Heaven, and Sister Lucia responded with a nod of her head. With the crucifix before her eyes, it was so beautiful to see the silent conversation she had with Him, making very significant gestures. Then she put her hand to her mouth, making a sign of wanting to kiss Him, but she did not have enough strength to give the kiss physically. It certainly was a kiss from her heart.

At 10 a.m., she received a blessing from the Holy Father, faxed over from the Nuncio and brought to her by our Bishop. She heard the text read to her, but she was not satisfied with this; she wanted to hold the fax in her hands and gestured for her glasses to read it personally, which she did carefully. The Holy Father said to her:

Reverend Sister Lucia of Jesus and the Immaculate Heart

Carmel of Santa Teresa – Coimbra

I was informed of the state of your health. I come to affirm our affectionate union with a special remembrance of your personal union with God, with all the comfort to help you overcome these worthily resigned serene moments of trial united to Christ the Redeemer, and let yourself be enlightened by your Easter. As a pledge of the best heavenly graces, I send to you and the Carmelite Community and families my apostolic blessing.

Johannes Paulus PP II

The Supreme Pastor of the Church came to bless the Shepherdess who was about to depart in the arms of her Mother.

Throughout the morning she made the sign of the cross often, her hands more free since the intravenous tube had been removed. The doctor and nurse returned in the afternoon to put it back in again.

Between noon and 1 p.m., her ultimate decline began; she was extremely weak and was breathing harder. The oxygen could no long enter her lungs that were closed. It was obvious she would *break the web of her sweet meeting*[496] with the Lord of her life.

About five o'clock, as promised, the doctor, nurse and finally the Bishop

---

496 St. John of the Cross, *Living Flame of Love*, Song 1.

returned. The Prioress asked the doctor not to try more intravenous feeding, because the beloved patient was very close to death. She confirmed her condition and the Community was called. They all surrounded the bed of their dying beloved Sister, as they accompanied the prayers of the ritual spoken by the Bishop. It was an intense time; no one was aware of their surroundings. Everyone concentrated on the Shepherdess preparing to enter into eternal life with so much serenity.

On completion of the prayers of the ritual, the Bishop closed the book and began to pray invocations from his heart:

-*Receive Jesus Christ Who gave you life!*
-*Receive the Lady more brilliant than the sun, who appeared to you!*
-*Receive the Angel of Portugal, who appeared to you!*
-*Receive Blessed Francisco, who with you saw the Virgin Mary!*
-*Receive Blessed Jacinta, who with you saw the Virgin Mary!*
-*Etc.... etc. ... etc. ...*

Just when we never expected to see those eyes again that had so often beheld the heavenly beauty of Our Lady, they opened! Her eyes went slowly to all the sisters that surrounded her and they, in turn, received her expression indicating her farewell with deep emotion. When her eyes stopped at the Prioress, they fixed deeply for a long time. She received this look and the message that emanated from it as if she were completely alone with the Shepherdess, as if she was outside of time. Then placing the crucifix before those eyes like two beams of light, Lucia set her eyes on Him and she closed them again.

It was the final farewell. Thus she departed, adorned in silence and simplicity, leaving her life here to find now eternal life. She went into the arms of the Lady brighter than the sun to meet her cousins, letting the scent of her virtues embalm each corner of the Monastery of St. Teresa.

8 | I Am Going to See Heaven

The news spread swiftly through the media and started the throngs of people wanting to see and bid farewell to the mortal remains of Sister Lucia, whose coffin was exposed in the lower choir, under the gaze of an image of the Immaculate Heart of Mary. Soon they had to form a line and pass by for only a few seconds. There were so many people! Some waited six hours to see her for a short moment. There were those who stepped into the line five times to be able to see her again. There was a flood of flowers. The superior placed them around her coffin, but then had to place them in a mound. Hundreds of bouquets and notes were passed through the bars; among them was a postcard with a well written stanza:

The coffin of Sister Lucia in the lower
choir of the Carmel of Coimbra.

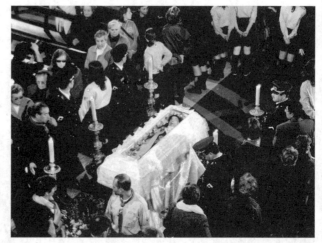

▲ Flag at half-mast at the
  University of Coimbra.

▶ Celebration of the
  Funeral Mass at the
  New Cathedral of Coimbra.

◄ Cardinal Tarcisio Bertone
praying the final prayer
before the tomb in the cloister
of the Carmel of Coimbra.

◄ The coffin in the tomb of Sister
Lucia in the cloister of the
Carmel of Coimbra.

◄ The tomb of Sister Lucia in
the cloister of the
Carmel of Coimbra.

Lucia,
The whole world becomes more alone
While going to Heaven, Sister, her own voice…
But the Mondego reverses its path
And makes our eyes an inlet!
Paulo llharco

Shortly thereafter, the author who sent this stanza placed it in a beautiful frame. At 9 p.m. the first Mass was celebrated in the presence of her body, leaving the chapel open until midnight. Some people were on the street waiting for the reopening of the chapel just before dawn. The next day after the morning Mass, there was no room. The line seemed never to end; the extent of it always the same. When the afternoon passage was interrupted by the celebration of the Eucharist, the people that could not enter because of lack of space stayed on the street and sang songs of Fatima and prayed. No one was bored waiting.

On February 15, the Portuguese government declared a day of national mourning, a beautiful gesture that represented the hearts of thousands of Portuguese who felt so much sadness for the Portuguese Sister who did so much good for the nation, and who was so well known and admired worldwide.

The funeral Mass was celebrated in the New Cathedral of Coimbra and presided by His Eminence, Cardinal Tarcisio Bertone, special envoy of the Holy Father and the bearer of a message sent by His Holiness as follows:

The Venerable Brother Albino Mamede Cleto, Bishop of Coimbra,

With deep emotion I learned that Sister Maria Lucia of Jesus and the Immaculate Heart, 97 years old, was called by the heavenly Father to the eternal mansions of Heaven. She reached the goal for which she always aspired in prayer and silence, in the convent.

The liturgy of these days reminds us that death is the common inheritance of the children of Adam, but at the same time gives us the assurance that Jesus, the sacrifice of the Cross, has opened the door to immortal life. We remember these certainties of the faith when we give our ultimate salute to this humble and devout Carmelite who consecrated her life to Christ, Savior of the world.

The visit of the Virgin Mary that little Lucia received in Fatima, along with her cousins Francisco and Jacinta in 1917, was for her the beginning of a unique mission to which she remained faithful until the end of her days. Sister Lucia leaves us with an example of great fidelity to the Lord and of joyful adherence to His divine will. I remember with emotion the various meetings I had with her and the bond of spiritual friendship that over time had become more intense. I have always felt supported by the daily gift of her prayer, especially in the hard times of trial and suffering. May the Lord reward her amply for her great and hidden service to the Church.

I like to think that Sister Lucia was welcomed in her prayerful passage from earth to Heaven and that it was precisely what she saw in Fatima so many years ago. I would like now that the Holy Virgin accompany the soul of her devoted daughter, a blissful encounter with the divine Bridegroom. I trust you, Venerable Brother, to the task of ensuring the religious of the Carmel of Coimbra my spiritual closeness to grant a pledge of consolation at the moment of separation, an affectionate Blessing extended to the families, to you Cardinal Tarcisio Bertone, my Special Envoy, and to all participants in the sacred rite of suffrage.

Vatican, February 14, 2005, John Paul II

After Mass in the Church of Carmel with the participation of only her family, the casket was taken to the Cathedral to be exposed in the afternoon. The hearse that made the entire journey separating the Carmel from the New Cathedral of Coimbra was surrounded by a group of people walking or standing beside these last steps of the Shepherdess on earth. Police officers and several members of the scouts were the honor guard at the casket, which was opened but protected by a covering of transparent acrylic. The Cathedral was too small for the number who wanted to participate and a large crowd had to stand outside.

Divine Providence decreed that almost all of the Portuguese Bishops be present. Sister Lucia died when the Portuguese Episcopal Conference was making the Spiritual Exercises in Fatima. All who were there went to Coimbra for the celebration of the Funeral Mass, returning then to continue with the Exercises.

After the Celebration the procession proceeded back to the Carmel, where there was once again a crowd of people, also Cardinal Tarcisio Bertone, a few bishops and many priests, who accompanied the coffin of Sister Lucia with great affection and devotion. When the casket was lifted up to be carried out of the Cathedral, someone started singing: '*In Heaven, In Heaven, in Heaven, one day I am going to see...*'

The whole assembly joined in the same chant with deep emotion amid a great round of applause. The funeral procession exited on the coats of college students who were waiting at the door of the Cathedral, making a carpet in honor of the one who lived so humbly!

In the Carmel, after the last response prayed by Cardinal Tarcisio Bertone, in the presence of the Apostolic Nuncio, Archbishop Alfio Rapisardo, the Bishop of Coimbra, Albino Cleto and some bishops and priests, the casket was prepared for burial in such a way that it would remain in perfect condition, so that in a year it could be transferred to Fatima.

There was still time to take one last photo of Sister Lucia's coffin with all her

Sisters of the Community and some Carmelite Fathers who were present.

Finally, her coffin was buried in grave No. 3, a new grave that was always abundantly adorned with candles and flowers throughout the year. Every day requests for prayer and letters arrived to be placed on her grave. A basket was put there because they received so many. Each person was entrusting his heart and intentions to Sister Lucia, knowing that she now heard them better and quicker. For the Sisters who had lived many years or just a few years with the Shepherdess, it was a great joy and consolation to be able to have her so near, to pray to her and ask for her intercession to God and Our Lady. They felt she was very close, that she had only changed the way in which she was present in their midst.

9 | Relocation to Fatima

By the decision of the Bishop of Leiria-Fatima, Serafim Ferreira de Silva, the transfer of the coffin of Sister Lucia from the Carmel of Coimbra to the Basilica of the Shrine of Fatima was set for February 19, 2006. It was a new suffering for the Community but, resigned to it, they accepted.

On the eve of this morning, her grave was opened in the presence of the Bishop of Coimbra, the mayor of Coimbra, the president of the parish of the New Cathedral, Bishop John Bosco and Bishop Ricardo, both of Brazil. The chaplain of the Carmel and Rev. Luciano Cristino stayed with her coffin in the inner chapel of the Carmel. In the afternoon there was a Solemn Celebration in the cloister in the presence of all the Provincial Carmelites of Europe, many priests and Carmelite priests and also the Rev. Father Kondor, a great friend and admirer of Sister Lucia. These priests that were spending the night in Fatima returned the next day to attend the Mass of Farewell for Sister Lucia from her beloved Carmel and accompanied her body back to her birthplace. During the whole night Sister Lucia's coffin was accompanied by the sisters, and the next morning she was taken to the Choir for the celebration of Mass at 8:30 a.m.

On the morning of the 19th, the Mass was celebrated by the Bishop of Coimbra, Bishop Albino Cleto, concelebrated by dozens of priests and attended by a crowd of faithful friends and devotees of Sister Lucia, as well as many journalists who followed and transmitted the events. They witnessed the greatness and importance of each moment, and the constant presence of a crowd of people throughout the transfer despite the persistent rain and bad weather.

After the Mass, it was time for her farewell to the Carmel. Six Sisters carried the casket from the Choir to the door of the enclosure. Two Sisters carried the image of the Immaculate Heart of Mary, followed by the rest of the Community in procession. The body of the Shepherdess passed for the last time from the cloister that she dreamed of when she left Fatima as a child and where she spent most of her life, to return to Fatima where it all began. The Sisters placed the casket on the floor by the door of the enclosure and tried to sing a song prepared for this moment, but almost could not because of their tears. Bishop Albino entered the enclosure with six police officers who carried the casket to the hearse and followed it to the New Cathedral. There was a great feeling of pain, sadness and emptiness among the Sisters! It was as if everything had vanished; no one said anything. Father Petro Ferreira, O.C.D., came to their side to comfort them, knowing how much this farewell hurt the hearts of those who lived more closely with Sister Lucia than anyone. He traced the Sign of the Cross on each of their foreheads and then turned to go to join the procession. The Mother Prioress Sister Maria Celina and two Sisters who were allowed outside of the Carmel of Coimbra were in the hearse with the casket of Sister Lucia. Hundreds of people lined the streets and highways as the funeral procession of Sister Lucia passed by, all the way to Fatima. A long line of people followed her on foot and by car along the way.

At 11:00 a.m., Mass was celebrated in the New Cathedral in Coimbra with large numbers of people attending, which was followed by a procession to Fatima at 1:00 p.m.

Bishop Seraphim received the procession as it arrived in the sanctuary where there were already many people who wanted to be able to see and touch the coffin of the Shepherdess Lucia. The Mother Prioress handed the keys of the coffin to the Bishop of Coimbra, and he in turn gave them to Bishop Seraphim. The procession continued to the Chapel of Apparitions where the casket was placed; there the Bishop recited the Rosary with meditations from Sister Lucia's book "Calls from Message of Fatima." Later her coffin was brought to a place prepared in front of the altar during the celebration of Mass.

Only a few people entered the Basilica for the burial—close family members and some bishops and priests. Lucia was buried on the left side of Blessed Jacinta, beneath a marble plate with the inscription of her name, her dates of birth and death, and the words, "Here lies the body that both walked the path in fulfilling the Will of God and in faithfulness to the requests of Our Lady.

In a silent gesture of affection, on the marble slab was placed a bouquet of 16 white roses representing all the Sisters. It was wrapped with a white ribbon that had all their signatures and the message:

In each rose is a longing
From each Sister of Carmel, forever!
United with us for Eternity,

Immersed with the Trinity
In our walk, you are our Model!

Here, the pilgrims continue to visit her, thanking her for favors received, asking her for help with their problems, leaving flowers and wanting always to remember her. As in her life when she received hundreds of letters, or was sought by both great and small, Sister Lucia will continue to say:

-It is all because of Our Lady! [497]

---

497   Oral Narration of Sister Lucia.

◀ The transfer of the body of
Sister Lucia to Fatima, farewell
Mass in the New Cathedral
of Coimbra, February 19, 2006.

Procession with the image of Our Lady of Fatima and the Body of Sister Lucia, in the Sanctuary.

▶ Tomb of Sister Lucia in the
Basilica of Our Lady of the
Rosary, next to her cousin
Jacinta Marto, Fatima.

With her we pray this prayer-poem that came from her heart:

At midday
We descended
To your open bosom, heavenly light!
Your Heart
Brings forgiveness
To a poor child that led to God!

In you O Mary,
The sun smiled,
Beautiful star from high Heaven!
With harmony,
Sweetly said:
You have sweet asylum in my bosom!

Gentle alliance,
Firm hope,
Under your mantle comes my shelter,
You who are pure,
All tenderness
Within your bosom I dwell.

My heart
Into your hand,
O living Mother, let it live;
Save your child
In the dark trail,
Not to return if requested.

Sister Lucia

CONCLUSION

It was with affection that the Sisters traveled alongside Sister Lucia on the long journey of her life, which was illuminated by a profound love for Our Lady. This love always filled Sister Lucia's soul and she was captured irresistibly in the Heart of God. There she found her treasure, the Precious Pearl in exchange for everything that was abandoned.

She felt the seductions of the world, the temptation of the devil and the complaints of her nature. But she won everything with heroic fidelity to her 'Yes' on May 13, 1917. The world was her only path to God, and although surrounded by many obstacles, she always took the path as a ray of light, as her intimate desire, purpose and generous offering in favor of her brothers and sisters in Christ: *I want my life to be a trail of light that shines on the path of my brothers and sisters showing them faith, hope and charity.* [498]

---

498 *My Pathway*, III, p. 183.

BIBLIOGRAPHY

ANTONIO MARIA MARTINS, S. J., New Documents of Fatima, Bookstore Editions, A.I., Porto.

BOOK OF PROFESSIONS, Archives of the Carmel of Saint Teresa, Coimbra.

CONGREGATION FOR THE DOCTRINE OF THE FAITH, The Message of Fatima (The Secret), Publisher Paulus, 1st Edition, June, 2000.

CARDINAL TARCISIO BERTONE WITH GIUSEPPE DE CARLI, The Last Secret of Fatima. My Conversations with Sister Lucia, Publisher Sphere Books, 1st edition, September, 2007.

C. BARTHAS, Fatima, 1917-1968
Edition of the Shrine of Fatima.

CRITICAL DOCUMENTATION of FATIMA, Shrine of Fatima.

FERNANDO LEITE, S.J., Jacinta, Edition of the Apostolate of Prayer, Braga, 1951.

FATIMA –Altar of the World, Western Publisher 1953, Volume I.

JOHN DE MARCHI, I.M.C., The Lady More Brilliant Than the Sun, Publisher Consolata Missions, Fatima, 9th Edition, 1966.

JOAQUÍN MARIA ALONSO, Dr. Formigão, Man of God and Apostle of Fatima, Graphics of Coimbra, 1979.

LUIS KONDOR, Do You Want to Offer Yourselves to God?, Secretary of the Shepherds and the Missionary Seminary of the Divine Word, 2011.

LUIS PERROY, S. J., Ascent to Calvary, Spanish version, 2nd Edition.

M.M. PHILIPON, O.P., Spiritual Doctrine of Sister Elizabeth of the Trinity, Publisher House of Castelo, Coimbra, 1949.

MARIA TERESA PEREIRA DA CUNHA, Our Lady of Fatima, Pilgrim of the World, First Journey: Start of the Pilgrimage in Europe.

MADRE MONFALIM, Institute of the Sisters of Saint Dorothy, Publisher Bookstore Bertrand, 1946.

RULE AND CONSTITUTIONS of the Order of the Blessed Virgin Mary of Mount Carmel, 1991.

SAINT AUGUSTINE, Confessions of Saint Augustine, Volume I, 11th Edition, 1984.

SAINT JOHN OF THE CROSS, Complete Works, Editions, Carmel.

SAINT TERESA OF AVILA, Complete Works, Editions, Carmel.

SAINT TERESA OF JESUS OF THE ANDES, Complete Works, Editorial Mount Carmel, Burgos.

SAINT THERESE OF THE CHILD JESUS, Complete Works, Editions, Carmel.

SEBASTIAN MARTINS DOS REIS, A Life in the Service of Fatima.

SISTER MARIA CELINA OF JESUS CRUCIFIED, Sister Lucia, The Memory That We Have of Her, edition of the Carmel of Coimbra and the Secretary Office of the Shepherds, 3rd Edition, March 2006.

SISTER MARIA LUCIA of JESUS and of the IMMACULATE HEART, Memoirs of Sister Lucia, Volume I (1st to 4th Memoir), Publisher Secretary Office of the Shepherds, Fatima, Portugal, 15th Edition, October 2011.

SISTER MARIA LUCIA of JESUS and of the IMMACULATE HEART, Memoirs of Sister Lucia, Volume II (5th and 6th Memoir), Publisher Secretary Office of the Shepherds, Fatima, Portugal, 4th and 5th Edition, May 2005.

SISTER MARIA LUCIA of JESUS and of the IMMACULATE HEART, How I See the Message, edition of the Carmel of Coimbra and the Secretary Office of the Shepherds, 2nd Edition, October 2007.

SISTER MARIA LUCIA of JESUS and of the IMMACULATE HEART, Calls from the Message of Fatima, edition of the Carmel of Coimbra and the Secretary Office of the Shepherds, 4th Edition, December 2007.

SISTER MARIA LUCIA of JESUS and of the IMMACULATE HEART, Letters of Sister Lucia, Archives of the Carmel of Saint Teresa, Coimbra.

SISTER MARIA LUCIA of JESUS and of the IMMACULATE HEART, My Pathway, Archives of the Carmel of Saint Teresa, Coimbra.

STANISLAO DZIWISZ, A Life with Karol, Conversations with Gian Franco Svidercoschi, Publisher Sphere Books, 1st Edition, May 2007.

PRAYER FOR THE BEATIFICATION OF SISTER LUCIA

Most Holy Trinity, Father, Son and Holy Spirit, I adore You profoundly.
By the infinite merits of the Sacred Heart of Jesus and through the intercession
of the Immaculate Heart of Mary, I implore You – if it should be for Your greater
glory and the good of our souls – to glorify in the sight of Your Holy Church,
Sister Lucia the Shepherdess of Fatima, granting us through her intercession the
grace which we implore.   Amen.

Our Father – Hail Mary – Glory be to the Father

With ecclesiastical authorization

Please send details of any graces received through Lucia's intercession to:

Carmel of Saint Teresa 3000-359
Coimbra - PORTUGAL

causabeatificacaolucia@lucia.pt